MAKING THE EAST LATIN

Dumbarton Oaks Medieval Humanities

Series Editor
Jan M. Ziolkowski

MAKING THE EAST LATIN

The Latin Literature of the Levant in the Era of the Crusades

JULIAN YOLLES

DUMBARTON OAKS RESEARCH LIBRARY AND COLLECTION
WASHINGTON, DC

Printed in the United States of America by Sheridan Books, Inc.

LIBRARY OF CONGRESS CATALOGING-IN-PUBLICATION DATA

NAMES: Yolles, Julian, author.
TITLE: Making the East Latin : the Latin literature of the Levant in the era of the Crusades / Julian Yolles.
OTHER TITLES: Dumbarton Oaks medieval humanities.
DESCRIPTION: Washington, DC : Dumbarton Oaks Research Library and Collection, [2022]
Series: Dumbarton Oaks medieval humanities | Originally presented as the author's thesis (Ph.D.)—Harvard University, 2015.
Includes bibliographical references and index.
In English; source text in Latin with parallel English translation.
Summary: "'This new day, new joy, the consummation of toil and devotion with ever new and eternal rejoicing, required new words, new songs from all!' So wrote Raymond of Aguilers, a Provençal priest, when an army of nobles, knights, footmen, and priests from across Europe managed to conquer Jerusalem after three years of traveling and fighting. And new words, and new songs, there were. These settlers produced a hybrid Latin literature—a 'Levantine Latinity'—distinct from that in Europe, and their new literary tradition both drew on and resisted Levantine Muslim, Christian, and Jewish cultures in the newly occupied territories. This volume analyzes the literary and rhetorical techniques of well-known authors such as William of Tyre, literary compositions of communities of canons in the Kingdom of Jerusalem, and individual scholars in the Principality of Antioch. These varied sources reveal the coherent and increasingly sophisticated ways in which Crusader settlers responded to their new environment while maintaining ties with their homelands in western Europe. In a short time, Levantine Latinity emerged to form an indispensable part of the literary history of both the Near East and of Europe."—Provided by publisher.
IDENTIFIERS: LCCN 2021019936 | ISBN 9780884024880 (hardback)
SUBJECTS: LCSH: Latin literature, Medieval and modern—Latin Orient—History and criticism. | Rhetoric, Medieval—Latin Orient—History and criticism. | Literature, Medieval—History and criticism.
CLASSIFICATION: LCC PA8035 .Y65 2022 | DDC 870.9/001—dc23
LC RECORD available at https://lccn.loc.gov/2021019936

Please visit www.doaks.org/publications
for other books in this series and all of the titles that we publish.

For Amanda

CONTENTS

ACKNOWLEDGMENTS

This project began as a doctoral dissertation, submitted in 2015 to the Department of the Classics at Harvard University. Over the years, I have benefited from the insights and support of innumerable friends, colleagues, and research institutions. In the following acknowledgments of my considerable debts of gratitude, I will inevitably have forgotten some; I hope that they will forgive the omission.

As a graduate student, my research was generously supported by the William R. Tyler Fellowship, offered by the Dumbarton Oaks Research Library and Collection. Subsequent research and reworking of the dissertation were made possible by the generous support of a Harvard College Fellowship and, more recently, by a postdoctoral fellowship offered by the Centre for Medieval Literature at the University of Southern Denmark and the University of York, funded by the Carlsberg Foundation and by the Danish National Research Foundation (project DNRF102ID).

I wish to express my gratitude to the many research libraries and institutions that made the research for this project possible. For the images in this volume, special thanks go to Andrea Langner and Thomas Bouillon of the Universitätsbibliothek of the University of Erfurt, to Eliana Calandra of the Biblioteca communale in Palermo, to the staff of the Harvard Art Museums, and to Jonathan Shea and Lucy Yan of the Dumbarton Oaks Research Library and Collection. The map for this volume was created by Tina Ross.

This book would not have been possible without the expert guidance at Dumbarton Oaks of Joel Kalvesmaki, Kathleen Sparkes, Sarah Spence, and Colin Whiting. I am also deeply grateful to the two anonymous readers who reviewed earlier versions and went above and beyond in providing feedback. Naturally, I take responsibility for any shortcomings that remain.

As a graduate student (and to this day), I benefited immensely from the advice and guidance of my dissertation committee: Marcus Bull, Benjamin Kedar, Richard Tarrant, and Jan Ziolkowski. Numerous generous scholars, colleagues, and friends have helped me to develop my ideas or assisted me with various queries and requests: Serena Ammirati, Cara Aspesi, Joseph Baxley, Robin Wahlsten Böckerman, Gil Fishhof, Konrad Hirschler, Steffen Hope, Valeria Flavia Lovato, Divna Manolova, Sandro Nikolaishvili, Michalis Olympios, Aglae Pizzone, Pietro Podolak, Rosa M. Rodríguez Porto, Jonathan Rubin, Christopher Schabel, Uri Shachar, Justin Stover, Elizabeth Tyler, and Wolf Zöller. I am especially grateful to Christian Høgel for his feedback on portions of the book, and to Lars Boje Mortensen for his invaluable comments on an earlier version of the entire manuscript. Special recognition is due to my dear friends Coleman Connelly, Julia Judge-Mulhall, John Mulhall, and Drew Rife, who offered intellectual and moral support in equal measure.

Finally, I am indebted to the encouragement of several families that I call my own: the Bos, Rife, and Yolles families. Special thanks go to my sister Bernadette Yolles for her unswerving support, and to the wonderful Amanda Burton for inspiring me to persevere and for never failing to make me laugh.

30 October 2020
Odense, Denmark

ILLUSTRATIONS

FIGURES

TABLE

NOTE ON NAMES, PLACES, DATES, AND TRANSLATIONS

Wherever possible, I have employed the most common English spelling for the names of places and individuals (e.g., "Antioch" rather than "Antiocheia" or "Antakiya"; "William" rather than "Guillelmus" or "Guillaume"). For transliteration of Greek, I employ the system used in Kazhdan et al., *Oxford Dictionary of Byzantium*. For transliteration of Arabic, I have adopted the widely followed scheme of the Deutsche Morgenländische Gesellschaft (DMG), as set forth in Brockelmann et al., *Die Transliteration der arabischen Schrift*. All dates are those of the Christian calendar, here indicated as BCE and CE. Because this is a study of Latin literature in the Levant that relies on precise philological analysis, I have opted to produce my own translations of quotations from Levantine Latin sources. For all other sources, I reproduce existing English translations wherever possible.

INTRODUCTION

Latinity at the Crossroads

On 15 July 1099, the armed expedition now known as the First Crusade captured Jerusalem. Its participants hailed from diverse regions in western Europe, including north-central France, Normandy, Provence, Flanders, and parts of Germany and Italy. While most Crusaders returned to their homes, some stayed behind to settle in the lands they had conquered. Over the following decades, these Crusader settlements grew to extend all the way from Edessa in the north (modern southeastern Turkey) to large swathes of the Sinai Peninsula in the south, covering much of the area of the Levant (fig. 1). Wedged between the Byzantine Empire and the Abbasid and Fatimid Caliphates, these Crusader settlements faced considerable challenges. That these new communities managed to survive and, gradually, to expand was to one settler nothing short of a miracle:

> Who can but marvel how we, a tiny people, were able not only to offer resistance, but even to live among so many kingdoms of our enemies? "Who has ever heard such things?" [Isa. 66:8] On one side, there is Egypt and Ethiopia, on another Arabia and Chaldea and Syria, on yet another Assyria and Media, Parthia and Mesopotamia, Persia and Scythia. A great sea, moreover, isolated us from the rest of Christianity, and, by God's will, trapped us among the hands of those seeking to harm us.[1]

The isolation expressed is palpable, yet there is also an emerging sense of community: despite their diverse backgrounds, the settlers considered themselves, in

1 FC prol. 4: *Quis potest non mirari, quomodo nos, exiguus populus inter tot hostium nostrorum regna non solum resistere, sed etiam vivere poteramus? Quis audivit unquam talia? Hinc Aegyptus et Aethiopia, hinc Arabia et Chaldaea atque Syria, hinc Assyria et Media, hinc Parthia et Mesopotamia, hinc Persida et Scythia; mare etiam magnum a Christianismo nos excludebat et inter manus nos laniantium, sicut permittebat Deus, concludebat.*

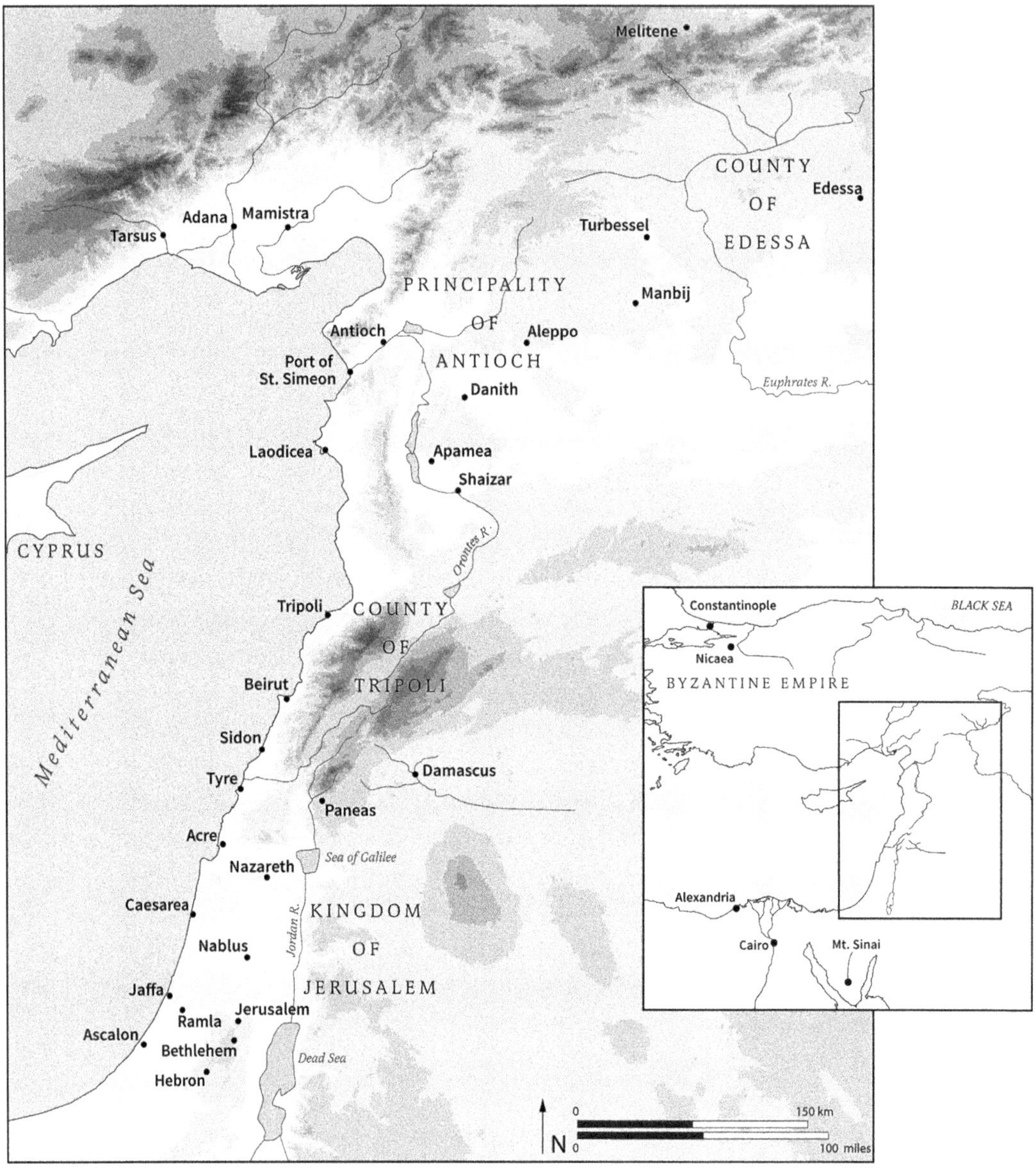

FIGURE 1

The twelfth-century Latin East. Map by Tina Ross.

contradistinction to those surrounding them, members of a single people whose origins lay beyond the Mediterranean. How these settlers and their descendants constructed a shared identity, often in response and in opposition to other Levantine communities, forms the subject of this book. The astonishing fact of the Crusade and the subsequent settlement of Crusaders in the Levant led to another unpredictable development: the creation of a Latin literary tradition of the Levant. For nearly two centuries, settlers from western Europe and their descendants produced literature in a wide array of genres, ranging from historical narratives in prose and verse to pilgrim guides and religious polemic. For the first hundred years, this literature was written almost exclusively in Latin.

Even though the Crusaders came from different cultural and linguistic backgrounds, they found cohesion in two closely related aspects. The rulers of the largest part of the Crusader settlements, the Kingdom of Jerusalem, proclaimed themselves "king of all Latinity in Jerusalem."[2] "Latinity" possesses in this context both a linguistic and a religious component, indicating those Christians who use the Latin rites, as opposed to Greek, Syriac, or Armenian. A late twelfth-century description of the Holy Land speaks explicitly about this dual aspect of Latinity in its treatment of the European settlers of the Levant: "The first among these [Christians of the Holy Land] are the Franks, more accurately called the Latins . . . all those who use the Latin letter [*latina littera*] and answer to the Roman Church are called Latins."[3]

Although the Crusader settlers possessed varied linguistic backgrounds, they all employed Latin as their written language of expression. In the Levant, Latin thus functioned as it did for much of medieval western Europe—as a medium that crossed temporal and geographical boundaries, a language ultimately inherited from the Romans used to communicate across linguistic divides. It was an acquired language of the intellectual elite and the mother tongue of no one.[4] Latin owed this preeminent position to the Roman Catholic Church, whose liturgy and scriptures guaranteed the preservation of the Latin idiom and its continued cultivation in schools housed in churches, cathedrals, and monasteries across Europe.

This book centers on the efforts of a small intellectual elite in the Levant to establish a Latin literary tradition—a tradition that I will refer to as Levantine

2 The earliest instance is in a charter issued by Baldwin I in 1115: *UKJ* 1:197, no. 64. Before that, Baldwin I had typically proclaimed himself to be *dei gratia Ierosolimorum/Ierusalem rex* (e.g., *UKJ* 1:187, no. 57), a title that occasionally reappears in charters of his successors (e.g., Baldwin II in *UKJ* 1:232, no. 86, although the end of the charter lists him as *Balduinus dei gratia secundus Latinorum rex Iherosolimitanus*).

3 *Tractatus de locis* 124: *Quorum primi sunt Franci, qui Latini verius appellantur . . . dicuntur Latini omnes qui latina littera utuntur et obediunt Romane ecclesie*. See appendix 1 for the dating of this work.

4 In Ziolkowski's words, a "father tongue" ("Towards a History," 506).

Latinity. One of the elements that sets this Latin tradition apart from that of medieval western Europe is the culturally and linguistically diverse Levantine environment, inhabited by various Eastern Christian, Muslim, and Jewish communities. Because of the influence of these groups on Latin literary culture, I have opted to refer to this emerging Latinity as "Levantine" rather than "Crusader."[5] Although this culture would not have existed without the First Crusade, many authors were not active in a crusading context: they had not taken a vow of crusading and had not come to the Levant as part of an expedition we would now qualify as a Crusade. Some Latin writers were in fact natives of the Levant. Moreover, their Latin works share little with the writings produced in other Crusading contexts, such as the Albigensian and Baltic Crusades. This book instead maintains that these Latin texts should be considered as part of the regional culture of the Levant.

At the same time, it has rightly been observed that the Crusades not only formed a primary impetus for western European conquest and settlement in the Levant but also continued to shape its literary culture.[6] It will become apparent that many—though not all—of the sources examined in this study discuss the First Crusade to a greater or lesser extent, and references to the Crusades permeated both textual and visual culture in the Latin East throughout the twelfth and thirteenth centuries. Nevertheless, I have eschewed the more cumbersome—though perhaps more accurate—nomenclature of "Latinity of the Crusader Levant" for ease of reference, and because I judged the regional component to be deserving of emphasis. However, throughout this study (including this book's title) I have sought to balance both the Levantine and Crusader components that characterized and shaped the literature of these settlements.

Based on a close examination of all surviving Latin literary works of the twelfth-century Levant and the role of these texts within religious, political, and intellectual life, this study argues that in the wake of the First Crusade, settlers from a range of different western European language groups established a distinctive and coherent Latin literary tradition that both drew on and resisted Levantine Christian, Muslim, and Jewish cultures in the newly occupied territories. In so doing, the settlements of the Levant produced a Latin literature distinct from that of Europe. The twelfth-century Levant presents scholars with a unique situation, in which settlers from across western Europe were transplanted to an area populated with several distinct intellectual cultures and in which various high-status written languages were current. Within this complex environment, the primacy of Latin as a language of intellectual and religious expression could no longer be taken for granted. While the Crusades are not typically associated with literary

5 MacEvitt (*Rough Tolerance*, 18–19; "What Was Crusader") made a similar appeal to scholars to move away from regarding the twelfth- and thirteenth-century Levant purely in a Crusading context.
6 Buck, "Settlement."

or intellectual pursuits, this study shows that the Crusader settlers responded to their new environment in increasingly sophisticated ways while maintaining ties with their European homelands. In a short time, Latin literary culture in the Levant emerged to form an indispensable part of the history of both the Near East and of Europe.

The Twelfth-Century Levant: Medieval and Modern Perspectives

Scholars commonly subdivide the Levantine settlements of the Crusaders and other travelers from western Europe according to their political organization, each with its own unique cultural composition (see fig. 1).[7] In the landlocked County of Edessa, stretching across northern Syria and Upper Mesopotamia, a minority of nobles from Flanders and north-central France governed a diverse population of Armenian Orthodox, Arabic-speaking Greek Orthodox (Melkite), West Syrian or Syrian Orthodox and East Syrian Christians (pejoratively known as Jacobites and Nestorians, respectively), and a small community of Latin Christians.[8] The equally diverse Principality of Antioch, situated on the Orontes River near the Mediterranean coast, was originally established by the Norman contingent of the First Crusade headed by Bohemond of Taranto. In 1136, however, a Provençal ruling class was introduced with the arrival of Raymond of Poitiers.[9] The leaders of the County of Tripoli, which stretched along the coast of much of modern Lebanon, similarly came from Provence and governed a mixed population of Muslims and Eastern Christians.[10] In the Kingdom of Jerusalem, a ruling class from Flanders and north-central France administered the largest territory, at one point extending from Tyre in the north to parts of the Sinai Peninsula in the south. Their subjects varied greatly within this extensive territory, with Eastern Christian communities living alongside Latin Christians in both urban and rural settlements throughout the kingdom, and sizeable Muslim and Jewish populations in the Galilean countryside.[11]

In light of the establishment of these disparate territories in the context of the First Crusade, they are often collectively referred to as the "Crusader States," although this appellation may give the misleading impression of modern political entities. In recent years, many scholars have preferred the term "Outremer," which

7 For recent overviews, see Barber, *Crusader States*; Jotischky, *Crusading and the Crusader States*.

8 Because of the County of Edessa's short duration (1097–1144) and the resulting paucity of evidence, it remains the least studied among the so-called Crusader States. The classic study of the County of Edessa remains Amouroux-Mourad, *Le comté d'Edesse*.

9 The expansive work of Cahen, *Syrie du nord*, has been superseded, at least in part, by Asbridge, *Creation of the Principality*, and Buck, *Principality of Antioch*.

10 Antweiler, *Bistum Tripolis*; Lewis, *Counts of Tripoli*.

11 Ellenblum, *Frankish Rural Settlement*.

derives from Old French ("[the lands] across the sea").[12] This term has the benefit of a medieval origin and is closely connected with the settlers from north-central France and their descendants, who spoke French as their native language. They grew to comprise the majority of the ruling class in the Kingdom of Jerusalem and the Principality of Antioch and, over the course of the thirteenth century, employed Old French also in written contexts that had previously been the domain of Latin.[13]

The medieval nomenclature for the Latin Christian inhabitants of the Levant changed during the twelfth century. Earlier sources, including the Latin narratives of the First Crusade, refer to the Crusaders and subsequent settlers as "Franks" (*Franci*), using the ethnonym as the umbrella term for an expansive cultural identity associated with the realm of the Carolingians and beyond.[14] This broad use of "Franks" was adopted by both Greek (*hoi Phrangoi*) and Arabic (*al-Ifranǧ*) speakers to refer in general terms to inhabitants of western Europe and the Latin settlers of the Levant.[15] Yet over the course of the twelfth century, the word "Frank" in Latin sources increasingly indicated inhabitants of the Kingdom of Francia, in the north-central region of modern France. Because of this growing specificity, a traveler from the Bavarian city of Würzburg took great offense when, during a visit to Jerusalem in ca. 1160, he learned that some attributed the capture of Jerusalem in the First Crusade solely to the merits of the Franks (*Franci*).[16] One late twelfth-century description of the Holy Land (the so-called *Tractatus de locis et statu sancte terre Ierosolimitane*, or *Treatise on the Places and Condition of the Holy Land of Jerusalem*) explicitly identifies this semantic development in referring to the settlers of the Levant as "the Franks, more accurately called the Latins."[17] Except when quoting earlier sources, the Levantine Latin author William of Tyre (ca. 1130–1184) likewise employed "Frank" in its specialized sense to refer to inhabitants and rulers of Francia, preferring "Latin" (*Latinus*) to describe his compatriots, sometimes differentiating between the Western Latins (*Latini occidentales*) of Europe and the Eastern Latins (*Latini orientales*) of the Levant.[18] Similarly, William referred to Latin settlements in the Levant collectively as the

12 Murray, "Franks and Indigenous Communities," 291.

13 For this transition, see chap. 5.

14 For the term *Francus* and related words of the same stem during the First Crusade, see Bull, "Overlapping and Competing Identities."

15 For the ethnonym "Franks" (*al-Ifranǧ*) and, less commonly, "Latins" (*al-Lāṭīnīyyūn*), see König, *Arabic-Islamic Views*, 215–21.

16 JW 1119–50.

17 *Tractatus de locis* 124.

18 For examples of William of Tyre's quotation of earlier sources using "Frank" to refer to the Levantines, see the letter of Baldwin I to the church of Bethlehem (WT 11.12.25 = *UKJ* 1:162, no. 40) and the privilege granted to the Venetians before the capture of Tyre (WT 12.25.100 = *UKJ* 3:1335, no. 764).

"Christian East" or "Our East," and it is likely through William's influence on modern Crusade historiography that the term "Latin East" has come to occupy a prominent place alongside "Crusader States" and "Outremer."

In the thirteenth century, another appellation for the Latins of the Levant appeared. When James of Vitry arrived in the Kingdom of Jerusalem in 1214 as the new bishop of Acre, he described the acculturated Latins of the Levant as *pullani*, a term that reappears in Old French sources (*poulains*), whose precise meaning and connotation remain a subject of scholarly debate.[19] Given the twelfth-century context of this study, I will refer to the Latin Christian inhabitants of the Levant as both "Franks" and "Latins," and to their settlements collectively as the "Latin East."

Just as Greek and Arabic (both Christian and Muslim) writers typically failed to distinguish between the various cultural and ethnic subdivisions among the Latins, so too did Latin authors identify the diverse Christian and Muslim communities of the Levant using ambiguous and inaccurate terms. While Latin authors often distinguished those Christians who either spoke Greek or used Greek rites (though they may have spoken Arabic in other settings) as "Greeks" (*Graeci*), they tended to lump Arabic-speaking Greek-rite Orthodox Melkites and Syriac-rite West Syrians and East Syrians together as "Syrians" (employing either *Suriani*, derived from the Arabic, or *Syri*) or "Syriacs" (*Syriaci*).[20] By contrast, Armenian and Georgian Orthodox Christians, who employed rites in their own distinctive languages and alphabets, often appear separately in Latin accounts.[21]

Initially Latin writers displayed similarly generalizing attitudes in referring to all Muslims as "Saracens" (*Sarraceni*) without differentiating between Sunni and Shiʿa Islam, let alone the many different branches of Shiʿites inhabiting the Levant, such as the Ismaʿili Fatimids, Alawites, Nizarites ("Assassins"), and Druze. William of Tyre is the first and only writer of the twelfth-century Latin East (and quite possibly the first Latin author in general) to distinguish between Sunni Islam and Shiʿism, the latter of which he characterized as appearing "to accord more with our faith."[22] In the subsequent references to his now lost history of "Eastern rulers," William hinted at a more extensive treatment of religious differences between Muslims. The lack of substantial twelfth-century Latin engagement with

19 Crawford, "Poulains."

20 In the past, some scholars assumed that the term *Suriani* generally referred to Melkites, but see Buck, *Principality of Antioch*, 168–74, on the mixed usage of this and related terms by Latin authors; for the Eastern Christian communities in the Kingdom of Jerusalem, see Pahlitzsch and Baraz, "Christian Communities."

21 See, e.g., *Tractatus de locis* 124–25.

22 WT 1.4.9–10. For William's attitude toward Islam, see Morton, "William of Tyre's Attitude"; for William as the first Western author to describe the schism between Sunni and Shiʿa Islam, see Hamilton, "Knowing the Enemy," 376.

Islam may be attributed to the separation between Christian and Muslim settlements in the Levant.[23] Muslims were barred from living in Frankish Jerusalem and, except for the towns along the coast in the County of Tripoli, generally lived in rural settlements and villages. Both rural Muslim and Eastern Christian communities under Latin rule were governed by a *rays* (from Arabic *raʾīs* or "headman") appointed by the local Frankish lord, eliminating the need for direct engagement between Frankish rulers and the native Levantine population.[24] But while Eastern Christians lived alongside Latins in the countryside as well as in cities, Latin contact with Muslims may not have been as prevalent. In the few discussions of Islam in twelfth-century Levantine Latin sources, knowledge of this religion seems to have been based not on direct interaction with Muslims but on Eastern Christian mediation: a mid-twelfth-century Latin account of the origins of Islam is framed as a conversation between a Latin and a Greek Christian in Antioch (the so-called "Adelphus" narrative), while William of Tyre's discussion of Shiʿa Islam appears to rely on Christian Arabic rather than Muslim sources.[25] It is possible, however, that in his lost work dedicated to "Eastern rulers" (presumably focused on Muslims, given his starting point with Muhammad), William utilized Muslim sources directly. Nevertheless, it has recently been shown that in thirteenth-century Acre, the indirect engagement of Islam through Eastern Christian (and, in some cases, Jewish) mediation continued to form the prevailing practice.[26]

Levantine Latinity and Medieval European Literature

Although Levantine Latin literature is unique, it offers avenues of research relevant to scholars of many seemingly unrelated aspects of medieval literature. This is because the development of Levantine Latinity speaks to the much larger issue of medieval Latin and its relation to European vernacular culture. Scholars have long struggled to explain and characterize the continued use of Latin in Europe, at times resorting to outlandish comparisons and metaphors. Celebrated medieval Latinist L. Traube infamously compared the language to a corpse whose hair and nails seem to grow after death.[27] Traube's student P. Lehmann instead likened medieval Latin to repotted plants, speaking of "flowers and trees that have been transplanted into foreign soil, far away from their origin, under a colder sky; they lose much of their former nature, but in spite of this they produce, under the right circumstances, new colors and shapes."[28] More recently, R. Hexter eloquently

23 Kedar, "Subjected Muslims"; Catlos, *Muslims of Medieval Latin Christendom*, 141–44.

24 Riley-Smith, "Some Lesser Officials."

25 For the "Adelphus" narrative, see chap. 4; for William of Tyre, see chap. 5.

26 Rubin, *Learning in a Crusader City*, 114–38.

27 Traube, *Vorlesungen und Abhandlungen*, 2:44.

28 Lehmann, "Vom Leben des Lateinischen."

characterized the Latin community of medieval clerics as "a group, born in exile . . . far from the longed-for home of Latinity. Like Ovid, they yearned always to return to Rome, but, of course, this yearning was for a Rome they had themselves never inhabited."[29]

One reason why medieval European Latin literature can be so difficult to pin down is because of its reticence on its own status, since it functioned as the default written discourse.[30] There did, of course, exist European vernacular literatures, and increasingly so over the course of the twelfth and thirteenth centuries. Yet as the modern adjective indicates, these vernacular languages (derived from the Latin *verna*, "servant") were deemed subservient to Latin, and writing in a vernacular usually occasioned self-reflection and justification. Prefacing Otfrid of Weissenburg's ninth-century biblical poem, composed in Old High German rhyming couplets, is a Latin dedication that sets out the author's rationale for the unprecedented composition.[31] Likewise, even in his revolutionary promotion of vernacular (or, as he put it, "vulgar") eloquence in its written form, Dante Alighieri (ca. 1265–1321) wrote in Latin.[32] In the Levant, Latinity encountered rivals of high-status literary and intellectual culture in Greek and Arabic, but also in Syriac, Armenian, Georgian, and Hebrew. It could no longer be taken for granted that Latin represented *the* written discourse par excellence. In linguistic terms, Latinity in the Levant was marked in a region where various competing language communities were brought into sharp contrast with one another.[33] Prompted by encounters with other established literary traditions, Latin authors in the Levant may be expected to have been more self-reflective about their own literary culture than their western European counterparts—or, barring that, to at least have reflected on the status of other literary traditions. Accordingly, my hope for this study is that an examination of medieval Latin literature within an entirely new linguistic context will produce fresh insights into the way Latin authors valorized their own continued usage of an ancient idiom.

Latin Literature in Crusades Scholarship

This book seeks to demonstrate that the writings from the western European settlements in the twelfth-century Levant form part of a distinctive and coherent Latin literary tradition by examining how authors used the literary, intellectual, and religious dimensions of Latin expression at their disposal to tell narratives

29 Hexter, "Ovid," 224.

30 Watson, "Idea of Latinity."

31 Otfrid of Weissenburg, *Das Evangelienbuch*.

32 Dante Alighieri, *De vulgari eloquentia*.

33 For the notions of marked and unmarked linguistic expression, see Andersen, "Markedness Theory."

about themselves, their institutions, and about their place in the Levant and their relation to the rest of the Latin world. This study therefore aims to fill a lacuna in Crusades historiography by approaching the sources primarily as literary works that were designed to speak to and create literary communities.

By contrast, earlier cultural histories of the Levantine Crusader settlements have at times tended to present an idealized picture extracted from the sources without paying adequate attention to the literary nature of these works. The two pioneering cultural histories of the Latin East, both published in 1883, spoke to a surging interest in interactions between Crusaders and the local Christian and Muslim populace of the Levant.[34] Previous histories of the Crusades had tended to be one-sided treatments largely told from a western European perspective that paid only limited attention to the cultural aspects of the conquered territories. However, the increased European colonial presence in the late nineteenth-century Middle East sparked an interest in more multifaceted approaches. E. Rey situated his work against the backdrop of the growing French colonial presence in the Middle East and Africa, painting a romanticized portrait of the cultural interactions between the indigenous population and the western European settlers. H. Prutz aimed at a comprehensive treatment of Levantine Latin society, drawing on a wide range of (mostly Latin) texts to show the development of a new culture in the Levant, distinct from western Europe and influenced by surrounding Levantine cultures. The sweeping approaches of Rey and Prutz found a successor, with a modified scope, in C. Cahen's celebrated cultural history of northern Syria in the period of the Crusades (1940).[35] Though covering a more limited geographical area, Cahen offered a similarly wide-ranging overview of social, political, religious, and cultural aspects of Syrian life under Latin rule.

After World War II, Crusades historiography's close association with European colonialism in the nineteenth and early twentieth centuries led to a critical reevaluation of the Latin East as a positive model for cultural interaction. S. Runciman, R. C. Smail, J. Prawer, and others corrected earlier idealizing portrayals by emphasizing the uneven power dynamics in the Latin East, depicting a system of cultural segregation in which a Latin urban minority governed a subjugated rural populace of indigenous Christians and Muslims. The supposed limited intellectual interests of the ruling Latin minority resulted in a culture that was but a pale reflection of the intellectual and cultural developments in western Europe and bore but little relation to the surrounding and more sophisticated Levantine cultures.[36] Comprehensive cultural studies subsequently gave way to specialized

34 Rey, *Colonies franques*; Prutz, *Kulturgeschichte der Kreuzzüge*.

35 Cahen, *Syrie du nord*.

36 Runciman, *History of the Crusades*, 3:328–33; Smail, *Crusading Warfare*; Prawer, *Latin Kingdom*. For the problems involved in identifying the Crusader States as European colonies, see Kedar, "Crusading Kingdom"; Ellenblum, *Frankish Rural Settlement*, 4–38.

efforts by R. Hiestand and B. Z. Kedar to chart the intellectual activities and cultural interactions in the Latin East.[37] Scholars increasingly focused on individual authors and provided detailed intellectual portraits of the most prominent Latin writers.[38]

The attention to literary technique yielded by this author-centric approach marked a significant shift in cultural studies on the Latin East. Where previous efforts had been broadly descriptive, aimed at enumerating various cultural characteristics of the Latin East, this new approach centered on analyzing the methods of Latin authors in composing their texts. Subsequently, scholars examined authors' attitudes as reflected in their works to draw larger conclusions about notions of communal identity in the Latin East.[39] Although these studies produced important new insights, they were limited by their excessive focus on the earliest Crusade narratives, in the use of outdated theoretical models, and through their portrayal of sources as more or less representative voices of Latin society.

At the same time, important new advances in the study of the cultural history of the Latin East were made in the field of art history. Scholars such as T. S. R. Boase, H. Buchthal, K. Weitzmann, and J. Folda demonstrated the development of a complex artistic culture that, depending on the artists involved, variously combined French, Italian, Byzantine, and diverse Eastern Christian (and, less commonly, Muslim) artistic designs in manuscript illumination, religious icons, and sculpture.[40] As we will see, this hybrid artistic culture—what Folda has termed "Crusader art"—represents an important parallel to developments in Latin literary works from the Levant, in which authors variously engaged with western European and Levantine traditions.

These art historical findings in turn stimulated a renewed focus on intercultural interactions, which greatly contributed to complicating the picture of the twelfth- and thirteenth-century Levant.[41] For instance, C. MacEvitt sought to reorient fundamentally the study of the culture of the Latin East from a

37 For Hiestand, see especially "Zum Leben und zur Laufbahn"; "*Plange, Syon et Iudea*"; "Un centre intellectuel"; "*Gaufridus abbas*." Kedar's many contributions to the study of the intellectual culture of the Levant have been collected in several volumes: *Franks in the Levant*; *Franks, Muslims and Oriental Christians*; *Crusaders and Franks*.

38 Schwinges, *Kreuzzugsideologie und Toleranz*; Giese, "Stadt- und Herrscherbeschreibungen"; Giese, "Untersuchungen zur *Historia Hierosolymitana*"; Epp, *Fulcher von Chartres*; Edbury and Rowe, *William of Tyre*; Rödig, *Zur politischen Ideenwelt*.

39 Epp, "Die Entstehung eines 'Nationalbewußtseins'"; Murray, "Ethnic Identity"; Elm, "Die Eroberung Jerusalems"; Elm, "*O beatas idus*"; Kirschberger, *Erster Kreuzzug und Ethnogenese*.

40 Boase, "Arts in the Latin Kingdom"; Boase, "Architecture and Sculpture"; Boase, "Mosaic, Painting, and Minor Arts"; Buchthal, *Miniature Painting*; Weitzmann, *Studies in the Arts at Sinai*; Folda, *Art of the Crusaders*; Folda, *Crusader Art*.

41 Folda, "Reflections on Christian Multiculturalism"; Georgopoulou, "Orientalism and Crusader Art"; Jotischky, "Ethnographic Attitudes"; Ciggaar, "Cultural Identities in Antioch"; Kedar and Aslanov, "Trans-Cultural Borrowing"; Murray, "Franks and Indigenous Communities."

Crusading, western European perspective by proposing a new model for interaction between Latins and Eastern Christians that takes Eastern Christian writings into account.[42]

Meanwhile, intellectual historians such as C. Burnett and, most recently, J. Rubin have sought to put to rest the notion prevailing among earlier scholars that the Latin East constituted an intellectual backwater of little consequence to the developments of European and Mediterranean intellectualism.[43] Burnett identified Latin Antioch as a hub of intellectual activity that, while not on the scale of other twelfth-century hotspots of intellectualism such as Toledo or Palermo, merits serious attention by intellectual historians. Rubin demonstrated that the intellectual culture of thirteenth-century Acre was far more innovative and diverse than previously assumed, with links to local Jewish and Eastern Christian communities as well as to the upper echelons of medieval Europe.

Most recently, scholars of medieval French literature have likewise demonstrated the significance of the Latin East for their field, pointing out that the most revolutionary developments in early French literature occurred not in metropolitan centers such as Paris, as has generally been assumed, but rather in so-called peripheries of the Francophone world, including the Latin East.[44]

A New Approach

Despite the quantum leap in our understanding of the cultural history of the Latin East that has occurred in recent years, a sizeable lacuna remains that this book seeks to fill: no single study has sought to trace the development of a brand-new Latin literary tradition in the Levant from its beginnings. In fact, rather than stimulating the study of Levantine Latin literature, the new appreciation for the achievements of thirteenth-century vernacular culture in the Latin East may lend the impression that the Latin tradition has, by comparison, little to offer to a literary scholar.[45] Moreover, despite the recent appearance of several excellent and sorely needed literary studies of the written sources of the Crusades, these have tended to focus on works produced in a western European context rather than in the Latin East.[46] The scholarly lacuna that remains may be a vestige of the fram-

42 MacEvitt, *Rough Tolerance.*

43 Burnett, "Antioch as a Link"; Rubin, *Learning in a Crusader City.*

44 Aslanov, *Evidence of Francophony*; Minervini, "La français dans l'orient"; Gaunt, "French Literature Abroad"; Morreale and Paul, *French of Outremer*; Morato and Schoenaers, "Medieval Francophone Literary Culture."

45 See, for instance, König's disappointed assessment that, contrary to the Romance languages, "Latin text production in the Eastern Mediterranean seems to have been limited to the ecclesiastical sphere" ("Latin-Arabic Entanglement," 87).

46 See the essays collected in Parsons and Paterson, *Literature of the Crusades*; Smith and Buck, *Remembering the Crusades*; Bale, *Cambridge Companion.* For a recent study of a literary genre

ing of the Latin East as culturally barren, intellectually passive colonies on the periphery of Europe. By definition, such a framing entails the denial of an autonomous literary or intellectual tradition.[47] Even as advances in art history, intellectual history, and French linguistics and literature have sought to examine the culture of the Latin East in its own right and not merely as a contributor to European cultural history, so it is necessary to study the Latin literature of the Levant on its own terms.[48]

As discussed in greater detail in chapter 1, the western European settlers of the Levant employed Latin in a wide range of settings and media: inscriptions on coins and seals, documents and legal texts, and letters. They expressed their most elaborate and explicit notions about their culture and identity in works of extended prose and poetry (and combinations of the two), some of which a modern reader would readily qualify as "literature" or even "belles-lettres." However, I will also examine texts perhaps less commonly considered by literary scholars, including abbreviated histories, accounts of the discovery of relics, sermons, liturgical texts, and even the prefaces to scientific works. In casting a wide net, I have chosen to err on the side of inclusiveness when selecting the source materials for this study. This approach finds support from the source texts themselves, which evince the need for a conception of literature not constrained by narrowly defined, clear-cut formal and generic characteristics. Many works of the Latin East defy easy categorization because they combine prose and verse or include elements of other genres. In attempting to be fairly comprehensive—only coins and seals, administrative and legal texts, and inscriptions are excluded from the analysis (though the latter are discussed wherever relevant)—I also aim to avoid the impression of circularity, of tailoring the analytical corpus to suit the argument. Brief descriptions of the sources used in this study and the evidence for their composition in the twelfth-century Latin East appear in appendix 1.

Based on these primary sources, the central argument advanced in this study is that settlers from a range of different language groups across western Europe in the wake of the First Crusade established a distinctive and coherent Latin literary tradition that both drew on and resisted Levantine Muslim, Christian, and Jewish cultures in the newly occupied territories. In so doing, the settlements of the Levant produced a Latin literature distinct from that in Europe. This argument relies on an analysis of the literary and rhetorical techniques employed in these sources, combined with cultural-historical methods that contextualize authors

---

related to the Crusades on a Mediterranean scale (covering European and Levantine sources), see Boyadjian, *City Lament*.

47 See most explicitly Prawer, *Latin Kingdom*, 530.

48 Compare Boase's early insistence that the literature of the Latin East possesses distinctive "local colour" ("Arts in the Latin Kingdom," 21), and note Kedar's plea for such an approach ("La *Via sancti sepulchri*," 181).

and their works and examine the literary communities addressed in and shaped by them. In writing a literary history, I have endeavored to produce a locally mapped study that considers not only literary techniques and motifs but also textual traditions, social and political circumstances, and institutional networks.[49]

This book's argument for the development of a Levantine Latin literary tradition over the course of the twelfth century seeks to balance two agents of change. On the one hand, I suggest that the development of Latin literature from Fulcher of Chartres to William of Tyre possessed an internal logic, driven by authors and their use of texts. On the other hand, I identify a variety of external factors (political, cultural, social, etc.) that exerted influences upon authors and their literary activity. I acknowledge that positing literary developments involves imposing a teleology on a set of sources. By attempting to balance these two agents, I have aimed to avoid the assumption that these developments were necessary. Other readers may view the Latin sources from the Levant differently, however, and it is not likely—nor desirable—that this study will remain the final word on the matter.

The Parameters and Organization of This Book

This study is limited to the twelfth century. More precisely, I have chosen as my chronological parameters the years 1099 and 1187, which mark the completion of the First Crusade and the end of the first Kingdom of Jerusalem with the conquest of the city by Ṣalāḥ al-Dīn (Saladin). This delimitation has several practical benefits. First, a focus on this early phase of the Latin East enables a sustained analysis of the genesis and development of a literary tradition without covering much of the same ground as previous scholarship. For the intellectual history of the Kingdom of Jerusalem, at least, the subsequent period has now received a full treatment by J. Rubin.[50] Moreover, these limits offer our study a degree of both geographical and linguistic coherence. Beginning in 1191, the settlements of the Latin East grew across large reaches of the eastern Mediterranean, including Cyprus and, following the Fourth Crusade (1204), also encompassing Constantinople (briefly) and large swathes of the Peloponnese. Furthermore, in the twelfth century the literary sources produced by the settlers in the Latin East were written almost exclusively in Latin. By contrast, the thirteenth-century Latin East witnessed the development of a growing body of French literature alongside the continued production of Latin texts. Much of the Latin composed in the thirteenth-century Latin East was connected with centers of study established there by the mendicant orders—religious institutions that did not exist prior to the thirteenth century—and may

49 For the case for such an approach, see the special issue of *Interfaces* on *Histories of Medieval European Literatures*, especially Müller, "Gute Geschichte/n."
50 Rubin, *Learning in a Crusader City*.

thus rightfully be regarded as a new literary development. This transition, in which vernacular (especially French) literature competed with Latin with increasing success, forms the end point of this study and is engaged with in the final chapter.

To chart the development of Levantine Latinity from its beginnings, this book is organized chronologically, starting with the genesis of a Levantine Latin literary tradition shortly after the end of the First Crusade (1099) in chapter 2 and concluding with William of Tyre's monumental history of the Latin East, completed shortly before the Battle of Hattin (1187), in chapter 5. Within this chronological organization, I have adopted a subdivision based on smaller subsets of literary communities. Chapter 2 examines the historical writings of Fulcher of Chartres, a priest at various points closely connected with the king of Jerusalem and quite possibly the Church of the Holy Sepulcher, whose work reveals the development of a Latin literary tradition in Jerusalem over several decades. Chapter 3 centers on the efforts of communities of regular canons in the Kingdom of Jerusalem to create institutional identities through Latin belles-lettres, while chapter 4 examines the development of a learned Latin discourse specific to the Principality of Antioch, yet very much connected to the Kingdom of Jerusalem. Chapter 5 treats the substantial historical writings of William, a royal chancellor and archbishop of Tyre, whose work represents the culmination of several literary and intellectual developments. Our study concludes with a reflection on the ways in which the literary culture of the Levant changed over the course of the late twelfth and early thirteenth centuries.

Chapter One

LEVANTINE LATINITY

THIS CHAPTER CENTERS ON THE ROLE of Latin as a unifying language among the western European settlers of the twelfth-century Levant, who established Latin as the language of law, religion, and intellectual pursuit and founded schools, libraries, and centers of book production. Because Latin possessed this cultural currency, settlers could obtain wealth, prestige, and influence by composing Latin literature.[1] After presenting an overview of the surviving sources from the Latin East, the chapter concludes by situating Levantine Latinity in the context of other Latin expansion movements in Europe and the Mediterranean during the twelfth century.

Varieties of Levantine Latinity

Amid the diverse cultural and linguistic landscape of the Levant, the Franks employed Latin in a variety of domains, including commerce, administration, and law and governance (both secular and ecclesiastical).

Latin was ubiquitous in legends on coins, which had either been brought from western Europe or were minted by the Franks themselves.[2] Except in the County of Edessa, where the limited evidence indicates that the counts favored Greek on their coinage, the Frankish rulers of the twelfth-century Levant employed Latin to identify themselves as the issuing authority (with or without title) and to record the place of issue. In the Principality of Antioch, the princes issued coins bearing Greek and Latin legends (occasionally both on a single coin) until the introduction of exclusively Latin coins with the arrival of the Provençal Raymond of

1 For the notion of Latin as providing cultural capital in the Middle Ages, see the essays in part two of Hexter and Townsend, *Oxford Handbook*. For an expansive recent overview of book culture in the Latin East, see Bale, "Reading and Writing in Outremer."

2 The standard studies of coins in the Latin East remain Porteous, "Crusader Coinage"; Bates and Metcalf, "Crusader Coinage"; Metcalf, *Coinage of the Crusades*.

FIGURE 2
Imitation of a dinar of al-Amīr, Misr. Cambridge, MA, Harvard Art Museums/Arthur M. Sackler Museum, bequest of Thomas Whittemore, 1951.31.4.2365. Photo © President and Fellows of Harvard College.

Poitiers in 1136. The early use of Greek by the Norman rulers of Antioch may reflect both their proximity to the Byzantines and a more widespread Norman tradition of Byzantine imitation.[3] In the County of Tripoli and the Kingdom of Jerusalem, rulers struck, in addition to Latin silver, copper, and billon (an alloy of silver and copper) coins, imitations of gold dinars known as bezants, with Arabic legends reproducing those of the Fatimid Caliphs al-Amīr (in the Kingdom of Jerusalem) and al-Mustanṣir (in the County of Tripoli) (fig. 2). While it is hazardous to draw ideological conclusions on the basis of numismatic evidence (where concerns over maintaining stable currencies were key factors), it is clear that Latin did not simply replace Greek and Arabic culture in the Levant.[4]

Although coins could be used by rulers for self-representation, seals were a more common way for members of the elite to express their identity and authority.[5] Both secular lords and ecclesiastical authorities (such as patriarchs, bishops, and abbots) used lead and wax seals to authenticate documents. While a scribe could forge a document, it was expensive and difficult to reproduce the attached seals. Intricately engraved, seals were miniature artworks that often featured the likeness of the associated individual or symbols representing an institution. The kings of Jerusalem famously depicted on their seals the three most prominent edifices in Jerusalem: the Church of the Holy Sepulcher, the Tower of David, and the Dome of the Rock (known to the Franks as the Templum Domini, or Lord's Temple) (fig. 3). In addition to a pictorial representation, seals bore identifying text. In contrast to the coinage of the Latin East, seals featured Latin almost exclusively, with the exception of the bilingual Greek and Latin inscriptions of the Latin patriarchs of Jerusalem, beginning with Fulcher of Angoulême (1147–1157) (see fig. 4 for a later example).[6]

3 Rheinheimer, "Tankred und das Siegel Boemunds."

4 See the caveats in Metcalf, "Six Unresolved Problems."

5 For seals from the Latin East, see Schlumberger and Chalandon, *Sigillographie*; Mayer, *Siegelwesen*; Mayer and Sode, *Die Siegel*.

6 Mayer, *Siegelwesen*, 12; Folda, *Art of the Crusaders*, 231.

FIGURE 3
Seal of Amalric, king of Jerusalem. Cambridge, MA, Harvard Art Museums/Arthur M. Sackler Museum, bequest of Thomas Whittemore, BZS.1951.31.5.2939. Scale 1:1. Photo © Dumbarton Oaks Research Library and Collection.

FIGURE 4
Seal of Amalric, Latin patriarch of Jerusalem. Washington, DC, Dumbarton Oaks Research Library and Collection, BZS 1970.21. Scale 1:1. Photo © Dumbarton Oaks Research Library and Collection.

The documents these seals authenticated were written in Latin. Secular and ecclesiastical authorities employed Latin documents to record contracts and transactions, to keep a record of the resolution of disputes, and to issue decrees. In the twelfth century, Latin thus functioned as a language of administration, governance, and law. While the documents were issued by Frankish authorities, the list of witnesses typically concluding them sometimes included Eastern Christians.[7]

The earliest extant laws from the Latin East (and the only ones dating to the twelfth century) are twenty-five canons, written in Latin and promulgated at a council convened at Nablus on 16 January 1120 by Warmund, patriarch of Jerusalem, and King Baldwin II of Jerusalem.[8] The canons show a sophisticated

7 For an example of Eastern Christian witnesses, see *Cart St-Sép*, 178–83, no. 77 (RRH no. 194; RRR no. 391).

8 Kedar, "Origins of the Earliest Laws."

incorporation of Latin Christian legal elements (such as the ordeal) into a Byzantine legal framework ultimately derived from the *Ecloga*, a legal code promulgated in 741 by the Byzantine emperors Leo III and Constantine V. In addition to combining Latin Christian and Byzantine law, the canons include innovations addressing issues specific to the Franks of the Levant: stringent laws forbidding sexual relations between Franks and "Saracens" (Muslims), a prohibition on Franks wearing Saracen dress, and permission for clerics to bear defensive arms. Like the numismatic and diplomatic evidence, the canons of Nablus thus paint a picture of a complex web of cultural interactions between Latins, Byzantines, and Muslims.

While coins, seals, and documents all employed Latin in its written form, oral and musical performance constituted an important dimension of Levantine Latinity. In fact, crusading itself can be said to have begun with a Latin oration. At the Council of Clermont in 1095, Pope Urban II preached his famous call for (what would later come to be known as) a Crusade to a broad audience of both clerical and lay members. He did so not in French—his mother tongue, and the language that was spoken by most of the attendees—but, as one contemporary writer noted with approval, in expertly spoken Latin.[9] This was the timeless language of prayer and of official ecclesiastical business in the Roman Catholic Church. In the many monasteries, convents, and churches dotting the Latin East, monks, canons, priests, bishops, and patriarchs preached Latin sermons and celebrated Latin liturgies.

Recent scholarship has significantly enhanced our knowledge of liturgical practices in the Latin East and shown how liturgies helped shape communal identities and functioned as sophisticated forms of intellectual expression.[10] The fact that no fewer than seven of the nine surviving manuscripts from the twelfth-century scriptorium at the Church of the Holy Sepulcher are liturgical manuscripts attests to the importance of Latin as a liturgical language. These and later manuscript witnesses offer tangible evidence that Latin was not only written and read in the Levant, but frequently spoken and heard. The liturgical instructions provided in so-called ordinals, as well as, in some instances, musical notations, offer a small window onto the oral dimension of Levantine Latinity. For many of those who were not members of the intellectual elite, the spoken (or sung) word was one of the few forms in which they were exposed to the Latin language.[11] Even for

9 Guibert of Nogent, *Dei gesta per Francos* 2.3, discussed in Haye, *Lateinische Oralität*, 20–24.

10 The literature has now assumed substantial proportions. See, for the most important recent contributions: Salvadó, "Liturgy of the Holy Sepulchre"; Shagrir and Gaposchkin, *Liturgy and Devotion*; Gaposchkin, *Invisible Weapons*; and Aspesi, "Breviary of Lucca." For groundbreaking earlier work, see Linder, "Liturgy of the Liberation," and Dondi, *Liturgy of the Canons*.

11 For musical notation of liturgical manuscripts of the Latin East, see Aspesi, "Breviary of Lucca," 92–128, 331. See also below, p. 40, on the liturgical fragments with musical notation from the Qubbat al-Ḫazna of Damascus.

most clergy, for whom access to complete collections of the Bible was rare until the thirteenth century, the liturgy provided their primary interaction with scripture.[12]

The importance of the liturgy in the day-to-day experience of settlers in the Latin East emerges from the many references to ritual processions through Jerusalem that involved communal song—presumably in Latin, given that they were led by Latin clergy.[13] Various remarks in narrative sources also indicate that Latin song was part of the daily life of clergy and monastic communities and to some extent even of lay people. When the canons at the church of Hebron began to excavate the tombs of the patriarchs and matriarchs hidden beneath their church, their priests reportedly celebrated mass while other clergy recited psalms and lay members of the community prayed.[14] After a lengthy captivity by Muslims near Tyre, the laywoman Margaret of Beverly was later said to have possessed only her rags and a psalter.[15] In the midst of a narrative of King Amalric's military exploits, the historian William of Tyre employed a liturgical reference to date a battle, thus evincing something of his own frame of reference as well as that of his anticipated readership.[16] In fact, liturgy and historiography were closely intertwined in the Latin East: two Latin histories from early twelfth-century Antioch include original poems in meters typically used in hymns, while readings from another early twelfth-century historian were incorporated into a liturgy at the Church of the Holy Sepulcher in Jerusalem.[17]

However, liturgy was likely not the only context for oral Latinity in the Levant, as both poetry and historiography may have been recited. The poem of Achard of Arrouaise, prior of the Templum Domini, may have been intended for a performance in song, either by Achard at the king's court or as part of a new commemorative tradition among the canons of the Templum Domini. This is suggested by the poet's frequent references to his activity in terms evoking orality, as well as the fact that the poem employs the meter of a hymn.[18] Likewise, the chronicler Fulcher of Chartres addressed his audience as comprising both readers and

12 Murray, "Biblical Quotations," 27.

13 See, for instance, Fulcher of Chartres's depiction of both clergy and lay people singing hymns in a procession through the city immediately after the Crusader conquest of Jerusalem: FC 1.29.2. For other examples of processions, see MacEvitt, "Processing Together."

14 *Tractatus de inventione* 301–6.

15 The episode occurs in the account of her life by her brother Thomas of Froidmont, *Hodoeporicon*. For a discussion, see Bale, "Reading and Writing," 85–86.

16 WT 19.24.70–72: *quarta deinde die, sabbato videlicet, que illam dominicam precedit qua in ecclesia cantatur Letare Ierusalem, nuntiatur hostes esse in proximo.*

17 RC 3166–95; WC 1.7.8–9, 2.6.7. For Fulcher of Chartres's incorporation of the Crusader capture into the liturgical commemoration, see chap. 2.

18 Poleg in GA, *Mac*, 14. For verbs indicating a potential oral performance, see AP ll. 9, 26, 40, 43–44, 680. See also chap. 3.

listeners and referred to his literary activity as an oral performance.[19] His contemporary Walter the Chancellor similarly seems to have expected an oral performance of his history.[20] Some limited evidence is also available about the potential audience for such recitations: William of Tyre famously portrayed King Baldwin III and Baldwin IV each as an avid "listener of histories" (*historiarum auditor*).[21] While, as several scholars have pointed out, such a characterization is a trope of royal and imperial biography that goes back to Einhard's depiction of Charlemagne and does not necessarily reflect these kings' true habits, the fact that William does not apply this description uniformly to all Latin kings of Jerusalem (in fact, he compares Amalric unfavorably to his brother Baldwin III precisely for his lack of interest in reading history) indicates that these portraits should not be dismissed out of hand.[22]

In addition to its role in commercial, administrative, legal, and liturgical settings, Latin functioned as a medium for literary expression and intellectual discourse by which speakers and writers communicated with an elite similarly trained in a classicizing program of education. As a learned language, Latin united scholars who, though removed from each other in time and space and culturally differentiated, considered themselves members of an intellectual tradition. The Latin sources from the twelfth-century Levant frequently appeal to this shared background in explicit terms. In one of the prefaces to his translation-cum-commentary of an Arabic cosmological treatise, the Antiochene scholar Stephen the Philosopher bewails the limited and often erroneous astronomical education of "Latinity" (*Latinitas*) that rested primarily on the fifth-century Roman author Macrobius. Stephen draws a line tracing a continuous linguistic and intellectual tradition from the late Roman Empire to his twelfth-century contemporaries across western Europe and the Mediterranean. When he describes his project as "transmitting into the power of Latin expression secrets unknown to the ears of our people" (*Latine tradere facultati nostratum incognita auribus archana*), his aim ranges beyond mere linguistic translation. Stephen wishes to introduce Ptolemaic cosmology, as preserved and developed in Arabic texts, into the Latin cultural and intellectual vocabulary.[23]

The Norman writer Ralph of Caen, Stephen's contemporary in Antioch, similarly situated Latin literary activity in a continuum extending from Roman

19 FC 1.26.7; 1.33.12; 3.50.15.

20 WC 1 prol. 1: *operae pretium est audire and auditis enim miraculorum virtutibus*; the prefatory poem to book 2: *Galterius hic recitavit*; 2 prol. 1 and 2 prol. 2: *auditorum*.

21 WT 16.2.12–19; 21.1.50.

22 Vessey, "William of Tyre," 438; Jaeger, *Origins of Courtliness*, 228; WT 16.2.12–19.

23 SP, *Liber Mamonis*, 2 pref. 1–2, 174. It is possible that Stephen employed *facultas* here in a technical rhetorical sense ("power" or "ability"), as in Cicero, *De inventione* 1.5.7. For Stephen's manuscript copy and use of this text, see chap. 4.

antiquity to an open-ended future. In the prologue to his ambitious narrative of Norman exploits during and after the First Crusade using a combination of prose and poetry, Ralph writes to his former schoolteacher (and, at the time of Ralph's writing, Latin patriarch of Jerusalem), "We ought to strive with every effort to read what has been written and to write what deserves to be read in order that, by reading ancient writings and by writing new ones, antiquity may satisfy us in our need, while we, having been satisfied, nourish posterity in its need."[24]

This book centers on Latin as a mode of literary discourse and on the efforts of twelfth-century writers such as Ralph of Caen to shape a learned Latin literature in a part of the world where no such tradition had existed. A variety of motives occupied authors in their endeavors, often at the same time. Some may have hoped to ingratiate themselves with a patron while earning undying literary fame (and generous financial compensation); others wrote as representatives of a community, aiming to set down authoritative foundational narratives of their brand-new institution; and still others sought to consolidate the position of the Latin Church in disputed areas of the Levant by formulating a program of religious polemic. To engage in these learned activities, authors required an infrastructure: schooling for those born in the Latin East, libraries of books to consult and to serve as repositories for the authors' own works, scriptoria or centers of book production for the more elaborate projects, and patrons to fund it all. In the following, I offer a brief sketch of the evidence for each of these elements in the twelfth-century Latin East.

Latin Education

In the twelfth century, Latin education was organized in parish churches, monasteries, court chapels, and cathedral schools. Additionally, over the course of this century new institutions of higher learning were founded that would, by the early thirteenth century, develop into universities.[25] While many Latin authors immigrated to the Levant as adults, secular and ecclesiastical institutions needed locally organized programs of schooling to instruct new generations and to ensure a steady influx of educated personnel without relying solely on newcomers from Europe. Already by 1103, less than four years after the capture of Jerusalem, provisions were made for Latin instruction at the Church of the Holy Sepulcher. In the period between October 1102 and March 1103, Evremar, patriarch of Jerusalem, ordered the disbursement of an annual sum of 150 bezants to each resident canon at the

24 RC prol. 1.6–9: *Debemus igitur summa ope niti et legere scripta et scribere legenda, quatinus, legendo vetera, scriptitando nova, hinc nos antiquitas egentes saciet, inde posteritatem saciati nutriamus egentem.*

25 For background on the developments of Latin schooling in the High Middle Ages, see Jaeger, *Envy of Angels*, and Orme, *Medieval Schools.*

Church of the Holy Sepulcher. Evremar listed among the offices of cantor, treasurer, and sacristan that of the *magister scholasticus* or "master of the school," the person normally responsible for instruction along with the succentor (*subcantor*).[26] These teachers and their students also played a role in liturgical celebrations at the Church of the Holy Sepulcher. For instance, during the Palm Sunday procession through the city, the succentor and the master of the school (here given as *magister scole*) reenacted with their students (*pueri*) the singing of the "children of the Hebrews" (*pueri Hebraeorum*) mentioned in the Palm Sunday antiphon.[27]

The various legal documents from the twelfth- and thirteenth-century Latin East enable us to piece together valuable information about the existence of schools outside of Jerusalem and the people who administered them. For example, one Mainardus, "teacher of the clerics of the church of Beirut" (*Berutensis ecclesie clericorum doctor*) witnessed a charter of the Hospital of Saint John of Jerusalem in 1133. If this is the same individual as one "Lord Mainardus, bishop of Beirut" (*domnus Mainardus Beritensis episcopus*) from a document of 1163, it seems that Mainardus assumed his teaching profession at a relatively early age.[28] The mention of a canon named Leonardus, master of the school, in a document issued by Aimery of Limoges, Latin patriarch of Antioch, attests to the existence of a school at the church of Antioch by 1185.[29] Several decades later, in 1213/1214, we learn that a deacon had been "in charge of the schools" of the church of Antioch for nine years before being given a canonry in the chapter of Antioch.[30] Unnamed masters of the schools (*magistri scolarum*) witnessed a document of Patriarch Albert of Antioch in 1233—these were presumably teachers at the church of Antioch, though perhaps also of the churches of Tyre, Tripoli, Sidon, and Beirut, whose bishops all witnessed the document.[31]

The cathedral teaching office seems to have been the first rung on the career of some promising clergy in the Latin East, such as the aforementioned Bishop Mainardus of Beirut and John of Pisa, who became a cardinal in Rome after instructing "young clergy" (*clericulos*) at the Holy Sepulcher in the early decades of the twelfth century.[32] Other clerics in the Latin East held a teaching office

26 *Cart St-Sép*, 72–74, no. 19; *UKJ* 1:128–30, no. 24 (RRH no. 40; RRR no. 69).

27 Rome, BAV, Barberini lat. 659, fol. 66r; Salvadó, "Liturgy of the Holy Sepulchre," 577: *Tunc subcantor et magister scole et pueri cum ipsis ascendunt super portam per quam Dominus Ihesus adveniens intravit, et ibi expectant donec ingressi congregentur.* For this observation, see Zöller, "Regular Canons," 381.

28 *Cart St-Sép*, 258–59, no. 132 (RRH no. 385; RRR no. 700).

29 *Cart Hosp*, 1:446–47, no. 665 (RRH no. 636; RRR no. 1152). In a slight variation, his office appears as *magister scolarum* in the witness list.

30 Antweiler, *Bistum Tripolis*, 268.

31 *Cart Hosp*, 2:455–57, no. 2058 (RRH no. 1043; RRR no. 2205).

32 *Cart St-Sép*, 222–23, no. 103 (RRH no. 166; RRR no. 348); Hotzelt, "Die Chorherren," 118. Dating to 1136, the charter bears the subscription "written by the hand of John of Pisa, who at that

before their arrival in the Levant. For example, Arnulf of Chocques, patriarch of Jerusalem (briefly in 1099, and later in 1112–15 and 1116–18), had taught Latin literature at the renowned abbey school of Saint-Étienne in Caen, in Normandy. One of his pupils there, Ralph of Caen, later traveled to Antioch and dedicated a historical composition to his former teacher, possibly after moving to Jerusalem.[33] Achard of Arrouaise had been a master of the schools at the Church of Saint Mary in northern French Arras before heading a community of canons at the Templum Domini.[34] Another former teacher was Elias, who taught grammar near southern French Narbonne before undertaking a pilgrimage to Jerusalem sometime between 1131–38. As a hermit in Jerusalem, Elias acquired a following with whom he retired to a nearby cave, but he eventually became abbot, first of the monastery of Saint Mary in the Valley of Jehoshaphat, in Jerusalem, and finally of the abbey of Palmaria, in Galilee, where he enjoyed renown for his austerity and scriptural learning. Elias's biographer Gerard of Nazareth may have been a native of Galilee, where he spent some time early in his life as a recluse in a small cell before making a career as bishop of Laodicea in the Principality of Antioch (ca. 1140–1161). During his time in Galilee, Gerard also engaged in teaching activities, unsuccessfully attempting to teach an illiterate anchorite to read the psalms.[35] Even in the thirteenth century, the Latin East continued to attract those who had been teachers in the Latin West, as exemplified by Nicholas Leccirius, who had been a master of the schools in Genoa before becoming cantor of Tripoli and eventually archbishop of Tyre (1251–1253).[36]

Churches did not have a monopoly on education in the Latin East, and it did not take long for military orders and other groups to secure privileges to organize their own schooling. An agreement between the bishop of Acre and the master of the Hospitallers dated to 1175 states that the bishop "shall not prevent the children who wish to receive an education in the house of the Hospital [from receiving an education there]." In securing the Hospitallers' right to run a school in Acre, the document implies the existence of a school at the city's cathedral.[37] In 1190, the Venetians sued for their right to have, among other privileges, their own schools in the Venetian third of Tyre, which similarly implies the existence of other schools there not run by Venetians.[38]

---

time was teaching the young clergy" (*scriptum per manum Iohannis Pisani qui eo tempore ad Sepulchrum clericulos docebat*).

33 RC prol. 58–64; see chap. 4.

34 Milis, *L'ordre des chanoines*, 1:100; see chap. 3.

35 Kedar, "Gerard of Nazareth," 72.

36 Antweiler, *Bistum Tripolis*, 268.

37 *Cart Hosp*, 1:87–88, no. 100 (RRH no. 144; RRR no. 316); Rubin, *Learning in a Crusader City*, 55.

38 Hiestand, *Papsturkunden*, 337–39, no. 161.

Aristocrats and royalty in the Latin East could afford to hire private tutors for their children. Given their proximity to centers of power and influence, these positions must have been highly sought after. In addition to teaching at Saint-Etienne, Arnulf of Chocques had previously served as tutor to Cecilia, daughter of William the Conqueror, before joining the First Crusade. Beginning in 1170, famed historian of the Latin East William of Tyre tutored the young prince Baldwin IV of Jerusalem (later known as the Leper King). At the time, William held the office of archdeacon of Tyre, already an elevated position in the church hierarchy. His next appointment came four years later as chancellor of the Kingdom of Jerusalem (the chief secular administrative office in charge of day-to-day governance), followed a year later by the archiepiscopate of Tyre. That William held the position of private tutor amid these prominent offices demonstrates the esteem associated with instructing a prince of the kingdom. Similarly, a charter from 1223 proudly identifies its author as one "W. Rostaig, master of the children of Lord Rainaldus of Mimars" (*W. Rostaig magister puerorum domni Rainaldi de Mimars*).[39]

A papal letter dating to 1212 gives some indication of the costs of education.[40] In this letter, Pope Innocent III orders an investigation into the disappearance of a sum of 1,000 bezants left to Iterius, a canon of the church of Antioch, and his brother by their uncle, Peter of Angoulême, former patriarch of Antioch (1196–1208). Peter of Angoulême had intended the money for his nephews' education (*in studiis scholasticis*) and deposited it for safekeeping with the master of the Hospital of Saint John of Jerusalem, who in turn transferred the funds to the new patriarch of Antioch, Peter of Ivrea. Peter of Ivrea, it seems, kept the money for himself. To put the 500 bezants per nephew apportioned for tuition into perspective, we may recall that in the year 1103, 150 bezants constituted the yearly allowance of a canon at the prestigious Church of the Holy Sepulcher. It is unclear whether Peter of Angoulême had intended to fund his nephews' schooling in the Latin East or whether he had planned to send them to Europe, as those of means appear to have been disposed to do. William of Tyre, who was born in Jerusalem and may have come from a wealthy merchant family, famously spent nineteen years studying all over Europe pursuing the liberal arts, theology, and law before returning to the Latin East.[41]

39 Mayer, *Marseilles Levantehandel*, 191–92, no. 8 (RRH no. 965; RRR no. 1953).

40 Innocent III, *Die Register Innocenz' III*, no. 181 (RRH no. 859a; RRR no. 1663); Antweiler, *Bistum Tripolis*, 204.

41 Edbury and Rowe (*William of Tyre*, 15) question the extent to which William's claim to have spent the period of his studies in "voluntary poverty" should be taken at face value (WT 19.12.13). Even if he did possess affluent origins, it is reasonable to assume that the high expenses he incurred necessitated a relatively modest lifestyle.

Scholars and students required book collections to consult materials and to serve as repositories for their own works. Most of the older monasteries and churches in the Levant predating the First Crusade would have built up libraries over the years, while new institutions established collections with books brought from western Europe or newly produced manuscripts from Levantine scriptoria (see below). Sometimes new foundations received books as donations from wealthy patrons, as in the case of the convent of Saint Lazarus of Bethany. Queen Melisende of Jerusalem established this convent in 1143 to spare her sister Iveta the indignity of having to serve under an abbess at the existing convent of Saint Anne's, endowing the new foundation with chalices and other liturgical objects, as well as books.[42] Individual bishops likewise enriched the libraries of their sees. For example, William of Tyre references his account of the Third Lateran Council (1179), for which "I had given orders to place it in the archives of the holy church of Tyre, along with the other books I had bestowed upon this church."[43]

In a rare instance, a charter from the Church of Saint Mary of the Valley of Jehoshaphat, dating to 1129 and drawn up by one "Hugo, priest and librarian of [the church of] Bethlehem" (*Hugo Bethleemitae sacerdos et bibliotecarius*), attests to the size of the library by virtue of having a dedicated librarian (though he apparently also engaged in scribal activities).[44] The absence of librarians in documents obscures the evidence for libraries in the Latin East, since at cathedrals the management of book collections was typically divided between the offices of the chanter (*cantor*) and treasurer (*thesaurarius*), who safeguarded liturgical books, vestments, and relics.[45]

A twelfth-century manuscript now held in Erfurt provides direct evidence for one library (fig. 5).[46] The verso of the last folio contains a list of books, announcing that "these are the books of the convent of the church of Nazareth" (*hii sunt libri conventus nazarene ecclesie*; a complete transcription and translation of this catalogue appear in appendix 2). The Cathedral of the Annunciation in Nazareth was one of the largest churches in the Kingdom of Jerusalem and hosted a church synod in the summer of 1160.[47] The "convent" referenced in the catalogue likely refers to the chapter of regular canons (clergy who observed a semimonastic rule)

42 WT 15.26.8–11, 43–45.
43 WT 21.25.73–79.
44 Kohler, "Chartes de l'abbaye," 125–27, no. 17 (RRH no. 129a; RRR no. 277).
45 Minervini, "Produzione e circolazione," 80.
46 Erfurt, Stadtbücherei, Ampl. Q. 102. See appendix 2 for a transcription.
47 Pringle, *Churches* 2:119; Hamilton, *Latin Church*, 76.

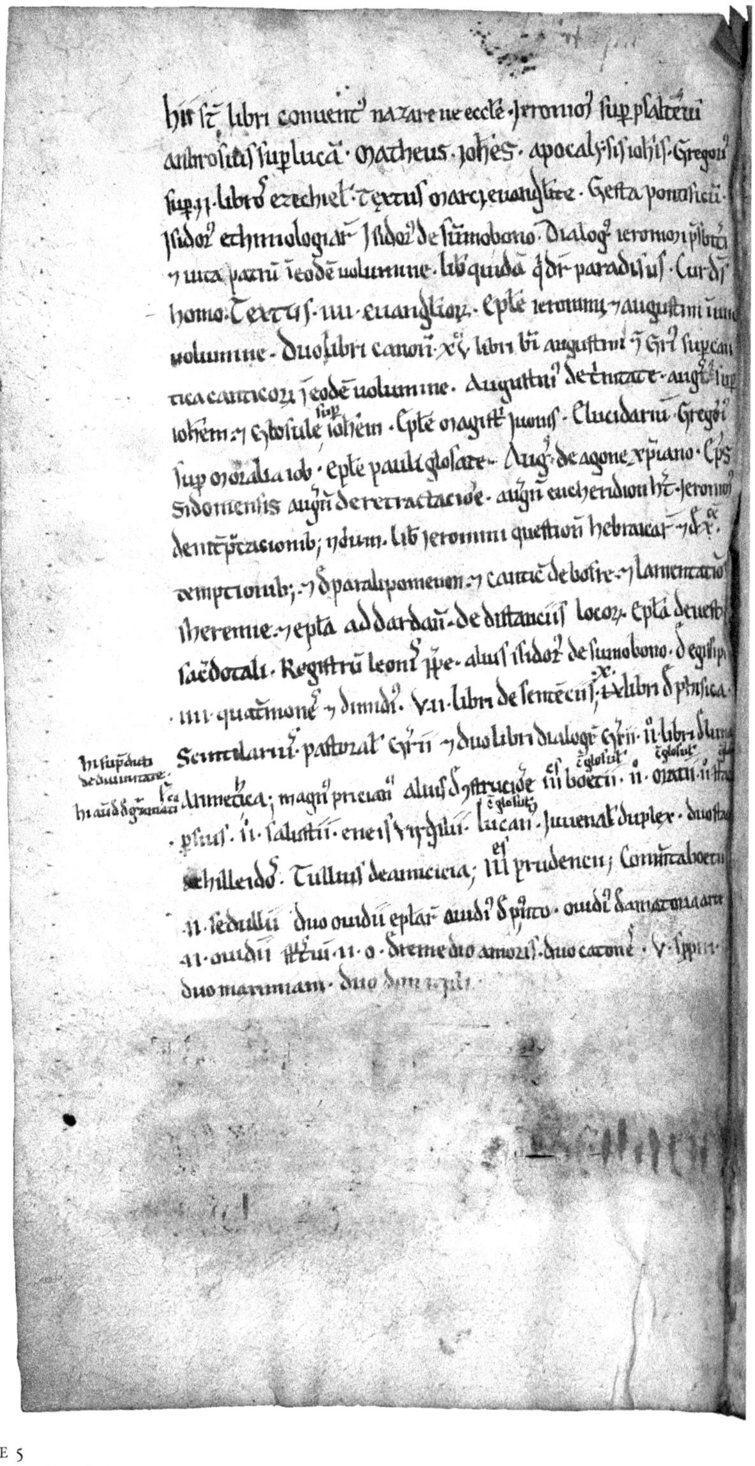

FIGURE 5
Catalogue of books belonging to the church of Nazareth. Universität Erfurt, UB Erfurt, Dep. Erf., CA 4° 102, fol. 167v. Photo courtesy the Universitätsbibliothek Erfurt.

attached to the cathedral.[48] The catalogue lists a total of sixty-nine different works, several of which were available in multiple copies. As B. Z. Kedar has observed, the library must have been even more extensive than the catalogue leads us to believe, since only two of the nine works copied in the manuscript containing the catalogue are listed.[49] Of the listed works, the cataloguer classified forty-three as "pertaining to theology" (*de divinitate*) and twenty-six as "pertaining to language and literature" (*de gramatica*).[50]

The "theological" texts include separate copies of the gospels and patristic commentaries on biblical texts, as well as Isidore's *Etymologies* and Anselm of Canterbury's *Cur deus homo* (Why God [became] man). The latter was especially relevant in a multiconfessional context, as it could have furnished Latin Christians with arguments against Jews and Muslims concerning the Incarnation of Christ. Moreover, Anselm's letter to Baldwin I of Jerusalem, in which he portrayed the king as a ruler of a biblical mold, may have excited particular interest in Anselm's other works among the canons of Nazareth.[51] Other works under the theological category speak more directly to the Levantine environment of the canons of Nazareth, such as Jerome's treatise on interpreting Hebrew place-names from the Bible and the letter to Dardanus (incorrectly ascribed to Jerome in the Middle Ages) on the distances between various sites mentioned in the Bible.

The books under the heading of *gramatica* cover a range of materials on the liberal arts, including grammar (the popular late ancient textbooks of Donatus and Priscian), astronomy or astrology (a work simply listed as *De luna* or "On the moon"), and arithmetic, as well as unspecified works of Boethius (perhaps his famous *Consolation of Philosophy* or his more technical logical treatises and translations). The majority of books in this category belong to classical Latin literature. The selection of classical texts represents the tastes of contemporary continental cathedral libraries, with common school texts such as Persius, Sallust, Virgil, Lucan, Juvenal, and presumably the *Thebaid* and *Achilleid* of Statius (with at least

48 *Chartes Josaphat*, 82–83, no. 35 (RRH no. 371; RRR no. 676), dating to 1163, references "Lethardus *ecclesie Nazarene archiepiscopus* and his convent." See also the reference to one "Radulfus and his convent" from 1168 in Mayer, *Kanzlei* 2:893–95, no. 5; *UKJ* 2:577–78, no. 335 (RRH no. 393a; RRR no. 806).

49 Kedar ("On Books and Hermits," 48) and Huygens (*Latijn in Outremer*, 12–14) both provide the number of volumes that the library possessed, arriving at a grand tally of 102. However, it is unclear in the catalogue where one volume ends and another begins, as not all works listed in the catalogue were contained in separate volumes. See, for example, the entries *scintilarius* (a work by Bede) and the immediately following *pastoralis Gregorii*: both works are in fact contained in the codex that also has the catalogue.

50 Different numbers can be found in Huygens (46:26) and Kedar (43:29), presumably resulting from a double count of some works. For example, I counted only once the gospels listed separately at the start of the catalogue and the later *textus iiii evangeliorum*.

51 Anselm of Canterbury, *Opera*, no. 324, 255.

one additional volume of the *Achilleid* by itself).[52] There were also two volumes of Horace's poetry (supplied with glosses), although it is not specified whether this refers to the whole or only to parts of his corpus. The final classical poet is Ovid, whose *Epistulae ex Ponto, Heroides, Ars amatoria, Tristia,* and *Remedia amoris* were all represented—most in several copies.[53] The fact that the convent possessed multiple copies of these classical poems strongly suggests that they were used in a school setting. As for classical prose, only Cicero's treatise *De amicitia* is listed. Finally, interspersed among the classical poets are the Christian Latin poets Prudentius, Sedulius, Prosper of Aquitaine, and Maximian.

Strikingly, the cataloguer noted that "the bishop of Sidon has in his possession Augustine's *Retractationes* [Revisions] and Augustine's *Enchiridion* [Handbook]" (*Episcopus Sidoniensis Augustinum de Retractatione, Augustinum encheiridion habet*). Various circumstances may have prompted Sidon to borrow a manuscript, including the need to make fresh copies (due to the damaged state of an existing copy or because of accidental loss, etc.). Moreover, the remark provides some indication of the traffic of books in the twelfth-century Latin East and the potential for texts to find circulation beyond the walls of a single library.

It so happens that several books belonging to the cathedral library of Sidon survive today. While cataloguing the Borghese manuscript collection of the Vatican Library, A. Maier encountered several books with the following ownership mark: "Belonging to the church of Sidon" (*Ecclesie Sidonensis*).[54] In all, thirteen manuscripts from Sidon survive, six of which (and part of one) date to the twelfth century. Their contents range from homilies to Jerome's biographies of celebrities (*De viris illustribus*), a twelfth-century commentary on Revelation, lives of the desert fathers, and Seneca the Younger's *De beneficiis* (On benefits), among other texts. Maier traced these codices to the collection of the Avignon pope Urban V, where they are listed in a catalogue dated to 1369. Maier plausibly suggested that the last bishop of Sidon, the Dominican Rostagnus de Candole, donated them to the papal library, or they could have ended up in papal possession after his death in 1329.[55] Based on records detailing the movement of books from the church of Beirut to Cyprus upon the Latin evacuation in 1291, it seems likely that Adam of Romery, de Candole's predecessor and last bishop to preside in Sidon, similarly

52 The phrase is *duo Stacii Achilleidos*, which could refer to one volume containing the two books of the *Achilleid* or two volumes containing the *Achilleid*.

53 I assume that the item *duo Ovidii epistularum*, listed separately from *Ovidius de Ponto*, refers to the *Heroides*, although it is possible, as apparently interpreted by Huygens (*Latijn in Outremer*, 14), that this item represents merely another copy of the *Epistulae ex Ponto*. See, for instance, the reference to *in epistolis* for Ovid's *Heroides* in the late eleventh-century Blaubeuren catalogue, distinct from the item *de Ponto*: Glauche, *Schullektüre im Mittelalter*, 102–3.

54 Maier, "Die Handschriften," "Die Homiliare," and "Noch einmal." Additional manuscripts were identified by Fohlen ("Un nouveau manuscrit") and Gasnault ("L'homéliaire").

55 Maier, "Die Handschriften," 44–45.

brought the books of the church of Sidon with him to Cyprus, along with other possessions of the church.[56]

The origins of the books of Sidon remain unclear. Given their resemblance to other manuscripts from the area, Maier posited that some may have been commissioned by the church of Sidon from a scriptorium in Tuscany. P. Gasnault alternatively suggested that they were brought by Italian pilgrims and donated to Sidon.[57] One particular manuscript among the books of Sidon contains the canons of the Council of Nablus (held in 1120) and the so-called Sentences of Sidon (*Sententiae Sidonenses*), a collection of canons that took shape in the Latin East from 1130 to 1135.[58] While it cannot be ruled out that some books may originally have been copied in Europe, the presence of this manuscript, which must have been produced in the Latin East, indicates that these books do not represent a single collection that was transported from western Europe to Sidon and then back again.

Scribal Activities and Manuscript Production

Manuscript production in the Latin East occurred in several settings. The kings and patriarchs of Jerusalem, the princes and patriarchs of Antioch, and the counts of Tripoli maintained chanceries or administrative centers overseen by a chancellor, who drew up official documents. Other secular rulers had their chaplains and minor clergy draw up charters on an ad hoc basis.[59]

The production of books took place in centers of manuscript production known as scriptoria (sing. scriptorium). Scriptoria were part of a monastery or cathedral with the resources and personnel to engage in the laborious and expensive task of book production, which involved preparing parchment, binding, copying text, and, for the more luxurious projects, illustrating the text with various pigments or gold leaf and adorning the covers with gold, ivory, and gems. A particularly large scriptorium like the one at the Church of the Holy Sepulcher in Jerusalem may have produced books not merely for its own needs but also to meet those of surrounding churches and monasteries and fulfilling royal commissions. The nine surviving manuscripts from this scriptorium demonstrate the diversity of their clientele. They range from relatively simple and unadorned liturgical books for use by priests to illuminated display copies of the gospels, to a sumptuous psalter intended for Queen Melisende of Jerusalem.[60] This famous manuscript

56 See below, "The Survival of Sources and Fragmentary Manuscripts."

57 Maier, "Noch einmal," 291; Gasnault, "L'homéliaire."

58 Rome, BAV, lat. 1345.

59 On the chancery of the Kingdom of Jerusalem, see Mayer, *Kanzlei*.

60 Rome, BAV, Biblioteca Angelica, 477, a sacramentary; Cambridge, Fitzwilliam Museum, McClean 49, formerly part of the previous manuscript; Paris, BNF, lat. 12056, a copy of the Angelica-McClean manuscript; London, British Museum, Egerton 1139, psalter of Queen Melisende; Paris,

exhibits in its artistic program a combination of Anglo-Angevin, Byzantine, and possibly Islamic features that render the book prototypical of what art historian J. Folda has termed "Crusader art."[61] Four artists were involved in the production of a cycle of miniatures depicting various biblical scenes. Given the Byzantine style, it has been suggested that they worked under the direction of a Greek artist or worked closely from Greek books in the library of the Church of the Holy Sepulcher.[62] One of the artists signed his name in Latin with the phrase "Basilius made me" (*Basilius me fecit*) above three persons identified in Greek. Since the artist did not follow Byzantine iconographic practices consistently and applied them imperfectly, it has been posited that he may have been of western European origin. Yet it is equally plausible that Basilius, whose name may also point to an Eastern Christian cultural identity, represents young, homegrown talent of early twelfth-century Jerusalem.[63] The scribes who copied the Latin texts at the scriptorium of the Holy Sepulcher appear to have been trained in French scriptoria, based on the shapes of the letter forms.[64] One manuscript, however, contains an Armenian numbering of the quires in the same hand that copied the Latin text, attesting the influence of Armenian scribes at the Church of the Holy Sepulcher.[65]

In addition to the one belonging to the Church of the Holy Sepulcher in Jerusalem, other scriptoria operated in the twelfth-century Latin East. After Jerusalem fell to Ṣalāḥ al-Dīn in 1187, the scriptorium of the Holy Sepulcher moved to the city of Acre in the north of the kingdom, where new manuscripts were produced after the arrival of the French king Louis IX in 1250. Given its prominence and the wealth of its patriarchs, the city of Antioch almost certainly possessed a scriptorium.[66] While Antiochene localization of some manuscripts has proven controversial,[67] traces of a patriarchal scriptorium may

---

BNF, lat. 9396, gospel of Saint John; Rome, BAV, Barb. lat. 659, an ordinal for the Knights Templar; Naples, Biblioteca Nazionale, VI. G. 11, a missal; Paris, BNF, lat. 276, four gospels; Rome, BAV, lat. 5974, four gospels.

61 For the Melisende Psalter, see Folda, *Art of the Crusaders*, 137–58; for the notion of "Crusader art," see Folda, *Crusader Art*, 511–27.

62 Buchthal, *Miniature Painting*, 2–13; Folda, *Art of the Crusaders*, 156; Maraszak, *Les manuscrits enluminés*, 93–98.

63 Folda, *Art of the Crusaders*, 155. This Basilius may be the same individual as the Basilius listed as *scriptor* of the mosaic angels in the upper nave in the Church of the Nativity in Bethlehem; see Boase, "Arts in the Latin Kingdom," 15. For an example of the name Basilius as used by Suriani, see *UKJ* 1:466–69, no. 256; 2:529, no. 302 (RRH no. 353; RRR no. 652), dating to 1160; for an Armenian example from 1207, see *Cart Hosp* 2:70–71, no. 1262 (RRH no. 820; RRR no. 1589).

64 Wormald (Buchthal, *Miniature Painting*, 135); Folda, *Art of the Crusaders*, 86–87.

65 Wormald (Buchthal, *Miniature Painting*, 135); Folda, *Art of the Crusaders*, 162.

66 On the wealth of the patriarchs of Antioch, especially Aimery of Limoges, see Hamilton, *Latin Church*, 154.

67 The so-called San Daniele Bible, which exhibits Syro-Armenian features in its coloring and patterning, may have come from the Principality of Antioch, as Folda (*Art of the Crusaders*,

be found in a fragmentary thirteenth-century psalter and in a thirteenth-century calendar of the Latin church of Antioch.[68] The opulent cathedral of Tyre likewise may have featured a scriptorium.[69] Its existence by the thirteenth century is confirmed in an extant liturgical handbook, the so-called pontifical of Tyre, while for the twelfth century a case has recently been made to assign another liturgical manuscript to the putative scriptorium of Tyre.[70] The presence of a scribe among the regular canons of the church of Hebron in 1119 may indicate a scriptorium or archive, even before the church's elevation to a cathedral in 1167.[71] Finally, the existence of an archiepiscopal archive or library in twelfth-century Caesarea may point to the presence of a scriptorium there.[72]

While highly placed ecclesiastical officials and members of the royal house required well-organized scriptoria to produce deluxe manuscripts, literary and scientific compositions involved manuscript production on a smaller scale. An extreme example is the sole surviving manuscript of Ralph of Caen's *Tancredus*, a history of the First Crusade and subsequent years in prose and poetry. The manuscript measures a mere 143 by 204 millimeters and possesses the marks of a draft handwritten by the author himself: it was copied in a coarse hand and features copious corrections and revisions, some on separate leaves intended to be inserted in the appropriate places.[73] By contrast, the scholar Stephen the Philosopher evidently possessed more extensive resources as resident at the convent of Saint Paul in Antioch, given that he employed a scribe to copy classical rhetorical works and had two scribes write down his Latin translation of a tenth-century medical treatise from Arabic. These scribes, identified as Alduinus and Pancus, may also have assisted Stephen in copying his translation-cum-commentary of an eleventh-century Arabic cosmological work.[74]

465–67) tentatively suggests, while Garrison ("Twelfth-Century Bible") and Hunt ("Syriac Buchanan Bible") propose a Jerusalemite origin. A thirteenth-century manuscript of an Old French translation of William of Tyre's history was also assigned by Folda ("Crusader Manuscript") to Antioch, though this attribution has recently been called into question by Handyside ("Crusader Manuscript").

68 On the psalter, see Folda, "Crusader Painting," 106–7; on the calendar, see Saxer, "Le calendrier."

69 For the grand design of the cathedral of Tyre, see Pringle, *Churches* 4:190–98.

70 Aspesi, "Breviary of Lucca."

71 *Tractatus de inventione* 284.

72 Aspesi, "Breviary of Lucca," 662. For the likelihood of the existence of an archive at the Church of Saint Peter in Caesarea, see Kool, "Deposit."

73 Brussels, Bibliothèque royale, 5369–73. See the description in RC xxiii–xxviii.

74 The colophon is missing from this twelfth-century manuscript: Cambrai, Médiathèque d'Agglomération, A 930. See, for a description, SP, *Liber Mamonis*, 16–17.

Patronage

To fund their literary and intellectual projects, authors in the Latin East depended on a system of patronage. Authors often declared the involvement of patrons in dedicatory introductions and addresses throughout the works. One should distinguish, however, between works commissioned by patrons as clear evidence of a patron-client relationship and prospective dedications that, on their own, may only provide evidence of an author's aspirations toward such a relationship. Broadly speaking, patrons can be subdivided into lay and ecclesiastical groups, with a further distinction between secular clergy (e.g., patriarchs and bishops) and monastic institutions (monasteries and convents, but for our purposes also regular canons or clergy living under a semimonastic rule) (table 1).

Lay patrons included the kings of Jerusalem (Baldwin I, Baldwin III, and Amalric I), the count of Tripoli (Raymond III of Tripoli), and a new member of the Knights Templar who had recently arrived from Toledo (Rodrigo González de Lara); they also included persons in western Europe with a connection to the Latin East (Geoffrey of Anjou, son of Fulk of Anjou, king of Jerusalem).

Secular ecclesiastical patrons were mostly patriarchs (of Jerusalem, Arnulf of Chocques; of Antioch, Aimery of Limoges), although a visiting bishop from Olomouc (Jindřich Zdík) saw opportunity to sponsor a pilgrim guide during his stay in the Latin East. The evidence for monastic patronage is more limited and confined to the Kingdom of Jerusalem (the regular canons of Hebron and the convent of Saint Mary of Bethany), although the institutional support Stephen the Philosopher received as treasurer of the convent of Saint Paul may arguably rise to the level of patronage.

Some authors did not write for a clearly defined patron (Walter the Chancellor, Stephen the Philosopher) or changed patrons at some point while writing. For example, after the death of Baldwin I in 1118, Fulcher of Chartres may have joined the canons of the Church of the Holy Sepulcher, while William of Tyre was first commissioned to write by King Amalric I and subsequently enjoyed the patronage of Count Raymond III of Tripoli.

Even this limited snapshot of literary patronage in the twelfth-century Latin East underlines the important role of lay patrons in sponsoring literature.[75] Clearly lay aristocrats and their courts valued association with learned Latin activity—or, in the case of prospective patronage, were perceived to value such association. Ecclesiastical patronage in the Latin East is less surprising, and there must have

75 It may be possible to add Raymond of Poitiers, prince of Antioch, as another lay patron. The late twelfth-century poet who reworked an Old French epic titled the *Chanson des Chétifs* claimed that the original poem had been composed at the Antiochene court of Raymond of Poitiers and was subsequently dispatched to western Europe by the patriarch, presumably referring to Aimery of Limoges. See Sweetenham, *Chanson des Chétifs*, 15–16.

TABLE 1. Literary Patronage of the Twelfth-Century Latin East

Lay	Ecclesiastical: Secular	Ecclesiastical: Monastic
Baldwin I: Fulcher of Chartres; Achard of Arrouaise*	Arnulf of Chocques: Ralph of Caen*	Canons of Hebron: *Tractatus de inventione*
Geoffrey of Anjou: Geoffrey the Abbot*	Jindřich Zdík: Rorgo Fretellus	Convent of Saint Mary of Bethany: Gerard of Nazareth
Rodrigo González de Lara: Rorgo Fretellus	Aimery of Limoges: Hugh Eterianus	
Baldwin III: *Balduini III Historia*		
Amalric I: William of Tyre		
Raymond III of Tripoli: William of Tyre		

* Authors whose patrons can only be identified as prospective.

been many more opportunities for budding authors than the record shows. With no fewer than thirty-five dioceses, the Latin East featured an extremely dense church organization outpacing even that of southern Italy and requiring a large number of clerics to sustain it.[76] Because of this demand, even minor clergy who might have struggled to make a name for themselves in Europe could hope for something more in the Latin East.

The correspondence of Aimery of Limoges, Latin patriarch of Antioch, with the Pisan scholar Hugh Eterianus (residing at the Byzantine court in Constantinople) proves illuminating for the practical aspects of literary patronage. In one letter from sometime in or after 1176–77, Aimery asked Hugh for Latin translations of three works. In recompense, Aimery offered him a "twofold payment" (*duplicatas . . . expensas*), as well as "commensurate acts of gratitude" (*condignas gratiarum actiones*).[77] Perhaps as a form of down payment, Aimery sent a silver chalice along with the letter, adding that he would have dispatched more objects if the couriers had not been in such haste. An earlier letter of Aimery to Hugh

76 Hiestand, "Der lateinische Klerus," 50.

77 Aimery of Limoges, *Letter to Hugh Eterianus*, 479–81 (PL 202:229–32).

from sometime after 1171 offers another glimpse into the financial side of literary patronage. In this recently uncovered letter, Aimery even sought to entice the scholar to take up residence in Antioch, promising him 1,000 bezants within eight days of his arrival (whether as a one-time payment or as a recurring income remains unclear).[78] While a pessimist may be inclined to adduce this information as evidence that the Latin East lacked in-house talent to supply its intellectual needs, I view the proposed exchange as a demonstration of the considerable interest of patrons in the Latin East in attracting renowned scholars and as an indication of the significant resources they were willing to commit (and apparently had at their disposal) to do so.

The Survival of Sources and Fragmentary Manuscripts

Only a few handfuls of Latin texts from the twelfth-century Levant survive, but they almost certainly represent but a portion of the total literary and intellectual output of this period. While in the past some scholars ventured assessments of the intellectual culture of the twelfth-century Latin East based on the absence of certain types of texts and genres, such arguments from silence fail to consider the many hazards involved in the textual transmission of twelfth-century Latin sources from the Levant. Apart from some fragmentary texts, all the Latin sources survive because they were brought to western Europe at some point. Some texts found their way to Europe at an early stage: the poem of Achard of Arrouaise, prior of the Templum Domini, may have accompanied the letter sent by his successor, Geoffrey, to Count Geoffrey of Anjou (along with two additional poems of his own composition) in 1135–37. Likewise, the knight known as W. Grassegals may have brought a collection of three Latin historical accounts from the Latin East to France, where he donated the book to Louis VII sometime before the king's departure for the Second Crusade in 1146.[79] Moreover, pilgrims returned to Europe with works composed in the Latin East. Jindřich Zdík, the bishop of Olomouc, brought back a pilgrim guide he commissioned from Rorgo Fretellus, a deacon in Antioch, while a marginal comment from the hand of Matthew Paris declares that he received a work of William of Tyre from Peter des Roches, bishop of Winchester, upon his return to England from a pilgrimage to the Holy Land in 1231.[80] In this process of transmission, the literary tastes of western Europeans were the decisive factor: they brought back and continued to copy primarily texts that were

78 Tarragona, Biblioteca Publica Provincial, 92, fol. 143r. These letters have been recently edited by P. Podolak for CCCM 298.

79 Rubenstein, "Putting History to Use."

80 Matthew Paris, *Historia Anglorum*, 1:163; Huygens, "La tradition manuscrite," 323–24.

of personal interest to them. This selection bias helps to explain the loss, baffling to modern scholars, of William of Tyre's history of "Oriental rulers." Unlike William's history of the Latin Kingdom of Jerusalem, a history of Levantine Muslims and Eastern Christians may have possessed little immediate relevance to a medieval European audience.

The survival rate for works not specifically addressed to patrons in Europe or brought there by travelers must have been slim, since books written in the Latin East passed through various stages of attrition.[81] First, books were lost as they were moved within the Latin East during evacuation efforts. After their initial conquests of the late eleventh and the early decades of the twelfth century, the Franks continuously suffered territorial losses in the Levant. The fall of the County of Edessa in 1144 marked the end of Latin expansion, with a precipitous decline of Latin presence following the 1187 Battle of Hattin until the complete dissolution of Frankish Levantine rule with the fall of Acre in 1291. Frankish refugees, especially monks and clergy, will have carried some books with them as they fled to areas of the Levant still under Latin control, but most of their libraries must have been lost. In the aftermath of the fall of Acre, the Dominican friar Riccoldo of Montecroce wrote vividly—and, it should be noted, polemically—of the fate of some of the Christian books, which he later encountered in Nineveh (i.e., Mosul in modern Iraq):

> In the great city of Nineveh I found a missal taken as if it were a slave along with the Christian booty from Acre; it contained the gospels and epistles. The Saracens have forbidden this book, they wish to destroy it, and have scraped the letters from its pages in order to make the drums and tambourines of which Easterners make great use. . . . Behold, the books of the Christians are being scattered throughout the world like captives and slaves of the Saracens and Tartars![82]

81 On the survival and circulation of books from the Latin East, see especially Minervini, "Produzione e circolazione," "Outremer," and "Modelli culturali," as well as Tessera, "Dalla liturgia."

82 George-Tvrtković, *Christian Pilgrim*, 157. For the Latin text, see Riccoldo of Montecroce, *Epistolae ad ecclesiam triumphantem*, 281: *Ego autem librum missale inveni quasi sclavum portatum de spoliis christianorum de Accon in Nynive, civitate grandi, ubi erant epistole et evangelia. Quem librum interdicebant Sarraceni, volebant destruere et cartas eius radere ad faciendum cartas pro tympanis et tamburis quibus orientales multum utuntur. . . . Ecce libri christianorum disperguntur per mundum quasi captivi et sclavi Sarracenorum et Tartarorum.* In his second letter from Baghdad, Riccoldo claims that "[t]he books of the prophets and the gospels have been thrown to the dogs" (George-Tvrtković, *Christian Pilgrim*, 147), and in the third letter, he writes that while searching for fellow Dominican friars among the captives taken by Muslims, "I have found habits and vestments, as well as books and breviaries, in the hands of the Saracens" (George-Tvrtković, *Christian Pilgrim*, 153). He goes on to say in this letter that the Muslims brought a copy of Gregory the Great's *Moralia in Iob* "all the way to the great city of Nineveh," where he "ransomed [the] book as if it were a captive slave who had found itself removed from Christendom more than a fifty days' journey by camel

Riccoldo's claim of Muslims repurposing Christian books accords to some extent with the evidence provided by fragmentary texts, including Gospels, which were used as protective wrappers for collections of *ḥadīṯ*, the Islamic biographical traditions on Muhammad (see below).[83] His polemical framing of such reuse as a destructive practice and a means of censure, however, must be read within the historical context of Riccoldo's letter and its rhetorical purpose. A widespread narrative originating from the early thirteenth-century Latin East presents an entirely different Muslim attitude toward gospel books. In the version recounted by Oliver, a German preacher who participated in the Fifth Crusade, a delegation of Muslim "wise men" (*sapientes*) traveled to Jerusalem where they asked to examine gospel books (*codices ewangeliorum*). These they kissed and venerated out of regard for the purity of the law they contained (*propter munditiam legis*), with particular appreciation for the role attributed to the archangel Gabriel in the gospel of Luke, for which Muslims found a parallel in Islam, where Gabriel is depicted as the channel of Qur'anic revelations to Muhammad.[84]

As the Latin presence in the Levant diminished in the second half of the thirteenth century, the Franks eventually sought refuge in parts of the Latin-controlled Mediterranean, such as Cyprus, Rhodes, and Sicily. Shortly before the fall of Acre, the entire scriptorium of the Hospital of Saint John may have moved to Cyprus, while the last bishop of Beirut, as mentioned, brought the books belonging to his church to Cyprus in the same year. The books of Sidon likely traversed a similar route before eventually making their way to the papal library of Avignon.[85] A letter from Pope John XXII on 24 August 1322 shows the value of such books, the distribution of which occupied the attentions even of the supreme pontiff. In the letter, the pope instructs the canons of the church of Beirut to hand over the liturgical books, chalices, crucifixes, censers, and other items that they had brought with them upon their evacuation to Cyprus, and to place them at the disposal of Balian, the archbishop of Rhodes, and his indigent church. Provisions

---

in all directions" (George-Tvrtković, *Christian Pilgrim*, 156). Finally, he claims that the epistles of Paul "have been scattered among the Saracens" (George-Tvrtković, *Christian Pilgrim*, 158). In the fourth letter, Riccoldo writes that in Baghdad "books and vestments were being sold" and repeats the account of his fruitless search for fellow friars, during which he found only their books and breviaries (George-Tvrtković, *Christian Pilgrim*, 165–66).

83 As an example from Sinai shows, Greek books were also subject to looting in this era: see Jotischky, "Fortunes of War."

84 Oliver of Paderborn, *Historia Damiatina*, 204. For references to other versions of the story, see Daniel, *Islam and the West*, 388, n. 15. For an earlier example of Muslim veneration of Christian Bibles, see Bruce, *Cluny and the Muslims*, 59–60.

85 The move of the Acre scriptorium to Cyprus was suggested by Edbury and Folda, "Two Thirteenth-Century Manuscripts," 250.

were also made, however, for the books' return to Beirut (or adequate compensation thereof) in the event of a Latin reconquest.[86]

The evacuation from the Levant must have resulted in a further loss of books. Once part of European libraries, the books were then subject to the usual vagaries of medieval manuscript survival: they could be erased and reused as so-called palimpsests, go up in flames, or fall prey to any number of accidents and conflicts. For example, while Ralph of Caen's *Tancredus* narrowly escaped a fire at the monastery of Gembloux, the original manuscript of the anonymous *Balduini III Historia* seems to have perished during the French Revolution.[87]

While it is impossible to make judgments about what does not survive, it is possible that further manuscripts of the Latin East may be identified in the future. Recently fragmentary manuscripts have come to light (or, in some cases, brought again to scholarly attention) that help to expand our picture of the literary culture of the Latin East. These fragments may be subdivided into the following groups: fragments from the so-called Cairo Genizah, fragments from the Qubbat al-Ḫazna of Damascus, and fragments formerly belonging to the private Schøyen collection.

The Cairo Genizah refers to the storeroom of the Ben Ezra Synagogue of the Palestinian Jewish community in Fustat, the old city of Cairo.[88] This community had moved at the end of the eleventh century to the city, which was under Fatimid rule at the time, because of the Crusader capture of Jerusalem. They brought with them their books, some of which they had had to ransom from the Crusaders.[89] The synagogue, which was the largest of three synagogues in the city, became a storehouse where Cairene Jews deposited all manner of books, scrolls, and documents, although it is likely that the other synagogues maintained similar archives. In the late nineteenth century, manuscripts of the Cairo Genizah were dispersed among private collectors during renovations to the synagogue; today they are distributed among fifty-four institutions and eighteen private owners.[90] Some medieval documents and fragmentary books of the Cairo Genizah demonstrate Latin influence, and recently three twelfth-century fragments of Baebius Italicus's Latin abbreviation

86 For the letter, see Rome, BAV, Reg. Vat. 73, fol. 418r, no. 1225; Reg. Aven. 17, fol. 214r–214v, no. 1225; see also the summary in Mollat, *Lettres communes*, 4:150, no. 16029. I am grateful to C. Schabel for supplying me with a transcription of the letter and to M. Olympios for his suggestions on the subsequent fate of the books of Beirut. The books probably remained in Rhodes after Balian moved to Split to become archbishop of Salona, as they were earmarked for the church of Rhodes. The books may have been lost in the subsequent destruction of the church in the siege of 1522, or they may have been dispersed by the Hospitallers before then.

87 See appendix 3.

88 Jefferson, "Deconstructing 'the Cairo Genizah.'"

89 Goitein, *Mediterranean Society*, 3:356.

90 For an overview of the Cairo Genizah collections, see the Friedberg Genizah Project, http://pr.genizah.org/Index.aspx%22.

of the *Iliad* (the *Ilias latina*, originally composed in the mid-first century CE) have been identified.[91] The provenance of this fragmentary manuscript is unclear. Other documents demonstrate that the twelfth-century Jewish community in Cairo maintained contacts with Jews across the Mediterranean as well as the Levant. It is possible, though unproven, that the book once belonged to a library in the Latin East.[92] If so, the work likely served as a school text, as it did in medieval Europe.[93]

The Qubbat al-Ḫazna of Damascus refers to the storehouse of the Umayyad Great Mosque in Damascus. Although its current location remains unknown, the textual materials it contained are now situated in the Syrian National Library.[94] Following a visit of Kaiser Wilhelm II to Damascus in 1898, the biblical philologist Bruno Violet obtained access to some of the materials of the Qubbat al-Ḫazna (though he was not permitted to enter it himself).[95] His preliminary catalogue included fragments in Arabic, Turkish, Hebrew, Armenian, Coptic, Syriac, Greek, Old French, and Latin. The 214 photos he took, from a selection of 1,558 fragments, are now at the Berlin-Brandenburg Academy of Sciences and Humanities.[96] A select number of additional photos were made after the fragments were brought to Berlin in 1903 until their return to Damascus in 1909.[97]

The identification of the texts in the Damascus fragments remains an ongoing process; in a recent survey based on the available photographs, S. Ammirati identified sixteen manuscripts (of separate fragments and groups) containing at

91 Some fragments contain Hebrew transliterations of Latin words. For example, one fragment lists in Hebrew the names of the months as derived from the Latin (T-S NS 98.51), while some fragments of medical texts include Latin-derived terms and transliterations (T-S K1.112, T-S K14.6, and T-S K14.48). One fragment of a medical text references the famous physician and philosopher Ibn Sina (Avicenna) using a Hebrew transliteration of the Latin version of his name (T-S K21.54). The *Ilias latina* fragment is T-S Misc. 27.2 c–e of the Taylor-Schechter Collection at the Cambridge University Library. For a description and digital reproductions, see https://cudl.lib.cam.ac.uk/view/MS-TS-MISC-00027-00002-C/1, accessed 30 October 2020. For a discussion, see Bohak and Ammirati, "Latin *Iliad*."

92 At the very least, as Ammirati's ("Reconsidering the Latin Fragments," 327–28) analysis has recently shown, the paleographical features and physical shape of the fragments correspond to those found in the Damascus Qubbat al-Ḫazna (see below). I am grateful to S. Ammirati for sharing with me an advance copy of this article.

93 Munk Olsen, *I classici*, 61–63.

94 Hirschler ("Books within Books") argues that the fragments now in the Syrian National Library originated from texts stored in the Qubbat al-Ḫazna. I am grateful to K. Hirschler for sending me an advance copy of the publication and for his comments.

95 Bandt and Rattmann, "Die Damaskusreise"; D'Ottone Rambach, "Manuscripts as Mirrors"; Bandt and Rattmann, "Bruno Violet."

96 The so-called Violet photos are Berlin-Brandenburg Academy of Sciences and Humanities, BBAW Akz.-Nr. 481. They are accessible online at https://bibelexegese.bbaw.de/handschriften/damaszener-handschriften/, accessed 30 October 2020.

97 For these 54 photos, see Berlin, Staatsbibliothek, simulata orientalia 6. They are accessible online at https://digital.staatsbibliothek-berlin.de/werkansicht?PPN=PPN685013049&PHYSID=PHYS_0002, accessed 30 October 2020.

least nineteen different texts written in Latin or, in the case of Old French texts, in Latin script.[98] The Latin fragments include the following:

- Liturgical texts and chants with musical notation.
- A safe-conduct issued by King Baldwin III of Jerusalem for a merchant from Tyre referred to as Bohali, son of Hebencstin (dating between 7 June 1156 and 10 February 1163).[99]
- A late twelfth- or early thirteenth-century fragment of the sequences of Notker Balbulus (originally late ninth century).
- An early twelfth-century fragment of epigrams of Prosper of Aquitaine (originally fifth century).
- A late eleventh- or early twelfth-century fragment of Bernard of Angers's *Liber miraculorum sanctae Fidis* (originally eleventh century).
- A late eleventh-century fragment of Bede's poem *De die iudicii* (originally eighth century) along with the opening lines of the popular Latin school text known as the *Disticha Catonis*.
- A thirteenth-century fragment of Vitalis of Blois's widespread comedy *Geta* (originally ca. mid-twelfth century).
- A fourteenth-century fragment of a penitential poem and accompanying excerpt of Jerome's *sententiae*.
- An early medieval fragment (ninth century) of an unknown version of the martyrdom account of Saints Eustathius and Pancras.

The inclusion among these fragments of Baldwin III's safe-conduct provides indisputable evidence that at least some of them originated in the Latin East. Given the tumultuous history of the Crusader settlements in the Levant, it may seem a safe assumption that the various Latin fragments and documents that ended up in the Qubbat al-Ḫazna did so due to violence and conflict. However, the safe-conduct, which apparently served its intended purpose, demonstrates that these were not the sole ways by which texts changed hands.[100]

The fragmentary manuscripts formerly part of the Schøyen collection bear similarities to the Damascus fragments and may ultimately derive from the Qubbat al-Ḫazna.[101] Four of the twelve fragments are in Latin, with the remainder written

98 Ammirati, "Latin Fragments" and "Reconsidering the Latin Fragments." For the Old French texts, see Giannini and Minervini, "Old French Texts."

99 Mayer, "Une lettre de sauf-conduit"; *UKJ* 1:492–94, no. 268 (RRH no. 598a; RRR no. 699).

100 Hirschler, "Saleroom Fiction."

101 These fragments were sold recently to a private individual at an auction on 8 July 2020. See the catalogue description: "The History of Western Script: A Selection from The Schøyen Collection, in Celebration of the Collector's Eightieth Birthday, Dreweatts (London), 8 July 2020, lot 46,"

in Greek and Armenian. The Latin fragments all date to the twelfth century and include fragments of the Old and New Testament (Malachi 1:4–10 and 1:14–2:10; Matthew 11:17–29 and 12:6–25), Burchard of Worms's collection of canon law (the *Decretum*, ca. 1023), and Gregory the Great's homilies on the gospels (book 2, homily 31, with a reading from Matthew 9:9). In addition to the collocation of Latin, Greek, and Armenian fragments, the presence of Arabic marginalia marks these fragments as likely belonging to a Levantine context. Arabic titles in the margins indicate that the fragments were preserved, not necessarily because of the inherent value placed on the texts, but to serve as protective wrappers of Arabic books, such as collections of ḥadīṯ.[102]

As digitization makes the study of sources more widely available to scholars, it is likely that more books and fragments from the Latin East will be identified. These identifications will help us achieve a fuller understanding of the Latin culture of the Levant. For example, while the Latin fragments from the Cairo Genizah, the Damascus Qubbat al-Ḫazna, and the Schøyen collection largely correspond with the types of texts contained in the Sidon books and those listed in the Nazareth catalogue, the presence of the twelfth-century comedy of Vitalis of Blois (in a thirteenth-century manuscript fragment) at the Qubbat al-Ḫazna demonstrates a Levantine interest in recently composed Latin entertainment from western Europe, for which previously there had been no evidence.[103]

Levantine Latinity in Context

For an understanding of the significance of Levantine Latinity as a twelfth-century cultural phenomenon, we may compare this general picture of Latin literary culture in the Levant to emerging Latin cultures elsewhere in Europe and the Mediterranean during the late eleventh and twelfth centuries. The spread of Latin literary activities in these areas was closely linked to the adoption of Latin Christianity, as ecclesiastical and monastic institutions sponsored the copying of Latin texts and stimulated the composition of new historiographical accounts and narratives centered on local history. In northern Europe, Latin Christianity gradually took root beginning in the tenth century in northern Germany and

---

https://auctions.dreweatts.com/auctions/7497/blooms1-10012/lot-details/f973e60e-9cd9-43a5-8e0d-abcd00be332b. I am grateful to K. Hirschler for bringing the sale to my attention.

102 For example, Schøyen fragment 1776/04 reads in the top margin "the first and second <part of> the reading to al-Wazīr on the authority of al-Baġawī," referring to the renowned twelfth-century Qurʾanic commentator and transmitter of ḥadīṯ. For transcriptions and translations of the Arabic marginalia in the Schøyen fragments, see Hirschler, "Saleroom Fiction."

103 Compare also the thirteenth-century fragments from the Qubbat al-Ḫazna of two French *chansons de geste*: *Fierabras*, set in the time of Charlemagne, and *Enfances Godefroi*, relating Godfrey of Bouillon's origins. See Giannini and Minervini, "Old French Texts."

Denmark, and subsequently in Norway, Sweden, and Iceland. In central and eastern Europe, the spread of Latin Christendom in Poland, Bohemia, and Hungary followed similar trajectories. In all these areas, there was a delay between the initial adoption of Christianity (ranging between the late ninth and tenth centuries) and the appearance of the first locally produced Latin texts (eleventh century). Not until the twelfth century can we speak of established local centers of manuscript production.[104]

In the south of Europe, Latin Christians gradually gained more footholds in Muslim Iberia (al-Andalus) from the ninth century onward. The situation there was different from that in northern and eastern Europe, where Latin was being introduced for the first time, since Latin had never disappeared from the Iberian Peninsula. As more areas came under Latin Christian control, they fell under the cultural, ecclesiastical, and political influence of established Latin Christian centers. However, the conquest of Toledo in 1085 represented a watershed in the so-called *reconquista* movement. It not only marked a sharp acceleration of Christian expansion, but also suddenly brought Latin Christians into direct contact with Arabic learning through its Arabic-speaking Christian and Jewish population (so-called Mozarabs) and through one of the finest libraries in the Muslim world.[105] In the twelfth century, the foremost scholars of Europe flocked to Toledo from areas as diverse as England, Austria, and Italy.

The Normans adopted Christianity in the tenth century, and their eleventh-century conquests significantly contributed to the spread of Latin culture in England (1066) and in the south of Italy and Sicily (completed in 1091). In England Normans became the head of a new French-speaking ruling class that sponsored the composition of Latin and French literature. Unlike other areas of Latin expansion, the subjects of the Normans were already Christian and possessed an Anglo-Latin literary tradition of their own. In Sicily, on the other hand, Normans reintroduced Latin culture to the island, which had since the dissolution of the Western Roman Empire in the fifth century variously come under Germanic, Greek-speaking Byzantine, and Arabic-speaking Muslim rule. The twelfth century saw the consolidation of Latin as a language of governance, literature, and religion at the Norman court of Palermo, alongside Arabic and Greek.

The conditions of the Latin culture of the Levant arguably most resemble those of Norman Sicily. The two areas came under Latin control in roughly the

104 Boje Mortensen, "Sanctified Beginnings," 252–62.

105 Little is known about the library of Toledo, but, judging from the copious Arabic texts translated by the so-called Toledan School of translators, it must have been extensive. On libraries in medieval Iberia, see Faulhaber, "Libraries." For an eleventh-century description of the more famous library of Córdoba, see Rodriguez, *Muslim and Christian Contact*, 370–79.

same period: the Norman conquest of Sicily was completed in 1091, while the first Levantine territory was conquered in 1098. Unlike the gradual and repeated spread of Latin Christianity in Iberia and in some areas of northern and central Europe, its introduction in Sicily and the Levant was abrupt, sparked by a sudden influx of armed expeditions. The rapid foundation of new secular, ecclesiastical, and monastic institutions subsequently gave rise to comparable literary creativity. Furthermore, Latins in both areas faced similar social and cultural situations, given that the ruling Latin elite was outnumbered by a diverse local population of Greek- and Arabic-speaking Christians and Arabic-speaking Muslims.

The 1989 publication of a volume on medieval frontier societies spurred a new scholarly trend attempting to chart, among other cultural frontiers, the expanding Latin frontier from the eleventh century onward.[106] Framing the study of these Latin cultural areas as frontiers on the Latin expansion has the drawback of reinforcing the notion that these cultures, as rudimentary frontier societies largely preoccupied with survival, merely aspired to reproduce from a distance the cultural trends of Latin Europe as best they could, given their limited resources and capabilities. Such a one-directional framework permits only a limited analysis that fails to consider the potential of these emerging cultures for innovation and creativity unburdened by the weight of tradition.[107]

In the past two decades, scholars have instead examined these areas of Latin expansion as peripheries of a putative center somewhere in Europe.[108] Geographically speaking, the Latin East belongs with these peripheral Latin cultures, given its far remove from the intellectual centers of western Europe, the political and ecclesiastical centers of the German Empire in northern Italy and Germany, and the papacy in Rome. Moreover, the Latin literary activities in the Levant exhibit similarities with those in other peripheral areas. For example, Latin authors' use of the genre of saints' lives to construct identities of local communities and institutions in northern and central Europe corresponds closely with the foundational texts of new Levantine communities, such as the account detailing the discovery of the tombs of the patriarchs by the canons of the church of Hebron (*Tractatus de inventione*). Latin interaction with Muslims and Arabic-speaking Christians in Iberia and Sicily similarly gave rise to Latin polemical literature against Islam as well as to translations of Arabic medical and astronomical texts into Latin (see the "Adelphus" narrative and Stephen the Philosopher).

106 Bartlett and MacKay, *Medieval Frontier Societies*; Abulafia and Berend, *Medieval Frontiers*; Merisalo, *Frontiers in the Middle Ages*; Murray, *North-Eastern Frontiers*; Muldoon and Fernández-Armesto, *Expansion of Latin Europe*.

107 Rubin, *Learning in a Crusader City*, 174.

108 See especially the following collections of essays: Boje Mortensen, *Making of Christian Myths*; Garipzanov, *Historical Narratives*; Agapitos and Boje Mortensen, *Medieval Narratives*.

However, the Latin East defies a straightforward categorization within the binary center/periphery framework. While residing on the periphery of Europe and Latin Christendom, the Latin East found itself at the center of several overlapping peripheries, including peripheries of the Byzantine Empire, the Fatimid Caliphate, and the Abbasid Caliphate. Although the Latin East did not comprise a center according to conventional definitions, at the very least it constituted a cultural crossroads.

The Latin texts from the Levant reflect the complicated status of the Latin East as both a periphery and a center of sorts. While looking westward to patrons in Europe for material and military aid, the Latin settlers of the Levant attributed a central position to the Latin East within Christianity. One pilgrim guide, composed in Antioch, holds that "according to philosophers, Jerusalem, the glorious metropolis of Judea, is situated in the center of the world," referring to an ancient Jewish tradition that located within the city was the *omphalos*, the life-giving navel of the world.[109] Other claims to centrality were more specifically tied to an institution or community. The leaders of the community of canons at the Templum Domini, Achard of Arrouaise and Geoffrey the Abbot, attributed to their institution a primacy and a central role within the Christian salvation narrative that rivaled the claims of the Church of the Holy Sepulcher in Jerusalem and of the papacy in Rome. Similarly, a poetic resume of the First Crusade commissioned by the young King Baldwin III (here referred to as *Balduini III Historia*) closely links the earthly Kingdom of Jerusalem with the kingdom of heaven.[110]

Even as a periphery, the Latin East should be considered not only in relation to western Europe, but also as one of the peripheries of the Byzantine Empire. Writing in the context of the medieval Georgian kingdoms and their connection to Byzantium, D. Braund noted that "imperial peripheries are regularly more dynamic than centres: it is precisely at their peripheries that political, cultural, and military systems change most quickly and radically as they face new challenges, new peoples, and new environments."[111] Similarly, as the work of Folda, Jacoby, and Rubin on thirteenth-century Acre has shown, far from a remote European outpost, this Levantine city was home to major artistic and intellectual innovations—especially in the French vernacular—that exerted lasting influences on European culture.[112] Centered on the twelfth century, this book tells the story

109 RF 50: *Jherusalem gloriosa Iudee metropolis iuxta phylosophos in medio mundi sita est.* The origin of this widespread notion is Ezekiel 38:12, which speaks of the tribe of Israel as inhabiting the center of the world (*omphalos* in the Greek Septuagint). For the Midrashic tradition, see Schein, *Gateway*, 141. Graeco-Roman tradition, on the other hand, situated the world's center at Delphi. On these two diverging discourses, see Ciholas, *Omphalos and the Cross*.

110 *Balduini III Historia*, prol. 21–22 (see appendix 3).

111 Braund, *Georgia in Antiquity*, 3

112 Folda, *Crusader Art*, 511–27; Rubin, *Learning in a Crusader City*, 168–75.

of the Latin literary culture that came before these developments. The following chapters examine how Levantine authors used the literary, intellectual, and religious dimensions of Latin expression to tell narratives about themselves, their institutions, and about their place in the Levant and their relation to the rest of the Latin world. Some writers utilized elements from other Levantine literary traditions in their narratives, while others sought to displace these altogether with a fresh Latin perspective. In comparison to other Latin peripheries of the eleventh and twelfth centuries, the development of a Latin literature of the Levant, where writers composed complex narratives within a few decades of the first Latin settlements, progressed at a rapid pace. Because of the rich diversity of the Latin East and its situation at the crossroads of several competing cultural spheres, a study of this particular Latin culture can enhance our understanding of a period of intense cultural expansion across Europe, the Mediterranean, and the Levant.

Chapter Two

FULCHER OF CHARTRES AND THE BEGINNINGS OF LEVANTINE LATIN LITERATURE

"New Words, New Songs"

On 15 July 1099, a motley collection of nobles, knights, footmen, and priests from various areas of Europe managed to conquer Jerusalem. They had been under way for three years, traveling from their homes in north-central France, Normandy, Provence, Flanders, and parts of Germany and Italy, and facing innumerable obstacles and casualties. To those who made it to the end, the successful completion of the expedition represented an astounding and unprecedented event. Raymond of Aguilers, a Provençal priest, jubilantly heralded the occasion: "This new day, new joy, the consummation of toil and devotion with ever new and eternal rejoicing, required new words, new songs from all."[1] Another priest named Fulcher described the joyful celebration that followed: "Then they went to the Lord's Sepulcher and his glorious Temple, clergy and laity alike, singing with loud praises a new song to the Lord, and all joyfully visited the sacred sites, which they had desired for so long, making offerings and uttering humble prayers."[2] The unusual occasion required innovative forms of expression: new songs, poems, and histories commemorating the expedition. As these writers would have it, the first moments after the conclusion of what is now known as the First Crusade did in fact witness the creation of a new literary culture.

Apart from letters, the earliest Latin texts to issue from the twelfth-century Levant were accounts of the First Crusade. These works are the *Gesta Francorum* (Deeds of the Franks), the accounts of Peter Tudebode and Raymond of Aguilers, and the history of Fulcher of Chartres. Although they have often been referred to as eyewitness accounts, this label gives the misleading impression of relatively

1 RA 151: *Nova dies, novum gaudium, nova et perpetua leticia laboris atque devotionis consummatio, nova verba, nova cantica, ab universis exigebat.*

2 FC 1.29.2: *Tunc autem ad Sepulcrum Domini et Templum eius gloriosum euntes, clerici simul et laici, exsultationis voce altisona canticum novum Domino decantando, loca sacrosancta tamdiu desiderata, cum oblationibus faciendis supplicationibusque humillimis, laetabundi omnes visitaverunt.*

accurate field reports rather than literary compositions composed in hindsight and subject to complex redaction processes.[3] The history of Fulcher, a priest from Chartres, is unique among these works. Unlike the other accounts, Fulcher did not end his history with the conclusion of the Crusade in 1099 or the Battle of Ascalon shortly thereafter. Instead he chronicled the vicissitudes of those who continued to live in the Levant. The initial chronicle covered events through the year 1105, but it was eventually extended through 1127.

Because it took nearly three decades to assume its final shape, Fulcher's history forms a lens through which to trace the early development of Latin literary culture in the Levant. Furthermore, his work enjoyed an extensive afterlife in the Kingdom of Jerusalem as it saw promotion by both the patriarch and king of Jerusalem. Fulcher's narrative of the First Crusade and his vision of Latin society in the Levant thus proved greatly influential and may rightfully be credited with inaugurating a new Levantine Latin literary tradition.

A Wandering Scholar

Little is known about the first three and a half decades of Fulcher's life before the First Crusade. He was born in 1059, possibly in Chartres, where he was ordained a priest.[4] He was not a member of the clergy at the cathedral of Chartres, however, for his name is absent from the chapter's records.[5] He accompanied the renowned reformer Ivo of Chartres to the Council of Clermont in 1095, where he witnessed Pope Urban II's call for the Crusade.[6] He subsequently departed for the Holy Land in the entourage of Stephen of Blois, serving as the count's personal chaplain.[7] Just before the party reached Antioch in mid-October 1097, he joined the contingent of Baldwin of Boulogne, brother of Godfrey of Bouillon.[8] As Baldwin's chaplain, Fulcher spent the next year and a half in Edessa and was therefore absent from the sieges of Antioch and Jerusalem. Fulcher wrote little of his time in Edessa, where Baldwin skillfully and ruthlessly positioned himself at the head of the ruling Armenian family. After the Crusader capture of Jerusalem in the summer of 1099, Fulcher accompanied Baldwin on a pilgrimage to Jerusalem, only to return

3 Bull, "Western Narratives."

4 For the life and work of Fulcher, see Epp, *Fulcher von Chartres*, 24–36. Fulcher refers to himself as *Carnotensis* ("from Chartres") and at one point describes his longing for Chartres and Orléans—either of which could therefore have been his place of origin.

5 Epp, *Fulcher von Chartres*, 25.

6 Giese, "Untersuchungen zur *Historia Hierosolymitana*," 63–64.

7 FC 1.7.1.

8 FC 1.14.2, 1.14.15. October, according to Epp, *Fulcher von Chartres*, 26. Runciman (*History of the Crusades*, 1:329) dates the event to June 1097.

to Jerusalem permanently in the fall of 1100, when Baldwin was summoned from Edessa to be crowned king of Jerusalem after Godfrey of Bouillon's death.[9]

The contours of Fulcher's career after settling in Jerusalem remain vague. While it is reasonable to assume that Fulcher continued his service to Baldwin, his absence from the witness lists of charters suggests that he did not occupy a prominent position at the court.[10] From 1116 onward, Fulcher seems to have been sidelined at the court, given that he did not accompany Baldwin on his expedition to the Red Sea that year. V. Epp has convincingly argued that Fulcher may have joined the canons at the Church of the Holy Sepulcher, possibly as early as 1114, when the canons were reformed in accordance with the rule of Ivo of Chartres.[11] Epp further adduced Fulcher's increasing emphasis on the relic of the True Cross as evidence for this association, given that it was safeguarded in the Church of the Holy Sepulcher,[12] while the fact that Fulcher refers in his revised text to the relic as a "treasure" (*thesaurus*) may indicate that he had been appointed its treasurer (*thesaurarius*).[13] Removed from the politics of the royal court, the position of treasurer may have afforded Fulcher the means and opportunity to write a chronicle at his leisure, given that treasurers were responsible for safeguarding liturgical vestments, relics, as well as books. Fulcher's working method from 1124 onward in particular suggests that he had at his disposal the resources of a sizeable library, such as that of the Church of the Holy Sepulcher.[14] Given the chronicle's abrupt ending with a description of a plague of mice in the spring or summer of 1127, Fulcher probably died shortly thereafter at the age of 68.[15]

Fulcher's life was marked by extraordinary upheavals. He did not acquire a degree of stability until his settlement in Jerusalem at the age of 41, and even then,

9 FC 1.33.

10 Fulcher may, however, be identified with a clergyman who appears as witness to a donation charter issued by Baldwin I to the Church of Saint Mary of the Valley of Josaphat in 1107/8: *UKJ* 1: no. 32; Mayer, "Die Hofkapelle," 493.

11 Epp, *Fulcher von Chartres*, 31–32.

12 Epp, *Fulcher von Chartres*, 27. Fulcher describes the cross as *alma* (2.21.14), *gloriosa* (2.32.2), *sanctissima et pretiosissima* (3.5.2), and *victoriosa* (3.9.2).

13 FC 1.30.4; see also 3.9.3–4. There is no record of Fulcher holding this office. Charters list a *Girardus tessaurarius/thesaurarius* in 1112 (*Cart Hosp*, 1:25–26, no. 25; *UKJ* 1:176–77, no. 51 [RRH no. 68; RRR no. 126], and *UKJ* 1:177–79, no. 52 [RRH no. 68a; RRR no. 129]) and a *Petrus thesaurarius* in 1129 (Kohler, "Chartes de l'abbaye," 125–27, no. 17 [RRH no. 129a; RRR no. 277]), so it is possible that Fulcher held the office for some time in the intervening years but, for some reason or other, did not witness any charters. Giese's speculation ("Untersuchungen zur *Historia Hierosolymitana*," 64) that Fulcher may be identified with a "Fulcher, prior of the Olive Mount Priory" (*Cart Hosp*, 1:25–26, no. 25; *UKJ* 1:176–77, no. 51 [RRH no. 68; RRR no. 126]) has been rejected by Mayer ("Die Hofkapelle," 493).

14 For Fulcher's access to the archives of the patriarch of Jerusalem, see Epp, *Fulcher von Chartres*, 29.

15 FC 3.62. See Epp, *Fulcher von Chartres*, 35.

he appears to have changed career paths in his mid-fifties. Through his chronicle, which took shape over nearly three decades, we may trace the evolution of the most consequential early writer of the Latin East.

From Crusade Account to Chronicle of the Kingdom of Jerusalem

Upon settling in Jerusalem, Fulcher probably began writing between the fall of 1100 and the end of 1101.[16] At this time, there was no single agreed-upon term for what is now known as a Crusade. The word is an early modern construct, and it was left to writers such as Fulcher to conceptualize the confusing events of the so-called First Crusade.[17] Compared to later, more centrally organized expeditions led by kings such as Louis VII (1147–49) and Richard the Lionheart (1189–91), the First Crusade was a chaotic undertaking of many groups from various areas in Europe over several years. Pope Urban II led the initial effort in a preaching tour of France in the fall of 1095, and here at least Fulcher found a useful starting point for his history. Yet an end did not present itself easily. It was not apparent that the capture of Jerusalem in July 1099 constituted the conclusion of a neatly defined historical event. For instance, another early account of the Crusade continues through the Battle of Ascalon later that summer before breaking off abruptly.[18]

Fulcher and other Franks who stayed in the Levant may not have viewed their expedition as having come to an end. Initially, at least, Fulcher did not separate the First Crusade from subsequent events and simply continued the narrative, ending with a battle between Franks and Turks near the city Ramla in 1105. This original version is not extant but was known to a few early twelfth-century writers in western Europe.[19] Fulcher portrayed the Franks' resounding victory as a gift from God, who "did not wish for those unbelievers to rout his Christians, who had come from distant parts to Jerusalem out of love for him and to spread his name."[20] In this presentation of the events, the expedition seems never to have ended.

16 Hagenmeyer in FC 44–45.

17 Tyerman, *Invention of the Crusades*, 2 and 28; Lock, *Routledge Companion*, 258.

18 *GF* 97.

19 Traces of Fulcher's early work can be found in Guibert of Nogent (*Dei gesta per Francos* 7.32), the anonymous *Gesta Francorum Iherusalem expugnantium*, and the so-called Codex L. The passage in FC 2.33, in which Fulcher directs authorial remarks to the reader, was reasonably proposed by Hagenmeyer (FC 45) to be a vestige of this first version of Fulcher's text, which would have ended at this point. This argument is corroborated by the fact that revision of Fulcher's chronicle in the *Gesta Francorum Iherusalem expugnantium* also ends with the same battle at Ramla in 1105, concluding with the words *finis hic est* ("this is the end"), before continuing briefly to recount an earthquake and some astronomical phenomena of the following year. See Hagenmeyer in FC 46 and Edgington, "'Bartolf of Nangis,'" 22.

20 FC 2.32.8: *Deus . . . nolens Christianos suos perfidis illis destrui, qui pro eius amore et nomine ampliando de longinquis partibus Hierusalem venerant.*

It is unclear precisely how the chronicle developed in subsequent years, but Fulcher appears to have added to it sporadically beginning in 1109 or 1110. A turning point for Fulcher's historiographic project came with the capture of Tyre in 1124. A Frankish alliance with the Venetian fleet led to the conquest of this illustrious and ancient coastal city. The location formed the backdrop to several episodes in both the Old and New Testament and figures at the start of Virgil's *Aeneid*.[21] Most educated western Europeans, however, may have associated the city with a popular late antique tale centering on the legendary king Apollonius of Tyre.[22]

In both practical and symbolic terms, the conquest of Tyre represented the most significant Frankish victory since the capture of Jerusalem. Having taken Jaffa and Acre, the Franks (and their Venetian allies) now controlled the entire Levantine coast. Fulcher may well have viewed the occasion as marking a new era in which the Franks had become firmly established in the Levant. Sometime after the capture of Tyre, Fulcher divided his history accordingly into three books, creating a conceptual division between the First Crusade (book 1) and subsequent history, organized by the reigns of the first two kings of Jerusalem (books 2–3).

Fulcher's history survives in two versions, transmitted in a roughly equal number of manuscripts. The first redaction ends with the conquest of Tyre in 1124.[23] Fulcher subsequently divided his chronicle into three books and thoroughly revised the entire text, continuing his work through 1127 for the second redaction. At this point he may also have changed the title of his work from *Gesta Francorum Iherusalem peregrinantium* (Deeds of the Franks that undertook a pilgrimage to Jerusalem) to *Historia Hierosolymitana* (History of Jerusalem), thereby highlighting the shift from a Crusade-centered narrative to the establishment of a new, localized historiographical tradition.[24] A comparison of these two redactions reveals Fulcher's evolution of thought and historiographical methodology over nearly three decades, offering a rare glimpse into the development of the earliest stages of the Levantine Latin literary tradition.

The final organization of Fulcher's work as a chronicle of the Kingdom of Jerusalem reflects traditional modes of historical writing in the Middle Ages. Before the First Crusade, writing about the past usually took several set forms. In prose, the most prevalent genre was the chronicle, or a yearly updated work

21 For example, Tyre's famous king Hiram appears at various points, including 2 Sam. 5, 1 Kings 5–9, 1 Chron. 14, 2 Chron. 2. Virgil (*Aeneid* 1.12–18) speaks of the Tyrian colonists who founded Carthage.

22 For the widespread textual tradition of the *Gesta Apollonii Regis Tyri*, see Archibald, *Apollonius of Tyre*.

23 FC 3.36.

24 The first title, which is found with minor variation across manuscripts of the first redaction, likely originated with Fulcher. The second title is not as well attested, and therefore may have been a scribal innovation. See the discussion in FC 19–20.

enumerating events of note. Chronicles were frequently written in an institutional context, such as a monastery, church, or royal archive. Other historical writing focused on the history of a people, such as Gregory of Tours's history of the Franks and Paul the Deacon's work on the Lombards. The First Crusade, on the other hand, challenged writers by presenting them with a series of events and the actions of disparate groups.[25] Fulcher's reframing of his work as a royal chronicle placed the history in an established literary tradition, simultaneously elevating Fulcher's writing to the status of famous works of historiography and placing the young Latin kingdom on par with older and more renowned royal institutions in Europe.

A Chosen People in a Promised Land

While Fulcher organized the last version of his text by the reigns of the kings of Jerusalem, his ambitions for the work far exceeded the scope of a royal chronicle. Throughout the history, he presents his account as the story of a people chosen by God. The narrative's dramatic arc depicts the Latin Crusaders as a divided, quarreling people who found common purpose under the guidance of a king. Creating unity among the infighting Latins represented a major motivation for the Crusade according to Fulcher, who highlights this theme in his presentation of Pope Urban II's famous sermon at Clermont.[26] When the main Crusader contingent finally departs, Fulcher stresses the camaraderie among the various armies and joyfully proclaims,

> But who has ever heard so many linguistic communities in a single army, since there were Franks, Flemish, Frisians, French, Allobrogians, Lotharingians, Alamans, Bavarians, Normans, Angles, Scots, Aquitanians, Italians, Dacians, Apulians, Iberians, Bretons, Greeks, Armenians? But if some Briton or Teuton wanted to ask me a question, I would be unable to respond to either of them. But though we were diverse with respect to language, we seemed to be as brothers with respect to our love of God and nearly of one mind.[27]

25 The histories of Abbo of Saint-Germain and Guy of Amiens—on the siege of Paris in 896 and the Battle of Hastings (1066), respectively—formed important precedents for independent historical works centered on events rather than institutional or national history.

26 FC 1.3.7.

27 FC 1.13.4–5: *Sed quis umquam audivit tot tribus linguae in uno exercitu, cum ibi adessent Franci, Flandri, Frisi, Galli, Allobroges, Lotharingi, Alemanni, Baioarii, Normanni, Angli, Scoti, Aquitani, Itali, Daci, Apuli, Iberi, Britones, Graeci, Armeni? Quod si vellet me aliquis Britannus vel Teutonicus interrogare, neutro respondere sapere possem. Sed qui linguis diversi eramus, tamquam fratres sub dilectione Dei et proximi unanimes esse videbamur.*

This newfound harmony was short lived, and the untold calamities the Crusaders soon faced led to bickering and even open brawls among the armies. Nevertheless, when Fulcher's party finally reached their destination several years later after a harrowing trek beset by inclement weather, he refers to the hardened participants of the expedition as God's people: "I, Fulcher of Chartres, who was present at these events, one day saw many men and women, as well as a great number of beasts of burden, die because of this freezing rain. It would take long to recite, and perhaps it would be tedious to listeners, that no form of distress, no ailment failed to afflict the people of God."[28] Letters composed during the First Crusade and other eyewitness accounts echo this sentiment, speaking consistently of the Crusader army as a "people of God" (*populus Dei*) and a "knighthood of Christ" (*militia Christi*).[29] Fulcher similarly refers to the Crusaders as "God's people" at two key moments: when they reach Antioch and upon their conquest of Jerusalem.[30]

Fulcher's conception of the Crusaders as a people of God drew on narratives from the Old Testament. In the prologue to the history, Fulcher compares the Crusaders to the Maccabees and the Israelites.[31] The Maccabees, who figure in the biblical (Deuterocanonical) books of the Maccabees as Jewish warriors resisting foreign rule, offered medieval Christians a model for religiously motivated warfare and martyrdom. In the Israelites, the Crusaders saw a meaningful parallel between their own expedition and the Exodus, which brought God's chosen people to the Promised Land—a trajectory that culminated in the establishment of a kingdom.

In comparing the Crusaders to their biblical counterparts in the prologue, Fulcher speaks of "*their* land" (emphasis added), referring to the Israelites and Maccabees. Being present in the Holy Land meant participation in the struggles of the Israelites and Maccabees and identification with them. Elsewhere in his account of the First Crusade, Fulcher displays a keen awareness that the Crusaders traversed the land that had once witnessed the deeds of the Maccabees. When the Crusaders pass by Modiʿin on their way to Jerusalem, Fulcher describes it as "the city of the Maccabees," referring to the site as a principal location in the books of the Maccabees where Mattathias and his sons Judas, Jonathan, and Simon were said to be interred.[32]

Fulcher likewise connected Baldwin I's first major expedition as king of Jerusalem with the Israelite journey to the Promised Land. In 1100 Baldwin I

28 FC 1.33.12: *Ego Fulcherus Carnotensis, qui his intereram, vidi quadam die plures utriusque sexus, bestiasque quamplurimas hac pluvia mori algidissima. Longum est recitandum et audiendi forsan taedium, quia nulla anxietas, nullus dolor defuit populo Dei.*

29 Hagenmeyer, *Epistulae et chartae*, no. 18, 168. See the list in *Anonymi Gesta Francorum*, 21–22.

30 FC 1.17.1, 1.29.4. See also FC 1.30.1, 1.33.12, and the discussion in Epp, *Fulcher von Chartres*, 153.

31 FC prol. 3.

32 FC 1.25.13; 1 Macc. 2:70, 9:19, 13:25, 13:30. See also WT 8.1.9 and RF 69, which state that their tombs are still visible.

explored the area surrounding Jerusalem, venturing as far as the Orthodox monastery of Saint Aaron, near Petra in modern Jordan. While the expedition must have served military and political purposes, Fulcher, who accompanied Baldwin, emphasizes the biblical resonances. He recognizes the rock that Moses struck to provide water to the wandering Israelites ("which even now flows no less than at that time") and identifies the monastery of Saint Aaron as situated on the mountain "where Moses and Aaron used to speak to God."[33] With these biblical associations, Fulcher portrays the first Frankish king of Jerusalem as retracing the path along which Moses had led the Israelites to the Promised Land.

Upon returning to the Kingdom of Jerusalem, Baldwin and his knights fought off a sudden ambush of Turks near Beirut. To Fulcher, the event represented a fulfillment of God's promise to the Israelites: "Truly [God] was there with us and on our behalf, fulfilling in us that which he spoke to the Israelites through a prophet: 'If you will keep safe my precepts, I will enrich you with this gift, so that five from among you may pursue a hundred foreigners, and a hundred from among you ten thousand.'"[34] Fulcher depicts both those who participated in the First Crusade and those who remained in the Latin East as a people of God, with the second group logically following from the first. For this characterization, a biblical model was readily available. A chosen people led by God into the Promised Land easily fit the trajectory of the Israelites brought to Canaan under Moses's guidance—a Promised Land that, for once, could be identified with precisely the same geographical area as the Holy Land.

Fulcher bookended Baldwin's reign with a similarly charged biblical reference. Relating Baldwin I's death in 1118, he ends his book with an epitaph for the king: "When that king fell, the pious Frankish people wept, for he was their shield, strength, and aid. He was a weapon to his people, but fear to his enemies, being an enemy also to them; he was a valiant leader of the homeland, very much like Joshua."[35] By comparing Baldwin to Joshua, leader of the Israelite tribes in their conquest of Canaan, Fulcher presented biblical history as repeating in the Latin Kingdom of Jerusalem.[36] Just as Joshua had led the Israelites into the Promised Land, marking the next phase in Israelite history after a forty-year trek through the desert, so had a new era begun with the foundation of the Kingdom of Jerusalem.

33 FC 2.5.8–9.

34 FC 2.3.4: *Vere pro nobis et nobiscum fuit complens in nobis quod Israeliticis per prophetam dixit: Si praecepta mea servaveritis, hoc dono vos ditabo, ut persequantur V de vobis C alienos, et C ex vobis X milia*. Compare Lev. 28:8.

35 FC 2.64.7: *Cum rex iste ruit, Francorum gens pia flevit, / Cuius erat scutum, robur et auxilium. / Nam fuit arma suis, timor hostibus, hostis et illis; / Dux validus patriae, consimilis Iosue.*

36 For the imagery of Joshua in the Crusader context, particularly in thirteenth-century France, see Gaposchkin, "Louis IX."

The notion that the Latin settlers could be identified with the Israelites was a sentiment shared more widely by Fulcher's contemporaries. An important early source is the Canons of Nablus, or the legal records of a council convened by Patriarch Warmund and King Baldwin II of Jerusalem on 16 January 1120 in the city of Nablus (some fifty kilometers north of Jerusalem). The location was well chosen: it was near the biblical city Shechem (also known as Sichem), where, according to the book of Genesis, God confirmed the covenant he had first made with Abraham in Harran regarding the possession of the land of Canaan. Here, too, the Israelites had chosen to serve the Lord after their exodus from Egypt.[37] The council convened in response to the rout of the army of Roger, the Norman regent of Antioch, at the Battle of the Field of Blood the year before (1119).[38] The preamble to the canons interprets the calamity as a divine punishment for Latin sinfulness and proposes a set of stringent laws to curtail further transgressions. The conveners hoped that, as a result, the Lord would continue to honor his covenant with his people and save them from their enemies "just as we read happened in the case of the Israelites" (*ut in populo Israelitico contigisse legimus*).[39]

Fulcher reinforced his equation of the Latins with the Israelites and Maccabees by frequently casting their Seljuk and Fatimid enemies as biblical foes. So, for instance, he refers anachronistically to "Parthians, Medes, and Chaldeans" attacking towns near Antioch and to the Turks as "Philistines" (*Allophylli*).[40] In a subtler allusion, Fulcher describes a sudden Seljuk incursion as "boiling up from Persia," closely mirroring a passage in 2 Maccabees, where God is said to cause enemies to "boil up from Persia" and to attack Jerusalem as a punishment for Jewish sins.[41]

Natural disasters, too, find their biblical analogues in Fulcher's history. Plagues of locusts in 1114 and 1117 recall the plague described in the book of Exodus sent to punish Pharaoh and the Egyptian populace. Fulcher's language echoes, moreover, a passage in Judges where the nomadic tribes of the Midianites and Amalekites resemble locusts roving around the Israelite countryside, indicating to Fulcher's Christian audience the troubling significance of such events beyond their immediate danger.[42] The description of the plague of 1117 represents a particularly skillful allusion in which Fulcher inverts the biblical simile by comparing the locusts to a devastating human army (*ad morem exercitus hominum*). In an extended aside

37 Gen. 12; Josh. 24.

38 See chap. 4. For a full-length treatment of this battle and its significance, see Morton, *Field of Blood.*

39 Preamble to the Canons of Nablus (1120) in Kedar, "Origins of the Earliest Laws," 331.

40 FC 2.27.1, 3.18.7 (in verse).

41 FC 2.45.1: *Ebulliit e Perside Turcorum gens maxima, qui, per Mesopotamiam meantes Euphratem fluvium transierunt, et obsederunt castrum quod Turbezel vocatur.* Compare 2 Macc. 1:12: *Ipse enim ebullire fecit de Perside eos qui pugnaverunt contra nos et sanctam civitatem.*

42 FC 2.52.1, 2.60.1; Exod. 10; Judg. 6:5 and 7:12.

Fulcher laments Frankish sinfulness, which required God to chastise the Franks through various instructive calamities (*documenta*).[43] Likewise, an infestation of mice in 1127 parallels an episode in Samuel, in which the Philistines receive divine punishment after confiscating the Ark of the Covenant, and could be interpreted as a warning to the Latins not to imperil their own cherished relic, the True Cross.[44]

As a priest writing a narrative in Latin, the language of scripture and liturgy in western European Christendom, it is unsurprising that Fulcher used narrative structure and biblical allusion to construct a sacral history of the settlers of the Latin East. Yet in the decades after he began writing his account, Fulcher also developed an increasingly academic voice and laid claim to a startlingly ambitious intellectual authority.

Levantine Intellectual Authority

While Fulcher structured his work as a royal history with strong biblical overtones, his scriptural references increasingly reflect academic concerns that point toward his evolving knowledge of Levantine geography and history. A comparison between Fulcher's final redaction of the history (post-1124) and the earlier version shows that as time went on, Fulcher inserted additional biblical references into earlier portions of his work. For example, in the final version, he has rendered the city Ramla as Ramatha and identified it with the obscure biblical town Arimathea. Elsewhere he has specified that the coastal city Jaffa "lies in [the land of] the tribe of Dan."[45]

In other instances, Fulcher corrected earlier statements with more up-to-date information.[46] In describing Hebron, a town south of Jerusalem renowned as the burial place of the biblical patriarchs, Fulcher struck his initial statement claiming that in addition to Abraham, Isaac, and Jacob, Joseph too was entombed at this location.[47] Fulcher had relied here on an earlier tradition of pilgrim narratives that placed Joseph's tomb at this site.[48] In 1119, however, the canons of Hebron rediscovered the tombs of the patriarchs and matriarchs, which did not include that of Joseph.[49] When Fulcher revised his history in 1124, he removed Joseph's name from the passage to reflect the recent discovery.

43 FC 2.60.3–5.
44 FC 3.62.1; 1 Sam. 1:5.
45 FC 1.25.12, 2.3.12.
46 For a list of passages in which Fulcher made factual corrections of details such as dates, see Epp, *Fulcher von Chartres*, 144–45.
47 FC 2.4.5.
48 Piacenza Pilgrim, 30; Sæwulf, 232, 487.
49 See chap. 3.

Other revisions show not only a striving for accuracy, but also betray a desire to be perceived as a reliable intellectual authority. When describing the Crusader journey southward along the coast in the spring of 1099, Fulcher takes issue with those who identified Acre with the biblical city Ekron, which he located near Ascalon (west of Jerusalem). In his earlier version, Fulcher had humbly included himself among those mistaken, admitting that "I too had this habit [of referring to the city as Ekron] when I first entered the land of Palestine." In the final redaction, however, he simply points out that "some of our people erroneously believe Acre to be Ekron."[50]

Such discussions on historical geography are not the idle musings of dusty antiquarianism but point toward a lively intellectual scene and to a shared interest on the part of Latins to interpret their surroundings through scripture. These explanations were commonly found in pilgrim guides to the Holy Land, which aided travelers by identifying the location of the holy sites. With the influx of ever greater numbers of pilgrims, such guides became popular and widespread texts. The biblical references in the earlier version of Fulcher's history show an affinity with these pilgrim guides. For his later redaction, on the other hand, Fulcher increasingly conceived of his work as a well-researched historical account furnished with accurate geographical information.[51] He assumed for himself an intellectual authority, first by quoting well-established authors of the Latin intellectual tradition and then by modeling himself after their example.

For instance, Fulcher's account of his return to Edessa after a visit to Jerusalem in 1100 leads into a digression on Lake Tiberias (better known as the Sea of Galilee). He references in quick succession Josephus and Jerome to indicate the lake's size and to explain its origins. Flavius Josephus was a first-century CE Jewish writer who composed Greek works under Roman patronage. Both his account of the Jewish uprising against the Romans and his sprawling history known as the *Jewish Antiquities* were available in Latin translations and were regarded as repositories of reliable historical and geographical information.[52] The fourth-century bishop and polymath Jerome, who eventually settled in Palestine, likewise furnished a Latin audience with a wealth of information on Levantine history and geography, and in his treatises and biblical commentaries, he provided etymologies of Hebrew names and toponyms.

Fulcher emphasizes his familiarity with both authors, expressly stating that he has read Jerome's commentary on the book of Amos, but he claims to go beyond

50 FC 1.25.11.

51 In addition to the passages discussed below, Fulcher's interest in physical geography also comes to the fore in his speculation on the source of the Nile and its relation to the Mediterranean Sea and the Red Sea at FC 2.57–58 and on the Euphrates River at 2.59.

52 For the reception of Josephus in the Latin West, see Kletter, "Christian Reception of Josephus"; for the reception of Josephus in the twelfth-century Latin East, see Yolles, "Josephus."

these two impressive authorities to propose an explanation for the lake's source. "In imitation of blessed Jerome," Fulcher writes, "I made a rather clever conjecture." Drawing on information supplied by Jerome, Fulcher hypothesizes that the Jordan River, which feeds Lake Tiberias, originates from two springs, one named "Jor" and the other "Dan." While claiming to offer his own theory, he neglectes to mention, however, that Jerome himself had proposed the very same explanation.[53]

Fulcher used similar language to claim an intellectual contribution when describing his visit to the Dead Sea. The unusual body of salt water south of Jerusalem drew his attention not only for its biblical associations as the supposed site of Sodom and Gomorrah, but also as a natural anomaly utterly foreign to the French priest.[54] Fulcher prominently records his own experiential observation ("I, Fulcher, learned by experiment"), describing in detail how he descended from his mule and dipped his hand into the water to bravely sample a draught of the unpotable liquid.[55] Again, Fulcher offers his learned hypothesis ("I conjecture") on the reasons for the Dead Sea's salinity: either the water continuously leeches salt off of a nearby salt mound or an underground passage connects the Mediterranean with the Dead Sea. The passage is littered with information drawn from a geographical digression in Josephus's *Jewish War* and even includes phrases lifted wholesale from Josephus. For instance, Fulcher gives the dimensions of the Dead Sea provided by Josephus and uses his wording to indicate the difficulty of submerging oneself into the water.[56] And while Fulcher's two-fold explanation appears to be his own, his subsequent observations on the so-called Sodom's apple closely resemble those of Josephus, even though they are likewise couched in language of personal observation ("wishing to know the nature [of these fruits], I broke the skin and found empty smoke billowing out like black dust").[57]

Josephus's works provided Fulcher not only with a wealth of information, but also with an intellectual model. Like Josephus, Fulcher wrote a historical account of events in the Levant, interspersed with geographical and other digressions. In so doing, he adopted a Josephan mode of intellectual inquiry. Elsewhere he followed Jerome's example in making linguistic observations, as when explaining the etymology of Damascus, which, according to Fulcher, "means 'kiss of blood,' or 'drinking blood,' for we read that Abel's blood was spilt in Damascus."[58]

53 FC 1.34.2–4; Jerome, *Commentarii in prophetas minores*, on Amos 8:12; Jerome, *Commentarii in evangelium Matthaei*, on Matt. 16:13. Rorgo Fretellus (RF 31), likely also drawing on Jerome, offered the same explanation.

54 Gen. 14.

55 FC 2.5.1.

56 Compare FC 2.5.1 and 2.5.2 with Flavius Josephus, *De bello Iudaico* 5.5.

57 FC 2.5.6; Flavius Josephus, *De bello Iudaico* 5.5.

58 Fulcher's sources were probably Jerome, *Liber interpretationis hebraicorum nominum* 5.5, and *Commentarii in Ezechielem* 8.27.18; he may also have looked to Haimo of Auxerre, *Annotatio libri Isaiae prophetae* 17.1.

Another example of how far Fulcher was willing to go in his imitation of Josephus is his tendency to pass off Josephus's references to ancient sources of information as his own. In his description of Tyre, Fulcher references the "archives of Tyre" and thereby gives the impression of having had access to a source he knew only from a quotation in Josephus. Earlier, Fulcher likewise cites both Josephus and the ancient historian Menander, even though he knew of the latter only from a passage of Josephus.[59]

Fulcher's writing shows an increasingly scholarly bent. In the portions written after 1124, he liberally quotes the works of Josephus (with attribution)—to such an extent that he must have had access to Latin copies of both *Jewish War* and *Jewish Antiquities* as he worked.[60] In the same period, Fulcher also incorporated extensive passages on natural history from a third-century CE encyclopedia by the Roman author Solinus, itself based on Pliny the Elder's *Natural History*. These lengthy excerpts baffle modern readers but may be explained by Fulcher's working method and by his posturing as a privileged intellectual authority on the Levant.[61]

Fulcher embedded the excerpts of Solinus within a narrative describing Baldwin II's unsuccessful raid in the pastures surrounding Ascalon. Fulcher attributes this failure to the fact that the Ascalonites had been forewarned of the king's arrival by carrier pigeons. Writing to a European audience to whom this means of communication was unknown, he explains that it was a widespread practice among the "Saracens" (i.e., Muslims) of Palestine.[62] Fulcher goes on to discuss the fact that different regions have varying customs and diverse natural environments.[63] Again relying on his own eyewitness testimony, he declares that he has never seen a whale or a lamprey in Palestine, nor a magpie or a warbler—animals that could be found in western Europe. Instead, Fulcher claims to have observed near Nablus a creature "with the head of a goat, a neck like a donkey, a cloven hoof, the tail of a calf, and larger than a ram." Reminded of the mythical chimaera, he proceeds to quote Solinus's description. With the book still open, Fulcher may have decided to

59 FC 3.30.3, 3.29.5.

60 FC 3.29.2–5 (references to Josephus); FC 3.46.6 and Flavius Josephus, *De bello Iudaico* 1.374; FC 3.51.4 and Flavius Josephus, *De bello Iudaico* 7.97–99; FC 3.52.1 and Flavius Josephus, *De bello Iudaico* 2.9.

61 See the remarks of Hagenmeyer in FC 3.49, n. 1, and Ryan, in her translation of Fulcher, *History of the Expedition* 3.48, n. 1.

62 FC 3.47. For the use of carrier pigeons in the Latin East, see Lohrmann, "Échanges techniques," 130–33.

63 FC 3.48.1. Fulcher speaks of *consuetudines*, meaning "mores" or "cultural practices," and *res*, literally "things," encompassing everything from animals to plants and trees (not "customs," as Ryan, *History of the Expedition*, translates, which would be redundant).

insert passages on a host of other animals, mythical and otherwise, with the occasional comment on whether they could be found in the Levant.[64]

Over the years, Fulcher's aims and methods in writing history developed considerably. By 1124 he seems to have viewed his task not only as chronicling the events surrounding God's people in the Levant, but also as building a storehouse of accurate and current information on diverse topics. Fulcher was increasingly concerned with developing and maintaining an image among the Latins of a reliable intellectual authority.

Latinizing the Levant

In claiming for himself the privileged position of Levantine intellectual authority, Fulcher might be expected to have consulted with local Christian communities of the Levant. There was a sizeable—and growing—population of Levantine Christians in Jerusalem and its environs. In 1116 Baldwin I resettled groups of "Syrians" (i.e., Eastern Christians) from Transjordan in Jerusalem to expand the city's population.[65] Moreover, Latins certainly encountered Orthodox Greek and other Eastern Christian clergy at the Church of the Holy Sepulcher during the Easter celebrations, even though these communities celebrated separately.[66]

Despite their visible presence in Fulcher's immediate vicinity, these local Christian communities are conspicuous in their absence from much of his history. Throughout the chronicle, Fulcher wrote entirely from a Latin Christian perspective. In his version of Pope Urban II's speech at the start of the work, for example, the expedition is principally aimed at reforming Latin Christendom by inviting rulers and their subjects to participate in an armed pilgrimage to the Holy Land. Only secondarily does the pope reference the Turkic conquests of the Levant and the recent suffering of Levantine Christians.[67] In narrating the Crusader capture of Jerusalem, Fulcher likewise frames the expedition's objective as an effort to purge Christ's sacred space from pagan defilement and to return it to its former state of dignity, without a single reference to Levantine Christians.[68] Even in the prologue, composed in 1118–20, when Fulcher had practically been living

64 For example, Fulcher observes that crocodiles plagued the coastal city of Caesarea and had been brought there not long ago to cause havoc and devour the Franks' cattle (FC 3.49.4).

65 WT 11.27; Prawer, *Crusader Institutions*, 92–93.

66 For Orthodox clergy at the Church of the Holy Sepulcher during the Easter celebrations, see Galadza, "Greek Liturgy," 430–31; for Greek Orthodox clergy in Latin Jerusalem more generally, see Pahlitzsch, *Graeci und Suriani*.

67 Munro, "Speech of Pope Urban II," 236–37. See for an opposing view MacEvitt, "Processing Together," 458.

68 FC 1.29.4.

side-by-side with Levantine Christians for nearly two decades, he still considers his subject matter to be the "expedition [of] . . . the entire Western people."[69]

When he does mention Levantine Christians, Fulcher exhibits a degree of ambivalence. He quotes at length a letter purportedly written by the Crusaders to the pope after the conquest of Antioch, in which the leaders of the expedition urge the pope to join them. While they have been successful in defeating "Turks and pagans," they suggest that only the pope can defeat the Greek, Armenian, Syrian, and Jacobite "heretics."[70] Fulcher saw fit to include this openly hostile letter in the first redaction of his work without any commentary or editorialization. His decision to strike the letter from the second redaction may reflect Fulcher's evolution toward a more positive appraisal of Eastern Christians.[71] However, such a change in attitude was carefully circumscribed, as shown by his decision to remove from his revision a reference to the Greek Orthodox patriarch of Jerusalem at the time of the Crusader capture.[72] The questionable legality of the installment of a Latin patriarch may have been a sore point, especially if Fulcher now belonged to the clergy of the Holy Sepulcher.[73]

Nonetheless, Fulcher depicted Levantine Christian communities as grateful beneficiaries of Latin aid and as trustworthy allies in times of crisis. According to Fulcher, the Eastern Christian clergy of Bethlehem rejoiced at Baldwin and Tancred's arrival in the summer of 1099.[74] Moreover, he painted a vivid portrait of a "Syrian Christian" entrusted by Baldwin I to deliver a message to Jerusalem in the spring of 1102.[75] Obeying his impetuous temper, Baldwin had rushed out with but a handful of soldiers to meet an oncoming threat from Ramla without waiting for reinforcements. After the rout of his army, Baldwin barely escaped the onslaught. Meanwhile, the rumor of the king's death reached Jerusalem, causing great consternation among the Latins. Having fled to nearby Jaffa, Baldwin desperately needed to get word to his men. Not knowing whom to trust, Fulcher describes how Baldwin found "a certain Syrian, a humble man and poorly clothed," who bravely undertook the hazardous journey on Baldwin's behalf.

An extended narrative episode in Fulcher's history further illustrates his complicated attitude toward Eastern Christian communities. The episode revolves around the daring escape from captivity of Joscelin I of Courtenay, count of

69 FC prol. 5.
70 FC 1.24.13–14; see also chap. 4.
71 Biddlecombe in Baudri of Bourgueil, *Historia Ierosolimitana*, xlviii.
72 FC 1.30.2.
73 Pahlitzsch, *Graeci und Suriani*, 90–92.
74 FC 1.25.14.
75 FC 2.21.5.

Edessa.[76] Joscelin had been taken captive in 1122 by Nūr al-Dawla Balak, Artuqid emir of Aleppo, and imprisoned in Harput, a stronghold near Melitene (in modern central Turkey). When Baldwin arrived the following year to free him, returning the favor Joscelin had done him by arranging for his ransom in 1108, he met with the same fate.[77] Fulcher recounts the botched attempt by hired local Armenians to free both Baldwin and Joscelin; in the end, only Joscelin succeeds in evading his captors. His eventual safe return is facilitated by another Armenian—a local farmer who recognizes the count and offers to accompany him along with his entire household to ensure his safe passage. Upon reaching Turbessel (Tall Bāšir, in modern southeastern Turkey), Joscelin rewards the Armenians generously. Fulcher concludes with the moral of the story:

> Blessed be the universal Lord, who directs his will and power such that, when he wishes, he casts down the powerful from on high and raises a pauper out of the dust. For in the morning Baldwin ruled as king, but in the evening he served as a slave; and it was no different with Joscelin. It is clear therefore that nothing is certain in this world, nothing is stable, nothing is agreeable for long. For this reason it is not good to long for earthly things, but rather to have a heart intent on God. And let us not put our faith in what will perish, so that we do not become estranged from what is eternal.[78]

Fulcher's emphasis on the mutability of fortune points to the precarious position held by Latins in the Levant and to their need to cooperate with Eastern Christian communities like the Armenians. That this notion was not a given, but required a long-winded narrative as a justification, shows that in the 1120s—at least in the mind of Fulcher—Eastern Christians still represented outsiders. A comparison with William of Tyre's treatment of the same episode (writing ca. 1169–84) reveals how much had changed in half a century. William omits the entire scene between Joscelin and the Armenian farmer, focusing instead on the cruel punishment suffered by the Armenians who failed to liberate Baldwin and Joscelin at Harput.[79]

76 For Joscelin of Courtenay, lord of Tiberias and later count of Edessa, see Murray, *Crusader Kingdom*, 214, no. 79.

77 The Latin, Arabic, Armenian, and Syriac sources differ widely in the details of the release of Baldwin and Joscelin in 1108. For an overview, see Nicholson, *Joscelyn I*, 13–15.

78 FC 3.24.16: *Benedictus autem sit universalis Dominus, qui voluntatem suam et potestatem ita modificat, ut potentem de excelso, cum vult, praecipitet et de pulvere pauperem sublimet. Mane itaque Balduinus rex imperavit, sero autem servus servivit; Goscelinus quoque nihilominus. Liquet utique nihil in hoc saeculo esse certum, nihil stabile, nec etiam diu gratum. Ideo terrenis inhiare non est bonum, sed cor habere ad Deum semper intentum. Nec confidamus in caducis, ne alienemur aeternis.* For a similar sentiment, compare Walter the Chancellor, writing in Antioch in the early 1120s: *ea nocte fuit idem servus et dominus* (WC 2.1.3).

79 WT 12.18–20; see also MacEvitt, *Rough Tolerance*, 94.

Unlike Fulcher, William takes the Armenians' integration within Frankish society for granted and even goes further by taking issue with those aspects of Fulcher's narrative that present Armenians as mercurial and motivated by anything other than Christian solidarity.

Fulcher similarly stresses the need for a cooperative mindset in relating the discovery of a fragment of the True Cross. The fragment had been found, Fulcher tells us, by "a certain Syrian" shortly after the capture of Jerusalem in 1099.[80] According to the Provençal priest Raymond of Aguilers, the relic was discovered by the Latin patriarch Arnulf of Chocques, who interrogated the "inhabitants" (*incolae*) of Jerusalem concerning the whereabouts of the relic venerated by pilgrims before the Crusade. Perceiving that the Latins were elected by God, the locals eventually handed over their relic, which they had buried in a church.[81]

Fulcher instead presents the episode not as the transfer of a relic from local Christians to divinely chosen Latins, but as the miraculous discovery of an object that had been hidden long ago by "religious men" and safeguarded by a Syrian and his father.[82] The event constituted a divine revelation from the perspective of the Latins, but Fulcher also emphasizes the specific role of Syrian Christians as keepers of the treasure. Fulcher, who as possible treasurer of the Church of the Holy Sepulcher may have written a so-called *inventio* account documenting the relic's discovery, frames the subsequent celebrations in emphatically inclusive terms, describing how "the entire populace jointly" (*omnes una*) carried the relic in a procession throughout the city.[83]

While acknowledging the role of local Christians in preserving the relic, Fulcher does not attribute to them any privileged information they might possess regarding the object. Two letters from Ansellus, cantor at the Church of the Holy Sepulcher, written to the congregation of Paris in 1120–21, offer a stark contrast.[84] These letters detail the provenance of a smaller relic of the Cross, which the cantor had sent to the bishop of Paris along with a stone relic from the Holy Sepulcher. Ansellus explains that the relic of the Cross had been acquired from the founder of a new convent in Jerusalem, a former consort of Giorgi II, king of Georgia. Ansellus treats in some detail the history of the Cross and the dispersion of its relics

80 FC 1.30.4.

81 RA 154.

82 FC 1.30.4. William of Tyre (WT 9.4) followed Fulcher's presentation of the event, emphasizing the extensive effort of the Syrian (*studio et opera cuiusdam hominis Syri*). For the sources, see Frolow, *La relique de la Vraie Croix*, no. 258.

83 FC 1.30.4. For joint processions in Frankish Jerusalem, see MacEvitt, "Processing Together." For the genre of the *inventio*, see chap. 3.

84 For Ansellus, see Frolow, *La relique de la Vraie Croix*, no. 298; Folda, *Art of the Crusaders*, 87; Dondi, *Liturgy of the Canons*, 58–59; and Aspesi, "Cantors of the Holy Sepulchre," 278–96. For the letters, see PL 168:729–32 (Barber and Bate, *Letters from the East*, no. 12). For the dating, see Bresc-Bautier, "L'envoi de la relique."

among various Christian communities. He identifies his source as the "writings/scriptures of the Greeks and Syriacs" (*Graecorum et Syriacorum scripturis*) and claims to have spoken with the "elders of the Suriani" (*seniorum Surianorum*). Remarkably, Ansellus explains that, while his Parisian addressees may have read a thing or two about the history of the Cross, "the Greeks possess many things, which the Latins do not" (*multa enim habent Graeci, quae non habent Latini*).[85]

In claiming for himself a position of privileged authority on the relic's authenticity, Ansellus possessed decidedly pragmatic motivations, for he requested that the congregation of Paris inscribe their books with his name as the relic's donor, even supplying the exact text they were to write. If Fulcher indeed held the position of treasurer at the Church of the Holy Sepulcher, Ansellus's authoritative history of the relic may have impinged on the activities of his colleague. An amusing letter from Pope Calixtus II to Patriarch Warmund of Jerusalem in 1121 shows that Ansellus did not shy from stirring up controversy, as a report had reached the pope that the cantor and succentor of the Holy Sepulcher had been "living like secular clerics in their houses" and ordered "others to replace them in the performance of the Divine Office."[86] Apparently the pair refused to submit to the reformed lifestyle that had been imposed on the canons of the Church of the Holy Sepulcher in 1114 by the Latin patriarch Arnulf of Chocques. If, as some scholars maintain, Fulcher had had a hand in the reform, he may have found in Ansellus a staunch opponent to his efforts.[87] Sadly we do not possess sufficient evidence regarding Fulcher's career in this period to definitively connect his activities with those of Ansellus.

Unlike the cantor of the Holy Sepulcher, Fulcher did not acknowledge the merits of other Levantine intellectual cultures that might possess information about the Holy Land unavailable to the Latins. However, as E. Andersen Oftestad has shown recently, Fulcher did make use of rabbinic traditions in his discussion of the sacred objects allegedly hidden underneath the Temple of Jerusalem.[88] Although he does not cite these sources, Fulcher references an oral tradition by attributing spoken discourse to unnamed individuals. In the first redaction, he writes, "they say (*aiunt*) that the Ark of the Covenant lies sealed within the rock, together with the rod [of Abraham] and the tablets of the law." In the second redaction, Fulcher's passage assumes a more theological tone, in keeping with other passages he wrote at this final stage of composition (see below): "[the rock,] in which they prophesied (*divinabant*) that the Ark of the Covenant lay sealed,

85 PL 168:731B.

86 Hiestand, *Papsturkunden*, 130–31, no. 23 (RRH no. 94; RRR no. 206).

87 Dondi, *Liturgy of the Canons*, 59; Shagrir, "*Adventus* in Jerusalem"; Gaposchkin, *Invisible Weapons*, 147.

88 Andersen Oftestad, *Lateran Church*, 100–105; see also Hagenmeyer's earlier comments (FC 1.26.7, n. 22).

together with the rod [of Abraham] and the tablets of the law."[89] The following discussion, in which Fulcher presents evidence arguing for and against the current presence of these objects underneath the Templum Domini, derives entirely from rabbinic sources. It is unclear how Fulcher accessed these sources—though his phrasing suggests an oral transmission of some kind—and whether or not he was aware of their Jewish origins. However, the fact that one manuscript, containing what is generally considered an elaboration of an early version of Fulcher's history, attributes the claims to Jews (*Hebraei*) may indicate that Fulcher deliberately suppressed their provenance.[90]

Only rarely did Fulcher acknowledge other linguistic and cultural traditions in the Levant. Once, for example, he explains that the animal, "which is called 'salamander' in Greek, [is called] *stellio* in Latin."[91] More commonly, Fulcher's references to other Levantine languages occur in the context of his discussions of place-names. Occasionally he offers Greek and Hebrew equivalents of toponyms; once he even explains that Caesarea Philippi "is called Paneas [Banyas] in the Syriac language (*lingua Syriaca*)."[92] Wherever possible, Fulcher preferred Latinized biblical or Greco-Roman place-names to more recent designations, since such toponyms had an ancient, established tradition. Classical pedigree mattered to authors such as Fulcher, who wrote not in their native tongue but in the language of the Romans.

Although Fulcher recognized Greek, Hebrew, and Syriac as ancient languages, he accorded no such status to Arabic. For instance, when describing the events occurring near Antioch in 1124, Fulcher refers to the ancient Syrian city of Hierapolis, but remarks that the common people (*vulgus*) call it Mombech (i.e., Manbij, in northern Syria).[93] He makes an even clearer distinction between Latin, the language of literature, and Arabic, spoken discourse of the masses, in his discussion of Baldwin I and Tancred's expedition in 1111. Describing their pursuit of raiding Turks, Fulcher explains that the army passed by a city called Sisara, "which city I do not know how to express in a literary manner (*litteratorie*), but the inhabitants of that region call it Chesar in the common language (*vulgariter*)."[94] Not content with the Arabic toponym, Fulcher or one of his fellow Latin settlers

89 FC 1.26.7; cf. 1.26.9.

90 The so-called Codex L. For the passage in question, see Fulcher of Chartres, *Historia Iherosolymitana*, 356, and Andersen Oftestad, *Lateran Church*, 103–4.

91 FC 3.49.13.

92 For Greek, FC 1.34.5, 2.64.1; for Hebrew, 2.46.1, 2.64.1; for Syriac, 1.34.2.

93 FC 3.31.1: *perrexit Hierapolim, quam urbem Mombech vulgus vocitat.*

94 FC 2.45.6; cf. FC 3.31.1. The first redaction of Fulcher's history read *grammatice* for *litteratorie*, which has much the same sense as "in accordance with literary standards." For more discussion of the medieval curriculum of *grammatica*, see chap. 4. For another twelfth-century parallel to the rare adverb *litteratorie*, see *Annales Rodenses*, 696 (ca. 1100–1157): *in loco videlicet qui litteratorie Clarus fons est dictus, vulgari autem nomine Clarefontanus.*

evidently tried coining their own Latinized form of the city Shaizar, possibly after the name of the Canaanite leader mentioned in the book of Judges.[95] In Fulcher's eyes, to be literary was to be Latin.

A comparison with William of Tyre once again reveals an entirely different attitude. Describing the city of Babylon near Cairo, he writes of "an excellent metropolis, which is commonly (*vulgo*) called Babilonia, but in the Arabic language (*lingua Arabica*) is called Macer" (i.e., Maṣr).[96] Unlike Fulcher, William identifies the Arabic language by name and, what is more, appears to reverse the literary/non-literary binary by using the word *vulgo* to refer to the Latin appellation.

Throughout his work, Fulcher prefers classical and biblical authorities over more recent sources. That his fellow Jerusalemite (and probable colleague at the Church of the Holy Sepulcher) Ansellus prided himself on his access to Greek and Syriac traditions demonstrates that Fulcher's refusal to credit non-Latin Christians with an intellectual tradition of their own, one that might contain knowledge beyond the ken of Latins, and his focus on Latin sources and naming conventions were not necessarily the result of a lack of information, but formed part of a deliberate strategy to promote his own brand of Levantine Latinity. Fulcher's history sought to return to a biblical and classical past. As he would have it, his Latin history, and not the traditions of local Jews or Greek, Syriac, and Arabic Christians in Jerusalem, possessed literary and intellectual authority.

"As in the Heavens, So on Earth"

Fulcher's efforts to cast the history of the Latins in a biblical mold and to control his own image as an intellectual authority of the Levant were not distinct projects. They converge most prominently in his many passages on celestial phenomena. Fulcher's interest in this topic reflects a more widely shared preoccupation with predicting and explaining celestial events in the High Middle Ages more generally and in the twelfth-century Levant specifically.[97] According to Ralph of Caen, Arnulf of Chocques was accompanied on the Crusade by a *didascalus* (astrologer).[98] By the thirteenth century, a set of astrological predictions circulated in Europe that claimed to have been compiled by the physician of King Amalric

95 For the biblical Sisara, see Judges 4–5; Fulcher references this person at FC 3.29.2. Other early Levantine Latin authors also employ *Sisara* as a Latin toponym for Shaizar: WC 1.2.7, 1.3.5–7, 1.4.1, 1.4.6; RC 4475. Some other early authors (at least one of whom wrote in the Latin West) mistook *Sisara* for Caesarea: *GF* 34.5; AA 11.39.

96 WT 19.15.1: *egregiam metropolim, que vulgo Babilonia dicitur, lingua vero Arabica Macer appellatur.*

97 For an overview of the scholarship on celestial portents during the High Middle Ages, see Williams, *Fiery Shapes.*

98 RC 266–67 and the discussion at XCII.

of Jerusalem (r. 1163–1174) and are therefore known as the *Sortes regis Amalrici* (Predictions of King Amalric).[99] There were also Latin writings in the Levant that centered on related fields. The catalogue of books belonging to the church of Nazareth lists *duo libri de luna* (two books about the moon), probably containing methods for calculating the lunar cycle.[100] Stephen the Philosopher, a Pisan scholar employed as treasurer of the convent of Saint Paul in Antioch in the 1120s, authored a cosmological translation-cum-commentary entitled *Liber Mamonis in astronomia* (The book of Mamon on astronomy), which contains fifteen diagrams depicting, among other things, the lunar cycle.[101] Nor was interest in celestial matters in the Levant confined to the Latins. To name but one example, the Armenian chronicler Matthew of Edessa (d. 1144) drew on an extensive Armenian historiographical tradition in which astrological omens functioned as interpretive keys and structural devices.[102]

Fulcher's interest in celestial events features prominently throughout his work. The verse epigrams concluding each book in the final redaction all contain references to astrological signs, while the narrative draws attention to celestial phenomena on numerous occasions.[103] These observations form part of a theological-historical argument. For example, Fulcher interpreted a lunar eclipse on the morning of 16 June 1117 as a portent sent by God.[104] He portrays such signs as urgent missives sent by God to his people, who ignore them at their peril.[105] Fulcher was not alone in this view, and he depicts lively debates about the meaning of such events. "Some conjectured," he writes, "that, because of the red glow, blood would be spilt in battle; others however interpreted the blackness as signifying that a famine would occur."[106] Fulcher generally declines to speculate about the correct interpretation, as in the instance of the lunar eclipse: "But we entrust this matter to the care and providence of God, who foretold to his disciples that signs would come in the sun and moon."[107] On another occasion, however, Fulcher humbly offers an explanation for the appearance of "a fiery,

99 See appendix 1.
100 See appendix 2.
101 Cambrai, Bibliothèque Municipale, 930, fol. 36r; see SP, *Liber Mamonis*, 44–46.
102 Andrews, *Matt'ēos Uřhayec'i*, 32–33.
103 For a list, see Epp, *Fulcher von Chartres*, 160. Epp considered Fulcher's overt astrological references part of an effort to anchor the kingdom of Jerusalem in a classical-mythological tradition.
104 FC 2.61.
105 FC 2.60.
106 FC 2.61: *ex hoc quidam coniectabant rubore in praelio fore fundendum sanguinem; alii vero nigredine significabant venturam famem.*
107 FC 2.61: *Nos vero dispositioni et providentiae Dei hoc commisimus, qui in sole et luna discipulis suis praedixit signa fore ventura.* This is a reference to Luke 21:25. Compare also Fulcher's reluctance to interpret the appearance of a comet in FC 3.55.4: *significantiam cuius Conditori omnium commisimus.*

blood-colored glow" following a lunar eclipse on 16 December 1117. Employing the same terminology he used elsewhere in promoting his intellectual contributions, Fulcher writes: "I conjectured (*coniiciebamus*) therefore that either a great amount of blood would be spilt in battle or that something else, a presage of no lesser threat, would occur. But what I considered to be uncertain, I humbly entrusted to the Lord God's care."[108]

In book 3, in what rightly may be termed the central passage of the work, Fulcher offers the most explicit expression of his theological-historical program:

> Consider, I ask, and reflect, how in our age God has transformed the West into the East. For we who were Westerners have now been turned into Easterners. He who was a Roman or Frank has become a Galilean in this land, or a Palestinian. He who was from Reims or Chartres has now become a citizen of Tyre or Antioch. We have already forgotten the places of our birth; already they have become unknown to many of us, and even unheard of. Some already own their own homes and households as if by hereditary right, while others have already married—and not just women of their own people, but even Syrian and Armenian women, and sometimes even Saracens, after they have received the grace of baptism. . . . Each uses the idioms and expressions of various languages in conversing. A mixed language has become a common tongue known to each nationality, and faith unites those who are of unknown descent. For it is written: "The lion and the bull shall eat straw together" [Isa. 65:25]. He who was born a stranger has now become a native, and he who was a foreigner has become indigenous. Day after day, [more of] our next of kin and family follow us, leaving behind all they possessed—indeed, not desiring it. For those who were poor there have been made wealthy by God here. Those who had but a few coins, here possess innumerable bezants, and he who did not have an estate, here, by God's generosity, owns a city. Indeed, why would one return to the West, who found the East to be like this? . . . You perceive, then, that this is a great miracle to be marveled at by the entire world. Who has ever heard such a thing?[109]

108 FC 2.63.3.

109 FC 3.37.2–8: *Considera, quaeso, et mente recogita, quomodo tempore in nostro transvertit Deus Occidentem in Orientem. Nam qui fuimus occidentales, nunc facti sumus orientales. Qui fuit Romanus aut Francus, hac in terra factus est Galilaeus, aut Palaestinus. Qui fuit Remensis aut Carnotensis, nunc efficitur Tyrius vel Antiochenus. Iam obliti sumus nativitatis nostrae loca; iam nobis pluribus vel sunt ignota, vel etiam inaudita. Hic iam possidet domos proprias et familias quasi iure paterno et hereditario, ille vero iam duxit uxorem non tantum compatriotam, sed et Syram aut Armenam et interdum Saracenam, baptismi autem gratiam adeptam . . . Diversarum linguarum coutitur alternatim eloquio et obsequio alteruter. Lingua diversa iam communis facta utrique nationi fit nota, et iungit fides quibus est ignota progenies. Scriptum quippe est: leo et bos simul comedent paleas* [Isa. 65:25].

Fulcher's extended apostrophe arrests the reader with carefully balanced clauses and a lofty rhetorical climax unparalleled elsewhere in his history. This famous passage has been cited as an expression of a multicultural sentiment and as evidence of Latin cultural assimilation to local inhabitants. Others have pointed out that the idealizing portrait Fulcher paints may have served pragmatic concerns—to draw European immigrants to a Levantine promised land by emphasizing the materialistic advantages of the Latin East.[110] Yet to grasp the full scope of Fulcher's claims in this passage, it is necessary to read from the beginning of the chapter in which the passage is embedded:

> Then the sun appeared to us, for nearly an hour, to be changed into a new, hyacinth-tinted appearance with colorful splendor, and to be transformed into the likeness of the half moon, as though in an eclipse . . . therefore do not wonder when you see signs in the heavens, because God works no less on earth. For as in the heavens, so also does he transform and combine among earthly matters whatever and however he wishes. If his actions are wondrous, even more wondrous is the one who causes them. Consider, I ask . . . [111]

Read within its proper context, the wondrous transformation of the Latins described by Fulcher bears a direct relation to the heavenly portent he witnessed. While on other occasions Fulcher demurred from claiming complete certainty in explaining celestial events, in this instance he confidently and exuberantly interprets the event as a fulfillment of Isaiah's prophecy that "the lion and the bull shall eat straw together" (Isa. 65:25). In the context of the Latin East, this interpretation meant that the Latins had been transformed into something new by living in close proximity to Eastern Christians ("Syrians" and "Armenians") and Muslims ("Saracens").

Qui erat alienigena, nunc est indigena, et qui inquilinus, est utique incola factus. Nos nostri sequuntur de die in diem propinqui et parentes, quaecumque possederant relinquentes, nec etiam volentes. Qui enim illic erant inopes, hic facit eos Deus locupletes. Qui habuerant nummos paucos, hic possident bisantios innumeros, et qui non habuerat villam, hic Deo dante iam possidet urbem. Quare ergo reverteretur in Occidentem, qui hic taliter invenit Orientem? . . . Percipitis igitur esse hoc miraculum immensum et universo mundo valde stupendum. Quis audivit hactenus tale?"

110 For the former view, see Folda, "Crusader Art," 80; for the latter interpretation, see Hagenmeyer in FC 61–62; Giese, "Untersuchungen zur *Historia Hierosolymitana*," 94; and Epp, *Fulcher von Chartres*, 138.

111 FC 3.37.1–2: *Deinde apparuit nobis sol per unam fere horam fulgore colorifico in novam vel hyacinthinam formam commutatus et in specie lunae tanquam eclipsi quadam bicornis transformatus . . . noli ergo mirari cum signa vides in caelis, quia nihilominus operatur Deus et in terris. sicut enim in caelestibus, ita et in terrenis transformat et componit quaecumque et quomodo vult. quod si mira sunt quae fecerit, mirabilior est qui ea fecit. Considera, quaeso . . .*

Remarkably, this transformation extended into the linguistic sphere. Rather than present all inhabitants of the Levant—settlers and indigenous populations alike—as united under the banner of Latin culture, Fulcher claims that out of the various languages used in the Latin East, a single, yet variegated idiom had become current among all communities (*lingua diversa iam communis facta utrique nationi fit nota*). Fulcher's idealized vision of a post-Latin culture—or, more accurately, of a culture not tied to any one specific language—belongs to the eschatological realm of both a heavenly future and a biblical past. It is as if time turned back on itself: by conquering the Holy Sepulcher and settling in the Holy Land, the Crusaders reversed the curse of the Babylonian confusion that had engendered linguistic diversity. Only now was the spiritual harmony among the Crusader armies that Fulcher had sketched at the start of his work accompanied by a mutual intelligibility.[112]

Fulcher's vivid depiction of a hybrid Levantine Latin culture at this early date finds partial support from other sources. The stringent laws proposed at the Council of Nablus in 1120 prohibiting Latins from having intercourse with Saracens or from wearing Saracen dress testify to growing relations between Latins and Levantines—as does the fact that the legal framework derived from a Byzantine model. Concerns about Norman assimilation to Eastern Christian cultural practices also appear to underlie the criticisms of Walter the Chancellor in Antioch during the same period.[113] However, the artistic evidence from the first half of the twelfth century does not yet reflect this extent of cultural hybridity. As J. Folda has observed, the manuscripts illuminated at the scriptorium of the Church of the Holy Sepulcher follow western European artistic practices (particularly northern French) and do not yet evince the blend of western European, Byzantine, Armenian, and Islamic styles that appears in the second half of the twelfth century.[114] Similarly, even though Fulcher promoted the notion of a transformed, Levantine Latin ruling class and utilized some local Jewish traditions on the history of the Temple (without attribution), he did not draw on local Eastern Christian or Muslim traditions in writing his history.

Crucially, this chapter (3.37) was the first passage Fulcher wrote for his newly revised version, which begins in 1124. The chapter therefore represents his latest vision of the scope and significance of his theological-historical project. Over the three decades in which his work took shape, Fulcher's history developed from a straightforward narrative into a complex work of intellectual and eschatological pretensions, one that claimed to offer a comprehensive interpretation of Latin society in the Levant as the fulfillment of a biblical prophecy. For an explanation

112 FC 1.13.4–5, quoted above, p. 52, n. 27.

113 See chap. 4.

114 Folda, *Art of the Crusaders*, 86–87.

of this dramatic evolution we may turn to his own portrayal of a hybrid Latin East. The possibilities for socioeconomic mobility, as enumerated by Fulcher, may have paralleled opportunities of a literary and intellectual nature. Fulcher remained a minor figure within the political and ecclesiastical hierarchy of Jerusalem—especially following the death of Baldwin I in 1118—and some evidence suggests Fulcher's relation with his patron had grown more distant in the latter years of Baldwin's reign. Even if he appears to have landed a position among the canons of the Church of the Holy Sepulcher, Fulcher's absence from the witness lists of charters points to a position of limited social and political influence. Without powerful patronage or institutional support, it is doubtful that a figure such as Fulcher could have aspired to such lofty ambitions in western Europe. Yet in the volatile Latin East, where there did not yet exist a Latin literary and intellectual tradition, Fulcher saw an opportunity to make a name for himself as a scholar with privileged access to ancient sources on the history and geography of the Levant and possessing the theological authority to interpret divine signs and their bearing on the Latins. In subsequent decades, Fulcher realized his grand ambitions to some extent in the success his work enjoyed among the upper echelons of the Kingdom of Jerusalem.

Fulcher's Early Reception in the West

An early version of Fulcher's history, which extended through 1105, had found a readership in north-central France by 1109. The author of an anonymous account of the First Crusade, now commonly referred to as the *Gesta Francorum Iherusalem expugnantium* (Deeds of the Franks who conquered Jerusalem), must have had access to this lost version of Fulcher's text.[115] While the circumstances of this account remain unclear, several pieces of evidence place it in northern France or southern Belgium. The two earliest manuscripts originated in Marchiennes and Saint-Omer, and the text served as source material for Lambert of Saint-Omer's encyclopedic *Liber floridus*, completed in 1121.[116] The identification of another early twelfth-century author with access to Fulcher's lost version is more straightforward. Guibert of Nogent, Benedictine abbot of Nogent-Sous-Coucy, reports that in the course of writing his own narrative of the First Crusade (*Dei gesta per*

115 *Historiae Hierosolymitanae secunda pars*. In earlier scholarship, the text was wrongly described as an abbreviation of Fulcher of Chartres's work made by one Bartolf of Nangis. For the nature and composition of the work, see Rubenstein, "Lambert of Saint-Omer"; Derolez, "Abbey of Saint-Bertin"; Edgington, "'Bartolf of Nangis'"; and Rubenstein, "Three Crusade Chronicles Intersect."
116 Edgington, "'Bartolf of Nangis.'" Derolez ("Abbey of Saint-Bertin") argued that Lambert of Saint Omer may himself have had a hand in the composition of the *Gesta Francorum Iherusalem expugnantium*.

Francos, written 1109), he had come across the work of "a certain Fulcher, a priest of Chartres, who had for a long time been the chaplain for Baldwin at Edessa."[117]

Both authors had their reservations about their source material, to say the least. The author of the *Gesta Francorum Iherusalem expugnantium* hints that the text that lay before him was long-winded and that he instead aimed to "transform the text of this book with care" by reducing it to its barebones.[118] Guibert of Nogent issued far harsher judgment. He lambasts Fulcher's literary style for "swollen, foot-and-a-half-long words" and for producing "the blaring colors of vapid rhetorical schemes."[119] In his most stringent critique, Guibert accuses Fulcher of factual inaccuracy bordering on fabrication. Guibert's destruction of Fulcher's credibility occurs over the course of a series of increasingly devastating passages. He begins by questioning Fulcher's account of a miraculous event in the initial stages of the Crusade, in which the washed-up bodies of drowned Crusaders exhibited the sign of the cross etched into the skin of their shoulders. While Guibert does not doubt God's ability to perform such a miracle, he encourages "the man who wrote it, if he is still alive, . . . to think carefully about whether it actually happened."[120] The problem, according to Guibert, is that "men of the lowest social class, and even worthless women" claim to have experienced similarly miraculous appearances of the cross. Fulcher, at the very least, was guilty of lending naive credence to "vulgar fables." Guibert attributes the flaw of credulity to the Crusaders more generally, referencing the story of "a certain abbot" who tricked the Crusader rabble by cutting the sign of the cross into his forehead and eventually being appointed archbishop of Caesarea.[121]

But naivete was not Fulcher's sole failing as a historian. Guibert found his account of the Crusader capture of Antioch contradictory to the letters he had personally received from eyewitnesses, in particular from Anselm of Ribémont, castellan of Bouchain and lord of Ostrevant and Valenciennes.[122] In pitting Anselm of Ribémont against Fulcher of Chartres, Guibert at once burnishes his own credentials and makes an unfavorable comparison between a prominent nobleman and a minor clergyman. Dripping with sarcasm, Guibert questions whether to believe the eyewitness accounts of the discovery of the so-called Holy

117 Guibert of Nogent, *Dei gesta per Francos* 7.32 (Levine, *Deeds of God*, 155).

118 *Gesta Francorum Iherusalem expugnantium* 2.

119 Guibert of Nogent, *Dei gesta per Francos* 7.32 (Levine, *Deeds of God*, 155).

120 Guibert of Nogent, *Dei gesta per Francos* 7.32 (Levine, *Deeds of God*, 155). For related passages, see Purkis, "'Zealous Imitation.'"

121 This individual is not identified by Guibert, but presumably refers to Baldwin I, archbishop of Caesarea (1101–1107).

122 Guibert of Nogent, *Dei gesta per Francos* 7.33 (Levine, *Deeds of God*, 156). The letter Guibert received from Anselm, if it ever existed, does not survive, but his paraphrase of it corresponds to Anselm's letter to Manasses, archbishop of Reims (July 1098); see Hagenmeyer, *Epistulae et chartae*, no. XV (Barber and Bate, *Letters from the East*, no. 7).

Lance of Antioch or to give preference to "the cleverness of the priest Fulcher, who, while our men were suffering from starvation at Antioch, was feasting at ease in Edessa."[123]

Guibert's criticism of Fulcher appears founded on an aristocratic disdain for a lowly priest's stylistic incompetence, lack of critical judgment, and limited access to influential individuals. Guibert, by contrast, hailed from a noble family and, as the well-educated head of a powerful abbey, prided himself on his Latinity and connections. Given the limited circulation of the *Dei gesta per Francos*, it is unlikely that Guibert's scathing review reached Fulcher, but his remarks are indicative of the gulf that could exist between the literary-intellectual pretensions of Levantine authors and their appreciation among the intellectual elites in Europe.[124] Viewed from a different perspective, the absence of established and well-connected intellectual institutions in the Latin East afforded relatively minor figures such as Fulcher the opportunity to enjoy a literary success they would have found difficult to achieve in Europe. The contrast between Guibert's appraisal of (an admittedly early and no longer extant version of) Fulcher's history and its reception in the Latin East will illustrate this point.

Fulcher's History as a Liturgical Text

Toward the end of his chronicle, Fulcher addresses his audience as listeners and refers to his literary activity as an oral performance.[125] Whether or not this anticipated performance ever occurred in the way he envisioned, ample evidence indicates that Fulcher's chronicle found a ready audience in the two foremost centers of power in the Latin East: the Church of the Holy Sepulcher and the royal court of Jerusalem.

An early testament to Fulcher's reception in the Latin East appears in a liturgy for the feast commemorating the capture of Jerusalem on 15 July 1099. This new "Feast of Jerusalem" was instituted by 1105 at the latest.[126] An early thirteenth-century manuscript, probably copied in France, contains both a mass and an office specially composed for the occasion.[127] As recently demonstrated, this liturgy

123 Guibert of Nogent, *Dei gesta per Francos* 7.34 (Levine, *Deeds of God*, 157).

124 Although the text survives in eight manuscript witnesses, it did not have much impact on Crusade narrative traditions.

125 FC 3.50.15: *taedebit forsan historiae auditores, si omnia, quae in bello vel belli gratia tam vi quam astutia gesta sunt, recitentur.*

126 John, "Feast of the Liberation"; Gaposchkin, "Feast of the Liberation," 159–60. The name of the feast occurs with minor variations as "the feast of holy Jerusalem" (London, British Library, Additional 8927, fol. 134r), "the feast of Jerusalem, when it was captured by the Christians" (Rome, Biblioteca Angelica, 477, fol. 4v), and "the feast of Jerusalem, when it was captured by the Franks" (Paris, BNF, lat. 12056, fol. 5v).

127 London, British Library, Additional 8927.

represents an early version of the liturgy used at the Church of the Holy Sepulcher in the beginning of the twelfth century.[128] The liturgy centers on the city of Jerusalem, using liberal quotations from Isaiah in particular to present an eschatological vision of the city and its place within the Christian salvation narrative. Strikingly, among the lessons (*lectiones*) that provided an interpretive framework to the chants, the liturgy for the office prescribes readings from Fulcher's history. For Matins, the instructions read, "the lessons from the *historia*, when Jerusalem was captured; they begin like this: 'the city of Jerusalem is situated in a mountainous location. . . .'"[129] It is unclear how much of Fulcher's history the celebrants were supposed to read, but the indicated starting point contains an extensive description of Jerusalem. Beginning with a discussion of the surrounding geography, Fulcher draws a textual map of the city, focusing on the outer perimeter and the locations that form the backdrop to the ensuing narrative of the capture of the city: the Tower of David, the Templum Domini (Dome of the Rock), and the Templum Salomonis (al-Aqṣā Mosque). Descriptions of the latter two structures, both situated on what Jews and Christians call the Temple Mount, leads into a detailed reflection on the various Jewish temples that had stood there in previous eras, including a discussion of contradictory scriptural evidence on the fate of the Ark of the Covenant.

As the only non-scriptural text prescribed for reading in this liturgy, the inclusion of Fulcher's history represents a stunning literary success. The liturgy bears testament to the fundamentally different reception Fulcher enjoyed in the Latin East, where his work seems to have acquired the status of a liturgical text. Several factors may have accounted for this achievement. The early dissemination of his Crusade account may simply have made Fulcher the standard, go-to authority. Alternatively, Fulcher's posturing as a well-informed intellectual with an increasingly theological bent may have appealed to the canons of the Holy Sepulcher. Finally, given that Fulcher was probably a canon at the Holy Sepulcher by 1116, his connections there likely played a role in the success of his history. In fact, several scholars have even argued that Fulcher himself had a hand in shaping the liturgy.[130] I. Shagrir, for example, has suggested that the numerous influences from Chartres on the canonical life at the Church of the Holy Sepulcher point to an active role of Fulcher, a former priest of Chartres, in introducing Chartrian

128 Gaposchkin, "Feast of the Liberation"; see also the earlier work of Linder, "Liturgy of the Liberation." For a detailed chronology, see Aspesi, "Cantors of the Holy Sepulchre," 283–96.

129 FC 1.26.1; London, British Library, Additional 8927, fols. 134r–v: *Lectiones de historia ubi capta fuit hierusalem, incipiuntur enim sic: Est enim civitas ierusalem in montano loco sita*. As Linder ("Liturgy of the Liberation," 122–23) has noted, the incipit does not correspond verbatim to either the first or second redaction of Fulcher's history and may reflect the text of Fulcher's earlier version of ca. 1105.

130 Dondi, *Liturgy of the Canons*, 59; Salvadó, "Augustinian Reform"; Gaposchkin, *Invisible Weapons*, 147.

practices to Jerusalem. These influences include similarities in the *adventus* processions and the reform of the canons of the Holy Sepulcher in 1114 according to the rule of Ivo of Chartres, Fulcher's former mentor.[131] Alternatively, as C. Aspesi has suggested, Cantor Ansellus may have been responsible both for the initial institution of the feast and for the confection of an appropriate liturgy.[132] In the absence of conclusive evidence regarding Fulcher's role at the Church of the Holy Sepulcher, it is difficult to establish which would have been the more exceptional achievement: the promotion of one's own literary work by the clergy of the Holy Sepulcher or success in implementing a comprehensive program of reform.

Although subsequent revisions of the liturgy for 15 July no longer included readings from Fulcher's history, his exclusion likely reflects a change in emphasis within the liturgy rather than a diminution of status.[133] The revised liturgy for this date consistently shifted the earlier focus on the city of Jerusalem as a whole to the Church of the Holy Sepulcher specifically. The passage from Fulcher's history, which barely mentions the Holy Sepulcher, would not have served this new program.[134] In fact, a sermon from the mid-twelfth century attests to Fulcher's continued influence on the ecclesiastical sphere of the Kingdom of Jerusalem.

The sermon is found in a manuscript comprising six distinct parts from the eleventh to the twelfth centuries, mostly containing saints' lives and sermons.[135] The sermon dates, on paleographical grounds, to the middle or second half of the twelfth century, while scribal errors indicate that the text is a copy of an earlier one.[136] The sermon bears the title *Sermo domini Fulcheri de Ierosolimitana civitate quomodo capta est a Latinis* (Sermon of Fulcher on how the city Jerusalem was captured by the Latins). C. Kohler, who edited the text, surmised that, given the quotations from Fulcher's history in the sermon, a scribe had misattributed the sermon to Fulcher of Chartres, even though the text makes clear that the preacher merely quotes from Fulcher, for he introduces one such quotation with *Fulcherius*

131 Shagrir, "*Adventus* in Jerusalem," 15–17.

132 Aspesi, "Cantors of the Holy Sepulchre," 295–96.

133 Linder, "'Like Purest Gold Resplendent,'" 31–32; Gaposchkin, "Echoes of Victory"; John, "Feast of the Liberation," 417–19; Aspesi, "Cantors of the Holy Sepulchre," 283–96; Salvadó, "Rewriting the Latin Liturgy."

134 For the surprising lack of prominence of the Church of the Holy Sepulcher in Fulcher's narrative, see Lees, "*Historia Hierosolymitana*."

135 See appendix 1.

136 Kohler in *Sermo domini Fulcheri* 159. The text contains several copying errors that were later corrected. In line 29 of folio 319r, *crucibus in pannis suis quod est consutis signum* (with crosses sewn onto their clothing, which is a sign), the phrase *quod est* should follow, and has been corrected by separating lines, demonstrating that this is not an autograph, but a copy. Additional evidence is provided by the incorrect month used to date the capture of Jerusalem (June instead of July), as well as by a nonsensical calendrical notation: *idibus in kalendis iunii sub tempore messis* (on the ides, on the kalends of June, at the time of harvest[?]).

dicit (Fulcher says).[137] Instead, the occasion for the sermon may present a clue as to the work's true authorship.

As the title indicates, the sermon's occasion was the same Feast of Jerusalem as that celebrated in the liturgy discussed above. By the mid-twelfth century, it had become customary for both clergy and the laity to participate in a procession from the Holy Sepulcher to the Templum Domini every year on this feast day. After reciting prayers in front of the Templum Domini, the procession moved toward the northern part of the city walls, where Godfrey of Bouillon had first entered the city. There the patriarch of Jerusalem delivered a sermon.[138] Given this context for the sermon, a more probable candidate for the authorship of the sermon is in fact a different Fulcher than our priest from Chartres: Fulcher of Angoulême, patriarch of Jerusalem (1146–1157).[139] More evidence for this identification may be found within the sermon itself and the way in which it utilizes the work of Fulcher of Chartres.

The sermon opens with an address to the congregation (*fratres dilectissimi*, "dearest brothers"), a doxology, and an acknowledgment of the liturgical occasion (*Celebremus ergo solennitatem*, "let us celebrate, therefore, the feast").[140] Reflecting on the long period during which Jerusalem labored under pagan rule, the preacher personifies the city as a newly liberated slave, depicting its streets and neighborhoods as participating in the celebration. A paraphrase follows of a passage from Fulcher's history on the destructions Jerusalem suffered at the hands of various rulers, culminating in the sack of the city under the Roman emperors Vespasian and Titus.[141] The sermon's use of this passage reflects a careful reading of the chronicle, drawing on Fulcher's extensive description of Tyre that precedes the account of its capture by the Latins in 1124. The passage, occurring toward the end of the history, would not have been an obvious choice for a preacher composing a sermon on the capture of Jerusalem. Its reference therefore indicates a thorough familiarity

137 *Sermo domini Fulcheri* 163.

138 Reference to the delivery of a sermon during this procession is made in Rome, BAV, Barberini, lat. 659, fol. 101v, edited in Salvadó, "Liturgy of the Holy Sepulchre," 630. This so-called Barberini Ordinal was copied between 1175 and 1187 for Templar use in Jerusalem and reflects, as Salvadó ("Rewriting the Latin Liturgy," 405) has shown, "the liturgy of the Holy Sepulchre at the time of its rededication in 1149."

139 Pringle (*Churches* 3:21, no. 283) first suggested that Patriarch Fulcher may have delivered the sermon on the fiftieth anniversary of the capture of Jerusalem (1149), during which the Church of the Holy Sepulcher was reconsecrated. For the argument that the title *domnus*, which appears in the sermon's rubric, more likely refers to Patriarch Fulcher, see Salvadó, "Liturgy of the Holy Sepulchre," 31; Aspesi, "Breviary of Lucca," 699–703; and Zöller, *Regularkanoniker*, 88. However, this argument is complicated by the fact that in at least three manuscripts of Fulcher's history, his name appears as *Domni Fulcheri*; see FC 115.

140 *Sermo domini Fulcheri* 163.

141 FC 3.30, at *Sermo domini Fulcheri* 161. For the motif of Titus and Vespasian in this sermon, see Schein, *Gateway to the Heavenly City*, 43.

with Fulcher's work and may even provide a further argument for identifying the author of the sermon with Fulcher of Angoulême, who, as archbishop of Tyre (1134–1146) prior to his appointment to the Jerusalemite see, would have had an interest in accounts of the capture of Tyre.

After quoting Luke and Isaiah, the preacher introduces the first direct quotation of Fulcher. The quoted passage occurs immediately after the capture of Jerusalem. In relating the Crusader occupation of the city, Fulcher erupts in a series of jubilant outbursts on the prophetic fulfillment this event represents.[142] This passage would have been highly apposite to the commemorative occasion, especially since Fulcher's exclamations occur directly after a description of a communal procession from the Holy Sepulcher to the Templum Domini. After a dramatic depiction of the First Crusade as a battle of Europe against the combined forces of Asia and Africa, the preacher introduces a lengthy quotation from Fulcher on the many sacrifices made by the Crusaders.[143] Upon drawing a liturgical connection by citing the passage from Isaiah used in the introit to the mass for the Feast of Jerusalem, the preacher inserts yet another series of quotes from Fulcher.[144] This time the preacher explicitly identifies the source: *Fulcherius dicit: hęc omnia oculis nostris vidimus* (Fulcher says: all of this we have seen with our own eyes). The quoted words do not occur verbatim in Fulcher's history, but paraphrase a passage in which Fulcher professes his eyewitness testimony.[145] The preacher subsequently presents an extremely condensed version of Fulcher's account of the Crusade by stitching together sentences and phrases from different sections. The emphasis of this Fulcherian patchwork falls squarely on the miraculous nature of the Crusade: drawn from disparate regions, the diverse Crusader army achieved unity by conquering Jerusalem, in a fulfillment of Isaiah's prophecy.

This sermon represents an emphatic endorsement of Fulcher and his work. It not only bolsters the importance of the chronicle as a historical document but also supports Fulcher's theological interpretation of the Crusade. While Guibert of Nogent questioned Fulcher's value as an eyewitness, the preacher wholeheartedly vouched for his authority as a primary witness to the events of the Crusade. If the preacher was indeed Patriarch Fulcher, this sermon represents a remarkable turn in the literary fortune of Fulcher of Chartres. Yet Fulcher's influence was

142 FC 1.29.3, at *Sermo domini Fulcheri* 161–62.

143 The addition of the African continent draws on widespread medieval visualizations in world maps that divide the world into three continents: Asia (at the top), Europe (on the left), and Africa (on the right), resulting in the so-called T-O map. The quotation (FC 1.6.11–12), which has *sequentibus* as opposed to *diligentibus* (1.6.12), demonstrates that the preacher used a copy of Fulcher's first redaction.

144 Isa. 66:18–20.

145 FC 1.5.12, at *Sermo domini Fulcheri* 163.

not confined to the ecclesiastical sphere, but also extended to the royal courts of France and Jerusalem.

Fulcher's History as a Royal Narrative

The oldest manuscript of Fulcher's history presents the text alongside two other Latin historical works from the early twelfth-century Levant: the *Bella Antiochena* (Wars of Antioch) by Walter, chancellor of the Norman Principality of Antioch, and the account of the First Crusade by the Provençal Raymond of Aguilers, chaplain to Count Raymond of Le Puy.[146] On a bifolium affixed to the manuscript, a scribe different from the hand that copied the historical texts inserted a letter dedicating the collection to the French king Louis VII. The book was, the letter declares, a gift from an otherwise unknown W. Grassegals, who identifies himself as a knight from Vélay and a veteran of the First Crusade. As J. Rubenstein has argued, it seems likely that the collection was made in the Latin East and subsequently made its way over to France—possibly via the scriptorium of Le Puy, where a copy of the collection was made.[147] Since the version of Fulcher's text in the collection belongs to the so-called first redaction, which was completed in 1124, I suggest that the collection was made sometime between 1124 and 1127, when Fulcher wrote his second redaction. At any rate, the book with the dedicatory letter was given to King Louis sometime between 1137 and 1146, when he departed for the Second Crusade.[148] The book was subsequently deposited in the library of Saint Victor and afterward gave rise to an additional five copies.

While Fulcher's inclusion in a book given to the king of France represents, in some ways, his vindication against Guibert's harsh judgments, still, the manuscript's context rendered his reception rather mixed. For example, the scribe disagreed with Fulcher's skeptical assessment of the authenticity of the Holy Lance of Antioch, prefacing the passage with a critical note referring the reader instead to the account of Raymond of Aguilers at the end of the book: "Where the Lance is found, [about which] Raymond's book speaks better and more truthfully than does Fulcher's."[149] Once again, Fulcher's truthfulness and eyewitness testimony (or lack thereof) were called into question.

Fulcher's work also received an audience at the royal court of Jerusalem. In 1718 the French Benedictine scholar Edmond Martène came upon a history of the First Crusade in a manuscript at the monastery of Himmerod, in the diocese of

146 Paris, BNF, lat. 14378.

147 Rubenstein, "Putting History to Use"; the Jerusalemite origin of the collection was first suggested by Hagenmeyer (FC 91–92).

148 Rubenstein ("Putting History to Use," 150–52) argues for a date closer to 1137.

149 Paris, BNF, lat. 14378, fol. 25v: *Ubi lancea fuit inventa. viiii. Veridice et melius loquitur liber Raimundi quam Fulcherii.*

Trier. The account bore the cumbersome title *Balduini III Historia Nicaena vel Antiochena necnon Ierosolymitana* (Baldwin III's history of Nicaea, Antioch, and Jerusalem).[150] Believing it to be a new source for the First Crusade, he proceeded to copy the manuscript with the intent to publish it. He quickly discovered, however, that most of the account is an abbreviation of the histories of Fulcher of Chartres and Robert the Monk, and decided to publish only the prologue, which he believed to be the sole original portion. The text then vanished for some time. While the original manuscript was probably destroyed along with the monastery of Himmerod during the French Revolution, in 1881 Paul Riant rediscovered Martène's transcription.

Thanks to the prologue, more is known about the historical circumstances of this text than the other adaptations of Fulcher's chronicle. Written in the prestigious classical quantitative dactylic hexameter but featuring the popular medieval internal (so-called leonine) rhyme, the prologue opens with a summary of the First Crusade. A brief history of the Kingdom of Jerusalem follows, consisting of a list of the kings and the length of their reigns (not always accurate).[151] The last king to appear is Baldwin III: "Three years after his father, Baldwin III <has been> placed at the head of the kingdom and already distinguished by the name of his grandfather. He compiled and had this work written down: may he be granted the reward of eternal life! The *History of Nicaea, Antioch, as well as the splendid city of Jerusalem* begins."[152] The prologue situates the commissioning of this work in the third year of the reign of Baldwin III, which began upon the death of Fulk of Anjou in 1143. Accordingly, the date of composition should be situated around the year 1146, when Baldwin III would have been fifteen or sixteen years old.[153] This was a particularly troublesome time in the Kingdom of Jerusalem. The reign of King Fulk had been marred by violent tensions between Fulk's supporters, who had accompanied him from Anjou in 1131, and the established Franks who had participated in the Crusade or were descended from those who had done so. The latter faction sought support from Queen Melisende, whom, as the daughter of the Crusader Baldwin II, they considered one of their own. Melisende's

150 See appendix 3.

151 At *Balduini III Historia*, prol. 24–28, Baldwin II (r. 1118–1131) is said to have reigned for fifteen years, while Fulk (r. 1131–1143) is said to have reigned for thirteen years. See appendix 3.

152 *Balduini III Historia*, prol. 29–34: *Post patrem ternis Baldwinus tertius annis, / Praefectus regno iam nomine clarus avito, / Qui compilavit simul et conscribere fecit / Hoc opus; aeternae sibi sit retributio vitae! / Incipit Historia Nicena vel Antiochena, / Urbis praeclarae necnon Ierosolymitanae.* See appendix 3.

153 For Fulk's death, see WT 15.27, although William incorrectly places Fulk's death in 1142. For Baldwin and Melisende's crowning, see WT 16.3. Gerish ("Remembering Kings in Jerusalem") has pointed out that the dating may be more complicated, since it is unclear whether the poet counted by regnal or ecclesiastical years (which usually began in Easter), and whether he counted partial years as whole ones.

intercession on behalf of the Crusader barons eventually led to a falling out with Fulk in 1134 that divided the royal court into two factions.[154] When Fulk died, the young Baldwin III was crowned together with his mother on Christmas Day in 1143. Nevertheless, Melisende largely governed autonomously, refusing to relinquish her role even after Baldwin III reached the age of majority in 1145. Baldwin continued to struggle to assert himself onto the political scene in the years that followed, while critical external threats exacerbated the internal division within the royal court in the 1140s. Edessa had fallen to the forces of Zengi in 1144, throwing the remaining Crusader settlements into a state of existential panic and eventually leading to the calamitous Second Crusade (1147–1149). The situation came to a head in 1152, when a full-scale civil war threatened to break out between mother and son. This conflict was averted only by Melisende's acquiescence to relinquish the reins of governance and retire from public life.

This historical context is crucial for understanding the significance of the *Balduini III Historia*, which scholars in the past dismissed as derivative of earlier accounts.[155] While the text largely consists of excerpts from Robert the Monk (for the period covering the First Crusade) and Fulcher of Chartres (up to Baldwin II's capture in 1123), the compilation constitutes a valuable witness to conceptions of royal identity in a period from which precious few primary sources survive.[156] As such, the *Balduini III Historia* holds importance for the cultural history of the Latin East, since it represents the earliest attested act of explicit royal literary patronage in the Kingdom of Jerusalem. The young king Baldwin III may have considered such an act a way to assert himself at the royal court and to rival his mother, who had established herself as a patron of the arts.[157] His decision to commission a history of the First Crusade and the early decades of the Kingdom of Jerusalem reinforces William of Tyre's portrait of the king as a ruler with literary interests:

154 For Queen Melisende's role in Jerusalemite politics, see Mayer, "Studies in the History"; Hamilton, "Women in the Crusader States"; Hodgson, *Women, Crusading and the Holy Land*, 134–35 and 185–88.

155 Kedar, "Jerusalem Massacre," 25, and Edbury, "Crusader Sources," 28. Compare also Hagenmeyer's judgment of the text as "ganzen wertlosen Erzählung" (FC 84). The *Balduini III Historia* has been suggested as a source for late medieval *exempla* in Dominican sermons by Maggioni (James of Voragine, *Legenda aurea*, 1:xlviii and 398, n. 139); however, this suggestion has been rejected by MacGregor, "First Crusade," 45.

156 The text that the compiler used was probably the first recension of Fulcher, which extended only to the year 1124. For an analysis of the *Balduini III Historia*'s importance to the royal identity of Jerusalem, see Gerish, "Remembering Kings in Jerusalem."

157 WT 15.26. The most notable example of this patronage is the so-called Melisende Psalter now in the British Library. See Folda, *Art of the Crusaders*, 130–63; Folda, "Melisende of Jerusalem"; and Nicholson, "Women's Writing," 79.

> He was suitably well-read and much more so than his brother, Lord Amaury, who succeeded him: whenever he was able to enjoy a bit of free time from his public obligations, he gladly engaged in reading; he listened to history in particular, and inquired sedulously into the deeds and characters of ancient kings and the best of rulers; he was greatly entertained by conversations with those who were well-read in particular, but also with prudent members of the laity.[158]

Given Baldwin's youthful age at the time of the work's commission, its author was likely an individual closely connected to the court who played a role in the king's education, such as the court chaplain.[159] The acute tensions between Melisende and Baldwin eliminate candidates principally associated with the queen mother, such as one Peter the Chaplain, who is listed as "chaplain of the queen" (*reginae capellanus*) in a charter from 1138.[160] A more likely author is one "Adam, chaplain of the king" (*Adam regis capellanus*), who in 1150 witnessed a charter that represents one of Baldwin's first independent political acts and has, given its amateurish nature, been described as "a diplomatic disaster."[161] The charter was written "by the hand of Daniel, cleric of the king, brother of Hugo Saliens in Bonum" (*per manum Danielis clerici regis, fratris Salientis in Bonum Hugonis*), who, given his association with the king, may constitute another candidate for the authorship of the *Balduini III Historia*.

Given the text's close connection with the Jerusalemite crown, the *Balduini III Historia* represents the first royally sanctioned account of the First Crusade and the subsequent establishment of the royal institution. Although Fulcher of Chartres had served as chaplain to Baldwin I, his influence with the king seems to have declined in precisely the period that saw his most productive literary activity. In fact, Fulcher instead may have found association with the Church of the Holy Sepulcher, where, as we have seen, his history saw prominent performance in a liturgy and sermon for the feast commemorating the capture of Jerusalem. The *Balduini III Historia* therefore offered the king of Jerusalem the opportunity to recontextualize the Crusade in a way that promoted the royal institution. The

158 WT 16.2.12–19: *erat autem et commode litteratus et fratre suo domino Amalrico, qui ei successit, multo amplius: cum vero quid ocii ex occupationibus publicis decerpere poterat, libenter incumbebat lectioni; historiarum precipue auditor, antiquorum regum et optimorum principum gesta moresque diligenter investigabat; litteratorum maxime, sed et prudentum laicorum confabulationibus plurimum recreabatur.*

159 On the role of chaplains within the kingdom of Jerusalem, see Mayer, "Die Hofkapelle."

160 *UKJ* 1: nos. 124, 138, 141. Another unlikely candidate in this period is a chaplain named Fredericus, whose connection extended only to Queen Melisende. See *UKJ* 1: no. 177 and Mayer, "Die Hofkapelle," 496.

161 *UKJ* 1:407, no. 221: "eine diplomatische Kalamität." This Adam witnessed three charters and would go on to become bishop of Paneas: *UKJ* 1: nos. 138, 244, 258.

poetic prologue does so by presenting all the events of the Crusade as culminating in the foundation of the kingdom:

> [They] drove the Turks from the Holy Sepulcher of the Lord. And with the aid of the Lord it becomes the famed seat of a kingdom—<the Lord who> restrains the rebellious kings and peoples with this kingdom. . . . These two brothers [Godfrey of Bouillon and Baldwin of Boulogne], worthy of the royal crown, celebrated for their knightly valor, brave, fearsome in war, waged many battles with but few men of their own, laying low with bloodshed the troops hostile to them, and through God they were brave against the enemies from Babylon. They expanded the realm, which they then held; now may they be blessed without end in the kingdom of Christ. A relative of theirs has taken hold of their empire,[162] —another Baldwin, renowned for his good morals.[163]

By this account, the establishment of the Kingdom of Jerusalem formed the logical and divinely ordained consequence of the traditional formulation of the Crusader mission to "liberate" the Holy Sepulcher. In addition to emphasizing the importance of the Jerusalemite crown, the prologue frames the institution's primary objective in highly classicizing terms. The kingdom's mission to conquer and subjugate the surrounding nations recalls the objectives of Roman rule as famously formulated by Virgil.[164] In an additional Virgilian echo, the author praises the first two rulers of the kingdom, Godfrey and his brother Baldwin, for expanding the realm. In recompense they will reap the reward of a celestial kingdom "without end" (*sine fine*); their successor, in turn, inherited an "empire" (*imperium*).[165] The juxtaposition of the words *sine fine* and *imperium* recall the famous words of Jupiter in the first book of the *Aeneid*, predicting that Roman imperial rule will know no spatial or temporal bounds.[166] The author thereby

162 The use of the word *imperium*, typically meaning "empire" in medieval Latin, is remarkable here.

163 *Balduini III Historia*, prol. 8–10, 16–24: *Ac Turcos sancto Domini pepulere sepulchro / Auxilio Domini; sedesque fit inclyta regni, / Hoc regno Reges reprimens populosque rebelles . . . Hi duo Germani digni diademate regni, / Militia clari, fortes, bello metuendi, / Pauca gente sua gesserunt praelia multa, / Illis infestas sternentes caede catervas, / Perque Deum fortes fuerant Babylonis in hostes. / Dilataverunt regnum, quod tunc habuerunt. / In Regno Christi nunc sint sine fine beati, / Imperium quorum cognatus sumsit eorum, / Alter Balwinus, morum probitate decorus*. See appendix 3.

164 The passage may be viewed as a combination of Virgil, *Aeneid* 6.851–53 and 6.858, conjoining the injunction to "rule nations with empire" (*regere imperio populos*) with the prediction that the Roman army "will lay low the Carthaginians and the rebellious Gaul" (*sternet Poenos Gallumque rebellem*). For a quotation of *Aeneid* 6.853, see Baudri of Bourgueil, *Historia Ierosolimitana* 112.

165 *Balduini III Historia*, prol. 21–23. See appendix 3.

166 Virgil, *Aeneid* 1.278–79: *His ego nec metas rerum nec tempora pono; / imperium sine fine dedi.*

places the newly established Kingdom of Jerusalem within the paradigm of classical empire (though necessarily a Christianized version), providing it with the legitimacy that newly founded institutions of the twelfth century eagerly sought and simultaneously situating his own work within the classical literary tradition.[167]

Other evidence corroborates Baldwin III's predilection for a classical model of rulership. By 1152 the young king was determined to step out of his mother's shadow and be crowned sole ruler of the kingdom on Easter Sunday. When Patriarch Fulcher of Angoulême refused to cooperate, Baldwin III, in what has been interpreted as a gesture of defiance to his mother, on the following day publicly presented himself wearing a laurel crown (*laureatus*)—a symbol of Roman imperial rulership.[168]

In reframing the Crusade in such classicizing terms, the prologue to the *Balduini III Historia* added a new dimension to the First Crusade narrative as told in the Latin East.[169] Viewed within the political context of mid-twelfth century Jerusalem, Baldwin's decision to commission this retelling represented an attempt to reclaim the Crusade narrative for the crown. This was a boldly assertive act for a young king, since the Church of the Holy Sepulcher, as the crown's greatest political rival in the Kingdom of Jerusalem, had prominently adopted the history of Fulcher of Chartres as a central liturgical text.

Conclusion

By taking seriously Fulcher's intellectual and literary ambitions and by examining not only his historical narrative but also the frequently neglected geographical, biblical, and astrological portions of his text, his evolution as a writer and a thinker over the course of nearly three decades comes into view. His most significant development involves an increasing tendency to cast Levantine history and geography in a biblical mold and, more broadly, in what he considered a literary—that is, Latin—form. By doing so, Fulcher aimed to position himself as a privileged Latin intellectual authority on the Levant who not only furnished his work with comprehensive and up-to-date information but also employed a scholarly persona modeled on respected Levantine authorities such as Jerome and Josephus.

As he revised his work in the mid-1120s, Fulcher must have realized that there was a lacuna in the literary scene of the Latin East: while various reports of the Crusade circulated, no comprehensive narrative had provided a theological

167 On the broader phenomenon of new twelfth-century institutions seeking legitimacy by resorting to classical antiquity, see Boje Mortensen, "Roman Past."

168 WT 17.13.46; Mayer, "Das Pontifikale von Tyrus," 170–71; John, "Royal Inauguration," 497.

169 In the Latin West, several classicizing poetic treatments of the First Crusade appeared by the first half of the twelfth century, notably the *Historia vie Hierosolimitane* of Gilo of Paris (d. after 1139) and the *Expeditio Jerosolimitana* of Metellus of Tegernsee (1146–1165).

underpinning for Latin society in the Levant. Although he did not possess the sterling credentials—in terms of family, connections, and education—that would normally have been prerequisites for such an undertaking in the Latin West, the Latin East provided opportunities for both social and literary mobility.

As he adapted his chronicle to present an increasingly Latin view of Levantine geography and history, Fulcher also introduced a more conventional organization. He imposed a new structure onto his chronicle by dividing it into books centered on the reigns of the rulers of Jerusalem. By creating a formal and conceptual distinction between the First Crusade and the subsequent Kingdom of Jerusalem, Fulcher fundamentally transformed his text from a Crusade account into a traditional royal chronicle.

Fulcher's intellectual and literary approach did not necessarily constitute the only way for early Levantine Latin authors to write. The contemporary letters of Cantor Ansellus, for example, demonstrate an entirely different attitude toward the dynamic between Latin and other Levantine intellectual cultures and did not emphatically subordinate the latter to the former. Yet Fulcher's literary afterlife made him a towering figure in the early decades of Levantine Latin literary culture. The prominent status his work achieved as a central ecclesiastical and secular text, used to promote the narratives of both the patriarch and king of Jerusalem, can only be reconstructed by piecing together evidence drawn from sources typically neglected in studies of the twelfth-century Latin East. The failure to recognize Fulcher's importance in the cultural life of the early Kingdom of Jerusalem may stem from reliance on William of Tyre. William never mentions Fulcher by name, and in the rare instance in which he alludes to his work, William disputes Fulcher's claims and cites him only as an anonymous "some" or "others."[170] Yet by examining liturgical evidence, an obscure sermon, and an abbreviated version of Fulcher's chronicle, the contours of an impressive literary legacy emerge. By the mid-twelfth century, Fulcher's history, though largely neglected in the Latin West, had achieved the status of a canonical text in the Latin East.

While Fulcher's chronicle became closely associated with both the Church of the Holy Sepulcher and the royal court, in the next chapter we will examine how authors who did not possess a connection with these centers of power used Latin literature to promote their new institutions.

170 WT 12.18.1–19.

Chapter Three

INSTITUTIONAL POLITICS AND LATIN POETICS IN THE KINGDOM OF JERUSALEM

Regular Canons in Europe and the Latin East

After the Crusaders captured Jerusalem in 1099, only a small fraction remained to settle in the newly conquered territories. Though they eventually built elaborate new structures to meet their growing needs, like the cathedrals of Tyre and Caesarea, initially the settlers occupied renowned Christian churches, such as the Church of the Nativity in Bethlehem, or appropriated other existing structures. The al-Aqṣā Mosque, and later the Herodian Tower of David, served as a royal palace for the new rulers of Jerusalem. Yet monks and clerics also began to cast about for suitable places of residence and worship. These new communities concentrated around sites of religious significance, such as the ancient Church of the Holy Sepulcher in Jerusalem.[1] There were many advantages in being associated with a long religious tradition, from attracting numerous pilgrims and the revenue associated with such traffic to commanding political influence and enjoying privileges granted by secular rulers and the church.

Not all institutions possessed such renown as the Church of the Holy Sepulcher, however, and as the ecclesiastical and monastic landscape became more populated, newcomers either resorted to creative means of self-promotion or were relegated to a position of diminished wealth and significance. While those belonging to prominent monastic orders such as Cluny or Cîteaux may have counted on at least some instititutional support, unaffiliated clerics who arrived in the Holy Land to lead more rigorously spiritual lives found themselves in the most precarious position of all. The Gregorian Reforms of the eleventh century sparked a movement of such clerics, and in Italy, France, and England canons began to live in communities, over time adopting the semimonastic rule of Saint Augustine. Unlike monks, however, so-called regular canons answered to a bishop and were

1 For the canons of the Church of the Holy Sepulcher, see Hotzelt, "Die Chorherren"; Hamilton, *Latin Church*; Elm, "Das Kapitel"; Zöller, *Regularkanoniker*, 57–107.

frequently forced to deal with local secular rulers to secure land and possessions.[2] In addition to these challenges, communities of canons in the Latin East faced the harsh reality of life in the politically unstable Latin settlements of the Levant. For instance, a document recording the fraternal assocation between the chapter of Saint Paul of Antioch and that of Mount Tabor in Galilee stipulates with stark candor that "if the Principality of Antioch should be overrun by the Turks and the prince exiled, the monks of Saint Paul will be received into [the chapter of] Mount Tabor and will be provided for."[3]

This chapter centers on two such communities of canons in the Kingdom of Jerusalem and how they employed Latin literature to elevate their fledgling institutions and navigate delicate relationships with secular and ecclesiastical powers. Both of these communities occupied sites without any spiritual significance in the Latin tradition, so they had to devise creative new narratives of their own. An examination of the shared rhetorical strategies and literary motifs employed in their works will enable us to observe the emergence of a remarkably coherent literary tradition across these communities.

The Templum Domini: From "Dung Heap" to Pilgrim Destination

Settlement of the eastern area of the walled city of Jerusalem that Jews and Christians call the Temple Mount began shortly after the conclusion of the First Crusade. After adopting the al-Aqṣā Mosque as his residence, Godfrey of Bouillon installed a chapter of canons at the nearby Muslim sanctuary of the Dome of the Rock (Qubbat al-Ṣaḫra).[4] While the al-Aqṣā Mosque was referred to as the Temple or House of Solomon (Templum / Domus Salomonis), thus evoking the first Jewish temple that figures prominently in the Christian Old Testament, the Dome of the Rock became known as the Templum Domini or Lord's Temple, a reference primarily to the Jewish temple built by Herod the Great that formed the backdrop to several episodes in the gospels. Chief among these were scenes of Jesus's childhood, including his presentation on the day of the Virgin Mary's purification and his teaching of the elders, and the episode later in Jesus's life when he confronted the moneychangers in the Temple. Eventually, the Templum Domini also came to be associated with various figures and episodes from the Old Testament, including Jacob's angelic vision and the Ark of the Covenant.

2 For the standard introductions to regular canons, see Dereine, "Chanoines"; Walker Bynum, *Docere verbo et exemplo*; Peters, *Story of Monasticism*, 155–70.

3 *Cart Hosp*, 2:910–11, no. 22 (RRH no. 634; RRR no. 1137). See the similar arrangement made with the abbey of Saint Mary of the Valley of Jehoshaphat in 1197: *Chartes Josaphat*, 92–94, no. 44 (RRH no. 738; RRR no. 1394).

4 WT 9.9; Mayer, *Bistümer*, 222–29; *UKJ*, 1:98, no. 2.

Despite these prominent biblical episodes associated with the site on which the Dome of the Rock stood, scripture itself problematized its veneration by European Christians. All four gospels present Jesus as prophesying the destruction of the Temple.[5] Medieval readers interpreted these passages as foretelling the Roman sack of Jerusalem by the emperors Vespasian and Titus in 70 CE, culminating in the destruction of the Temple. Christians viewed this event as a divine rebuke of Judaism, and the physical destruction of its most sacred sanctuary as a symbolic evacuation of Jewish legitimacy and as a confirmation of the triumph of the New Covenant over the Old. So it was that in the centuries before the Islamic conquest of Jerusalem in 637/8 there was no attempt to repopulate the former site of the Temple with churches, leading to Jerome's infamous description of the Temple Mount as a "dung heap."[6]

The conspicuous void in Jerusalem's sacred topography was filled in 691–92 CE with the completion of an ambitious project by the Ummayad caliph ʿAbd al-Malik to construct a sanctuary surrounding a large rock formation on the Temple Mount.[7] The rock was associated with various persons and episodes known also from the Old Testament and was believed to be the location of Muhammad's ascent to heaven.[8] Commensurate with the site's development into the most important destination for Muslim pilgrims outside of Mecca and Medina, extraordinary wealth concentrated in and around the sanctuary. An endowment was established at least by the early tenth century to administer sums for the upkeep of the Dome of the Rock and to supply it continually with precious incense and oil, among other goods.[9] According to Ibn al-Aṯīr, more than forty large silver candelabra were stolen from the Dome of the Rock by the Crusaders, as well as a great silver lamp, a hundred and fifty small silver candelabra, and more than twenty gold ones—among other treasures.[10]

When the Crusaders conquered and began to settle Jerusalem, they had to confront the fact that in the place where western European Christians had for centuries imagined a divinely ordained lacuna, there stood instead a magnificent structure that dominated the skyline of the holy city.[11] As early as 1102–3, the pilgrim Sæwulf gave the impression that the Templum Domini was the original temple built by Solomon by refraining from any reference to the destruction of the various Jewish temples on the site.[12] One early chronicler referred to the Templum

5 Matt. 24:2; Mark 13:2; Luke 19:44; John 2:19.

6 Jerome, *Commentarii in Esaiam* 240.

7 Grabar, *Dome of the Rock*.

8 Hillenbrand, "Medieval Muslim Veneration." For a twelfth-century example, see Harawī, *Kitāb al-Ishārāt* 70–72.

9 Hillenbrand, "Medieval Muslim Veneration," 143.

10 Gabrieli, *Arab Historians*, 7.

11 Berger, *Crescent on the Temple*, 75–91; Andersen Oftestad, *Lateran Church*, 85–86.

12 Sæwulf, 270–323.

Domini as a "simulacrum" of Solomon's Temple, "built by I don't know whom, as tribute to the noble ancient House," and went on to praise its splendors: "It certainly was a place of very great beauty, built out of gold and silver, of immeasurable price, and of incredible variety, with walls and gates plated with layers of precious metals."[13] Another writer suggested that it had been built recently by Christians.[14] Fulcher of Chartres clarified that the Templum Domini stood on the site "where Solomon first built another wondrous [temple]," but allowed that, although the modern structure "is in no way comparable to that first one, still it has been constructed with wondrous workmanship and a most beautiful appearance."[15]

Accommodating Jerusalem's sacred topography to fit the Templum Domini was part of a larger reconfiguration by Frankish settlers and pilgrims that occurred in the early years of the twelfth century. For many western European Christians prior to the First Crusade, the geographical distance of the earthly city had favored its conception in purely abstract terms. Those who now occupied the city were forced not only to confront the physical realities of the sacred sites but also became invested in promoting the earthly dimension as a gateway to the spiritual.[16]

The growing importance of the earthly Jerusalem in Latin Christendom cannot be extricated from another spiritual trend in twelfth-century western Europe, in which Christians sought to follow in the footsteps of Christ. Some pilgrims took this *imitatio Christi* quite literally, by retracing Christ's geographical trajectory and visiting the principal sites associated with his life. To Fulcher of Chartres, the Crusader conquest of the earthly Jerusalem, where Jesus Christ "lived as man among men on earth," served to renew and celebrate Christ's acts and teachings while validating the Crusaders as a divinely chosen people.[17] A sequence from a twelfth-century liturgy used at the Church of the Holy Sepulcher makes a similar connection, drawing a parallel between Christ's ascension to heaven and the journey to the Holy Land of Crusaders and pilgrims: "Each carries the sign of the cross as he seeks out the holy sites of the highest ruler. . . . Let us worship him who was crucified, through whom we see the empires of demons destroyed. Let us worship him who rises again to make a journey to the kingdom of heaven for us."[18] A twelfth-century hymn that may have been composed in the Latin East links the earthly and heavenly cities in unequivocal terms, stating quite simply that "the

13 Guibert of Nogent, *Dei gesta per Francos* 7.4.10 (Levine, *Deeds of God*, 132).

14 AA 6.24.

15 FC 1.26.5.

16 Schein, *Gateway to the Heavenly City*, 63–90. Boyadjian (*City Lament*, 83–93) views this development as part of the Crusaders' appropriation of a Jewish conception of Jerusalem, as expressed most explicitly in the biblical Book of Lamentations.

17 FC 1.29.4.

18 *Manu plaudant*, ll. 20–28 (Linder, "Liturgy of the Liberation," 119–20): *Quisque portat signum crucis / dum requirit summi ducis / loca pia. . . . Crucifixum adoremus / per quem demonum videmus / destructa imperia. / Adoremus resurgentem iter nobis facientem / ad regna celestia.*

earthly Jerusalem [is] the starting point of the heavenly [Jerusalem]" (*Iherusalem terrestris / principium celestis*), before drawing a connection between the capture of Jerusalem and the hour of Christ's crucifixion: "On this hour the city was captured, so let there be no delay, let our voice be sonorous, exult, Jerusalem!"[19] Given the increasing spiritual importance attached to the physical holy sites in Jerusalem, the stakes were high for new institutions like the Templum Domini to lay claim to a variety of biblical traditions.

When the Crusaders first set foot in Jerusalem on 15 July 1099, attitudes toward the Templum Domini evolved rapidly and in contradictory ways. The Norman Tancred, who breached the north wall of the city, plundered the Dome of the Rock and stripped it of its considerable treasure. According to one chronicler, Tancred spent two full days systematically extracting "an incomparable quantity of gold and silver from the walls." He then shared the spoils, which could scarcely be carried by six camels or mules, with Godfrey of Bouillon.[20] Yet, when the fighting and looting subsided, the Crusaders' first course of action was a communal procession to the Holy Sepulcher and the Dome of the Rock—now christened the Templum Domini—while both clergy and lay members sang hymns.[21] Similarly, upon the discovery of the True Cross shortly after the capture of Jerusalem, the Crusaders formed a ritual procession through the city from the Church of the Holy Sepulcher to the Templum Domini.[22] The Templum Domini appears at crucial moments in the early days of the Crusader rule of Jerusalem as a spiritual focal point along with the Church of the Holy Sepulcher.[23] Notably, before the Battle of Ascalon in August 1099, the Crusader army prayed in front of the Templum Domini; after the Holy Fire failed to appear in the Church of the Holy Sepulcher on Holy Saturday in 1101, the patriarch, king, and papal legate performed public penance at the Templum Domini until the miracle was successfully enacted.[24] Even the first king of Jerusalem, Baldwin I, sought prominent assocation with the Templum Domini from the very beginning, for both his earliest coinage and royal seal depict it alongside the Tower of David and the Church of the Holy Sepulcher.[25]

Given the paucity of written sources for this early period, it is difficult to determine what significance the Templum Domini held for Jerusalem's new

19 *Ripoll Hymn*, l. 29: *Urbs capitur hac ora, / nulla sit ergo mora, / nostra sit vox canora, / Iherusalem, exulta!*

20 AA 6.23. For other accounts of Tancred's looting, see FC 1.28.2; *Gesta Francorum Iherusalem expugnantium* 37; RC 3630–79.

21 FC 1.29.2.

22 FC 1.30.4.

23 Zöller, *Regularkanoniker*, 119.

24 WT 9.11.

25 Metcalf, *Coinage of the Crusades*, 41; Mayer and Sode, *Die Siegel*, 61.

inhabitants. While some sources may have been lost, a prime reason for our lack of knowledge on this subject is probably that this meaning had yet to be articulated and codified. Despite the prominent visibility of the edifice, the community of canons that established themselves at the Templum Domini in the early twelfth century had their work cut out for them if they wished their institution to acquire spiritual and political significance. Over the following decades, the leaders of this community resorted to creative new ways to enhance their institutional standing within the ecclesiastical and secular landscape of early Frankish Jerusalem by composing Latin poetry.

Achard of Arrouaise: In Search of Treasure and Patronage

Leading the endeavor was the prior of the canons of the Templum Domini, Achard of Arrouaise. Having ruffled some feathers early in his career, Achard was no stranger to controversy. Before coming to Jerusalem, he had been a canon and provost of the Church of Saint Mary in Arras, in northern France, where he also assumed a role as master of the schools (*magister scholarum*).[26] In the latter capacity, he accompanied Lambert, bishop of Arras, to the Council of Clermont in 1095, where he witnessed Pope Urban II preaching the First Crusade.[27] Given his evident proximity to the bishop, Achard seemed to be well on track for a comfortable life as a senior member of the clergy.

Suddenly in 1097, Achard abandoned his post as provost and retreated to a cell at the monastery of Watten in the northern French diocese of Thérouanne. At this monastery, a number of canons, referring to themselves as "the poor of Christ" (*pauperes Christi*), had taken up residence to lead a clerical life informed by monastic practices.[28] Achard's decision seems to have been made without consulting Lambert, who promptly attempted to retrieve his canon. When the other canons prevented him from doing so, Lambert sent a series of letters to the monastery indicating the severity of the affront and arguing that their actions were in violation of canon law.[29] From Watten, Achard joined the newly formed community in nearby Arrouaise, becoming archdeacon and the right-hand man of its charismatic founder, Cono of Praeneste.[30] Achard seems to have made amends with his former bishop, for the following year both he and Cono bore witness to a charter issued by Lambert.[31]

26 Milis, *L'ordre des chanoines*, 1:100; Zöller, *Regularkanoniker*, 73–74.

27 PL 162:646B.

28 For an overview of this community, see Meijns, "De *pauperes Christi* van Watten."

29 Letters 25 and 29 in PL 162:657B–657D and 658B–659A, respectively.

30 For Cono of Praeneste, see Dereine, "Conon de Préneste"; Hiestand, "Legat, Kaiser und Basileus"; Cadderi, *Conone di Preneste*; Tessera, "La croce del legato."

31 Van Drival, *Cartulaire*, 67 and 70.

Shortly after 1100, Achard moved to reside at the nearby cathedral of Thérouanne, joining the reform-minded bishop John of Warneton. Once again, Achard's career could have carried on there, but by 1104 we encounter him in Jerusalem. He had arrived there to deliver a letter from Lambert of Arras to the Latin patriarch of Jerusalem, Evremar of Chocques.[32] He appears to have decided to settle in Jerusalem, because two years later, Achard, now a deacon of the "church of Jerusalem" (possibly the Church of the Holy Sepulcher), traveled to the papal Curia in Rome with Arnulf of Chocques to assist him in his dispute with Evremar.[33] The erstwhile compatriots Evremar and Arnulf had both been deposed as patriarch of Jerusalem and were vying for reinstatement after the death of the previous patriarch, Daibert of Pisa. After his deposition, Arnulf became a prelate at the Templum Domini. When he finally regained his position as patrarich of Jerusalem in 1112, he likely repaid Achard for his earlier support by designating him his successor at the Templum Domini, for on 20 June that same year, Achard appears as prior of the Templum Domini among the witnesses to a charter of King Baldwin I of Jerusalem.[34] Over the course of his tenure at the Templum Domini, Achard bore witness to numerous charters of Baldwin I and Baldwin II and attended the Council of Nablus in 1120.[35] He must have died sometime between late 1135 and the end of 1137.[36]

After his appointment at the head of the Templum Domini, Achard addressed a lengthy poem to the king of Jerusalem in which he boldly demanded the return of the treasures taken from the Dome of the Rock upon the Crusader capture. The poem consists of 817 lines of 15 syllables with end-rhyming couplets in a meter typically employed in hymns.[37] The meter, along with the frequent references by the poet to his activity in terms evoking orality, suggests that the poem was intended to be performed in song, either by Achard at the king's court or as part of a new commemorative tradition among the canons of the Templum Domini.[38]

32 Giordanengo, *Le registre de Lambert*, no. 77, 434; Milis, *L'ordre des chanoines*, 1:93–106.

33 WT 11.12; Hiestand, *Die päpstlichen Legaten*, 1:150.

34 *UKJ* 1: no. 52.

35 Achard's name appears ninth in the list of witnesses: Kedar, "Canons of the Council," 332.

36 He is mentioned for the last time in a charter dating between Christmas 1135 and 1 September 1136 (*Cart St-Sép*, 78–80, no. 22 [RRH no. 167; RRR no. 345]), and his successor Geoffrey is mentioned in two charters dating between 24 September and 24 December 1137 (*Cart St-Sép*, 80–83, no. 23 [RRH no. 172; RRR no. 360]; *Cart Temp*, 99, no. 141 [RRH no. 173; RRR no. 364]).

37 The meter amounts to a rhythmical imitation of the quantitative trochaic septenarius, known as *versus caudati* in medieval classifications, but these rigid constraints are not followed by Achard in any consistent manner. See Meyer, *Gesammelte Abhandlungen*, 1:79; Erdmann, "Leonitas," 18–19; and Norberg, *Medieval Latin Versification*, 62, n. 20, 107–8.

38 So suggested Poleg in GA, *Mac*, 14. For verbs indicating a potential oral performance, see AP 9, 26, 40, 43–44, 680.

Achard's poem opens with an acrostic identifying poet and addressee as "Achard, prior of the Temple, to King Baldwin" (*Balduino regi prior Templi Acardus*). Although either King Baldwin I (r. 1100–1118) or Baldwin II (r. 1118–1131) could have been the intended addressee, a remark by Achard that he knows the identity of the robbers of the Templum Domini but chooses to suppress their names may indicate that the poem dates to the reign of Baldwin I. Tancred, the main culprit responsible for the looting, died on 12 December 1112, rendering Achard's reticence less poignant if the poem had been composed during the reign of Baldwin II.[39] Given that Achard had assumed his office at the Templum Domini just earlier that year, this poem would then have constituted one of his first actions as prior and would need to be dated within the narrow window between the spring of 1112 and 12 December of the same year.[40] Alternatively, Achard may have had in mind other Frankish nobles who had obtained a portion of the treasure—including the king himself. Since, according to Albert of Aachen, Tancred shared his spoils from the Dome of the Rock with Godfrey of Bouillon, it is not implausible that these treasures subsequently passed into the possession of his brother, King Baldwin I.

Although there is some conflicting evidence, Achard likely had little to complain about regarding the financial situation of the Templum Domini when he assumed its reins. Sometime in 1109–10, King Baldwin I approved the decision of Gibelin, patriarch of Jerusalem, to pay the Templum Domini an annual rent of 1,000 bezants. When Arnulf took Gibelin's place in 1112, he confirmed the grant.[41] However, the chronicler Albert of Aachen reports that, in 1109, King Baldwin I "returned" to Tancred, among other sizeable possessions, the Templum Domini along with its revenues.[42] In this period, Baldwin sought to settle the growing dispute between Tancred and his nephew Baldwin of Bourcq, then count of Edessa (later King Baldwin II). If the report is to be believed, King Baldwin I granted Tancred the revenues of the Templum Domini, to which Tancred may have laid claim for his role in the capture of Jerusalem. Nevertheless, Tancred's dwindling influence in the Kingdom of Jerusalem likely limited the impact of

39 AP ll. 21–23; Schein, "Between Mount Moriah," 181, n. 21; Prawer, *History of the Jews*, 47. Lehmann (AP, 300) argued that the poem's ending (AP ll. 811–15), expressing the hope that the return of the Templum Domini's stolen treasure will allow it to be dedicated during a summer in the near future, suggests that the composition of the poem should be placed later rather than earlier, given that the dedication did not occur until the spring of 1141.

40 Achard is first attested as prior of the Templum Domini on 20 June 1112, but likely succeeded Arnulf shortly after his election as patriarch of Jerusalem following Gibelin's death on 6 April that year.

41 The charter is not extant, but the grant is confirmed in a subsequent charter issued by King Amalric in 1166: Mayer, *Bistümer*, 228; *UKJ* 1: no. 49; *UKJ* 2: no. 316.

42 AA 11.12.

this arrangement and is unlikely to have constituted Achard's sole motivation in drafting his poem. Naturally, if Achard wrote after Tancred's death at the end of 1112, the agreement is less likely still to have played a role, since it would have been annulled and of little further consequence to the canons.[43]

Regardless of the state of the Templum Domini's finances, its interior must have been completely barren after Tancred's rigorous spoliation of all its marble, gold, and silver decoration. The sources describing the looting are unanimous in their emphasis that the loot consisted primarily of architectural ornament on the sanctuary's walls and many columns.[44] The bare walls and columns greeting the canons that took up residence in the Templum Domini would have been a stark and perpetual reminder of lost splendor. In his final exhortation to the king, Achard attests to this sentiment in his—probably hyperbolic—description of the Templum Domini as a ruin.[45] But for Achard to stir up new controversy with his poem, there must have been something more at stake than the mere outward appearance of the Templum Domini, something that also involved the site's spiritual significance. These two themes—lost material splendor and abiding spiritual dignity—form the heart of Achard's poem.

Opening his poem with a conventional literary device known as a priamel, Achard enumerates topics that have been the subject of poetry in the past, but which he will spurn: warfare, ekphrasis (elaborate descriptions of objects or places), and mythology. Focusing on the latter, Achard relates how previous poets composed poetry in praise of gods "created by men," proceeding to qualify their verse as "fanciful tales" (*fabulae* and *mendacium*). The priamel functions as a truth claim: the poem will relate unadulterated truths that, unlike classical texts of the school curriculum, require no allegorical unpacking.[46] Instead of calling upon the muse to inspire him, Achard invokes the Holy Spirit to enlighten him:

> Bestow, I ask, upon your supplicant the ability to relate in a worthy manner the work of King Solomon, about which I intend to write. And make well-disposed to me the person to whom I write, in order that he may wish to alleviate all our poverty, and return the property of the Temple that has been held ever since the capture of Jerusalem—to their own destruction!

43 So also Zöller, *Regularkanoniker*, 113. For the view that this arrangement was Achard's prime motivation, see Mayer, *Bistümer*, 225 and 227. For Tancred's limited involvement in the Kingdom of Jerusalem toward the end of his life as diminishing the impact of the arrangement, see Rheinheimer, "Tankred und das Siegel Boemunds," 84–85; Asbridge, *Creation of the Principality*, 119.

44 AA 6.23; FC 1.28.2; *Gesta Francorum Iherusalem expugnantium* 37; RC 3630–79.

45 AP 806.

46 On the notion of "truth claim" as a function of medieval literature, see Otter, "Functions of Fiction," 112–13.

—by those who claim to be the defenders of the faith, but are proven to be the Lord's enemies.[47]

The opening of the poem leaves little doubt about its purpose and intended audience: the poet writes to King Baldwin to request the return of the treasures taken from the Templum Domini during the capture of Jerusalem on 15 July 1099. With the Holy Spirit as his inspiration, Achard claims the requisite authority to make his urgent exhortation to the king. Notwithstanding the opening, the poem goes far beyond the plea of a mere suppliant. Achard states in no uncertain terms that the king's salvation depends on the rightful return of the stolen treasure.[48] As Achard would have been well aware, the king was in all likelihood not a neutral party to his suit and may have received the spoils Tancred shared with Godfrey of Bouillon (the king's brother, if the addressee was Baldwin I, or nephew, if he was Baldwin II). Even if Achard could not compel Tancred to return his part of the loot, he could hope to prevail upon the king.

Achard's persuasive strategy is to enumerate various biblical episodes that not only indicate the significance of the site of the Templum Domini but also provide Baldwin with a guide on how to act as king. Taking as his point of departure the foundation of the Temple as described in Kings and Chronicles, Achard relates how King David constructed an altar at the site of the Templum Domini to atone for his sin of pride and to escape the wrath of the avenging angel, making sure to specify that David bought the land from the Jebusite Ornan at full price.[49] The passage would have left little ambiguity for Baldwin, earlier addressed by Achard as "the successor to renowned King David," to take the biblical lesson to heart.[50] Similarly, when relating the events of the Maccabean revolt against Antiochus IV, Achard emphasizes Judas Maccabeus and his brothers' roles as restorers of the Temple and vanquishers of its despoilers. Clearly, these figures represented crucial examples to be followed by King Baldwin.[51]

This was a clever tactic, particularly given the fact that Baldwin I was explicitly associated with the rulers of Jerusalem described in the Old Testament. As early as ca. 1104, Anselm of Canterbury had written in a letter that Baldwin had "King David as his predecessor," while Ralph of Caen, sometime between around 1114

47 AP 13–20: *Presta, queso, supplicanti digne posse promere / Regis opus Salomonis, quod intendo scribere. / Ipsum quoque, cui scribo, michi fac placabilem, / Omnem nostram sublevare quo velit pauperiem. / Reddi cogat, que ad suam ipsorum perniciem / Templi bona tenent, ex quo capta est Ierusalem, / Esse se qui profitentur defensores fidei, / Magis autem comprobantur inimici domini.*

48 AP 26–32.

49 AP 110–27.

50 AP 24–25.

51 AP 544–69. For the biblical imagery in the poetry of Achard of Arrouaise and his successor, Geoffrey the Abbot, see Yolles, "Maccabees in the Lord's Temple."

and 1130, claimed that Baldwin I "was born divinely as one who was to take his seat on David's throne."[52] In the late 1130s, Rorgo Fretellus referred in a pilgrim guide to the realm of Baldwin I as the "Kingdom of David."[53]

As for the Maccabees, there are reports that the tomb of Baldwin I contained an epitaph that associated the king with Judas Maccabeus:

> King Baldwin, a second Judas Maccabeus,
> Hope of the nation, strength of the church, virtue of both,
> Whom Lebanon and Egypt, Dan and murderous
> Damascus feared and brought tribute to,
> Alas is enclosed in this humble tomb.[54]

Achard's point is clear. If, as seems to have been the case, Baldwin cultivated an image of himself as a biblically inspired ruler, he ought to emulate these figures in their good deeds while avoiding their sinful behavior. It comes as no surprise that for Achard, virtuous behavior of the biblical rulers coincides with observing the dignity of the site of the Templum Domini.

Achard establishes this dignity by crafting a narrative concatenation of biblical episodes centered on the site of the Temple, giving the impression that the Temple—and by implication, the Templum Domini—lay at the heart of Jewish and Christian history. While the Old Testatment poses few problems for this reading of the Bible, Achard must have struggled to find an equal number of relevant episodes from the New Testament. Notwithstanding a few episodes pertaining to Jesus's childhood, he would have been all too aware that the climactic events related in the gospels—the Crucifixion and Resurrection—distinctly favored the veneration of the Templum Domini's greatest competitor within the sacred topography of Jerusalem: the Church of the Holy Sepulcher. To address this imbalance, Achard resorted to relating several episodes drawn from extrabiblical sources, such as the works of Josephus and Eusebius.

From Josephus, Achard borrowed the story of the Jewish uprising against Rome and the subsequent destruction of Jerusalem, as told in the *Jewish War*. Following the commonly accepted narrative in which the Romans are viewed as divine avengers of Jesus's Crucifixion, Achard explains that the Jews' refusal to acknowledge Christ as Son of God led to the eventual destruction of Jerusalem,

52 Anselm of Canterbury, *Opera*, no. 324, 255; RC 1142–45.

53 RF 24. Compare RF 26 and JW 563–66.

54 *Rex Baldewinus, Iudas alter Machabeus, / Spes patriae, vigor ecclesiae, virt<us> utriusq<ue>, / quem formidabant, cui dona tributa ferebant / Cedar & Egypt<us> / Dan ac homicida Damascus / proh dolor in modico clauditur hoc tumulo.* I have followed here the transcription of Elzear Horn, who visited Jerusalem from 1724 to 1744: Elzear Horn, *Ichnographiae monumentorum*, 71. The epitaph also occurs, with a few variants, in the earlier account of Theoderich (*Peregrinatio*, 360).

including the Temple.[55] Toward the end of the work, however, he also offers an alternative explanation that places greater emphasis on the Temple. According to one Jewish tradition (*quidam Iudeorum*), the Jews were punished not for their role in bringing about the death of Christ, but rather for the execution of James the Less, Jesus's brother. Achard presents James as the first bishop of the Temple and depicts his appointment by the apostles Peter and the brothers John and Jacob, sons of Zebedee, as the starting point of the early Christian church (*Hinc accepit formam illam primitus eclesia*).[56] Achard thus invests the Temple with a tradition as an ecclesiastical institution that far predates the Church of the Holy Sepulcher. This was not a novel notion but assumed new significance within the context of the ecclesiastical politics of Frankish Jerusalem.[57] Achard's codification of this tradition in a poem addressed to the king may well have been perceived as a challenge to the patriarch.

But Achard went even further by recounting James's dramatic fate: while preaching the message of Christ, James was cast headlong from the Temple by the Jews and struck by a fuller's staff for good measure. This narrative, which was abbreviated into a few verses and inscribed inside the Frankish Chapel of Saint James on the Temple Mount, appears in some fragments of an early Christian author preserved by Eusebius and referred to as Hegesippus.[58] By utilizing this source, Achard brings the narrative of the destruction of the Temple by the Romans into connection with the Temple as a site of Christian martyrdom.

For additional insight into the way Achard crafted his institutional narrative, it is worth examining the elements he decided to omit. For instance, he does not cite Christ's famous prediction that the Temple would be destroyed, as presented in the four canonical gospels.[59] These passages were inconvenient to Achard's argument that the Templum Domini possessed a dignity, based on the religious history of the site, that warranted the king's reverence. On the contrary, the passages had laid the foundation for centuries of Christian neglect of the Temple Mount area. The passage from John was particularly problematic for the canons of the Templum Domini, since it interprets Jesus's statement about the Temple's destruction and subsequent reconstruction as a reference to his Crucifixion and Resurrection.[60] The passage makes reverence for a physical temple obsolete and

55 AP 683–86.

56 AP 765.

57 Andersen Oftestad, *Lateran Church*, 117.

58 AP 759–78. See AP 304–5, and Eusebius, *Historia ecclesiastica* 2.1, for the passage in question. This is a different Hegesippus than the one discussed below, who is referred to as Pseudo-Hegesippus.

59 Matt. 24:2; Mark 13:2; Luke 19:44; John 2:19.

60 Zöller, *Regularkanoniker*, 127–28.

instead supports veneration of those aspects of Jesus's life that were most closely connected with the Church of the Holy Sepulcher.

Achard concludes his poem with a reflection on the origins of the present edifice of the Templum Domini, presumably in the hope of preempting criticisms that the building had no connection whatsoever with the Judeo-Christian tradition.[61] He claims that no written record exists (*non legitur*) of the founder of the structure, but that some think that the building was constructed by the emperor Constantine or perhaps his mother, Helena. Both, of course, were intimately associated with the construction of the Church of the Holy Sepulcher and the finding of the True Cross. Achard ends the list of possible founders with the other renowned figure associated with the True Cross: Emperor Heraclius, who recovered the Cross in his defeat of the Sassanians in 630. The search for a foundational history as illustrious as that of the Church of the Holy Sepulcher is nowhere more patently obvious. Equally apparent is Achard's failure to even consider the possibility that the structure was built by Muslims.[62]

A pilgrim guide, written by a deacon in Antioch named Rorgo Fretellus in 1137–38, offers evidence that, at least by this time, Achard's suggestions were not the only ones circulating. After proposing (like Achard) Constantine, Helena, and Heraclius as founders, Rorgo expands the list with the emperor Justinian, concluding with the theory that the Templum Domini had been built by "a certain emir [*ammyratore*] from Memphis [or named Memphis] in Egypt in reverence of Allachiber, that is, 'the greatest god,' since [the building] is devoutly venerated by every tongue to worship [Allachiber]."[63] While it is possible that Achard of Arrouaise and Rorgo Fretellus availed themselves of the same source, the similarities between the passages may point to a wider dissemination of the institutional claims of the canons of the Templum Domini that extended to Antioch.[64]

Although Achard refuses to consider Muslims as the builders of the Dome of the Rock, he does attribute to them an important role in preserving the edifice as

61 AP 491–574.

62 Di Cesare ("Qubbat al-Ṣaḫrah"), by contrast, argues that Achard's depiction of the Templum Domini as an originally Christian shrine reflects attempts to mitigate the eschatological claims of Jewish and Islamic traditions and forms part of a broader tendency to subordinate the Templum Domini to the Church of the Holy Sepulcher.

63 RF 53: *Quidam enim sub Constantino imperatore ab Helena matre sua reedificatum esse perhibent, pro reverentia sancte Crucis ab ea reperte. Alii ab Heraclyo imperatore pro reverentia ligni Domini, quod de Perside triumphans gloriose retulerat. Alii a Iustiniano augusto; alii a quodam Ammyratore Memphis Egypti sub honore Allachiber, id est summi Dei. Et quoniam ad ipsum colendum ab omni lingua reverende veneratur. Quod verius Saracena superscriptio nobis manifeste declarat.* Similar passages occur in later pilgrim guides: see JW 87–88; Innominatus VI 434; and *Descriptio locorum circa Hierusalem adiacentum*, 426.

64 Lehmann in AP 302–5. Since Lehmann proposed a date of 1136 for the composition of Achard's poem, he posited this pilgrim guide (or its source) as the basis for Achard.

a site of worship. On the cusp of ending his poem, Achard gives thanks to God for delivering the Templum Domini and the Holy Sepulcher from the "hands of the unfaithful Turks," but points out that the "unfaithful" (*infideles*) preserved the Templum Domini along with its treasures and revenues. The many works of marble and mosaics adorning both the interior and exterior, he argues, could only have been funded through significant streams of income.[65] Strikingly, Achard's argument that the Templum Domini merited the status of a revered ecclesiastical institution rested on its prior history as a well maintained and richly endowed Muslim sanctuary. In promoting the notion of an unbroken historical tradition, Achard was willing to embrace a degree of institutional continuity with the site as a Muslim sanctuary.

Whereas Muslims had preserved the site and endowed it with riches, Achard berates the Christian people (*Christianus populus*) for despoiling it promptly upon their capture of Jerusalem. Thus, while Achard conceived of Baldwin as a ruler of a biblical mold, that did not exempt him, or the Franks of Jerusalem more generally, from scathing rebuke. The poem ends with a final plea to the king to compel the thieves to return the treasures so that the Franks as a whole might not suffer the Lord's opprobrium, and so the Templum Domini might fittingly be rededicated to usher in a new Christian era.

Whether Achard succeeded in his plea to the king remains unknown. It is unclear when Tancred compensated the Templum Domini, although the shared testimony of Fulcher of Chartres and Ralph of Caen indicates that he did so at some point. Fulcher initially (i.e., sometime before 1124) wrote that Tancred did so "afterward" (*postea*), but he struck even this vague specification from his post-1124 redaction. Fulcher, who was not present at the 1099 capture of Jerusalem, couches his remarks in the context of Tancred's alleged discovery in the Dome of the Rock of "an idol made in the name of Muhammad." In treating Tancred's subsequent spoiling, he hastens to add that Tancred had "sent back to this sacred place all the same things [he had looted], or things equal to their value." In his post-1124 redaction, Fulcher thought it necessary to include a more emphatic exculpation for Tancred's actions, adding that "at that time nothing godly was enacted there, when the Saracens observed their religion with the superstitious rite of idolatry."[66]

The Norman writer Ralph of Caen likewise sought to exonerate Tancred's despoiling of the sanctuary. Having come to Antioch around 1108, Ralph composed a Latin history celebrating in prose and verse the exploits of Tancred during and after the First Crusade (most of it written ca. 1114–18, with additions after 1130) and may have moved from Antioch to Jerusalem to cultivate the patronage of

65 AP 790–800.
66 FC 1.28.2.

his former teacher Arnulf of Chocques.[67] Ralph claimed that when Tancred burst into the Dome of the Rock during the Crusader capture of the city, he found there to his consternation a statue of Muhammad of "shining gold and entirely covered in gems and porphyry."[68] Ralph implies that Tancred's subsequent spoliation of the Dome of the Rock was fully justified, given that the treasures belonged to idolatrous worship rather than Christian piety. Unlike Fulcher (or any other source), Ralph depicts a vivid public debate between Tancred and Arnulf of Chocques over the restitution of the treasures immediately following the Latin conquest of Jerusalem. Arnulf argues that Tancred despoiled not a Muslim sanctuary but the house of God:

> The Temple, I say, of the Lord, which was not built yesterday or the day before, nor disturbed by the decree of just anyone, it was founded not at some random place, time, manner, or by just anyone: for this is the house of the Lord, firmly built—the Lord himself founded it. This is the very place, in which the patriarch Jacob declared the Lord to reside truly, the place he called the gate to heaven, where he saw the ladder reaching the heavens and the angels ascending and descending. This is the place Lord Christ illuminated with his presence as an infant and, after casting out the moneychangers with zealous reverence, praised with the following words: "It is written: my house shall be called the house of prayer." It would take too long to enumerate all the praises heaped on the majesty of this holy house by the Writ of the Old and New Testament.[69]

In the end, according to Ralph, the Frankish nobles decreed that Tancred could keep the treasures but must compensate the Templum Domini, which Tancred did "not unwillingly."[70] We may note that Arnulf's biblical argument echoes both in substance and in phrasing that of Achard. Like Achard, Arnulf refrains from

67 See appendix 1.
68 RC 3639–40. Following Muratova ("Western Chronicles"), a common misconception has situated Ralph's description of this scene at the al-Aqṣā Mosque (Domus Salomonis / Domus Salomoniaca) next to the Dome of the Rock (Templum Domini). However, at RC 3631, Ralph indicates that Tancred entered the "*Domini Templum*."
69 RC 3818–29: *Templum, inquam, Domini non ab heri et nudiustertius constructum, non quolibet dispensante circumactum, non ubivis, non quando, non quomodo, non a quovis fundatum: haec est enim domus Domini firmiter edificata, ipse Dominus fundavit eam. Hic ille est locus, in quo patriarcha Iacob vere Dominum esse asseruit, quem portam celi vocavit, ubi scalam celos tangentem et angelos ascendentes et descendentes vidit. Hunc Christus dominus et presentatione sui illustravit infans; et reverentiae zelo, mercimoniis eiectis, sic extulit adolescens: "Scriptum est: Domus mea domus orationis vocabitur." Longum est autem enumerare, quibus Paginae Veteris aut Novae laudibus huius sanctae domus cumulatur maiestas.*
70 RC 3941–42.

referencing the problematic gospel passages on the destruction of the Temple while citing the same biblical episodes. Moreover, Arnulf's reference to the "majesty of this holy house" (*huius sanctae domus . . . maiestas*) and its founder neatly parallels Achard's programmatic statement: "No one who reads the book of Kings can be ignorant of the great dignity always possessed by the Temple of God, or why, where, and by whom it was founded."[71] If Ralph's version of the events is to be believed and Tancred repaid the Templum Domini shortly after the conquest of Jerusalem in 1099, Achard's institutional narrative had taken shape already under Arnulf's leadership at the Templum Domini. Achard subsequently elaborated and codified this narrative in a poem, while seeking to compel the king to return his portion of the treasure. Alternatively, if Tancred compensated the Templum Domini as a result of Achard's poem in 1112, Ralph may have retroactively attributed the core elements of Achard's narrative to his (prospective) new patron, Arnulf of Chocques.

Regardless of the precise circumstances of composition, Achard's poem could hardly have had more grandiose pretentions, considering the relatively minor stature of his institution in the early twelfth century. But perhaps his bluster bore fruit. Sources indicate that restorations to the Templum Domini began as early as 1114, during which a large marble covering was erected over the rock formation inside, as well as an altar and choir.[72] While Achard's poem may have helped him secure at least some portion of the lost treasure, its lasting legacy is codifying an institutional history of the Templum Domini as a site sacred to Christendom and at least as worthy of the attentions of pilgrims as the Church of the Holy Sepulcher.

From an upstart canon in northern France to the head of an increasingly prominent institution in Frankish Jerusalem, Achard's life traced a remarkable trajectory. But he was not forgotten at home. A poem composed in Thérouanne in the early twelfth century boasts of the striking number of individuals from this diocese that had held key positions in the Latin East, from Godfrey of Bouillon and his brother Baldwin (both listed as kings of Jerusalem) to the first patriarchs of Jerusalem, Evremar and Arnulf. Amid these illustrious figures, the person to receive the most emphatic praise is none other than Achard of Arrouaise:

> In charge of the Temple was Achard, once your archdeacon:
> An upright, wise, and pious man.[73]

71 AP 33–35: *Quante semper dignitatis Templum Dei fuerit, / Qua de causa quove loco vel quis hoc fundaverit, / Nullus legens libros regum ignorare poterit.*

72 FC 1.26.7–9 and WT 8.3.94–98.

73 *Versus de viris* 191: *Praefuit et templo tuus archidiaconus ante / Vir probus et sapiens et religiosus Achardus*. See also Hiestand, "*Gaufridus abbas*," 49, n. 5. For a discussion of this poem, see Demyttenaere and Meijer, "Walter van Terwaan," 971–74.

Geoffrey, Abbot of the Templum Domini

With his Latin poem, Achard may well have helped the Templum Domini acquire crucial spiritual and political capital in its early stages by emphasizing the scriptural importance of the site. Shortly after his tenure, the Templum Domini was promoted from a priory to an abbey, indicating the increased stature the institution had achieved by the late 1130s. Where the institution would go from there was in the hands of Achard's successor, Geoffrey, who became the first abbot of the Templum Domini.

Nothing is known about Geoffrey before his arrival in Jerusalem.[74] His name occurs in a charter of the Knights Templar dating to the period of 24 September to 24 December 1137, during which he is listed as prior of the Templum Domini.[75] A charter belonging to the Holy Sepulcher from the same period lists Geoffrey as abbot of the Templum Domini, indicating that the institutional change of priory to abbey must have occurred at some point in the fall of 1137.[76] We may therefore conclude that Geoffrey succeeded Achard as prior of the Temple before its status changed from a priory to an abbey sometime between 25 December 1135 and 24 December 1137. Geoffrey disappears from the record after 1160, and in April of 1166 his successor, Hugh, appears as a witness to charters.[77]

Geoffrey enjoyed considerable prominence in the Kingdom of Jerusalem.[78] He was sent as an envoy on two different embassies to the Byzantine emperors John II Komnenos and Manuel Komnenos (in 1142/1143 and in 1158/1159, respectively), and William of Tyre explains that the reason for these assignments was his fluency in Greek.[79] Geoffrey's frequent appearance as a witness to charters further attests to his prominence within the Kingdom of Jerusalem.[80] One charter, confirming the purchase of a house in the enclosed Temple Mount area (*septa Templi*) by one otherwise unknown Arnaldus the Baker, bears Geoffrey's personal seal showing a figure seated on a throne holding an abbot's crosier, with the dome of the Templum Domini on the reverse (fig. 6).[81]

74 For the life of Geoffrey, see Linder, "Unpublished Charter"; Hiestand, "*Gaufridus abbas*"; Barber, *Crusader States*, 177–78.

75 *Cart Temp*, 99, no. 141 (RRH no. 173; RRR no. 364). Note the incorrect date here of 1 September 1137–2 April 1138, and see *UKJ* 2:857. The significant fact that Geoffrey is listed here as *prior* rather than *abbas* seems to have gone unnoticed by earlier scholars.

76 *Cart St-Sép*, 80–83, no. 23 (RRH no. 172; RRR no. 360). Note the incorrect date of 1 January–5 February 1138, and see Mayer, *Kanzlei*, 2:856–57, for a date of 24 September–24 December 1137.

77 *UKJ* 1: no. 260; *UKJ* 2: no. 316.

78 See Linder, "Unpublished Charter," and Hiestand, "*Gaufridus abbas*."

79 WT 15.21.11–12, 18.24.6–7.

80 *UKJ* 1: nos. 138–39, 143, 160–61, 164, 171, 173, 177, 179, 187–88, 205–6, 210, 214, 216, 220, 233, 237, 239, 258; *UKJ* 2: nos. 272, 274–75, 277; 281–82, 285, 288, 297–98, 303; *Cart St-Sép*, nos. 23–24, 50–51, 107; *Chartes Josaphat*, no. 23; Hiestand, "*Gaufridus abbas*," 58–59.

81 Hiestand "*Gaufridus abbas*," 58–59 (RRH, no. 173b; RRR no. 663).

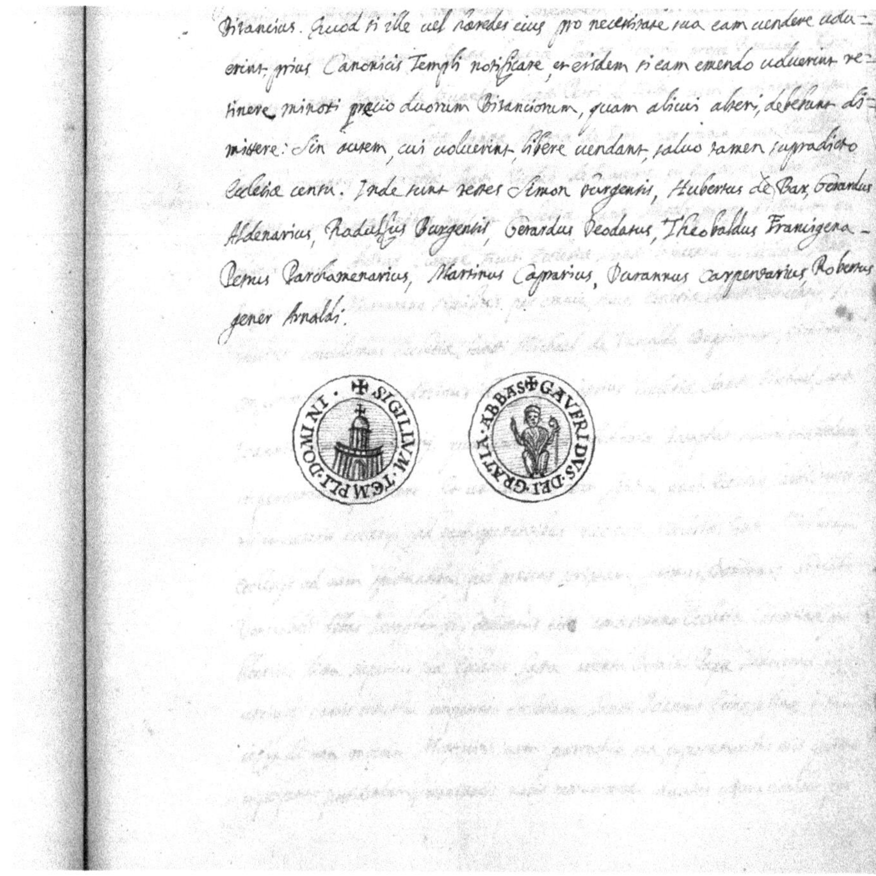

FIGURE 6
Seal of Geoffrey, abbot of the Templum Domini, copied by Antonino Amico. Palermo, Biblioteca comunale, Qq.H.11, fol. 70r, detail. Photo courtesy the Comune di Palermo.

However, little evidence indicates that Geoffrey enjoyed a similar position outside of the Latin East. One charter issued by Geoffrey in the period 1146–66 concerns the confirmation by Ernaldus Ruffus II of the donation of Woodbridge Priory to the abbey of the Templum Domini.[82] The charter records Geoffrey's confirmation that Ernaldus and his heirs would maintain the privilege of electing its prior. In this instance at least, Geoffrey appears to have been powerless to assert the rights of the Templum Domini more forcefully.[83] More importantly, as discussed below, this charter represents a flagrant contradiction of Geoffrey's

82 Linder, "Unpublished Charter," 121.
83 So too concludes Linder, "Unpublished Charter," 129.

self-promotion as a champion against the practice of simony, the buying and selling of ecclesiastical favors and offices.[84]

Nevertheless, Geoffrey's interest in expanding his influence beyond Jerusalem is attested by a letter he wrote to Count Geoffrey of Anjou, eldest son of Fulk of Anjou, king of Jerusalem from 1131 to 1143.[85] In this letter, Geoffrey describes himself as "prior of the most sacred Temple of the Lord which is in Jerusalem" (*dominici ac sanctissimi Templi quod est in Ierusalem prior*), indicating that it must have been written before the institutional change to an abbey in the fall of 1137.[86] The ostensible purpose of the letter is to solicit material aid from the count, presumably for the renovation of the Templum Domini that would be completed in 1141. At the start of the letter, Geoffrey writes, "Since I believe that you are not ignorant of the great dignity always possessed by the Temple of God, and by whom and how it was founded, or what great miracles took place in that very place, I did not wish to write of this. Indeed, to write of the dignity and the profound mystery would be proper to a book rather than a letter."[87] The book in question, historian R. Hiestand argues, was not a mere commonplace but referred to Achard of Arrouaise's poem on the history of the Temple.[88] To sollicit the count of Anjou's patronage, Geoffrey appears to have revised his predecessor's work and appended it to the letter.

But Achard's poem was not the only verse to issue from the Templum Domini. In fact, Geoffrey himself composed two lengthy Latin poems frequently transmitted along with Achard's: a versification of the biblical books of the Maccabees (763 lines) and a versified account of Josephus's *Jewish War* (980 lines). In his edition of Geoffrey's poem on the Maccabees, E. Poleg argued that Geoffrey's letter primarily refers to this poem rather than to Achard's poem on the history of the Temple.[89] Given the significant differences in style, content, and purpose between Achard's poem and Geoffrey's poem on the Maccabees, he deems it unlikely that Achard's poem was revised by Geoffrey. Instead, he argues, the use of the term *mysterium* in the letter points to the typological connections made in Geoffrey's poem, while the letter's reference to the story of the expulsion of the moneylenders from the Temple accords closely with Geoffrey's concern with simony in his versification of the Maccabees.[90]

84 I am grateful to A. T. Jotischky for this observation.

85 For the career of Geoffrey of Anjou, see Bradbury, "Geoffrey V of Anjou."

86 See Hiestand "*Gaufridus abbas,*" 52–53, 58.

87 Hiestand "*Gaufridus abbas,*" 58: *Quoniam credimus vobis non esse incognitum, quante dignitatis semper, a quibus vel qualiter fundatum Templum Dei fuerit, queve aut quanta inibi fuerint facta miracula, scribere noluimus. Ipsius enim dignitatem et mysterii profunditatem scribere libri potius esset quam epistole.*

88 Hiestand "*Gaufridus abbas,*" 53–54.

89 Poleg in GA, *Mac*, 22–23.

90 See, for instance, *misticam . . . sententiam* in GA, *Mac*, 110, but also the *dona mistica* in GA, *Ios*, 421, and *munera . . . mistica* in 432. The principal passage on simony occurs in GA, *Mac*, 214–40.

Poleg's arguments, though persuasive, do not account for the fact that Geoffrey's poem on the Maccabees does not deal with the founding of the Temple by any means—an aspect explicitly associated with the hypothetical book Geoffrey mentions in his letter. Moreover, the language employed in describing the proposed subject matter in the letter is almost identical with the programmatic statement near the beginning of Achard's poem (as cited earlier): "No one who reads the book of Kings can be ignorant of the great dignity always possessed by the Temple of God, or why, where, and who founded it."[91] These remarkable resemblences alone demonstrate that at the very least Geoffrey had Achard's poem in mind when he wrote his letter (whether he revised it or not). Yet even the episode of Christ expelling the moneylenders from the Temple, which is referred to in the letter and indicates for Poleg a connection with Geoffrey's concern for "buyers" and "sellers" (*emptores* and *venditores*) of spiritual goods, finds a more literal parallel in Achard's poem.[92] Achard, who diligently paraphrased in verse all biblical episodes concerning the various Jewish temples (or at least all that supported his argument), also relates this particular episode, and even quotes the same verse from Matthew as Geoffrey does in his letter.[93] This particular biblical episode, moreover, is so closely tied to the Temple that it did not require any particular justification for its inclusion, since it represented an episode that evocatively linked the Templum Domini to the gospels and the life of Christ.[94]

Finally, despite Poleg's claim to the contrary, a direct parallel to the *mysterium* mentioned in Geoffrey's letter appears in Achard's poem.[95] Toward the end of the poem, Achard apologizes for the fact that his poem cannot treat in detail all of the *mysteria* that took place in the Temple: "There are many great miracles that the Lord performed in the Temple and showed to the elders. But let it suffice to have spoken about just a few of the many; for my slight knowledge does not presume to write about so many great mysteries of the Savior."[96]

In sum, the nearly identical phrases in Achard's poem and Geoffrey's letter indicate that Achard's poem most likely accompanied the letter. In fact, there is no reason on the basis of the letter alone to suppose that either of Geoffrey's own

91 AP 33–35: *Quante semper dignitatis Templum Dei fuerit, / Qua de causa quove loco vel quis hoc fundaverit, / Nullus legens libros regum ignorare poterit.*

92 GA, *Mac*, 22. The relevant passage in Geoffrey's versification of the Maccabees occurs in the digression in lines 214–40. Although Geoffrey's use of the phrases *emptores* and *venditores* resembles the *ementes* and *vendentes* mentioned in Matthew 21:12–13 and in Geoffrey's letter, there is no reference to the story of the expulsion of the moneylenders in the passage from Geoffrey's poem.

93 Matt. 21:13: *domus mea domus orationis vocabitur*. This is itself a quotation from Isaiah 56:7.

94 See, for example, the references to this story in RF 55, JW 283, WT 1.15.46.

95 Poleg in GA, *Mac*, 22.

96 AP 678–82: *Multa sunt et mira valde, que in templo dominus / Signa fecit docuitque coram senioribus. / Sed sufficiat dixisse perpauca de pluribus; / Non presumpsit enim nostra tenuis scientia / tot et tanta salvatoris scribere misteria.*

poems accompanied it. On the other hand, he may have wished to increase the prestige of his gift by adding poems to a work originally directed to another patron (as would have been evident from the acrostic in the opening lines of Achard's poem). The timeline of the poems' composition corroborates this suggestion. As indicated by the designation of the poet as prior, both of Geoffrey's poems as well as the letter to Geoffrey of Anjou were written in the same short period (1135–37).[97]

Moreover, if all three poems accompanied the letter, this would account for the fact that they are found circulating together in twelfth-century manuscripts from France.[98] As P. Lehmann demonstrated, the manuscript tradition strongly indicates that Geoffrey (or someone else) revised an earlier version of Achard's poem.[99] This early version survives in a single early twelfth-century manuscript from the monastery of Saint-Michel en l'Herm in Poitiers, in which the incipit identifies the author as "a certain wise man" (*cuiusdam sapientis*).[100] Since this version of the poem is missing nearly 300 verses, the manuscript is unlikely to constitute Achard's autograph, as Hiestand had suggested, but may instead be an early incomplete or abbreviated copy.[101] In revising Achard's poem, Geoffrey corrected a few grammatical and morphological errors and made minor stylistic modifications by changing the word order or substituting synonyms.[102] While Geoffrey's interventions were largely superficial, in some instances they betray a different poetic strategy from that of his predecessor. For instance, in referencing the martyrdom of James the Less, Achard had placed greater emphasis on James's passion ("but for the death of his brother James, who suffered there"), while Geoffrey was more concerned with providing clarity ("but for James, who was said to be the brother of the lord").[103] Geoffrey's didactic tendency also manifests in his addition

97 In Geoffrey's letter to the count of Anjou (quoted above), he refers to himself as a prior, while the one manuscript identifying Geoffrey's authorship of the two poems attributes them (along with Achard's poem) to Geoffrey in his capacity as prior; see Oxford, Bodleian Library, Laudianus misc. 406, fol. 1r: *Incipit opus Gaufridi prioris de templo super libros Machabeorum*.

98 Some manuscript evidence suggests that Geoffrey's first poem circulated separately at some point. The fragment discovered by Poleg contains the poem's last forty-one lines, which are immediately followed by another text (see Poleg's description of the manuscript in GA, *Mac*, 17). It is possible, therefore, as Poleg suggests, that Geoffrey sent his versification of the Maccabees with the letter and not that of Josephus. However, the lack of rubrication and explicit indicates that the text may have been excerpted; at the very least, it does not provide compelling evidence that the poem ever gained wider circulation separate from the other two poems, unlike Geoffrey's versification of Josephus.

99 Lehmann in AP 305–6.

100 Rome, BAV, Reg. lat. 150, fol. 159v (early twelfth century).

101 Hiestand, "*Gaufridus* abbas," 53.

102 For Geoffrey's corrections of errors, see AP 69, 76, 82, 574, 773; for stylistic changes, see AP 86–87, 120–21, 152, 154, 159, 164, 168, 170–71, 176, 189–90, 525, 529, 621, 633, 686, 688, 746, 761, 766, 799.

103 AP 761. Compare Achard's original *sed pro morte fratris eius ibi passi Iacobi* with Geoffrey's *sed pro Iacobo qui frater dicebatur domini*.

of verses to make the moral lessons more explicit or to clarify a point.[104] After revising Achard's poem, Geoffrey added two of his own poems and circulated the combined production under his own name.

The manuscript evidence may provide a further clue to support the suggestion that Geoffrey conceived of the three poems as a unified production. Although scholars have been aware of the existence of ten lines of dactylic hexameter dealing with the founding and destruction of the Temple at the end of the three poems, they have not received any scholarly attention.[105] These verses were probably composed by Geoffrey rather than Achard, since they appear only at the end of Geoffrey's poems and are absent from the one manuscript containing only Achard's poem. The lines of dactylic hexameter deal with the foundation of the Temple by Solomon, its destruction by Nebuchadnezzar, and the destruction of the subsequent Temple by Titus. The poem therefore manages to achieve a unity between the three poetic productions, so that—if Geoffrey indeed authored these verses—this poem strongly suggests that he intended for both his own poems and that of his predecessor to circulate together.

On the Books of Maccabees

Unlike Achard's poem to King Baldwin, there remain many questions concerning the circumstances, purpose, and intended audience of Geoffrey's versifications. While Geoffrey's letter to the count of Anjou may indicate that his poems circulated in the Latin West, the content of his verses primarily points to an audience within the Latin East. The books of the Maccabees and Josephus's *Jewish War* resonated with the Franks in the East, who at every turn perceived themselves and the space around them as part of a continuum with a sacralized past. Over the course of the First Crusade, the Maccabees became symbols of Christian valor. The narrative of First Maccabees, centered on the resistance of Judas Maccabeus and his brothers against the gentile Antiochus IV, spoke to Christians who perceived in their Turkic and Fatimid opponents a pagan foe. After the conclusion of the Crusade, the Maccabees continued to be held up as prime examples, particularly among the new military orders of the Knights Templar and the Hospitallers.[106]

Geoffrey utilized the popular religious cachet enjoyed by the Maccabees in the Latin East to increase the standing of the Templum Domini. His versification of the Maccabees in a poem entitled *On the Books of the Maccabees* represents a significant expansion of the poetic program begun by his predecessor Achard, who

104 See Lehmann's critical apparatus for AP 36, 54, and 137.

105 See Lehmann in AP 299; for the verses, see GA, *Ios*, 971–80.

106 For overviews, see Morton, "Defence of the Holy Land"; Lapina, "Maccabees"; and Yolles, "Maccabees in the Lord's Temple."

briefly paraphrased a series of biblical episodes. Geoffrey, instead, offers a highly accessible extended narrative interspersed with authorial comments identifying his purpose and the significance of the biblical text. The first such passage occurs near the start of the poem, after the poet has set the stage:

> With this poem I urge the readers to consider carefully how unlawful it is, and in opposition to the Holy Spirit, at this moment in time to attempt to acquire the priesthood through purchase. For now we do not sacrifice the fat of bulls or rams to the Lord, nay, instead the flesh and blood assumed by the Son of God from the Virgin Mary for us sinners. If the fire was extinguished when Jason acquired the priestly glory by bribing the king, what do we believe will happen now with the fire of the Holy Spirit? It is extinguished both to the buyers and the sellers.[107]

Far from merely rephrasing the biblical text in verse, Geoffrey offers his own interpretative guide embedded within the poem: the books of the Maccabees can be read allegorically as an injunction not to engage in simony. The Gregorian Reforms of the eleventh century focused on eradicating the corrupting influence of secular bribes on the church by encouraging clergy members to lead stricter lives. The canons of the Templum Domini, who observed the monastic rule of Augustine from at least 1114, must have viewed themselves as champions of this issue. Achard of Arrouaise had already laid some of the groundwork for Geoffrey in recounting the famous passage from Matthew in which Jesus casts out the moneychangers from the Temple. Tellingly, Achard describes the episode as Jesus's greatest miracle, since it represents his complete victory over secular might (*seculari potestate*).[108] By 1160 the passage was inscribed below a painting of Christ inside the Templum Domini.[109] Here we may recall the Woodbridge Priory charter from 1146–66, in which Geoffrey granted a secular lord and his heirs the privilege of electing the prior. This fact renders Geoffrey's claim to a considerable amount of moral authority on the issue of simony even more extraordinary.

What is more, Geoffrey presents the trajectory of salvation history as centered on the location of the Templum Domini, from the first altar constructed by David (as related by Achard) to Christ's incarnation through the Virgin Mary. Like

107 GA, *Mac*, 214–24: *Ammonemus hoc carmine lectores ut sollicite / Perpendant, quam nefarium sit contra sanctum spiritum / Nunc temporis per pretium ambire sacerdotium. / Non enim adeps pinguium, taurorum vel arietum / Nunc immolatur domino in nostro sacrificio, / Immo caro cum sanguine quam de Maria virgine / Assumpsit dei filius pro nobis peccatoribus. / Si ignis tunc extinctus est, quando Iason potitus est / Pontificali gloria data regi pecunia, / Quid fieri nunc, credimus, de igne sancti spiritus? / Extinguitur emptoribus simul ac venditoribus.*

108 AP 648–53.

109 JW 119–29; Theoderich, *Peregrinatio*, 22–24. See also Schein, "Between Mount Moriah," 183.

David's altar, the mention of Mary was likely intended to evoke the Templum Domini, which would be dedicated to the Virgin Mary just a few years later in 1141. With this version of salvation history, Geoffrey utterly elides the Crucifixion and Resurrection, thus bypassing the religious traditions associated with the Church of the Holy Sepulcher. Where Achard primarily claimed spiritual authority to rebuke those who had transgressed against the Templum Domini, Geoffrey assumes an even more grandiose voice, asserting that his institution forms the heart of Christianity itself. As the head of a community of reformist canons, Geoffrey viewed himself as a champion against ecclesiastical vices, quite possibly including the patriarch of Jerusalem in his censure of simony.

Geoffrey, moreover, devised an ingenious explanation that placed the issue of simony at the heart of his institution's history. While the term was generally associated with a passage in Acts, in which Simon Magus offers Peter payment in return for the gifts of the Holy Spirit, Geoffrey presents an alternative origin toward the end of his poem on the Maccabees: "The history has been treated with the utmost brevity, for I have omitted much and spoken but little about many things. My intention is to show through these books that the vice of simony arose in ancient times, from Simon and afterward from a certain Jason."[110] Geoffrey refers not to Simon Magus but to Simon the Benjamite, an overseer of the Temple who tried to persuade Apollonius to rob the Temple's treasury (2 Maccabees 3), and to the high priest Jason, who promoted a policy of Hellenization (2 Maccabees 4). Like Achard, Geoffrey resorts to creative strategies to promote the Templum Domini and, as its head, his own spiritual authority. He does so by reframing the books of the Maccabees from a text viewed as containing examples of religiously inspired valor to a narrative filled with lessons for clergy and secular rulers.

A passage at the very end of his poem on the Maccabees indicates the extent to which Geoffrey perceives his own literary activity as instrumental in promoting ecclesiastical reform: "But now many, ignorant of the past, say that never was there a time like that of our own; but if they knew the past, they would call these happy times."[111] Geoffrey chastises his fellow Franks for a presentist mindset that, still in the heady rush of the successful completion of the First Crusade, happily proclaimed the dawn of "a new day, new joy" requiring "new words and new songs."[112] Such a way of thinking not only erodes the very basis for Geoffrey's spiritual authority and the dignity of the Templum Domini, but fails to learn the

110 GA, *Mac*, 1148–52: *Digesta est hystoria sub brevitate maxima / Nam plura pretermisimus de multis pauca diximus. / Et nostra est intentio de symonie vitio / Ex his libris ostendere quod ab antiquo tempore / Exortum est a Symone et post a quodam Iasone.*

111 GA, *Mac*, 1168–70: *Nunc autem dicunt plurimi preteritorum nescii / Huic nostro similia nunquam fuisse tempora, / Qui si nossent preterita hec dicerent felicia.* For a discussion, see Yolles, "Maccabees in the Lord's Temple," 437–38.

112 RA 151.

valuable lessons of the past. To demonstrate the potential dangers of such ignorance, Geoffrey composed a sequel to his versification of the Maccabees in the form of a poem on Josephus's *Jewish War* titled *On the Seven Books of Josephus*.

On the Seven Books of Josephus

The first-century Jewish author Flavius Josephus penned his Greek account of the Jewish rebellion in Rome, where he enjoyed the patronage of the emperors Vespasian and Titus. Given the accolades Geoffrey received from William of Tyre for his Greek fluency (the only Frank to receive such praise from William), it is tempting to imagine him working directly from the Greek original.[113] A close comparison between Geoffrey's poem and the available Latin translations of Josephus reveals, however, that Geoffrey was following these to such an extent that it seems unlikely that he ever had the Greek text in front of him.[114]

There existed two such translations in the Middle Ages. The first is a fourth-century translation often attributed to one "Hegesippus," comprising an abbreviated revision of Josephus's text into five books, with a notable Christian slant.[115] The second, more faithful translation also dates to the fourth century and was often (most likely erroneously) attributed to Rufinus of Aquileia, the prolific translator of Greek patristic works.[116] Remarkably, rather than relying upon a single Latin translation, Geoffrey appears to have consulted both texts for his poem. Given the practicalities of medieval composition and the difficulty involving the simultaneous consultation of multiple codices (or the awkward flipping back and forth within one codex), Geoffrey's combined use of these two translations represents a noteworthy achievement. While it is possible that Geoffrey had access to a text of Pseudo-Rufinus that was glossed or interpolated with Pseudo-Hegesippus, I have been unable to find evidence for the existence of such an interpolated version. In any case, both translations likely circulated in the twelfth-century Latin East, given that William of Tyre invokes both Pseudo-Hegesippus and Josephus as "excellent writers and renowned historiographers" (*egregii scriptores et illustres historiographi*) in his description of Jerusalem.[117]

As in his versification of the Maccabees, Geoffrey was no slavish imitator of his source texts. For instance, he prefaces the narrative with a clear and concise overview of the Jewish priests of the Temple from the time of the Maccabees until

113 WT 15.21.11–12, 18.24.6–7. For this observation, see the remarks of Huygens in WT ad loc., on the first of these passages, as well as Hiestand, "*Gaufridus abbas*," 50–51.

114 GA, *Ios*, 87–88.

115 Pseudo-Hegesippus, *Historiae libri quinque*.

116 For the authorship, see Schreckenberg and Schubert, *Jewish Historiography*, 71–73.

117 WT 8.2.18.

the beginning of the Jewish revolt of 66–73 CE.[118] At other points, he brings the events of Josephus's narrative in line with episodes in the book of Acts, or provides a helpful differentiation between the three individuals referred to by Josephus as "Herod." Once he even refers readers with an interest in the civil war that erupted in the wake of Julius Caesar's assassination to the poet Lucan and draws on the Christian Latin historian Orosius to relate a memorable anecdote regarding Hannibal's crossing of the Alps.[119]

In perhaps his greatest departure from the Josephan source material, Geoffrey refers to a passage in the Gospel of Luke to explain the Roman siege of Jerusalem as a fulfillment of Christ's prophecy.[120] This passage would have held particular poignancy for the community of canons at the Templum Domini, since it immediately precedes the episode in which Christ evicts the moneylenders from the Temple. Moreover, Christ's famous quotation of Isaiah ("My house shall be a house of prayer") in the biblical passage was inscribed within the Templum Domini after the renovations of the early twelfth century.[121] Geoffrey therefore draws an intimate connection between Christ's prophecy, the Roman siege of Jerusalem, and the Frankish Templum Domini. The link becomes explicit when Geoffrey describes how Titus attempts to persuade the Jews to surrender: "Frequently Titus commiserated with them and beseeched them to look out for themselves and to live in peace, and not to allow the city and the Templum Domini to be destroyed."[122] In this passage, Geoffrey nearly transforms Titus from a warlord into a pacifist. Here Geoffrey relied on a long tradition that stretched back as far as the church fathers Lactantius and Eusebius, in which Vespasian and Titus were perceived as divine agents and were sometimes portrayed as actively attempting to prevent the destruction of Jerusalem.[123] Isidore ensured the wider dissemination of the narrative, which later gave rise to numerous dramatized retellings in the vernacular.[124] Yet Geoffrey renders the story more immediately relevant to his community by having Titus warn against the destruction not only of Jerusalem, but specifically of the Temple, here given the same name as that used by Geoffrey and his fellow canons to refer to their own institution.

Similarly, when urging his compatriots to surrender to the Romans, the Jewish ruler Herod Agrippa II states that if they are unwilling to comply, they may as well commit suicide and burn the city and the Templum Domini to the ground

118 GA, *Ios*, 1–11.

119 GA, *Ios*, 294–95 and 759–67, respectively.

120 GA, *Ios*, 539–41.

121 Luke 19:46, quoting Isaiah 56:7.

122 GA, *Ios*, 557–59: *Sepe Tytus misertus est eosque deprecatus est / Ut sibimet consulerent et ut in pace viverent, / Nec paterentur destrui urbem Templumque Domini.*

123 See Jacobsen, "Die Eroberung von Jerusalem," 342–43.

124 On the vernacular reworking, see Yeager, *Jerusalem in Medieval Narrative*, 78–107, and Thiolier-Méjean, *La prise de Jérusalem*.

themselves. The speech contains a lengthy encomium of the Romans, presented as the all-powerful rulers of the world who govern with divine assistance. Another speech, this time by Josephus himself, contains a catalogue of various peoples throughout history unable to resist the might of the Romans. The speaker makes an exception for the Gauls, "mighty in strength," who receive extended praise.[125] While both speeches were present in his source materials, Geoffrey elaborated them to the point of rhetorical set pieces in direct speech. The point was to capture the attention of Geoffrey's contemporaries and to render ancient history more immediate with a nod to twelfth-century Franks who prided themselves on their supposed Gallic heritage.[126]

Geoffrey required his compatriots' attention, for, as a new Josephus, he desperately sought to warn his fellow Franks to learn from history and not to allow Jerusalem and the Templum Domini to be destroyed by God's wrath over their sinful behavior. We observed a similar mindset in the preamble to the Canons of the Council of Nablus of 1120, in which the conveners drew attention to the vicissitudes of the Israelites as recounted in the Bible. In 1184, some fifty years after Geoffrey's poem, William of Tyre expressed a similar moral urgency in warning his contemporaries to learn the lessons of history.[127] In the short preface to the last extant book of his chronicle, William looks upon the current state of the Latin East with pessimism yet perceives for himself an essential task as historiographer in preventing future calamity by pointing out the moral failings of his compatriots. Compared to the Canons of Nablus and to William of Tyre, Geoffrey's innovation is to make the survival of Jerusalem—and, by extension, of all the Latin settlements in the Levant—contingent solely upon the continued well-being of the Templum Domini.

Geoffrey's moral authority rested on the illustrious history that his institution laid claim to—a history that Achard had helped to construct and upon which Geoffrey's own poems elaborated. Geoffrey hoped to accomplish his ambitions by casting them, as his predecessor had done, in an artful form. Like Achard's poem, Geoffrey's poetic endeavors may have been driven by a motivation to produce an institutional history for the benefit of the canons of the Templum Domini that could provide spiritual guidance to the community under his care. In this context, the poetic form could have had several advantages over a prose treatise: the rhyming scheme and meter rendered Geoffrey's words more conducive to memorization

125 GA, *Ios*, 726–45. Morin ("Hégésippe en rimes latines," 176) believed this passage to be an original composition on the part of the poet, since it is not in Pseudo-Hegesippus; however, it does occur in Pseudo-Rufinus. See GA, *Ios*, 78.

126 Note that these same speeches were used earlier by Widukind of Corvey (d. after 973) as a testament of the prowess of the Saxons. See Widukind of Corvey, *Res gestae Saxonicae*, 3:418. See also Schreckenberg, *Die Flavius-Josephus-Tradition*, 127–28.

127 WT 23 prol. 32–49.

and performance, while at the same time helping to establish a fixed institutional narrative by making it more difficult to introduce changes.

Such a fixed narrative could prove resilient even when treated subsequently in prose. Traces of Geoffrey's versification of Josephus's *Jewish War* can be found within a year or two in the pilgrim guide written by Rorgo Fretellus in Antioch, attesting to an early circulation of his poem beyond Jerusalem.[128] The passage in question centers on the death of Herod Agrippa, for which Geoffrey produced a unique combination of elements drawn from Josephus's *Jewish War* and *Jewish Antiquities* and the book of Acts from the New Testament.[129] In his treatment of Caesarea, Rorgo included a similar descriptive vignette and even followed Geoffrey's portrayal of Herod's clothing as made of gems and gold rather than of silver (as described in the Vulgate translation of Acts).[130] Geoffrey's condensed version of the Josephan text, combined with the relevant biblical passages, may have made for a convenient reference work that saved authors such as Rorgo Fretellus the trouble of sifting through several lengthy historical accounts.[131]

In addition to providing an institutional narrative for the canons of the Templum Domini, a Latin versification of a text so closely tied to the history of Jerusalem must also be viewed as part of a careful strategy to solicit patronage—either from local rulers or from those in the Latin West who sought prestigious association with the Holy Land. That association with Jerusalem was particularly prized is clear from the example of Geoffrey of Anjou. After his father, Fulk of Anjou, ascended to the throne of Jerusalem in 1131, Geoffrey proudly identified himself in charters as "Geoffrey, count of Anjou, son of the king of Jerusalem."[132] A figure of Geoffrey of Anjou's standing may have hoped to acquire greater influence and cultural capital through acts of patronage. The increased relations between the Templum Domini and the court of Anjou seem to indicate that Geoffrey the Abbot's solicitations for patronage garnered success. In a letter dating to ca. 1140, the canons of the Templum Domini recommend one of their fellow canons to the count in return for his inclusion in their prayer services.[133]

While Geoffrey's letter and poems may have helped persuade the count of Anjou to contribute funds for the extensive renovation and redecoration of the Templum Domini, documentary evidence also indicates Geoffrey's succesful

128 Yolles, "Josephus"; for Rorgo Fretellus, see appendix 1.

129 GA, *Ios*, 667–76.

130 RF 74: *In qua et Herodes Iunior Agrippa videlicet in throno suo residens purpureis vestibus gemmis auroque contextis regie decoratus est velut Deum se sublimans ulcione divina percussus in publico pessumdatus expiravit.*

131 The one instance in which Rorgo refers to Josephus is sufficiently vague (*Iosepho testante*) that it could have come from an intermediary, such as Geoffrey's versification: RF 62.

132 See, e.g., Chartrou, *L'Anjou de 1109 à 1151*, "Pièces justificatives," nos. 46–47, 49, 53–54, 57. I am grateful to M. Blincoe for this observation.

133 Chartrou, *L'Anjou de 1109 à 1151*, "Catalogue," no. 134.

cultivation of a wide range of ecclesiastical and secular patrons in the Latin East, including Melisende, queen of Jerusalem and wife of Fulk of Anjou. A charter from 1166 confirms the many grants, possessions, and privileges the canons of the Templum Domini had amassed up to that point, including properties and revenue streams in Jerusalem, Hebron, Ascalon, Nablus, the Transjordan, Caesarea, Acre, Tyre, Arabia Petraea, and Montréal.[134]

Through the combined energetic efforts of Achard of Arrouaise and Geoffrey the Abbot, the barren interior of the Templum Domini was eventually transformed. Already during Achard's tenure, a marble altar and choir had been erected on top of the rock formation; these were subsequently girt with an exquisitely wrought iron grill. The workmanship impressed such diverse visitors as an Icelandic pilgrim and a Muslim pilgrim from Mosul named al-Harawī, who compared it to a house.[135] Also during Geoffrey's tenure, a range of mosaic inscriptions were made to adorn both the exterior and the interior of the Templum Domini. In keeping with Achard and Geoffrey's poems, the Latin inscription on the exterior represents an innovative concatenation of verses from the Old and New Testament that, as J. Folda has put it, "reconstruct a 'new psalm' in praise of this building as the house of the lord founded on a rock."[136] Moreover, an extensive program of textual and visual decoration of the interior was completed by around 1160, during Geoffrey's tenure. Original verse inscriptions in rhymed dactylic hexameters marked important sites, indicating Jacob's vision of the heavenly ladder, Jesus's presentation in the Temple (both accompanied by paintings or mosaic portraits), and the Virgin Mary's purification.[137] Evidently, for the canons of the Templum Domini, Latin verse continued to function as an important medium in which to promote their institution.

Finding Prestige: The Canons of Hebron

Jerusalem was not the only place in the Latin East populated by newly formed communities of monks and canons. By 1112, a community of Augustinian canons had taken up residence in Hebron, some twenty miles south of Jerusalem. While the heads of the Templum Domini had made the unusual decision to compose a series of poems, a more common strategy for a new community to enhance its prestige took the form of prose institutional histories documenting miraculous events.

134 *UKJ* 2:550–53, no. 316 (RRH no. 422a; RRR no. 760).

135 Icelandic Pilgrim (Wilkinson, *Jerusalem Pilgrimage*, 220–22); Harawī, *Kitāb al-Ishārāt* 71.

136 Folda, *Art of the Crusaders*, 252.

137 For these inscriptions, see Folda, *Art of the Crusaders*, 252–53. They are recorded (sometimes in different versions) by the twelfth-century pilgrims John of Würzburg and Theoderich. For the exterior inscription, see JW 388–99; Theoderich, *Peregrinatio*, 545–60; for the interior inscriptions, see JW 279–314, 576–612.

Such events were frequently associated with saints' relics, giving rise to accounts of *inventio* (discovery of a saint's relic) and *translatio* (the transfer of a relic to an institutional context of veneration).[138] The sanctuary in Hebron, known today as the Ḥaram al-Ḫalīl, presented the canons with just such an opportunity.[139]

Below the sanctuary lay the Cave of Machpelah, said to house the tombs of the patriarchs Abraham, Isaac, and Jacob, along with those of the matriarchs Sarah, Rebekah, and Leah. Originally the site of Jewish worship, it continued to be a place of prominence under Muslim rule and functioned as a mosque by the tenth century.[140] Six cenotaphs had been placed within the Ḥaram as early as the time of Egeria, toward the end of the fourth century, but by the twelfth century, the location of the original tombs had been lost from memory.[141] Thus their rediscovery by the canons in 1119 represented a momentous event for the community of Hebron, which documented the incident by commissioning an eloquent Latin narrative.

An account detailing the *inventio* and *translatio* of saints' relics fulfilled a range of important functions. First, it offered an authoritative version of the miraculous discovery of a saint's relic, thus giving meaning to an object and investing it with sanctity. Second, the text provided the community with a formalized narrative for use in rituals of communal commemoration (such as liturgical celebration), and so contributed to the cohesion of the community and the development of communal identity. Furthermore, such accounts presented a credible narrative for the outside world of how the community acquired the relic in question. These narratives were especially helpful in situations where the authenticity or rightful possession of the relic was in dispute. Finally, the text was intended to spread the word, as a form of marketing to attract pilgrim traffic and the associated revenue streams to the community.

No fewer than three Latin accounts detailing the *inventio* survive. The first and most extensive version was discovered by P. Riant in 1884 and likely represents the oldest account that is most closely connected with the community of Hebron.[142] Titled *Tractatus de inventione sanctorum patriarcharum Abraham, Ysaac et Jacob* (Treatise on the discovery of the patriarch saints Abraham, Isaac, and Jacob) and spanning sixteen pages in the modern edition, this version was written by an anonymous author who addresses the canons of Hebron, by whom

138 For overviews of the genre, see Aigrain, *L'hagiographie*; Heinzelmann, *Translationsberichte*; and Heffernan, *Sacred Biography*.

139 Hamilton, *Latin Church*, 77, n. 4.

140 For the history of the Ḥaram al-Ḫalīl, see Vincent et al., *Hébron*, and Pringle, *Churches*, 1, no. 100.

141 As preserved in a passage from Peter the Deacon, *Liber de locis sanctis* 93–98, 252–78.

142 See *Tractatus de inventione* in appendix 1.

he had been commissioned to write the account.[143] The earliest possible date for the composition of this account is 1128, given the reference to Warmund, Latin patriarch of Jerusalem, as deceased, while the church's elevation to a bishopric in 1167 provides the terminus ante quem.[144] The author's claim to have interviewed Odo and Arnulf, the two canons who discovered the relics in 1119, suggests that the account was penned not much later than the mid-twelfth century.[145]

The second account, *Breviarium*, represents an abbreviated version of the first text (five and a half pages in the modern edition); it was most likely written at a later date and will not concern us here.[146]

The third account, *Translatio beatorum patriarcharum Abrahe, Ysaac et Iacob* (Translation of the blessed patriarchs Abraham, Isaac, and Jacob), was discovered in 1896 by C. Kohler and presents a version of the events that differs markedly from that in the first two accounts.[147] It is a third of the length of the first account and gives a different year in which the discovery took place, which it describes not as a communal effort but rather as the result of several visions sent by the patriarch Abraham to an unnamed monk from the monastery of Saint Martin in Tours.[148] The text fails to mention any of the canons of Hebron or their prior by name and also omits the conflict between Patriarch Warmund and the canons of Hebron. This third account was likely written later, and there is nothing in it that suggests a composition in the Latin East. The reference to the community as the "church of Hebron" (*Ebronica ecclesia*) indicates that this account, unlike the version discovered by Riant, was written after the church's elevation to a bishopric in 1167 but likely before Ṣalāḥ al-Dīn's conquest of Hebron in 1187

143 *Tractatus de inventione* 1–2: *fratres karissimi qui Cariatarbe estis, vestris volens parere iussionibus opus michi iniunctum incipere nequaquam distuli.*

144 *Tractatus de inventione* 398–99: *sancte recordationis Guarmundo patriarche, qui tunc temporis illic preerat.* For the redating of the church of Hebron's elevation from 1168 to 1167, see Mayer, *Bistümer*, 197–214. The imperfect tense verb used to refer to Baldwin, lord of Hebron, at *Tractatus de inventione* 300 (*qui eodem tempore ibidem principabatur, nomine Balduini*), provides inconclusive evidence, as the passage could mean that Baldwin was "also at that time" in charge. For Baldwin of Saint-Abraham, last attested in 1136, see *UKJ* 1: no. 135; Mayer, "Die Herrschaftsbildung in Hebron."

145 *Tractatus de inventione* 24–25. Whalen ("*Discovery of the Holy Patriarchs*," 145) argues instead for a date nearer to the church's elevation (i.e., 1167), not taking into account that the canons Arnulf and Odo, presented as still alive in the text, would likely have passed away.

146 BHL no. 10. It is found in a single manuscript: Lille, 450, fols. 57r–58v (second foliation; second half of the thirteenth century), from Loos-Notre-Dame. First edited by Riant (*Tractatus eiusdem Breviarium*), it resembles the first account to such an extent that it was relegated to the *apparatus criticus* by Huygens ("Inventio Patriarcharum").

147 Kohler, "Un nouveau récit." The text was edited anew as "Text II" in Huygens, "Inventio Patriarcharum," 150–55. The only manuscript witness is Avranches, 130, fols. 79v–81v (second half of the thirteenth century).

148 "Text II" in Huygens, "Inventio Patriarcharum," ll. 20–21.

and may have originated from Tours.[149] For the present purposes, I will restrict my discussion to the first account.

The *Tractatus de inventione*

The author begins by asking the community of Hebron for prayers and by identifying his chief sources: the oral account of two canons, Arnulf and Odo, who were intimately involved in the events, as well as a Greek monk from Mount Sinai, later identified as John, who related to him the history of the sanctuary up to the time of Emperor Theodosius II (r. 402–450). A summary of relevant biblical passages follows, intended to remind readers of the biblical authority for the claim that the tombs of the patriarchs Abraham, Isaac, and Jacob lie in Hebron.[150] After citing a passage from Genesis, the author argues that the bones of Adam were also interred in Hebron, supporting his claim with a tendentious misquotation from the book of Joshua and with reference to an otherwise unattested work of Ambrose titled *De creatione Ade* (On the creation of Adam).[151] This extraordinary claim is sure to have rankled the canons of the Church of the Holy Sepulcher, whose traditions famously posited that Jesus had been crucified on the very spot in which Adam's bones lay, thus establishing a meaningful trajectory from original sin to the redemption of mankind.[152]

The treatise proceeds with a detailed description of the Ḥaram to indicate the difficulty of reaching the patriarchal tombs below, thereby laying the foundation for the claim that the tombs could not have been found without the aid of a divine miracle.[153] Next follows a brief history of the sanctuary, specifying its maintenance by a Jewish priestly cast of Levites, who safeguarded the site until their persecution at the hands of the Roman emperors Titus and Vespasian (in that order). He dwells at some length on the horrors suffered by early Christians, who took up the protection of the Cave of the Patriarchs after the Jews had been driven away. Assisted by an ecumenical body of clergy of various confessions, the

149 Elm, "*Nec minori celebritate*," 338. Some (Kohler, "Un nouveau récit," 490–94, followed by Vincent et al., *Hébron*, 168) have suggested that the text may have been composed as a school exercise in variation and rhetorical embellishment based on the older account. Elm ("*Nec minori celebritate*," 335–38), on the other hand, viewed the differences in style, content (the dating of the events), and purpose as indicative of another source altogether and pointed to the abundant use of rhyme to suggest that this source may have been a rhythmical poem of the sort produced by Achard of Arrouaise and Geoffrey the Abbot.

150 *Tractatus de inventione* 28–38.

151 The quotation of Joshua 14:14–15 at *Tractatus de inventione* 39–40 conveniently omits the words "among the Enacims" from the sentence "Adam, the greatest among the Enacims, was laid there" (Douay-Rheims).

152 Zöller, *Regularkanoniker*, 342–44.

153 *Tractatus de inventione* 53–55.

Christians were united in their willingness to lay down their lives to protect the relics. In the contention that these Christians subsequently established bishops and archbishops in various Levantine cities, including Hebron, the importance of the Frankish institutional context emerges. Although the author had claimed at the beginning that he had been instructed by the canons to relate "how the bodies of the holy patriarchs Abraham, Isaac, and Jacob had been discovered," the aspirations of the clergy of Hebron to elevate their church to an episcopal see constituted a key motivation for the composition of this account.[154] According to the author, the renowned authorities of Jerome, Josephus, and Eusebius established Hebron's right to an episcopate. While a passage in Jerome's *Liber de situ et nominibus locorum Hebraicorum* (Book on the location and names of Hebrew places) has recently been identified that offers some support to the author's claim that Hebron was known in antiquity as a "metropolis of the Philistines" (*metropolis Philistinorum*), his unqualified statement is misleading at best.[155]

Puzzlingly, the author fails to mention a passage from the fifth-century Roman historian Socrates of Constantinople, set during the reign of Theodosius II, that would have supported the canons' position.[156] In the sixth century, Cassiodorus and Epiphanius Scholasticus translated selections of Socrates' *Historia ecclesiastica* and the histories of Sozomen and Theodoret from Greek into Latin, collating them into a single narrative; this history, known as the *Historia ecclesiastica tripartita* (Threefold history of the church), became quite popular throughout the Latin world. Socrates relates that when an unnamed bishop of Hebron (*episcopus Chebronensis*) died during a visit to Constantinople, Theodosius II sought to keep the holy man's rough cloak, "believing that he might acquire some of the deceased's holiness." Although this text was widely available in the Latin translation commissioned by Cassiodorus, the author of the *Tractatus de inventione* may simply have overlooked this minor notice.

Next is the account of the Greek monk in a lengthy digression on Emperor Theodosius II's fruitless efforts to uncover the tombs of the patriarchs. The author concludes this section by again naming the Greek monk from Sinai as his source, this time also mentioning that he was named John and adding a reference to a Syrian priest (or a priest named Sirus).[157] The author explains why it was necessary to include their account:

> To the truthfulness of these events, dearest brothers, which we recounted as having occurred during the reign of Emperor Theodosius, testified to

154 *Tractatus de inventione* 3–4.

155 Zöller, *Regularkanoniker*, 333; PL 23:862.

156 *Historia ecclesiastica tripartita*, 4:17.46–50.

157 *Tractatus de inventione* 234–36.

> us a certain John, monk of Mount Sinai, and a certain Syrian priest, who seemed to me pious men. These things we have included in this account, so that when you hear that the bones of the patriarchs, which could not be discovered by so many and such pious men—indeed, over the course of one hundred generations—were discovered by the Latins, you might clearly understand the extent of the benevolence that God, creator of all, has bestowed upon them, more than upon the other peoples, and also in order that those who claim that Hebron is not a metropolis may become sensible and repent. And if they do not wish to believe Eusebius of Caesarea, and Jerome, confessor of Christ, and Josephus, let them at least agree with what is found in Greek books, as I have written.[158]

The author's statement regarding his sources raises many questions about the way he acquired his information. Initially he appears to indicate an oral transaction with a Greek monk and a Syrian priest ("testified to us"), yet he subsequently refers to documents written in Greek ("Greek books"). Possibly the two may be the authors of the Greek books in question, which our Latin author consulted on his own. More likely, however, the anonymous author sought to indicate that Greek and Syrian monks testified about what they had learned from Greek books. The reference both to an oral interaction with Greek and Syrian experts and to their authoritative written sources would correspond to Cantor Ansellus's reference to conversations with the "elders of the Suriani" (*seniorum Surianorum*) and to consultation of the "writings of the Greeks and Syriacs" (*Graecorum et Syriacorum scripturis*).[159] The Greek texts referred to by our anonymous author remain a mystery, as does the monks' identity (assuming that they are distinct).

Eager to arrive at the avowed subject matter of his treatise—the *inventio* or discovery—the author briefly summarizes the centuries following Theodosius, when Hebron came under Muslim rule. In a remarkable resemblance to Achard of Arrouaise's praise of Muslim safeguarding of the Templum Domini, the author extends his argument of the institutional continuity of the church of Hebron across the centuries to include also the site's history as a place of Jewish and Muslim worship. Although the author describes the Muslims who conquered

158 *Tractatus de inventione* 236–43: *Hec, fratres karissimi, que sub Theodosio imperatore facta memoravimus, a quodam Iohanne montis Synai monacho et a quodam Siro sacerdote, religiosis ut videbantur viris, nobis sub veritate testificata sunt. Que ideo huic operi inseruimus, ut cum patriarcharum ossa, que a tantis et tam religiosis viris, immo a C iam transactis generationibus non potuerunt inveniri, a Latinis inventa esse audieritis, aperte intelligatis quantam benivolentiam creator omnium deus eis plus quam ceteris gentibus exibuerit, et insuper ut resipiscant et peniteant qui dicunt civitatem Ebron metropolim non esse. Qui si Eusebio Cesariensi et Christi confessori Ieronimo Iosephoque credere nolunt, his saltem, que in grecis voluminibus, ut scripsimus, continentur assentiant.*

159 See chap. 2.

Jerusalem and Hebron as barbarians (*barbari*), he claims that their priests (*sacerdotes*) took possession (*possederunt*) of the Templum Domini in Jerusalem and of the city of Hebron, presumably to suggest that the dignity of these sacred sites was respected and maintained inviolate by the Muslims. Explaining that a local Jewish community was appointed custodian of the site by the new Muslim regime and permitted to build a synagogue, the author emphasizes the veneration and respect accorded by Muslims, "even though they were infidels" (*gens illa, licet infidelis*), who entered the sanctuary barefoot and with washed feet, and constructed a place of prayer (*oratorium*) "with miraculous workmanship, which they decorated with gold, silver, and silk cloth."[160] Just like Achard, the author of the *Tractatus de inventione* contrasts Muslim veneration of the site with its spoliation by the Crusaders, singling out an unnamed archbishop of Apamea (who can be identified as Peter of Narbonne). The section ends with a note on the foundation of the convent of Augustinian canons at Hebron in 1112.

The remainder of the treatise contains a vivid description of the discovery of the tombs. One afternoon in the summer of 1119, one of the canons (a scribe, the author specifies) was resting near the cenotaph of Isaac when he felt a cool breeze coming from below. Noticing an aperture, he proceeded to measure the depth by lowering a piece of lead attached to a string. After obtaining permission from Baldwin, lord of Hebron, and the assent of the entire community of canons—the author carefully specifies—excavations of the site began.

When the canons finally succeeded in penetrating to the lower caverns and found the tombs, the prior immediately departed to Jerusalem to ask the patriarch—for the church of Hebron was under his authority—to bring the bones up to the surface where they could be labeled and displayed for veneration (in other words, a *translatio*). When Patriarch Warmund reneged on his promise to attend the festive occasion, the canons proceeded without him. Two years passed, during which unnamed individuals urged Warmund to prevail upon the canons of Hebron to return the relics to their original resting place. They did, and there, we are told, the relics are still venerated to this day.

While the author's identity remains unknown, the text may provide some clues. First, the author was absent from the events he describes, given his reliance on the accounts of others. Further evidence indicates that the author probably did not belong to the chapter of the canons of the church of Hebron. He exclusively refers to the canons with pronouns of the second person plural rather than the inclusive first person, while using demonstratives suggesting distance rather than proximity, speaking of "there" and "that place" rather than "here."[161] In a

160 *Tractatus de inventione* 251–66.

161 *Tractatus de inventione* 1–2: *fratres karissimi qui Cariatarbe estis*. For possessive pronouns in the second person plural, see, e.g., *Tractatus de inventione* 1–2 and 7. For demonstratives denoting

particularly revealing passage at the start of the treatise, the author states that "*our* Redeemer . . . deigned to reveal to *you* the bodies of the saints" (emphasis added).[162] On the other hand, the author must have maintained a close connection with the canons of Hebron, given that he was able to interview the two main witnesses, Arnulf and Odo, in person and that the chapter entrusted him with his task. He may have been a regular canon himself, since he addresses the canons of Hebron consistently as "brothers" (*fratres*) and displays detailed knowledge of the customs of regular canons.[163] It may be significant that, when describing the Muslim occupation of Jerusalem, the only sacred site mentioned by the author is the Templum Domini, possibly indicating an association with it.[164]

Whatever his identity, the author was a highly competent writer who grasped the institutional concerns of the canons of Hebron. He utilized the persuasive potential of the *inventio* genre to provide a scriptural and theological basis on which the community could claim its place among the pilgrim destinations. He argues that the discovery of the tombs of the patriarchs signified God's election of the resident Latin Christians above all others who had attempted to find the relics before them and failed.

The author's use of source materials betrays a great deal of sophistication. If we take him at his word, he consulted both a Greek monk and a Syrian priest in composing his account, expertly weaving their narrative into the structure of his text. Given the identification of the Greek John as a "monk of Mount Sinai," it seems probable that he (and possibly the unnamed Syrian priest) belonged to the monastic community of the Orthodox monastery of Saint Catherine on Mount Sinai. Founded in the mid-sixth century by the Roman emperor Justinian, the monastery of Saint Catherine is the oldest continuously run monastic institution.[165] Although it was an Orthodox community, the monastery enjoyed good relations with the Latins. There was a Latin community of monks at the monastery during the twelfth century, and by the early thirteenth century the monastery owned possessions in Jerusalem, Jaffa, Acre, Laodicea, and Antioch, among others.[166] The author may have interacted with the Greek monk and Syrian priest at the

---

distance, see, e.g., *Tractatus de inventione* 44–45: *Non inconvenienter ergo veteres locum illum Cariatarbe . . . appellare voluerunt.*

162 *Tractatus de inventione* 20–21: *Redemptoris nostri . . . qui sanctorum corpora vobis revelare dignatus est.*

163 See especially *Tractatus de inventione* 282–83: *sicut mos est Regularium canonicis post meridiem in lectulis suis quiescentibus.*

164 *Tractatus de inventione* 251–53: *Irrumpentes igitur barbari obtinuerunt totam regionem illam et Ierusalem civitatem quam elegit dominus, sacerdotes quoque eorum possederunt Templum Domini, quod erat in ea, et civitatem Ebron.*

165 For an overview of the monastery of Saint Catherine of Sinai during the twelfth and thirteenth centuries, see Lafontaine-Dosogne, "Le monastère du Sinaï."

166 Pringle, *Churches*, 2:52.

monastery or perhaps in one of its churches in Jerusalem or Acre. Alternatively, he may have encountered them in Hebron when they visited the sanctuary. While the specifics remain elusive, the *inventio* account offers an intriguing glimpse into intellectual interactions between Latins and the Orthodox monks of Mount Sinai. Though few, the details of this embedded story, including the names and affiliation of the informants, render it unlikely that the narrative was entirely the author's invention. At the same time, the way the story is told shows heavy editorialization to reflect a Latin perspective. The author may therefore have reworked a local legend, as recounted to him by the Greek monk and Syrian priest, for the canons to promote their relatively young institution.

Like the poems of the Templum Domini, the *inventio* account also sought to enhance the prestige of their site by associating it with a history of Christian martyrdom and simultaneously issued a warning to the local secular ruler not to interfere with the sacred site. The author does so in recounting the story of the Roman emperor Theodosius II's failed attempts to remove the relics of the patriarchs from their resting place and transfer them to Constantinople. The men he had sent to Hebron were first struck with blindness and then, as they touched the sanctuary's walls and tried to feel their way in, stuck to the wall and could only retreat. Despite Theodosius's piety, there is a kind of poetic retribution for the persecutions staged by previous emperors, described by the author as "his wicked predecessor emperors" (*iniqui predecessores sui imperatores*).[167] In addition to housing the venerable relics, the church now becomes the site of Christian martyrdom—a similar strategy to the one Achard had employed in promoting the Templum Domini as the site of the martyrdom of James the Less.

The history of Emperor Theodosius II as presented in the *inventio* can be read as a parable and as a way for the canons of Hebron to express implicit criticism of outside intervention seeking to remove the relics of the patriarchs from their resting place. A further *translatio* from the church of Hebron to Jerusalem would have resulted in a loss of status as well as income for the canons, who would have become less likely to benefit from the revenue generated by pilgrimage. Moreover, as the *inventio* account indicates, the canons of Hebron mistrusted the involvement of Baldwin, lord of Hebron, in the excavations of the newly discovered relics, having experienced only a few years earlier a pillaging at the hands of Peter of Narbonne, bishop of Albara and later archbishop of Apamea. The remarkable failure even of a celebrated Christian emperor to remove the patriarchal relics should be read within this context.[168]

167 *Tractatus de inventione* 110–11. On this aspect, see Elm, "*Nec minori celebritate*," 324.

168 At *Tractatus de inventione* 365–68, the canon Arnulf fears that Baldwin might think that there is plunder in the form of gold or silver to be had in the Cave of the Patriarchs. On the plundering of the Ḥaram al-Ḳalīl under the Franks, see *Tractatus de inventione* 264–65. One may

The increased profile of a major pilgrim destination brought distinct material advantages, and rather than hand the patriarchal relics over to the patriarch in Jerusalem or to the secular lord of Hebron, the canons made the case that, like Bethlehem and Nazareth, the dignity of their sanctuary warranted elevation to an episcopal see. Unsurprisingly, Patriarch Warmund was not keen to acquiesce to a loss of considerable revenue.[169]

As W. Zöller has suggested, we may tentatively assign the composition of the *Tractatus de inventione* to 1128–1131, the period immediately following the death of Warmund, by combining archaeological and textual evidence.[170] The *Tractatus de inventione* may have formed part of a broader effort by the canons to promote the church of Hebron, which included redesigning the eleventh-century mosque they occupied into a basilica. A remark by the pilgrim al-Harawī seems to indicate that the lower caverns were renovated with the support of King Baldwin II, an effort possibly accompanying the construction project of the basilica above.[171] More persuasive evidence is the inclusion of the Feast of the Patriarchs commemorating the *inventio* on 6 October in the liturgical calendars of two sacramentaries composed in the scriptorium of the Church of the Holy Sepulcher in the period 1128–32. Although the feast does not yet have a proper office and appears instead as a special mass, the early inclusion of the feast may indicate a partial acceptance of the canons' narrative as outlined in the *Tractatus de inventione*.[172] Alternatively, it could point to an effort on the part of the Church of the Holy Sepulcher to appropriate the feast.

Regardless, the commission of a treatise detailing the discovery of the patriarchal relics would neatly parallel contemporaneous construction efforts and result in the early creation of a commemorative feast at the church of Hebron. Like the poems of the Templum Domini, the *Tractatus de inventione* may have formed part of a liturgical celebration there, as suggested by the reference within the text to the canons "singing with ringing voices and chanting [the hymn] *Te deum laudamus*" (*vocibus altisonis modulantibus et Te deum laudamus decantantibus*) as the relics were brought up from the caverns and transferred to the church.[173]

Strikingly, despite the canons' efforts in promoting the enhanced status of their church and the partial success they may have enjoyed in the liturgical traditions of the Church of the Holy Sepulcher, they did not achieve their stated goal

---

compare this situation with Tancred's plundering of the Dome of the Rock, resulting in similar reactions from the canons who took residence there.

169 For the relations between Warmund and Hebron, see Kirstein, *Die lateinischen Patriarchen*, 215–18.

170 Zöller, *Regularkanoniker*, 349–50.

171 Harawī, *Kitāb al-Ishārāt* 83.

172 Dondi, *Liturgy of the Canons*, 61–63; Zöller, *Regularkanoniker*, 351–52.

173 *Tractatus de inventione* 404–5.

for elevation to a bishopric until 1167—some thirty-seven years after the likely composition of the *Tractatus de inventione*, by which point most of the canons involved in commissioning the treatise would have passed away. Possibly, the canons' literary strategy to claim their church also as the burial site of Adam backfired, causing such affront to the canons of the Church of the Holy Sepulcher that it took several more decades for the canons of Hebron to meet with success. Ultimately, however, the canons' bid proved successful, for William of Tyre references precisely their association with the relics of the patriarchs (though not of Adam!) as the reason for the church's elevation in 1167.[174]

Conclusion

The twelfth-century Latin East teemed with communities of canons, monks, nuns, and even entirely new orders that defied previous conceptions of spirituality, such as the Knights Templar. These groups jockeyed for prominence in an increasingly complex and populated religious landscape. We have observed how, in their own ways, the canons of the Templum Domini and the church of Hebron successfully employed Latin literature to promote their respective institutions.

The canons of the Templum Domini possessed no relics, and there existed only a tenuous link between their site and the biblical tradition. Prior Achard devised a creative solution to this quandary by composing a gift for the most powerful individual in the Latin East: a poem addressed to the king of Jerusalem in a language associated with intellectual sophistication as well as ecclesiastical authority. In making his case for the return of the treasures looted from the Dome of the Rock, Achard at once formulated a moral guide for the king based on biblical models and articulated an institutional history that posited a historical continuity with the previous Jewish temples on the site. His successor Geoffrey seized on this strategy and expanded Achard's project to establish the Templum Domini as the spiritual center of Jerusalem—and, implicitly, of salvation history.

The canons of Hebron, on the other hand, resorted to more conventional methods to promote their community by associating it with relics. While their sanctuary, too, had been pillaged by the Crusaders, the fortuitous discovery of the subterranean chambers afforded the canons an opportunity to attract pilgrims and, eventually, to elevate their church to a prestigious metropolitan see. As part of this promotional effort, they commissioned a gifted writer to draw up a compelling Latin narrative that constructed the history of the site from the time of the

174 WT 20.3.12–14: *Ebronensis* [sc. *ecclesia*] *quoque intuitu servorum dei, quorum memoria in benedictione est, Abraham videlicet, Ysaac et Iacob, eadem tunc primum dignitate* [sc. *cathedrali prerogativa*] *meruit insigniri.*

patriarchs Abraham, Isaac, and Jacob to the miraculous discovery of the tombs by the canons, and even went so far as to lay claim to housing the remains of Adam.

Despite differences in genre and in the formal characteristics of the texts produced by each community, the canons employed remarkably similar rhetorical strategies in making their case. Both communities crafted complicated arguments in which they posited an unbroken historical continuity, as attested by local Jewish, Greek, and Syriac traditions, while promoting the notion that Latin Christians were divinely elected and superior to other, non-Latin traditions. In the previous chapter, we likewise observed the explicit invocation of Greek and Syriac authorities by the cantor Ansellus to authenticate relics as well as Fulcher of Chartres's unacknowledged use of Jewish traditions on the sacred objects of the Temple. A new phenomenon here is the promotion by the canons of the Templum Domini and the church of Hebron of the history of their institutions as Muslim sanctuaries. Both communities argued that the Muslim institutions that predated their own provided a legitimate basis for continued material, political, and spiritual capital, while berating the Crusaders for looting the treasures bestowed upon their sites by Muslims. One further shared rhetorical element between these communities of canons is their willingness to promote their own institutions at the cost of the Church of the Holy Sepulcher. Both communities were willing to challenge the centrality of the Church of the Holy Sepulcher—not merely within the sacred topography of the Holy Land, but even within the Christian salvation narrative.

Ultimately, both communities of canons grasped the potential of literature for achieving their objectives and for contributing to the continued survival of their communities. A successful institution required a good story, a memorable narrative that helped pilgrims, secular officials, and ecclesiastical functionaries to bridge the centuries and bring a twelfth-century sanctuary into connection with a perceived biblical past. Such a connection, in turn, enabled institutions to persuade others to donate land, goods, and funds, and to make their case for a degree of financial and political independence. Both communities accomplished this feat by crafting artful yet accessible Latin narratives that incorporated biblical episodes.

As was the case with Fulcher of Chartres's literary afterlife, the subsequent fate of the works of these communities of canons differed substantially between the Latin West and East. The poems from the Templum Domini and the *Tractatus de inventione* saw only a limited circulation in Europe and do not appear to have exerted any influence on subsequent historiographical or spiritual traditions in western Europe. In the Latin East, the narratives of the canons of the Templum Domini and of the church of Hebron proved more influential, as witnessed by the reemergence of elements of the poems of Achard of Arrouaise and Geoffrey the Abbot in pilgrim guides and in the chronicle of William of Tyre later in the twelfth century. In treating the history of Jerusalem under Muslim rule, William relied on a history written in Arabic by a Melkite Christian, but he deviated from this source to introduce details first encountered in Achard of Arrouaise's poem. William refers to the site of the later al-Aqṣā Mosque as the "Temple" destroyed by Titus and touted the resources and possessions accorded by Muslims to maintain the sanctuary.[175] In relating the church of Hebron's elevation to a bishopric in 1167, William similarly reflected the argument made by the canons in referring to the tombs of the patriarchs. Whether this constituted the sole reason for Hebron's elevation is in doubt; it is likely that military considerations also played a role, as an episcopal see would have been expected to make contributions to the defense of the realm.[176]

Of the astounding number of new religious communities in the twelfth-century Latin East, the regular canons of the Templum Domini and the church of Hebron proved to be exceptionally successful in elevating their status from humble, virtually unknown collectives of canons to powerful institutions of the Frankish realm. In the Latin works they left behind, we observe the tantalizingly limited traces of what must have been a dynamic and lively literary scene, in which Latin literature functioned as both a legitimate and legitimizing method of self-representation.

175 WT 1.2.30–52; see the discussion of this passage in chap. 5.
176 Hamilton, *Latin Church*, 77.

Chapter Four

LEARNED LATINITY AND LATIN ORTHODOXY IN THE PRINCIPALITY OF ANTIOCH

THE FIRST MAJOR LEVANTINE CITY CONQUERED during the First Crusade—and arguably the most strategically important—was the city of Antioch. Situated on the Orontes River near the Mediterranean coast and flanked by the Amanus Mountains, the city governed both the overland and coastal routes between the Levant and the Anatolian plateau. To the north, Antioch controlled the Belen Pass through the mountains to the Cilician plain and the cities Mamistra, Adana, and Tarsus. To the southwest, the city had coastal access via the nearby port of Saint Simeon, but more important was the port city of Laodicea further south, situated within striking distance of Byzantine Cyprus.

In addition to its strategic significance, the ancient city held a venerable position in Christendom as the site of the first missionary activities of both Peter and Paul and the place where Christianity's adherents first received the name "Christian." In the early centuries of Christianity, Antioch was home to several renowned church fathers, including Ignatius of Antioch, Severus of Antioch, Theophilus of Antioch, and later John Chrysostom and Theodore of Mopsuestia. Antioch's symbolic significance as the cradle of the Christian church attracted a plethora of Christian communities, including West and East Syrian Christians, Armenians, Georgians, and, above all, Greek and Arabic-speaking Orthodox Christians, or Melkites.

When the Crusaders conquered Antioch, they encountered a flourishing and diverse intellectual culture that had maintained a far greater degree of continuity than Jerusalem. This chapter examines how Latins shaped a learned literary culture within this unique environment. Under the influence of and in response to this intellectual milieu, Latin writers in Antioch embarked on ambitious projects that ranged from historiography to medicine, cosmology, exegesis, and religious polemic and doctrinal debate. While the six Latin authors and works under discussion in this chapter addressed different audiences and operated in various forms and genres, a literary and rhetorical analysis of their works exposes common characteristics that reveal the emergence of a Latin literary tradition within Antioch, yet one that was closely connected to other literary communities of the Latin East.

Antioch before and after the First Crusade

Following the Byzantine reconquest of Antioch from the Hamdanids in 969, the ancient city blossomed into an intellectual center. Spurred by the immigration of Christians fleeing the increasingly oppressive Fatimid regime in northern Africa, Antioch enjoyed a flourishing period of scholarly activity, the full extent of which has only recently begun to receive recognition.[1] During the centuries of Muslim rule, the Christian communities of Antioch had adopted Arabic modes of expression that they continued to employ when the city reverted to Greek-speaking Byzantine governance.[2] Antiochene Arabic-speaking Christians subsequently embarked on an expansive program to translate Greek texts into Arabic from the late tenth century onward, drawing comparisons to the more famous ninth-century translation movement in Baghdad.[3]

Prominent Melkites such as Ibrāhīm ibn Yūḥannā al-Anṭākī (d. 1025), ʿAbdallāh ibn al-Faḍl (eleventh century), Abū l-Farağ Yaḥyā ibn Saʿīd ibn Yaḥyā (eleventh century), and Antony, abbot of the monastery of Saint Simeon the Younger (first half of the eleventh century), translated patristic and philosophical works from Greek into Arabic. They also composed original theological works and polemics against Islam.[4] In the same period, Symeon Seth (d. ca. 1112), who appears to have had Antiochene origins, composed Greek treatises on dietetics, natural philosophy, and astronomy, and translated the celebrated Indian collection

1 Noble and Treiger, "Christian Arabic Theology"; Treiger, "ʿAbdallāh ibn al-Faḍl al-Anṭākī" and "Graeco-Syro-Arabic Melkite Translation"; Roberts, *Reason and Revelation*. Antioch's cultural renaissance during the tenth and eleventh centuries is the subject of several recent and ongoing dissertations: Tokay, "Continuity and Transformation"; Mugler, "Martyr with Too Many Causes"; J. Glynias (Princeton University, ongoing). For Christian displacement by the Fatimids as a contributing factor to Antioch's revival, see Brett, "Badr al-Ǧamali."

2 For Eastern Christian literature in Antioch generally, see Baumstark, *Geschichte der syrischen Literatur*; Graf, *Geschichte der christlichen arabischen Literatur*, vol. 2; and Edgington, "Antioch: Medieval City of Culture."

3 Treiger, "Greek into Arabic."

4 Ibrāhīm ibn Yūḥannā al-Anṭākī translated Greek patristic works, including those by Pseudo-Dionysius, Ephrem, Gregory Nazianzen, and John Chrysostom. He also wrote *Life of Christopher*, a hagiography of a patriarch of Antioch who was martyred by the Hamdanids. See Lamoreaux, "Ibrāhīm ibn Yūḥannā al-Anṭākī"; Swanson, "Arabic Hagiography," 356; and Mugler, "Ibrāhīm ibn Yūḥannā." ʿAbdallāh ibn al-Faḍl was a prolific translator of Greek patristic and philosophical works: Treiger, "ʿAbdallāh ibn al-Faḍl al-Antākī." Abū l-Farağ Yaḥyā ibn Saʿīd ibn Yaḥyā was a Melkite physician whose writings include both religious apology and polemic: Swanson, "Abū l-Faraj Yaḥyā ibn Saʿīd ibn Yaḥyā." Antony of Saint Simeon the Younger translated the works of John of Damascus against Nestorians as well as works of John Chrysostom; see Ibrahim, "Some Notes on Antonios" and "Jean Chrysostome arabe."

of animal fables *Kalīla wa-Dimna* into Greek from an Arabic version. He had a successful career that took him to the upper echelons of the Byzantine court, and he is credited as an astrologer (*mathematikos*) by Anna Komnene.[5] Antioch was, moreover, home to thriving West Syrian, East Syrian, Georgian, Armenian, and Maronite populations, whose scholarly activities closely intertwined with those of the Melkites. For example, the famed physician Ibn Buṭlān (d. 1066), an East Syrian Christian who settled in Antioch toward the end of his life, wrote the immensely influential *Taqwīm al-Siḥḥa* (Almanac of health), later transmitted in the West as *Tacuinum sanitatis in medicina* (The *Tacuinum* of medical healthcare); his Melkite student Yūḥannā al-Anṭākī, in turn, wrote a theological tract on the Trinity.[6]

Byzantine control of the region declined with their defeat at the Battle of Manzikert in 1071. In 1085 Antioch once again came under Muslim rule, this time as the subject of the Seljuk sultanate of Rūm. The Seljuk occupation was of short duration: just thirteen years later, in June 1098, the city was conquered by the Crusaders on their way to Jerusalem. According to William of Tyre, while the period of Seljuk rule had proved oppressive to the Christian population, who had been permitted only to practice trade and crafts, it did little to reduce their numbers.[7] Given the predominantly Christian character of the Antiochene populace, it is hardly surprising that support for Yaghi-Siyan, the Muslim governor of Antioch at the time of the Crusade, was minimal. As William of Tyre later wrote, Yaghi-Siyan harbored such mistrust of the local populace during the Crusader siege of Antioch that he instituted a strict curfew and ordered the disarmament of all Christians residing in the city.[8]

However, initially positive relations between Antioch's Eastern Christian population and its Latin Christian conquerors quickly gave way to religious and political tension. A passage in a letter purporting to have been written by the leaders of the Crusade to the pope three months after the city's capture assumes a remarkably hostile tone toward Eastern Christians in Antioch. The leaders invite the pope to join the Crusade in Antioch, proclaiming that, while they had successfully defeated "Turks and pagans" (*Turcos et paganos*), only the pope could defeat the "Greek, Armenian, Syrian, and Jacobite heretics" (*haereticos... Graecos et Armenos, Syros Iacobitasque*).[9] As R. Hiestand has argued, this openly polemical passage may not have reflected the sentiment of all the leaders, but may instead have

5 For Symeon Seth, see Magdalino, "Porphyrogenita and the Astrologers," 19–21. For his scientific works, see Bouras-Vallianatos, "Galen's Reception in Byzantium." For Anna Komnene's reference, see *Alexiad* 6.7.

6 Swanson, "Yūḥannā al-Anṭākī."

7 WT 5.11.17–21. The predominance of the Christian population in Antioch in this period is supported in modern scholarship; see Korobeinikov, "Orthodox Communities."

8 WT 5.19.

9 *Epistulae et chartae*, no. XVI, 161–65 (Barber and Bate, *Letters from the East*, no. 8, 30–33).

been added later by the Norman leader Bohemond of Taranto, who quickly established himself as ruler over a new princedom of Antioch.[10] In doing so, Bohemond violated the oath he and some of the other leaders had sworn to the Byzantine emperor to return to the Byzantines any conquered lands that had previously belonged to their empire.[11] On other occasions, too, Bohemond did not eschew employing religious arguments to portray Eastern Christians as dangerous and untrustworthy in his quest for territory and political influence. Shortly after the Crusader conquest of Antioch, Bohemond persuaded the newly arrived papal legate to assist him in his siege of the Byzantine-held port city of Laodicea by portraying its Eastern Christian population as "false Christians" (*falsos Christianos*) who aided Turks and Saracens in attacking Christian pilgrims.[12] The following summer, Bohemond further escalated tensions by ousting the Greek Orthodox patriarch of Antioch, John IV, and replacing him with the Latin Christian Bernard of Valence.[13] Yet despite the tumultuous early history under Latin rule, the city maintained its unique cultural character and provided a fertile environment for a distinctively Antiochene tradition of Latin literature in the following decades.

Classroom Learning on Display: Ralph of Caen and Stephen the Philosopher

At first glance, Ralph of Caen and Stephen the Philosopher have little in common. One hailed from Normandy and wrote belletristic prose and poetry, the other came from Pisa and engaged mainly in scientific pursuits. By juxtaposing these two authors from Antioch, however, an important shared characteristic emerges: both employed emphatic displays of a specific type of learning rooted in a Latin school tradition. This Latin "classroom learning" connected them to a broader world of Latin erudition far beyond Antioch's city walls, and it also provides evidence for early attempts to establish a Latin tradition of learning within Antioch.

Ralph of Caen came to the Levant several years after the First Crusade. In May 1106 he joined the expedition of Bohemond of Taranto, who passed by Rouen to solicit aid for his campaign against the Byzantines. After the unsuccessful siege of Durazzo in 1107–8, Ralph continued on to Antioch, where he entered the circle of

10 Hiestand ("Boemondo I e la prima Crociata") argued that this passage was added later and reflects Bohemond's anti-Byzantine attitude in 1105–7. For the passage as an authentic reflection of broader Latin mistrust of non-Latin Christians, see García-Guijarro, "Some Considerations."

11 For the establishment of the Principality of Antioch, see Asbridge, *Creation of the Principality*, and the classic study of Cahen, *Syrie du nord*.

12 AA 6.57.

13 For the conflicts between the Latin and Byzantine Orthodox churches in Antioch, see Hamilton, *Latin Church*, 158–87; Asbridge, *Creation of the Principality*, 195–213; and Buck, *Principality of Antioch*, 189–217.

Tancred of Hauteville, Bohemond's nephew and new ruler of Antioch.[14] There he conceived of a literary work celebrating the deeds of both Tancred and Bohemond in mannerist prose and verse. Simply titled *Tancredus*, the focus of this prosimetrum falls squarely on the younger of the two Norman leaders, although Ralph frequently emphasizes Tancred's relation to Bohemond and to the renowned Norman conqueror Robert Guiscard. *Tancredus* is thus rightly considered a Norman cultural expression that forms part of a longer Norman tradition of prosimetric encomium, inaugurated by Dudo of Saint Quentin in the tenth century.[15]

An aspect of his work that has received less attention is the sheer amount of rhetorical skill and literary learning with which Ralph infused the *Tancredus*.[16] His writing abounds with aphoristic language, witty juxtapositions of words and phrases, and a variety of rhetorical figures, with particular fondness for metaphor, *figura etymologica*, paronomasia, asyndeton, alliteration, polyptoton, and hyperbaton. Unlike Fulcher's chronicle, rousing rhetorical speeches of the protagonists figure prominently in *Tancredus*.[17] Ralph's sentences and verses brim with quotations, paraphrases, and skillful allusions to various biblical and, especially, classical texts. As a result, *Tancredus* often resembles a patchwork of classical phrases and (half-)quotes, drawn from such mainstays of the twelfth-century school curriculum as Cicero, Sallust, Horace, Ovid, Lucan, Prudentius, and, above all, Virgil.[18]

Ralph parades his classroom learning in a prefatory letter in which he dedicates *Tancredus* to his former schoolteacher Arnulf of Chocques, who had by then ascended to the post of Latin patriarch of Jerusalem.[19] Ralph had studied under Arnulf at the abbey of Saint-Étienne in Caen in Normandy, an important center of intellectual activity in the eleventh and first half of the twelfth century. Saint-Étienne boasted William the Conqueror as its founder in 1059 and had hosted such renowned scholars as Lanfranc of Bec in 1063, William Bona Anima (who had become a monk at Caen after returning from a pilgrimage to the Holy Land) in 1070, and Theobald of Étampes (one of the founders of the school of Oxford)

14 Asbridge (*Creation of the Principality*, 134–43) has convincingly challenged the simplistic traditional narrative that Tancred ruled as Bohemond's regent, citing as evidence that he styled himself as a full-fledged prince.

15 Cantarella, "La frontiera della crociata," 225–46; Albu Hanawalt, *Normans in Their Histories*; Russo, "Tancredi e i Bizantini"; d'Angelo in RC xlvi–lxiii.

16 For earlier work on Ralph's style and use of the classics, see the brief discussions of Manitius, *Geschichte der lateinischen Literatur*, 3:422–24; De Ghellinck, *L'essor*, 118–19; Glaesener, "Raoul de Caen"; Boehm, "Die *Gesta Tancredi*"; Manselli, *Italia e Italiani*, 139; Elm, "'*O beatas idus*,'" 168–69; and, most important, d'Angelo in RC lxv–lxxxii.

17 For the longer speeches, see RC 314–41, 386–426, 559–76, 607–28, 1205–81, 1973–2010, 2878–909, 2943–64, 3051–75, 3227–42, 3797–871, 3873–932, 4347–62, 4363–86.

18 RC lxxvii–lxxix.

19 RC prol. 58–64.

in 1089.[20] While Arnulf was a divisive figure in Jerusalemite church politics, he possessed a respectable reputation as a scholar.[21] In a letter to another of Arnulf's students, Anselm of Canterbury remarked upon Arnulf's wide-ranging knowledge of classical literature, with particular reference to Virgil.[22] Guibert of Nogent similarly commented on Arnulf's knowledge of dialectic (i.e., logic) and especially grammar as qualifications for undertaking the tutelage of Cecilia, daughter of William the Conqueror and sister of Robert Curthose.[23]

With his dedication to Arnulf, Ralph transplants, as it were, a Latin classroom from Normandy to the Latin East. Ralph addresses Arnulf as a teacher (*doctorem*) and as a "most learned patriarch" (*patriarcha doctissime*), "not lacking in [expertise in] any liberal art" (*nullius . . . liberalis scientiae . . . exortem*). Ralph indulges in an obligatory cliché by asking Arnulf to correct the work as he sees fit—a commonplace that also appears in Fulcher's history as a request to the general reader for rhetorical embellishment—but Ralph adds a personal touch:[24] "Your correction—whatever it is—will be especially sweet to me, now that I am a young man, since in you, now that you are an old man, I will have obtained as a corrector the same person that I had as a teacher (*preceptorem*), when you were a young man and I was but a boy."[25] The learned and highly allusive *Tancredus* contains valuable evidence for the ways in which Latin schooling structured the thought of a medieval writer and attests to a coterie of similarly trained individuals. As E. R. Curtius has examined in detail, the shared use of classical texts and rhetorical conventions enabled an educational elite to form part of a Latin commonwealth, a world connected by a shared linguistic expression and literary language.[26]

20 On the school of Caen, see Foreville, "L'école de Caen"; RC lxxxii–lxxxv.

21 Arnulf acquired the epithet *mala corona* (wicked crown): see *GF* 8.20, 45–46; PT 85; and WT 11.15.2. For Arnulf of Chocques as patriarch, see Foreville, "Un chef de la première croisade," and Kirstein, *Die lateinischen Patriarchen*, 91–128. For Arnulf as teacher of Ralph of Caen, see Foreville, "L'école de Caen," 83–91; Boehm, "Die *Gesta Tancredi*," 49–51; Spear, "School of Caen Revisited"; Manselli, *Italia e Italiani*, 140; Murray, *Crusader Kingdom*, 182–83; Hodgson, "Reinventing Normans," 117; and RC lxxxii.

22 Anselm of Canterbury, *Opera*, *epistola* 64, 3:180: *audivi quod legas a domno Arnulfo . . . audivi quoque quod ipse multum valeat in declinatione . . . et volo quatenus ut fiat, quantum potes satagas, et praecipue de Virgilio et aliis auctoribus quos a me non legisti, exceptis his in quibus aliqua turpitudo sonat.*

23 Guibert of Nogent, *Dei gesta per Francos* 7.637–41: *Erat ibi tunc temporis quidam sub censura clericali agens, sub quo autem gradu nescio, qui vocaretur Arnulfus. Is, in dialecticae eruditione non hebes, cum minime haberetur ad grammaticae documenta rudis, regis Anglorum filiam monacham ea quam premisimus diu disciplina docuerat.* It is possible to view Guibert's words as disparaging Arnulf by emphasizing his position as a woman's tutor (see Hodgson, "Reinventing Normans," 64).

24 FC 2.34.1–2.

25 RC prol. 61–64.

26 Curtius, *Europäische Literatur*.

We can see this Latin school tradition clearly at work in *Tancredus*. Take, for example, the very opening of the prologue:

> We ought to strive with every effort (*summa ope niti*) to read what has been written and to write what deserves to be read in order that, by reading ancient writings and by writing new ones, antiquity may satisfy us in our need, while we, having been satisfied, nourish posterity in its need.[27]

In his opening exhortation both to read ancient works and to produce new classics, Ralph aptly alludes to the beginning of Sallust's *Bellum Catilinae* (War of Catiline), where the Roman author claims that the human effort (*summa ope niti*) to leave behind a written legacy is what separates us from cattle (*pecora*).[28] Ralph's very call to read and produce classics thus evokes the famous opening of a standard work in the Latin curriculum. A few sentences later, Ralph artfully moves from Sallust to Virgil's description of drone bees by placing in the mouths of his former patrons Bohemond and Tancred a lament over the state of modern literature compared to antiquity:

> How sloth ruins the modern generation, while for the ancient poets the greatest pleasure lay in composition! The ancient poets spoke only of fictional fables, but poets today ignore the victories of Christ's knights: idle cattle, to be compared to drones![29]

The link between the two passages is the Latin word for cattle, *pecus* (plural, *pecora*), first evoked by quoting Sallust, then quoted from a passage of Virgil, who applied it unusually to describe bees.[30] Note how Ralph draws attention to the unfamiliar sense of *pecus* here with the word *astruendi* (to be compared to, to be construed as) in a phrase that would not have been out of place as a teacher's gloss to the Virgilian passages.

Ralph's hyper-learned playfulness is not confined to the prologue but pervades the narrative of *Tancredus* as well. He depicts as follows the reaction of the

27 RC prol. 1.6–9: *Debemus igitur summa ope niti et legere scripta et scribere legenda, quatinus, legendo vetera, scriptitando nova, hinc nos antiquitas egentes saciet, inde posteritatem saciati nutriamus egentem.*

28 Sallust, *Bellum Catilinae* 1: *Omnis homines, qui sese student praestare ceteris animalibus, summa ope niti decet, ne vitam silentio transeant veluti pecora, quae natura prona atque ventri oboedientia finxit.*

29 RC prol. 22–23: *Quonam modernos segnicies perdit, cum priscis summa vatibus fuerit scribere voluptas! Et illi quidem adinventiones fabulosas ordiuntur, miliciae Christi victorias tacent hodierni: ignavum equidem pecus, et fucis astruendi!*

30 Virgil, *Georgics* 4.168; *Aeneid* 1.435.

Byzantine emperor Alexios Komnenos upon learning of the arrival of the feared Norman leader Bohemond:

> Struck by these rumors, the wily emperor "turns over in his mind new deceptions and new schemes," seeking to trap in his net the lions he does not dare to challenge with a hunting spear. So he furnishes his messengers with snares, [instructing them to] meet Bohemond upon his arrival with the following blandishments.[31]

Ralph's portrayal of Alexios plays into Greek stereotypes of effeminacy and deceitfulness by drawing on Virgil's description of Venus, who sought to trick Dido into falling for Aeneas.[32] Upon closer examination, we can see that Ralph has in fact combined two anti-Greek allusions in this passage, since the phrase *dolos versare* (to turn over deceptions) occurs in Virgil's description of the Greek arch-deceiver Sinon in book 2 of the *Aeneid*.[33] Ever showing himself the diligent student, Ralph may also have picked up on the related word *versutus* (wily), which he applies to Alexios, from Servius's late antique school commentary on this very passage.[34]

Here, as elsewhere, Ralph demonstrates an affinity for the medieval discipline of *grammatica*. This branch of Latin learning involved not only the rules of correct grammatical usage but extended to the careful reading and exposition of authoritative texts, including classical, biblical, and patristic works.[35] One final example suffices to show the extent to which Ralph integrated into his narrative the classroom reading of authoritative *exempla* (exemplary texts/passages) as taught by the *grammaticus*. When a messenger sent by Alexios Komnenos seeks to compel Bohemond and Tancred to return to his court, they ignore his pleas since, according to Ralph, they have learned the proper lessons from classical and biblical literature:

> The call to return made by him in his absence is neglected, whose person was despised in his presence; intending to go to the manger of the highest king, they do not listen to the betrayal of Herod calling them back. With their hands pressed down on the plough, they do not turn their eyes back, having learned how ruinous a single glance backward can be;

31 RC 256–61: *His versutus imperator percussus rumoribus, novos corde dolos "nova pectore versat consilia," retibus studet leones implicare, quos venabulo lacessere non audet. Igitur nuncios laqueis onerat, qui Boamundo venienti cum huiusmodi blandiciis occurrant.*

32 Virgil, *Aeneid* 1.657–58: *At Cytherea novas artis, nova pectore versat / consilia.*

33 Virgil, *Aeneid* 2.61–62: *fidens animi atque in utrumque paratus, / seu versare dolos seu certae occumbere morti.*

34 Servius, *In Vergilii Aeneidos* 2.62.1.

35 Reynolds, *Medieval Reading*; Copeland and Sluiter, *Medieval Grammar and Rhetoric.*

> and the examples of those two women, one of whom looked back at the chaos of Sodom, the other of whom was looked at by her Thracian husband [Orpheus], keep them from being pulled back into the darkness now that they have emerged into the light. Forewarned by so many examples, they considered that they avoided all such punishments by eluding this one punisher.[36]

In an elaborate intertextual game, Ralph depicts Bohemond and Tancred as readers: they have understood the lessons of the story of Lot's wife at Sodom and of Orpheus's failed attempt to save Eurydice. Raised on the same diet of literary *exempla*, Ralph's readers are intended to recognize the allusions and to conclude with Ralph that the protagonists have acted wisely.

A contemporary of Ralph named Stephen engaged in learning of a different sort. He specialized in translating scientific works that cohere with Antioch's pre-Crusade culture of translation. In the process, he likely enlisted the assistance of a local Arabic-speaking Eastern Christian community of scholars and thus evinces a level of engagement with Levantine intellectual culture unmatched by Ralph of Caen (or, for that matter, any of the authors discussed so far). Yet a less commonly noted aspect of Stephen's intellectual outlook enables a degree of comparison between the two authors: throughout his work, Stephen cultivated and promoted the discipline of rhetoric (*rhetorica*). So, like Ralph, he transported a Latin tradition of classroom learning into twelfth-century Antioch.

Stephen had traveled from Pisa to Antioch sometime after 1115 and was active there throughout the 1120s.[37] For their role in the capture of the coastal city of Laodicea in 1108, Tancred had given the Pisans a quarter in both this city and in Antioch.[38] While official Pisan expeditions to the Levant ceased after the deposition of Daibert of Pisa as patriarch of Jerusalem in 1102, Stephen probably came to Antioch as a member of the continuous stream of private Pisan shipowners and pilgrims to the Latin East. There, he seems to have been employed as treasurer at

36 RC 641–47: *Sordet revocatio absentis, cuius presens contempta est persona; neque, adituri summi regis cunabula, Herodis audiunt perfidiam revocantis. Immissave aratro manu, lumina non reflectunt, semel quam sit illa reflexio damnosa experti; sed et illae, quarum altera chaos Sodomae respexit, altera Threicio coniugi est respecta, emersos ad lucem rursus prohibent tenebris immergi. Tot admoniti exemplis, omnia haec visi sunt sibi evadere tormenta, dum hunc unum pretereunt tortorem.*

37 Burnett ("ʿAbd al-Masīḥ of Winchester," 162 and n. 13) discovered Stephen's connection to Pisa from a remark by the twelfth-century medical author Matheus Ferarius, who wrote that "a certain Stephen of Pisa went to those parts [i.e., the Levant] and, having learned the language, translated it [i.e., the *Practica*] in its entirety." Burnett suggests elsewhere ("Antioch as a Link," 7–8) that Stephen's departure for the Levant must have occurred sometime after 1115, since a revised translation of al-Maǧūsī's *Kāmil al-ṣināʿa al-ṭibbīyya*, made in 1114–15, was known to Stephen before his departure.

38 Matzke, "Pisa," 964.

the Benedictine convent of Saint Paul, where he was given a house by Bernard of Valence, patriarch of Antioch.[39] Since, according to one document, Stephen was the patriarch's nephew, their familial connection may have played a part in Stephen's career and fortunes in Antioch.[40] As appears to have been the case for Fulcher of Chartres at the Church of the Holy Sepulcher in Jerusalem, Stephen's employment as a treasurer at Saint Paul's may have afforded him the opportunity to pursue scholarly activities by placing him in close proximity to the abbey's collection of books.[41]

Stephen took full advantage of this opportunity to engage in a remarkable range of disciplines, including medicine, pharmacology, astronomy, cosmology, and possibly even physics and metaphysics.[42] In 1127, with the help of two scribes named Alduinus and Pancus, he translated ʿAlī ibn al-ʿAbbās al-Mağūsī's *Kāmil al-ṣināʿa al-ṭibbīyya* (The complete medical art), a popular mid-tenth century medical textbook, from Arabic into Latin and gave it the title *Regalis dispositio* (The royal arrangement).[43] He appended to this work the *Medicaminum omnium breviarium* (Compendium of all medicines), comprising a glossary of pharmacological terms taken from the ancient Greek physician Dioscorides and supplemented with their Arabic and Latin equivalents.

As Stephen explained in the preface to the *Regalis dispositio*, his translation of this work represented merely the first step in an ambitious program of philosophical study.[44] In his promise to address "far loftier matters" (*longe altiora*) in subsequent endeavors, Stephen hinted at his next projects: astronomy and cosmology. He composed (now lost) astronomical tables with instructions (*Regule canonis*) and wrote the *Liber Mamonis in astronomia* (*Book of Mamon on astronomy*), which contains a Latin translation of an eleventh-century Arabic cosmological treatise by Ḥasan ibn al-Hayṯam, interspersed with Stephen's own commentary and original observations.[45] The success of his *Regalis dispositio* appears to

39 Hunt ("Stephen of Antioch") combined information from a subscription in Milan, Biblioteca Ambrosiana, E. 7 sup., fol. 52r, referencing a "Stephen, treasurer of Antioch" (*Stephano thesaurario antiochie*) in the year 1121, with a document stating that Patriarch Bernard of Valence had given a house to "Stephen, treasurer of the Church of Saint Paul" (*Stephani, thesaurarii ecclesie Sancti Pauli*) in the time of Prince Bohemond II (1126–1130). See *Cart St-Sép*, 178–83, no. 77, partially reproduced in Burnett, "Antioch as a Link," 60.

40 Talbot, "Stephen of Antioch."

41 See chap. 2.

42 For the possibility that two Latin translations of Aristotle, the so-called *Physica Vaticana* and the *Metaphysica media*, originated with Stephen the Philosopher's circle, see Burnett, "Note on the Origins."

43 This work and the accompanying *Medicaminum omnium breviarium* have not yet been edited. For an edition of Stephen's prefaces in these works, see Burnett "Antioch as a Link."

44 *Regalis dispositio*, pref. 17 (Burnett, "Antioch as a Link," 28–29).

45 Stephen's use of Ibn al-Hayṯam's *Maqāla fī hayʾat al-ʿālam* was discovered by R. Lemay in an unpublished study, as Grupe (SP, *Liber Mamonis* 15) notes. The text is extant in a single manuscript,

have boosted his confidence: whereas in the preface to his earlier work Stephen self-identifies as a "student of philosophy" (*philosophie discipulus*), he now confidently claims the title of philosopher.[46]

The *Liber Mamonis* is closely related to the first Latin translation of Ptolemy's *Almagest*, made by one ʿAbd al-Masīḥ of Winchester.[47] Correspondences in content, as well as style, vocabulary, and an idiosyncratic alphanumeric system of numbering, indicate that the two authors likely worked in close cooperation.[48] Based on the name and the text's connection to Stephen's works, C. Burnett has plausibly suggested that this individual may have been an Arabic-speaking Christian of Antioch who later relocated to Winchester. D. Weltecke has further proposed identifying this person with a philosopher named ʿAbd al-Masīḥ, who, according to Michael Rabbo, helped the West Syrian patriarch Athanasius VII escape the house arrest the Latins placed him under in Antioch.[49] In a recent study of Stephen's *Liber Mamonis* and ʿAbd al-Masīḥ's translation of the *Almagest*, D. Grupe argues that the *Liber Mamonis* contains evidence of close scholarly collaboration between Stephen and ʿAbd al-Masīḥ, who may have instructed Stephen in astronomy.[50] In Stephen's deployment of jargon used by practitioners of astronomy and his remarks on the didactic aspects of astronomy and cosmology, Grupe perceives the presence of a lively scholarly community in Antioch that enabled a neophyte such as Stephen to attain a sophisticated understanding of Ptolemaic cosmology.

Stephen directed his learned ambitions to a wider community of Latin scholars across the Mediterranean. In his outward gaze to the Latin intellectual community, Stephen presented himself as residing on an intellectual frontier—literally and figuratively. In the preface to the second part of the *Regalis dispositio*, Stephen writes:

> And I did not abandon the reader entirely to anxiety over inaccuracies, but at the end of the whole work I added, as far as I was able and inasmuch as the East possessed, a *Compendium of all medicines* in Dioscorides,

now Cambrai, Médiathèque d'Agglomération, A 930. The manuscript, which dates to the late twelfth century, was not Stephen's autograph but a later copy.

46 As Burnett notes ("Antioch as a Link," 9, n. 29), the title "student of philosophy" (*philosophie discipulus*) occurs throughout Stephen's translation of al-Maǧūsī's *Kāmil al-ṣināʿa al-ṭibbīyya*. The full title of the *Liber Mamonis in astronomia* declares him a "philosopher": *Liber Mamonis in astronomia a Stephano philosopho translatus* (The book of Mamon on astronomy, translated by Stephen the philosopher).

47 Dresden, Landesbibliothek, Db. 87, fols. 1–71 (thirteenth century).

48 See Burnett, "ʿAbd al-Masīḥ of Winchester"; Burnett, "Antioch as a Link," 12–13; and Burnett, "Transmission of Arabic Astronomy."

49 Weltecke, "On the Syriac Orthodox," 101, n. 28.

50 SP, *Liber Mamonis* 10–13.

presenting them in Greek on the one side, in Arabic on the other, so that, whoever might obtain this work, would be able to ascertain what each thing is—provided he finds a Greek, or indeed an Arab.[51]

In the conclusion to the *Breviarium*, Stephen similarly declares:

> This is what we have found up to now by our own effort in Syria concerning the interpretation [of the names] of medications in Greek and Arabic.[52]

Stephen keenly exploited his location in the Syrian "East" (*Oriens*) to provide his readership in the broader Latin community with as much learning as possible—even if his audience required access to Greek and Arabic speakers to take full advantage of it.[53] Through his innovative and iconoclastic approach, Stephen thus sought to establish an "Oriental" brand of Latin learning that involved not only the adoption of new ideas but also the repudiation of older authorities of learning. For example, in his criticism of the narrow conception of the world's habitable zones as espoused by the fourth-century scholar Macrobius, Stephen promoted a worldview that was, quite literally, broader than that of his Latin contemporaries in western Europe, among whom Macrobius's works enjoyed a renewed vogue in the twelfth century.[54]

Rather than uncritically extolling the Latin intellectual tradition, Stephen recognized its deficiencies and sought to overcome them by learning from other traditions. Earlier, Stephen explains that he "took pains to explore not only the Latin, but also the Arabic language for the sake of wisdom," and even went so far as to claim that "the Arabic language has, hidden within it . . . all the secrets of philosophy."[55] Where Ralph of Caen criticized "the moderns" (*moderni*) for slothful reluctance in producing new literary works, Stephen lambasted them (also referring to *moderni*) for stubbornly refusing to adopt a critical mindset and

51 *Regalis dispositio*, pref. to part 2 (Burnett, "Antioch as a Link," 37–38): *Nec vero omnino lectorem errori et sollicitudini remisimus, set quod posse nobis fuit et Oriens habebat in totius operis fine omnium que apud Diascoridem sunt medicaminum breviarium subdidimus, hinc eorum Grece, illinc Arabice habens, ut in cuius venerit hoc opus manus, quid queque res sit aut Grecum si invenit aut certe Arabem, sit illi posse consulere.*

52 *Medicaminum omnium breviarium*, explicit 1 (Burnett, "Antioch as a Link," 39–40): *Hec sunt que in Siria ad presens nostra invenit manus de medicaminum interpretatione grece et arabice.*

53 In the first preface to the *Medicaminum omnium breviarium*, Stephen similarly suggests that those in Sicily and Salerno consult Greek and Arabic speakers if they wish more accurate definitions of medical terms: Burnett, "Antioch as a Link," 38–39.

54 SP, *Liber Mamonis* 112–14. See on this passage Dalché, *La Géographie*, 98–101, and "Géographie Arabe," 418–19. For the renewed study of Macrobius at the "school" of Chartres in the twelfth century, see Wetherbee, "Philosophy, Cosmology."

55 *Regalis dispositio*, pref. 1.12 (Burnett, "Antioch as a Link," 26); *Regalis dispositio*, pref. 1.17 (Burnett, "Antioch as a Link," 28).

to accept more accurate information.[56] In touting his Arabic learning and his privileged access to "the truth of the Arabs" (*Arabum veritas*), Stephen utilized his location in "the East" to promote himself as an intellectual authority indispensable to Latinity.[57]

Yet despite his willingness to embrace new channels of knowledge, Stephen's learning was still rooted in and committed to the Latin tradition. This aspect is nowhere more apparent than in Stephen's deployment of rhetorical learning as taught in the Latin curriculum of rhetorica. The earliest trace of Stephen's intellectual activity belongs to this branch of learning. A colophon at the end of a manuscript containing the ancient rhetorical treatise *Rhetorica ad Herennium* (Rhetorical work addressed to Herennius) declares that the work was copied at Stephen's behest in Antioch: "***, scribe to Stephen, treasurer in Antioch, wrote this book of the *Rhetorics* in the year 1121 since the Passion of the Lord."[58] The layout of the text, with ample space for marginal annotations, indicates that the manuscript could have been used in a classroom setting or may have served as a copy for Stephen's personal study. The copious glosses to the section on rhetorical figures in the fourth book demonstrate Stephen's interest in having a ready reference work on this particular topic. Moreover, the scribe assigned each rhetorical figure an alphanumeric number, allowing the user to locate these figures with ease.[59]

Although Stephen's manuscript of the *Rhetorica ad Herennium* has been known to scholars for some time, compelling evidence indicates that he also commissioned a copy of another widely available work on rhetoric: Cicero's *De inventione* (On invention). It has gone unnoticed that the same alphanumeric system used

56 *Regalis dispositio*, pref. 1.19 (Burnett, "Antioch as a Link," 29).

57 For the phrase "the truth of the Arabs" (*Arabum veritate*), see *Regalis dispositio*, pref. 1.19 (Burnett, "Antioch as a Link," 29).

58 Milan, Biblioteca Ambrosiana, E. 7 sup., fol. 52r: *Scribsit hunc rethoricorum librum* *** [erasure of 3 or 4 letters] *scriba Stephano. thesaurario antiochie. anno a passio(n)e d(omi)ni millesimo ce(n)tesimo uicesimo primo*. Although the colophon could have been copied along with the text by a later scribe, codicological and paleographical features (dry-point ruling, tironian note for *et* alongside the ampersand, large open lower lobe of *g*, and the occasional use of the "e caudata") indicate a date of the twelfth century, so the manuscript is most likely the one that was copied in Antioch. The colophon is edited in Hunt, "Stephen of Antioch," and in Burnett, "Antioch as a Link," 9–10 (and see plate on 77); see for a reproduction Steffens, *Lateinische Paläographie*, no. 83C and plate. The scribe's name, consisting of three or four letters, has been erased. The scribe may have been Pancus, one of two scribes mentioned in the colophon of the *Regalis dispositio*, which was translated by Stephen the Philosopher; see Burnett, "Antioch as a Link," 67–68. The peculiar dating by reference to "the passion of the Lord" probably is to be interpreted as a practice of beginning the year with Easter rather than counting from the year of Jesus's crucifixion; see Haskins, *Studies in the History*, 134. See also Burnett, "Antioch as a Link," 67–69, with respect to a similar dating found in Stephen's *Regalis dispositio*, and the summary in Burnett, "Stephen, the Disciple of Philosophy."

59 Sabbadini, "Spogli Ambrosiani Latini," 272–76; see also Burnett, "Antioch as a Link," 63–64.

to number the books and rhetorical figures was also employed (by the same hand as the main text) to number the quires that make up the manuscript. The first letter that occurs (on folio 8v, the last folio of the first quire) is not ".a." as one would expect, but ".h." Seven quires, which are now lost, must have originally preceded this quire. Assuming that all the quires were prepared at the same time, a simple calculation based on the number of folios per quire and number of lines per folio allows for a rough estimate of the amount of missing text. The most likely text to have accompanied the *Rhetorica ad Herennium* (which was attributed to Cicero in the Middle Ages) is Cicero's *De inventione*, since this work was frequently copied along with it and matches the approximate length required.[60] John of Antioch's thirteenth-century French translation of both the *De inventione* and the *Rhetorica ad Herennium* (though made on the basis of a different manuscript) further attests to the tendency for these works to circulate together, even in the Latin East.[61]

Stephen put the rhetorical learning he acquired from these school texts to good use, particularly in the *Liber Mamonis*. The prefaces and digressions in this work exhibit what Grupe describes as a "flowery style" characterized by the use of synonyms to achieve stylistic variety.[62] Stephen also employed a diverse array of rhetorical figures, particularly metaphor, *figura etymologica*, hyperbaton, and the occasional assonance and alliteration. To give but one striking example, the following appears near the opening of Stephen's prologue:

> If there had not been such a great crowd of critics, Latinity would have had more fruitful scholarly authorities, and a more fertile crop of philosophy would have sprouted. Since there were a great many armies of critics, but few who offered benevolent support, an even smaller number of writers of

60 Assuming that the missing quires feature the same number of folios per quire (8) and the same number of lines per folio (33), the approximate length of the text contained in the missing part would have been 3,696 lines. If the same scribe who copied the *Rhetorica ad Herennium* also copied the text or texts preceding it, we arrive at a more specific approximation by multiplying times the average number of words per line (about 9 words, including abbreviations), or roughly 33,264 words, corresponding closely to the 33,879 words of the *De inventione*. On the shared textual tradition of the *De inventione* and the *Rhetorica ad Herennium*, see Winterbottom, "*De inventione*, and *ad Herennium*." The plural in the subscription (*hunc rhetoricorum librum*) cannot be used as evidence for the existence of multiple rhetorical texts in this codex, since it frequently occurs in titles of the *Rhetorica ad Herennium*, even when it occurs by itself. Presumably the noun *rhetorica* was construed as a neuter plural (rhetorical topics) rather than a feminine singular implying the noun *ars*. See for examples the exhaustive survey of eleventh- and twelfth-century manuscripts of Cicero in Munk Olsen, *L'étude des auteurs*, 1:135–320.

61 John of Antioch, *La Rectorique de Cyceron*. John of Antioch's independence from Stephen's text is apparent from the fact that key features of the Latin recension used by John (as identified by Guadagnini in John of Antioch, *La Rectorique de Cyceron*, 28–31) do not appear in the text copied for Stephen.

62 Grupe in SP, *Liber Mamonis* 40.

> the scholarly curriculum were more terrified by the crowd's cruelty than were united by the kind support of the others.[63]

Note how artfully Stephen moves from agrarian metaphors to martial imagery to contrast peaceful and productive scholarship with hostile and destructive criticism. At the same time, Stephen deftly employs hyperbaton (*tanta . . . multitudo, feraciores . . . auctores, fertilior . . . seges, pauciores . . . scriptores*) and uses both assonance and alliteration for emphasis (*tanta obtrectantium multitudo, multitudinis immanitate*).

Yet Stephen drew on ancient rhetoric for far more than stylistic devices. Immediately following the passage just quoted, he employs legal concepts and argues that rhetorical study is indispensable to civilized society. Stephen contrasts his own humility and open-minded spirit of philosophical disputation with the prevailing hypercritical attitudes that he holds responsible for a period of intellectual decline in Europe as compared to its neighbors:

> As a result, Europe, who could be in the possession of all scientific knowledge and skills, meanwhile seems inferior to any other peoples. . . . This has discredited the science of letters so much that those who had to venerate it most, namely the leaders of the states, despise it utterly. . . . As kings and the other respectable classes have been installed for the same reason for which the laws have been enacted, namely to protect a just balance, and one part of the law is the natural law and another part the positive law, but the knowledge of one of these parts is gained almost entirely, and that of the other part to a great extent, through intensive studies of written works, those who should be kings unlearned the way that leads to the truth and preserved merely the name of kings while acting as tyrants. Passively bound to inconsiderate "observance of consuetudes," they still judge the people by the same law that was brought into use by tyrants.[64]

63 SP, *Liber Mamonis* 1.1, 90: *Hec autem ideo, quia nisi tanta foret obtrectantium multitudo, feraciores habuisset Latinitas auctores, fertiliorque apud nos philosophie seges pullularet. Cum etenim plurimi essent exercitus detrahentium, pauci qui benigne susciperent, pauciores certe artium scriptores magis exterrebantur multitudinis immanitate, quam adunarentur aliquorum benigno studio.* I employ here a more literal translation than Grupe's in order to bring out the rhetorical qualities of the Latin. With Burnett ("Antioch as a Link," 43) I read *feraciores* for the manuscript reading *ferociores* (as followed by Grupe) as more suitable to the context and easily explained as a scribal error.

64 SP, *Liber Mamonis* 1.1, 90: *Unde factum est, ut que fere plenitudinem posset habere artium, nunc ceteris gentibus Europa videatur humilior . . . Que res tantum attulerit litteralis scientie odium, ut a quibus summe venerari debuerat, rerum publicarum rectoribus, summe odiretur . . . quoniam cum equitatis observande causa reges ceterique bonorum ordines, qua et leges constitute sunt, eius autem quedam pars naturalis, quedam sit posita, quarum alterius omnem fere scientiam, alterius maiorem partem, litterali plus exercicio adipiscamur, ignorata semita veritatis qui reges esse debuerant nomen*

Stephen explains that this intellectual malaise had wide-ranging ramifications. With no one left to cultivate *litteralis scientia* (literally, "the science of letters")—a broad concept presumably involving the study of both *grammatica* and *rhetorica*—codified law gave way to the caprices of rulers.[65] Stephen's usage of the legal term *consuetudines* to refer to customary (as opposed to natural) law may well draw on passages from Cicero's *De inventione* and the *Rhetorica ad Herennium*.[66] More importantly, Stephen argues that "training in letters" (*litterale exercicium*), as the foundation of legal interpretation, was indispensable to a civilization founded on justice and morality. Stephen expands on the moral and religious ramifications in the preface to the third book of the *Liber Mamonis* by evoking another work of Cicero:

> But, just as Cicero says that, by the rashness of G. I. Caesar, all was thrown into turmoil in the entire Roman Empire in his time, although afterwards, when the most true empire of Christ spread more deeply and widely, its roots were put to rest in the times of Constantine and the emperors who immediately succeeded him, [so] nevertheless it happened to us, just as it happened then, but much more severely. For all things among us, by the rashness of certain people, are mixed with greed, pride, idleness, negligence, and, above all, false traditions; shame has left, purity has fled, faith is lacking, the sacraments have disappeared. But about these things elsewhere! Yet I have said these few things to indicate that in our time the virtues have been put to flight and a tumult of vices has grown strong. Therefore, since it is agreed that the hosts of evil men are many, and of good men, the number is considered small but their value great, it is fitting to keep vigilant to confute the wicked wiles of the Devil.[67]

---

tantum retinentes tirannos se operibus exibebant. Ad consuetudinum enim inconsultam observantiam delapsi eadem populum lege iudicant, qua qui induxerunt in usum tiranni.

65 Grupe translates *litteralis scientie* simply as "scholarship," though the widespread medieval Latin use of this term to describe *grammatica* suggests something more specifically akin to "philology." See Marino, *Biography*," 47.

66 See Cicero, *De inventione* 2.65.1–67.1; 2.160.1–162.1; *Rhetorica ad Herennium* 2.19.1.

67 SP, *Liber Mamonis* 3 pref. 23–28, 1–5, 246–48: *Set, quemadmodum ait Tullius, temeritate G. I. Cesaris omnia suo tempore confusa in Romani imperii universitate fuisse, tametsi postea propagante altius diffusiusque Christi verissimo imperio radices sue composite sub Constantini proximeque sequentium imperatorum temporibus fuerint, nobis tamen sicut et tunc multoque durius contigit. Omnia enim apud nos quorundam temeritate, avaritia, superbia, ignavia, negligentia, falsis denique traditionibus permixta sunt, recessit pudor, fugit munditia, deest fides, sacramenta diffluxerunt. Set de his alias. Verum hec pauca diximus ut significaremus nostro tempore fugatis virtutibus vitiorum tumultus invaluisse. Quare multas esse improborum cum constet turbas, proborumque pauci numero magni re habentur, decet invigilare ad confutandas diaboli ingenii nequitias.* I have slightly modified Grupe's translation, which minimizes the charged religious sense of *fides* by rendering it as "trust."

Stephen bolsters his argument that his era was one of moral decline by paraphrasing a passage from Cicero's moral-philosophical treatise *De officiis* (On duties).[68] Comparing the current Latin status quo to the Roman Empire before the spread of Christianity, Stephen bewails the prevalence of moral vices and people's failure to adhere to the Christian faith and the sacraments. Stephen proposes an intellectual approach to avert a Latin religious crisis with a new program of Levantine Latin learning. The wakeful vigilance against the Devil's snares to which he exhorts his readership corresponds to the sleepless nights he claimed earlier to have devoted to the study of philosophical secrets so that he might transmit them to Latinity—used here in both a linguistic and religious sense.[69] Stephen's use of Cicero here as a moral authority underlines his firm commitment to a decidedly Latin tradition of learning.

In the preface to the second book of the *Liber Mamonis*, Stephen explains why rhetoric is crucial to his intellectual and religious project. Renewing his critique of Macrobius, Stephen depicts himself as engaging with Macrobius in a courtroom debate in which plaintiff and defendant provide evidence to the reader as to a jury:

> After we have presented our view with argumentative support brought together like for a contest with Macrobius's arguments, they shall finally by fair weighing settle the conflict, that is, the one between plaintiff and defendant or witness. Bringing up firmness of character, they shall hold court by sacred legal ceremony and, without favouritism, grant equal and unbiased support to the conflicting parties. When my own and Macrobius's statements are presented, and also what either of us brings forth as support for the understanding of his view, they shall judge whom they recognise as refuted or less convincing, or as unknowing of the facts, or as falsifier of well-understood facts, and, finally, whose side deserves more willing approval, by exclusive consideration of its truth.[70]

68 Cicero, *De officiis* 1.26: *Declaravit id modo temeritas C. Caesaris, qui omnia iura divina et humana pervertit propter eum, quem sibi ipse opinionis errore finxerat principatum. Est autem in hoc genere molestum, quod in maximis animis splendidissimisque ingeniis plerumque existunt honoris, imperii, potentiae, gloriae cupiditates.*

69 SP, *Liber Mamonis* 2 pref. 6, 174: *archana, que cum frequentibus vigiliis diuturnis cogitationum recessibus exquisita comparaverim.*

70 SP, *Liber Mamonis* 2 pref. 16–24, 174: *tum demum, cum nos in sententie nostre subsidium attulimus rationum cum Macrobianis in unum tamquam certaminis discrimen collatarum, equa lance partiantur conflictum, agentis scilicet et defendentis seu testis. Omissa per sancta iuridicaria sedentes constantia omni vacuum passione parem confligentibus assensum prebeant, enodatisque meis Macrobiique sententiis, quodque in sui patrocinium intellectus uterque asserit, quem de statu deiectum aut forte inferiorem animadvertunt ipsum aut inscium horum aut intellectorum depravatorem iudicent, ac tamen demum cuius sit secte amicitior assensus sub veritatis indagine.*

In what amounts to far more than an extended metaphor, Stephen depicts philosophical disputation—and therefore the distinction of truth from falsehood—as an inherently rhetorical exercise. Stephen's understanding of philosophy and of what we would call "science" was thus conditioned by the rhetorical learning that was a cornerstone of the medieval Latin curriculum.

In comparison to the Latin works from early twelfth-century Jerusalem, Ralph of Caen and Stephen the Philosopher stand out for their emphatic displays of specific types of learning taught in Latin schools all over western Europe. By cultivating and promoting this Latin classroom learning, Ralph and Stephen reproduced familiar models of learning while seeking to form part of a much broader community of Latin scholars. As prominent passages by both authors show, this desire to remain attached to a Latin "republic of letters" did not preclude stringent criticism of their erudite Latin contemporaries. In fact, Stephen presented his position on the Latin periphery as a distinct intellectual advantage, as it enabled him to access more accurate sources of knowledge and to transmit them to the broader community of Latin scholars. As the first explicit and serious engagement with intellectual traditions beyond Latin, his works represent a watershed in the Levantine Latin tradition. Specifically, Stephen is the first Latin author in the twelfth-century Levant to consider Arabic an intellectual idiom. Importantly, however, Stephen's interchangeable use of the concepts of "Latinity" and "Europe" shows that he did not yet perceive the Levant as a place of Latin learning.

Surprisingly, neither Stephen nor Ralph employed their learning to participate in any substantial religious engagement. As discussed in the previous chapter, Ralph restricted his comments on other religions to a memorable passage describing Tancred's reaction upon his alleged encounter with an idol of Muhammad in the Dome of the Rock.[71] Stephen, on the other hand, reserved his few religious critiques for his Latin Christian coreligionists. Over the following decades, however, religious engagement with both Muslims and Eastern Christians became an increasingly prominent feature of Latin literature in Antioch.

Little is known about the later fortunes of Ralph of Caen and Stephen of Antioch. Sometime after the death of his patron Tancred (1112), Ralph may have moved to Jerusalem to cultivate the patronage of his former teacher Arnulf of Chocques. Although his presence in Jerusalem is not attested by any document, Ralph's later additions to and revisions of *Tancredus* (the last of which can be dated to 1130) suggest increasing attempts to shift the focus of his work from Antioch to Jerusalem.[72] Stephen's name, on the other hand, comes up in a document from 1140, detailing a dispute between the abbey of Saint Paul and the canons of the Holy Sepulcher. The canons claimed that Stephen's house had been

71 RC 3639–40.

72 D'Angelo in RC xxxv–xxxviii.

confiscated from them by Bernard of Valence, Latin patriarch of Antioch (and, reportedly, Stephen's uncle). In a twist of irony, the case was eventually decided in favor of the canons, who proved their claims with the testimony of "Greek witnesses, mature in morals and age" (*Grecos testes, moribus et senio maturos*).[73] The willingness of these Eastern Christian clergy to testify against the abbey of Saint Paul indicates that, while Stephen may have collaborated closely with at least one Eastern Christian scholar, relations among the communities in Antioch remained complicated. Perhaps, like Ralph, Stephen relocated elsewhere in the Latin East: a "Stephen of Antioch" (*Stephanus de Antiochia*) witnessed two charters in Jerusalem in 1141.[74]

The Beginnings of Religious Polemic: Walter the Chancellor and "Adelphus"

Two works roughly contemporaneous with Ralph of Caen and Stephen the Philosopher combine prominent displays of Latin learning with a critique of other religious traditions in the Levant. Walter, a Norman chancellor of Antioch, wrote a short history of the Latin principality in which he not only documented military exploits but also sought to reform the moral lapses of Antioch's Eastern Christian communities. Another work, known as the "Adelphus" narrative, depicts a conversation between a Latin and a Greek Christian in Antioch on the origins of Islam, here presented as a dangerous perversion of learning. Although written in different genres, these two texts show the early development of a learned Latin religious discourse in Antioch.

Nothing is known of Walter the Chancellor beyond the sparse autobiographical references in his *Bella Antiochena* (Wars of Antioch). He occupied the chief administrative office of chancellor at the Antiochene court, at least during the period 1114–22, the outer limits of the events he covered in his writing.[75] Given his overt support of the Antiochene clergy, and of Patriarch Bernard of Valence in particular, Walter probably possessed a clerical background.[76] According to

73 *Cart St-Sép*, 178–83, no. 77. The witnesses were called Gregorius, cantor of the Church of Saint Mary (*ęcclesię Sanctę Marię cantor*), Thomas the succentor (*subcantor*), Michael, son of Molkim (*filius Molkim/Molkem*), and Abraham, son of Sucar (*filius Sucar*). In an interesting confluence, the charter was witnessed by, among others, Aimery of Limoges, in his capacity as deacon (*decanus*) before his ascent to the patriarchate later that year (see below).

74 Mayer, *Von der Cour*, 238–42, no. 7 (RRH no. 204; RRR no. 409), and *Cart St-Sép*, 226–28, no. 107 (RRH no. 205; RRR no. 410).

75 Walter identifies his office in WC 2 prol. 2: "I myself, Walter the Chancellor" (*ego ipse Galterius cancellarius*). Although no charters or administrative documents bear his name, his intimate knowledge of the inner workings of the court lend credence to the title he claimed for himself.

76 For example, when King Baldwin II first enters Antioch after Roger dies in the Battle of the Field of Blood in 1119, Walter (WC 2.9.8) approvingly presents his first point of action as consulting with Patriarch Bernard and the clergy, "as befitted a king."

his own statements, he was present at the Battle of the Field of Blood in 1119 and subsequently taken captive for a period of time by Il-ghāzi, the Artukid ruler of Aleppo. He had probably died by 1127.[77]

Walter composed a Latin historiographical work (largely in prose) in two short books, entitled *Bella Antiochena*. He likely wrote the first book from late 1115 to mid-1119, as it does not reference the Battle of the Field of Blood (summer 1119).[78] He composed the second book sometime after 1122, probably in two stages.[79]

Walter's history is unique in Latin historiography from the twelfth-century Levant in focusing exclusively on events occurring after the First Crusade—to the extent that he fails even to mention the Crusade at all. Instead, as the work's title indicates, Walter's history centers squarely on the early history of Latin Antioch, with detailed accounts of the military exploits of its rulers. His intended audience must therefore primarily have been the educated Latin elite of the principality responsible for its physical and spiritual defense, including both learned members of the knightly class and the clergy.[80] Nevertheless, Walter's work circulated beyond Antioch at an early date, as it was copied between 1137 and 1146 in a manuscript presented to the French king Louis VII.[81] As discussed previously, this collection of texts, in which Walter's *Bella Antiochena* sits awkwardly between Fulcher of Chartres's First Crusade narrative and that of Raymond of Aguilers, likely originated in the Latin East.

Despite the early textual transmission linking Walter's history with those of Fulcher and Raymond, the work possesses far greater affinities to Ralph of Caen's *Tancredus*. Most obviously, several correspondences in phrasing suggest that Walter the Chancellor had read *Tancredus*.[82] If so, Walter may have decided to compose a sequel of sorts. Beyond these verbal parallels, Walter and Ralph share stylistic features.[83] Like Ralph, Walter employed a wide range of rhetorical figures (especially the metaphor, *figura etymologica*, paronomasia, asyndeton, and polyptoton) and, unlike Fulcher, relished in dramatic speeches of the narrative's protagonists.[84] In a passage especially illustrative of the difference between Walter and Fulcher, Walter even identifies the metaphor he employed: "The metaphorical

77 In this year, his successor, one *Radulphus cancellarius*, appears in a charter: *I libri iurium della Repubblica* 1.2:154, no. 337.

78 Asbridge and Edgington, in their translation of Walter the Chancellor, *Antiochene Wars*, 8.

79 Book 2, chapter 12, contains a concluding formula that closely resembles those at the end of book 1 and the end of book 2, suggesting that Walter initially decided to end his book before continuing it at a later date.

80 In the prologue to book 1 (WC 1.prol.1), Walter addresses this audience as "the defenders of the true faith, who have the capacity for reason" (*capaces rationis et verae fidei defensores*).

81 See chap. 2.

82 D'Angelo (RC xcii–xciv) identified eleven such correspondences.

83 See Hagenmeyer's discussion in WC 25–28.

84 For the longer speeches in Walter the Chancellor, see the list in WC 27–28.

battle lines of hostile locusts, stirred up far and wide, completely devoured all the necessary foodstuffs belonging to the inhabitants of Syria."[85] The metaphor closely resembles Fulcher's description of a plague of locusts in 1117. But where Fulcher offered a simile comparing the movement of the locusts to a roving army (*ad morem exercitus hominum*), Walter exhibits his classroom learning by identifying the metaphor he employs as such (*locustarum agmina . . . sub metaphora hostium*).[86]

While Ralph and Walter share stylistic characteristics, a key difference between their works is Walter's prominent engagement with the religious communities of Antioch—a feature largely absent from *Tancredus*. For all his negative portrayals of Byzantines, Ralph never once engages in a religious critique of Orthodox Christians in his *Tancredus*. Walter, by contrast, places Eastern Christians (*orientales Christicolae*) and their alleged spiritual shortcomings front and center in the first book of the *Bella Antiochena*.[87] He prefaces the *Bella Antiochena* with a catalogue of moral vices committed by the population of Antioch, above all by its Eastern Christian communities, and presents their transgressions as the direct cause of the catastrophic earthquake that struck Antioch in 1114. The excesses Walter specifies are those stereotypically associated by Latin authors with decadent "eastern" behavior: excessive feasting, wearing luxurious garments (decorated with "Arabian gold"), and lascivious activities.[88] Walter's specificity in this passage, however, points to the lived experience of a cleric transplanted into an unfamiliar cultural realm.

As Walter claims in the prologue, the lifestyles of Eastern Christians of Antioch had resulted in frequent, but ineffective, punishment over the years:

> The Author of the highest justice allowed these [inhabitants of Antioch], who did not bewail the evils they had committed but voluntarily and publicly committed acts worthy of bewailing, to be afflicted by signs, prodigies, plagues, and even the tribulation [caused by] people hostile to them, all of which were brought upon them over the course of many years, not in order to destroy them but rather to have mercy on them. For when the Greeks ruled, they were compelled to be subservient to their rule. When the same [Greeks] had been driven from Asia, they passed to the lordship of the ruling Parthians; finally, by God's will, they gave way to the less tolerant power of the Gauls. And since they could not be brought to mend

85 WC 1 prol. 2: *locustarum agmina longe lateque sub metaphora hostium agitata, accolarum Syriae penitus omnia abstulere victui necessaria.*

86 FC 2.60.2. Fulcher also described the same plague of locusts discussed by Walter (FC 2.52.1) but did not employ similes or metaphors in this passage.

87 WC 1 prol. 2.

88 Compare the denigrating remarks about Eastern Christians in Guibert of Nogent, *Dei gesta per Francos* 1.2 (Levine, *Deeds of God*, 30–32).

their ways in this manner or that, the aforementioned Syrians and their overlords suffered such a great disaster and destruction from the earthquake that occurred, as no history has ever told of before.[89]

Walter justifies Norman rule of Antioch by claiming that God had sent the Normans as rightful successors to the Byzantine Greeks and the Seljuk Turks to punish its inhabitants for their immorality. Walter's urgency for moral reform stems not purely from a sense of Christian solidarity, but rather from the fact that the latest chastening in the form of an earthquake punished, in Walter's words, both "the aforementioned Syrians and their overlords" (*praefati Syri et eorum dominatores*).[90]

Although Walter does not say, it is distinctly possible, as some scholars have suggested, that he was also reacting to Norman cultural assimilation to their Eastern Christian subjects.[91] Some evidence in fact suggests an early willingness on the part of the Latin rulers of Antioch to adopt linguistic and other cultural practices of their subjects. Prince Roger minted coins in both Latin and Greek, perhaps reflecting the diversity of his subjects.[92] More tellingly, when the Antiochene legates Roland and Pontius attended a synod in Benevento in 1113, their Eastern hair and beard styles reportedly elicited great astonishment among their Western peers.[93] Walter's solution to the perceived growing moral decadence was to promote a model of Christian interaction in Antioch that amounted instead to Eastern Christian assimilation, in which Eastern Christians abandoned their cultural practices and embraced the divinely sanctioned Latin Christian ecclesiastical leadership and Norman rule.

The central narrative of book 1 focuses on the external threat to the Principality of Antioch in the form of an invasion by Bursuq of Hamadan, an agent of the Seljuk sultanate, and recounts the removal of this threat. Antioch's Norman ruler, Prince Roger of Salerno, first attempts to do so through an alliance with two local Muslim potentates, the Artukids Tughtekin of Damascus and Il-ghāzi of Mardin, but eventually defeats Bursuq without their aid.[94] After recounting Roger's

89 WC 1 prol. 6: *Hos itaque perpetrata mala non plangentes et plangenda voluntarie et publice perpetrantes auctor summae iustitiae signis, prodigiis, plagis, tribulatione etiam adversarum gentium, multis annorum curriculis inlatis, non perdendo sed parcendo permisit adfligi. Graecis namque regnantibus ipsorum imperio servisse convincuntur. Eisdem ex Asia propulsis Parthorum regnantium cessere dominio; tandem, Deo volente, intolerabiliori succubuere Gallorum potestati. Qui cum neque hinc neque inde corrigerentur, praefati Syri et eorum dominatores tantam a contingente terrae motu sunt passi calamitatem et ruinam, quantam antea fuisse nulla commemoravit historia.*

90 WC 1 prol. 6.

91 Skottki, "Of 'Pious Traitors,'" 94–104; Rubenstein, *Nebuchadnezzar's Dream*, 91–96.

92 Metcalf, *Coinage of the Crusades*, 22–30.

93 Hiestand, *Papsturkunden*, 3:119, no. 15.

94 On the nature of this alliance, see Köhler, *Alliances and Treaties*, 103–5.

successful military campaign, Walter returns to the theme of moral correction and once again attributes a central role to the Latin patriarch, who leads a triumphal procession into the city toward the Church of Saint Peter. Walter commemorates the occasion with a jubilant hymn representing the songs sung by the entire populace.

While the hymn has largely been ignored by scholars, a close examination shows that Walter used it to reinforce the theme of communal penance he introduced at the opening of the book by developing parallels between the Eastern Christians' public penance for their sinful acts and the communal procession after Roger's victory. At the beginning of book 1, Walter had recounted how, following the earthquake, Latins, Greeks, Syrians, Armenians, foreigners, and pilgrims alike confessed their sins, each in their own tongue (*pro diverso linguarum genere*) proclaiming in the streets, "Lord, spare your people!"[95] They flocked to the Church of Saint Peter, where they confessed to the Latin patriarch, Bernard of Valence, and promised to lead a virtuous life. "Through his faith, merits, and prayers," concluded Walter, "as well as the humble prayers of the rest of the clergy and other faithful, I believe, the Lord had pity on what remained of his people of Antioch."[96]

When the populace reconvened for a triumphal procession led by Bernard toward the Church of Saint Peter, as described at the end of book 1, their song conveys their newfound unity out of various ethnically and culturally diverse Christian communities. The hymn begins with an address to God and a portrayal of Antiochenes of all walks of life united as "his flock." Both free citizens and slaves (*Liber, servus et ancilla*) of various ethnicities (*diversarum / nationum populus*) decorated the streets and neighborhoods of the city with gold, gems, silks, and spices, such that "one might very well say that it was an earthly paradise" (*tantus odor funditur, / quod terrestris paradisus / possit dici penitus*).[97] Eventually the procession arrived at the Church of Saint Peter, where Roger dedicated his banner to the church and its community (*Ergo princeps ad altare / Fert vexillum triumphale, / Offert illud speciale, / Post haec munus principale*). After the clergy gave thanks and prayed, the congregation departed from the church to salute Roger: "All shout with their heart's voice: 'Greetings, king! Champion of truth! God's enemies fear you, and may you have continuous peace, salvation, and victory, for all times! Amen!'"[98] This concluding scene of book 1 of the *Bella Antiochena* closely corresponds to the prologue. Those who had brought the destructive earthquake upon themselves the previous year had learned their lesson and become a

95 WC 1.2–3.

96 WC 1.2.

97 WC 1.7.8.

98 WC 1.7.9: *Clamant omnes cordis voce: / "Salve rex! Athleta veri! / Te formidant hostes Dei, / Tibique sit continua / Pax, salus et victoria / Per saeculorum saecula! / Amen!"*

God-fearing people. Walter develops this parallelism throughout the hymn: the sinful coveting of gold, gems, and other jewelry, principally by immoral women prostituting themselves "in the streets and neighborhoods," corresponds to the decoration of the same streets and neighborhoods with gold and gems during the triumphal procession.[99]

While T. Asbridge and S. Edgington have focused on Walter's account of Roger's military exploits to argue that his purpose in book 1 consisted in conveying the notion that "Christian warfare must be carried out with divine sanction and with pure intention," the passages with which Walter bookended this campaign also suggest a preoccupation with the formation of a united Christian populace of Antioch.[100] Although the Antiochenes were initially divided by creed, language, and ethnicity, at the end of book 1 they fuse into a single populace united behind Latin secular and ecclesiastical leadership. Just as Fulcher of Chartres had promoted the notion of a linguistically unified Christian society of Jerusalem as a prefiguration of the heavenly city, so did Walter's newfound unity also extend to the linguistic diversity of Antioch. Where earlier all confessed their sins in their own tongue, the Antiochenes subsequently saluted Prince Roger in unison "with their heart's voice" (*clamant omnes cordis voce*).[101]

In addition to promoting Bernard as Antioch's ecclesiastical leader, Walter also seeks to make its secular ruler, Prince Roger, a rallying figure for both Eastern Christians and Latins. Strikingly, the hymn presents the Antiochenes saluting Roger as a king. Earlier in the narrative, Walter subtly develops Roger's transformation into a king when depicting his dramatic entrance onto the battlefield. Walter's phrasing, "the prince's banners go forth" (*vexilla principis prodeunt*), alludes to the opening of Venantius Fortunatus's famous sixth-century hymn on the relic of the True Cross, "the king's banners go forth" (*vexilla regis prodeunt*). This was an especially meaningful allusion, given that the battle was enjoined on 14 September 1115, on the Feast of the Holy Cross, for which occasion Fortunatus's hymn had originally been composed. Moreover, scholars have overlooked the fact that Walter's hymn at the end of the book employs the same meter as Fortunatus's hymn.[102] By making an emphatic connection between his own hymn and that of Venantius Fortunatus, Walter associates Prince Roger's banners

99 WC 1 prol. 4; 1.7.8. Compare especially the phrases *auro Arabico pretiosarumque gemmarum* (1 prol. 4) and *per plateas et per vicos* (1 prol. 5) in the prologue with the phrases *vicos sternunt et plateas . . . auro, gemmis adornantur* (1.7.8) in the hymn.

100 Asbridge and Edgington, *Antiochene Wars*, 11.

101 WC 1.7.9.

102 For the allusion, see WC 1.6.3: *Vexilla principis prodeunt*. The hymn in WC 1.7.8–9 consists of alternating strophes composed in 2 × 8 (with final paroxytone cadence) + 7 (with final proparoxytone cadence), with some exceptions. Likewise, the rhyming scheme is flexible, varying from ABAB to AABB or AAAA.

with the relic of the True Cross, thereby drawing on the relic's potential to unify the diverse Christian population of Antioch.

Walter's decision to end book 1 of the *Bella Antiochena* with a hymn strongly points to an ambition to incorporate his historiographical project into a commemorative liturgy. Unlike at the Church of the Holy Sepulcher, no evidence survives for the Latin liturgy at the Church of Saint Peter in twelfth-century Antioch. Yet the case of Walter's contemporary, Fulcher of Chartres, demonstrates that Latin historical narrative could achieve the status of a central liturgical text for a commemorative occasion. Just as passages of Fulcher's history were used to commemorate the capture of Jerusalem in 1099 in the early decades of the twelfth century, Walter may have sought to inaugurate a liturgical tradition centered on the Antiochene victory at the Battle of Sarmin in 1115. Unlike Fulcher, however, Walter designed the end of book one of the *Bella Antiochena* to be a commemorative liturgy from the very start. Such a move need not have been purely of Walter's own design. As S. John and J. Rubenstein have shown, the kings of Jerusalem were skilled at using liturgical celebration for their own political agenda, by timing key political events such as coronation ceremonies to coincide with prominent liturgical feasts to maximize the symbolic significance of their accession and by manipulating liturgical ceremonies to achieve favorable political outcomes.[103] While less source material survives from early Latin Antioch, it is plausible that Roger may similarly have perceived the institution of a liturgical celebration as a means to cement his own position.

Book 2 of Walter the Chancellor's *Bella Antiochena* exposes the unity achieved at the end of the first book as a fragile, superficial state that could not hold in the face of adversity. The contrast in tone between the two books is striking: where the first book ended on a note of celebration and a commemorative hymn that presented Antioch as "an earthly paradise," its sequel resembles a fire-and-brimstone sermon that concludes with a terrifying depiction of hell. The reason for this discrepancy lies in the subject matter, which no longer consists of a simple coming together of a divided populace, crowned by a resounding victory. Instead, Walter chronicles the disastrous rout of Prince Roger and the Antiochene army at the Battle of the Field of Blood in 1119, followed by the disturbing events he witnessed as a prisoner of Il-ghāzi and Tughtekin. These setbacks must have created rifts among the Antiochenes, and Walter expresses some of the anxiety of the Latin clergy in the immediate aftermath of the Battle of the Field of Blood:

> Meanwhile . . . whatever care, labor, fear, terror, or loss could befall Christianity, it all now, in turn, necessarily devolved to the clergy, since the military and almost all the Frankish citizens' guard was now lost. The situation was such that, I say, they feared much more to be deceived by

103 John, "Royal Inauguration"; Rubenstein, "Holy Fire."

> the betrayal of internal enemies than to come under attack of any external violence. This was not surprising: for if the people of Antioch, deprived of their possessions through force and the malevolence of our people, and given over to wicked behavior and depression, had wished to return wickedness for wickedness, as a just retribution, they could, in that intervening period, have caused great aggravation to our people through betrayal or some other means.[104]

While Walter had painstakingly crafted a narrative of a unified people of Antioch in the first book of his history, he now differentiates between the indigenous "people of Antioch" (*Antiocheni*) and "our people" (*nostri*) or "the Franks" (*Franci*).[105] In a move that recalls Yaghi-Siyan's suspicion of Antioch's Christian populace during the Crusader siege, the Franks harbored such mistrust that they ordered all non-Latin Antiochenes to surrender their weapons. Walter addresses the anxieties over the Eastern Christian population in two ways: through the creation of a new unity narrative focused on the entire Latin East and by externalizing the threat of division.

When Baldwin II, king of Jerusalem, stepped in as regent of Antioch to fill the vacuum left by Roger, Walter enthusiastically champions his involvement in Antiochene affairs. Walter heralds Baldwin's entry into Antioch: "Here is Baldwin, the aforementioned king, great in the expectation of all Christian people, greater still in his arrival, and greatest in the protection [he offered]."[106] In Baldwin, Walter has found a more perfectly Christian ruler to replace Roger and even goes so far as to declare him "the king, who, second only to the Lord, was the lord and defender of Christianity."[107] By embracing Baldwin as the supreme Christian ruler of the Latin East, and elsewhere promoting the valor of Pons, count of Tripoli, Walter reorients his history from an inward focus on Antioch to an outward gaze toward the rest of the Latin East.[108] Yet it is doubtful that

104 WC 2.8.5: *Interim . . . quidquid curae, laboris, timoris, metus vel damni Christianitati contingere poterat, iam destituto militari officio et iam paene toto amisso Francorum civium auxilio, ea vice in clerum necessario totum redactum exstitit, ita, inquam, ut multo acrius timerent interiorum hostium proditione falli quam vi exteriorum ullo modo intrinsecus posse comprimi. Nec id mirum: gens etenim Antiochena vi et pravo ingenio gentis nostrae privata suis bonis et addicta pravae consuetudini saepius maerore concussa, si, quod est vicissitudo iustitiae, malum pro malo reddere voluisset, eo temporis intervallo nostros proditione vel alio modo admodum gravare potuisset.*

105 Murray ("Franks and Eastern Christians," 119) highlights the importance of this passage as a demonstration that the Franks of Antioch developed an identity separate from Eastern Christians.

106 WC 2.9.8: *adest Balduinus, rex memoratus, omni populo Christiano exspectatione magnus, adventu maior, protectione maximus.*

107 WC 2.11.6: *rex, qui solus post Dominum dominus et defensor Christ[i]anitatis exstitit.*

108 For Pons of Tripoli, see WC 1.3.2, 1.4.1, 1.4.5, 2.8.9, 2.12.1; toward the end of the work, Walter (WC 2.16.5–9) also extolls David IV ("the Builder"), king of Georgia, as "a true and most perfect Christian."

Baldwin's arrival truly created the kind of unity among the Christians of Antioch that Walter had envisioned. As Walter relates, Baldwin's first actions as regent consisted of convening a council to confirm the possessions of the Frankish lords (*domini*) and to establish their hereditary rights over them—possessions that, as Walter had earlier admitted, had been confiscated from the indigenous population.[109]

Rather than dwell on the problematic internal politics of Antioch, Walter spends the remainder of the *Bella Antiochena* on external affairs, concentrating on Il-ghāzi and Tughtekin and their horrific treatment of prisoners. Walter's deeply negative portrayal of Il-ghāzi in particular has led to a characterization of the *Bella Antiochena* as a Christian polemic against Islam used to justify the Crusades.[110] However, while Walter had few qualms about offering generalizing critiques of Eastern Christians, there is only one passage in the *Bella Antiochena* in which he generalizes about Muslims, and even this sentiment leads into a critique of Christians. After recounting the horrendous tortures to which he and the other captives were subjected after the Battle of the Field of Blood, Walter cuts his account short with the following explanation:

> [Concerning] the various kinds of torture by which the captives were worn down in the prisons of the Saracens, I could describe and detail at length many strange and stupefying things; however, since kings, princes, and other rulers of the world, as well as men not in a position of power who belong to the same culture and religion as [their rulers], sometimes take prisoners justly, other times unjustly, and since they punish their captives with various afflictions to extort money from them, and since nearly all mortals typically follow examples of the wicked instead of the virtuous (this is the devil's doing), I considered it more beneficial to keep silent about the nature and number of tortures than to express them in detail, so that Christians would not do similar things toward other Christians and turn them into custom.[111]

109 WC 2.10.2.

110 Mallett, "'Other' in the Crusading Period," followed in part by Skottki, "Of 'Pious Traitors,'" and Latiff, *Cutting Edge*, 148.

111 WC 2.15.8: *Diversis itaque tormentorum generibus, quibus captivi in carceribus Saracenorum conterebantur, multa quidem miranda ac stupenda haberem describere et verbis edisserere; sed quia reges, principes mundique alii potentes, etiam et inpotentes eiusdem conditionis eiusdemque fidei homines, cuius et ipsi sunt, aliquando iuste, aliquando iniuste capiunt, captosque pro extorquenda pecunia diversis poenis puniunt, et cum paene omne genus mortalium instinctu diabolico a malis potius quam a bonis exempla sumere consueverint, utilius mecum reputo formam et quantitatem tormentorum tacere quam exprimere, ne Christicolae Christicolis similia inferant et in consuetudinem vertant.*

Walter presents the prison he and his fellow captives were held in as belonging to "Saracens"—the only passage in the entire work that employs this term, which was the word used by Latin authors to refer to Muslims. Yet rather than engage in an extended polemic against "Saracen" treatment of prisoners as a practice informed by Islam, Walter opts to provide beneficial rather than harmful examples to his Christian readers, who, he reminds them, are not immune from sin. As N. Morton has recently observed, other passages undercut a perception of the work as a wholesale polemic against Muslims and Islam.[112] One scene in particular, in which a Muslim religious leader, "pricked by his conscience" (*mente compunctus*), declines Il-ghāzi's order to kill a Frankish captive and passes the assignment on to someone else, evinces Walter's commitment to nuance and accuracy.[113]

Although Walter engages far more readily in a critique of Eastern Christians (and at times even Latin Christians) than in anything approaching a polemic against Islam, in a few instances his depiction of individual Muslims like Il-ghāzi is clearly informed by an ideological bias. This is nowhere more apparent than in the unsavory description of Il-ghāzi's death. Having been paralyzed after his defeat by the Georgian king David IV ("the Builder"), Il-ghāzi suffers a grisly end as he is carried off:

> It happened that, while he was carried in the litter, in which he was transported both as a symbol of honor and of his inability [to walk], his foul soul exited through his anus along with an evacuation of filth from his stomach; snatched by the claws of infernal scorpions, it was hurled into the vats of the lowest hell, filled with dreadful fires that burn endlessly, scorching and unquenchable.[114]

Il-ghāzi's unusual death bears a marked similarity to depictions of the infamous demise of Arius in the early fourth century. The fifth-century chronicle of Socrates of Constantinople, widely disseminated in the Latin translation commissioned and selected from by Cassiodorus as part of his *Historia ecclesiastica tripartita*, described that death as follows:

> A sudden terror from the innermost part of his conscience seized him, and his fright was followed by an evacuation from his stomach. . . . Afterward, a kind of faintness seized him as he evacuated [his bowels], and his bowels

112 Morton, "Walter the Chancellor."

113 WC 2.15.5.

114 WC 2.16.11: *Contigit autem in lectica, qua ferebatur pro honore et inpotentia, cum egressione fimi ventris ipsius sordidam per anum exiisse animam et abstractam infernalium scorpionum unguibus corruisse in inferni inferioris ollas, plenas diris ignibus ardentibus sine fine, comburentibus et inextinguibilibus.*

> protruded along with the excrement. Then he collapsed, and a mass of blood and smaller intestines flowed out, as well as portions of his liver and his spleen.[115]

Arius, who had received his education in Antioch, occupied a place in the Christian imagination as a sower of discord in the early church, and it is likely not a coincidence that his death, as recounted by his opponents, in turn resembles that of Judas (as told in Acts 1:18).[116] At an early stage, Christian writings against Islam marshalled the established polemical discourse against Arianism in their attacks on Islam by associating Muhammad with Arius. In the eighth century, John of Damascus claimed that Muhammad had received instruction from an Arian monk, while a century later Eulogius and Paulus Albarus of Córdoba cast Muhammad in the anti-Arian framework developed in the fourth century by Hilary of Poitiers.[117] As recently as 1109, Guibert of Nogent had compared the hermit who instructed Muhammad to Arius.[118] The association between Arius and Muhammad was motivated not only by a perceived resemblance between Arian Christology and Islamic monotheism, but also by the threat each figure was deemed to pose to the unity of the Christian church. The connection would go on to have a long and rich tradition, among such diverse authors as Peter the Venerable, Gerald of Wales, Riccoldo of Montecroce, and even Dante.[119]

Although Walter did not pen a treatise against Islam, he may have borrowed from anti-Islamic polemical literature to present Il-ghāzi to the Antiochene community as a dangerous force of division. Walter's literary strategy becomes apparent in his renewed use of the ring composition: book 2 of the *Bella Antiochena* begins and ends with a depiction of Il-ghāzi as an agent of discord. The opening sentence (after the prologue) describes Il-ghāzi as "the prince of the error of the Turcomans and of division" (*Turcomannorum erroris et dissidiae principem*), while Il-ghāzi's death at the end of the book is closely modeled on polemical depictions of Arius, viewed as the archdivider within the church.[120] It is possible that behind Walter's polemical treatment of Il-ghāzi lies an anxiety over division—division

115 *Historia ecclesiastica tripartita* 1:3.10: *terror eum subito ex quodam conscientiae secreto constrinxit, et cum formidine secuta est ventris effusio . . . Quo facto defectus eum quidam cum effusione corripuit, et una cum stercoribus meatus quoque prolapsus est. Tunc ergo concidit, et sanguinis multitudo cum subtilibus intestinis subsequenter effluxit, decurrebantque pariter cum splene etiam interna iecoris.*

116 For the development of the legend of Arius's death, see Muehlberger, "Legend of Arius' Death."

117 Esposito Frank, "Dante's Muhammad."

118 Guibert of Nogent, *Dei gesta per Francos* 1.4.273–77; see also the discussion of Arianism in 1.2.

119 Esposito Frank, "Dante's Muhammad."

120 WC 2.1.1. Hagenmeyer plausibly interpreted the otherwise unattested *dissidiae* as related to the Latin word *discidium* (separation, discord), and it has been translated as such by Asbridge and Edgington (*Antiochene Wars*, 110). Alternatively, the word could be a different spelling of the Latin

within Christianity and particularly division between the Eastern and Latin Christian populations of Antioch.

A short Latin work from Antioch on the origins of Islam is just the sort of text Walter may have looked to for his *Bella Antiochena*. The first Latin work from Antioch (and the Latin East in general) centered on Islam, this text largely consists of a narrative purportedly told by a Greek Christian to a Latin Christian newly arrived in Antioch from Jerusalem. Surviving in a single manuscript copy from the mid-twelfth century, it has only rarely received attention in Crusades studies, possibly owing to uncertainties about the authorship and place of composition.[121]

The work's explicit attributes the narrative to one "Adelphus," likely as the result of a scribe's misunderstanding of a passage in which the Greek interlocutor addresses the Latin Christian as *adelphe*, the vocative of the Greek word for "brother."[122] This misunderstanding may subsequently have led scholars of the fifteenth and seventeenth/eighteenth centuries to attribute the work to an otherwise unknown abbot named Adelphus.[123] Moreover, despite the overt setting in Antioch, scholars typically have viewed the work as a product of the Latin West composed in Europe after the author's return from a presumed pilgrimage to Jerusalem.[124] However, the text does not claim that the author merely passed through Antioch, while several narrative motifs shared only with Greek and Latin works from the Levant suggest, as I have discussed elsewhere, that the text should be viewed primarily in a Levantine context.[125]

The "Adelphus" narrative belongs to a literary genre purporting to explain the origins of Islam by relating a biography of Muhammad. More accurately, these "lives of Muhammad" typically depict an inversion of a saint's life, earning them J. Tolan's moniker "anti-hagiographies."[126] Unusually for the genre, this narrative opens with the Latin narrator's critical assessment of Greek intellectualism:

> The Greeks, who are the inventors or writers of almost all the arts, and with whose urbane cleverness, extracted from an old wineskin into a new container, teems many a Latin page, have left behind nothing composed in so fantastical a manner that the pure truth inside—hidden, as it were—

---

desidia (sloth) and thus possibly refer to Il-ghāzi's penchant for drunkenness, though this connection is less clear.

121 Trier, Stadtbibliothek 1897, fols. 1r–21v, described in Keuffer and Kentenich, *Beschreibendes Verzeichnis* 8:277.

122 "Adelphus" 3.

123 Bischoff, "Ein Leben Mohammeds," 106.

124 Bischoff, "Ein Leben Mohammeds," 111; Tolan, *Saracens*, 138; González Muñoz, *Mahometrica*, 80.

125 Yolles, "Latin Vigilance."

126 Tolan, "Anti-Hagiography."

> could not be found, if one searches carefully with the light that Latin vigilance struck from their flint. It is of course from the ideas of these Greeks, with which they are accustomed to debate with the Saracens, that I have assembled what I have undertaken to entrust at present to the office of the pen, like one of the diligent writers of the epic cycle.[127]

The Latin narrator forewarns readers against taking Greek wisdom at face value, urging them instead to utilize Latin learning to penetrate the truth deeply hidden away in Greek discourse. The narrator thus prepares readers for a critical assessment of the following account of the Greek interlocutor, disparagingly described as "a little Greek" (*Graeculus*). Despite its overall focus on Islam and its prophet, the "Adelphus" account shares with Walter the Chancellor a preoccupation with the relationship between Latin and Eastern Christians in Antioch. Yet unlike Walter, who depicted Eastern Christians as little more than a potential moral hazard to Latins, the "Adelphus" account acknowledges that Greeks of Antioch do possess learning, even if this learning requires diligent scrutiny by Latins.

Drawing on an established polemical tradition presenting Muhammad as the pupil of a Christian heretic, the Greek speaker situates the origins of Islam with the fifth-century heretic Nestorius. Banished from Constantinople for his heretical teachings, Nestorius chances upon an illiterate swineherd named Muhammad (*Machomet*) in the deserts of Lebanon. He decides to take up the young man's tutelage as part of a scheme to found a religion to rival Christianity. Together, teacher and student trick the local populace with feigned miracles. Eventually, Muhammad establishes himself as the sole ruler by murdering Nestorius and blaming a drunken follower.

Although this narrative is purportedly told by a Greek Christian, like other Latin works from Antioch, it showcases Latin classroom learning and counts on the reader's ability to decipher erudite references and jokes. For example, when Muhammad is first introduced, the Greek narrator describes him as follows: "For that swineherd had an exceedingly wicked craft, and a very wily mind. He was a man well-versed in necromancy, a student of diabolical teaching, a peerless magician, 'whom neither harmful plant nor hidden voice has escaped.'"[128] In concluding his depiction of Muhammad as a dark mage, the Greek narrator adds a verse that draws on Horace's fifth *Epode*. As the Latin reader was expected to know, this

127 "Adelphus" 1: *Graeci omnium paene artium aut inventores aut scriptores, quorum urbana facetia de veteri utre in novum vas deducta plurima Latina turget pagina, nil tam fabulose editum reliquere, in quo non pura veritas intus—quasi tecta—reperiatur, si eo lumine, quod ab ipsorum silice Latina vigilantia cudebat, curiose investigatur. Quorum nimirum Graecorum ex sententia, qua ipsi cum Saracenis disceptare solent, hoc, quod stili offcio commendare in praesens disposui, quasi unus de curiosis cyclicis collegi.*

128 "Adelphus" 6; Horace, *Epodes* 5.67.

classical poem centers on the efforts of a group of witches to brew a love potion by sacrificing a young boy. The allusion thus evokes a suitably ominous atmosphere while heightening the dramatic tension.

Elsewhere, classical references convey dramatic irony. For instance, when Nestorius urges his student to preach their new religion to his people, he paraphrases a verse from book 2 of Virgil's *Aeneid*: "And since with this plan in mind he thought that it was worth the effort to make Muhammad his ally, 'at last he compelled his student with friendly words.'"[129] In the Virgilian passage to which the narrator alludes, the Greek Androgeos mistakes Aeneas's band of warriors for Greeks, and thus brings about his own demise. The original *inscius* (unknowing), indicating Androgeos, becomes *discipulum* (pupil), referring to Muhammad, who is far cleverer than his teacher and will use this position of authority to bring about Nestorius's demise.

Although the "Adelphus" narrative centers on Islam, surprisingly little attention is paid to Islamic doctrine or religious practices. At the start of his account, the Greek narrator explains his decision not to expound on the heretical teachings for which Nestorius was banished: "As to the idea of this heresy, since it lacks reason, I think it better that you be in complete ignorance of it than that you discuss it at all. For it often happens that something is an obstacle if it is known that would be no obstacle, but rather a benefit, if it were not known."[130] Like Walter the Chancellor, the Greek narrator opts to withhold information from his audience to protect them from potentially harmful knowledge. Rather than focus on the content of Nestorius's (ultimately Islamic, according to this account) teachings, the greatest interest of the "Adelphus" narrative lay in providing an entertaining story about Muhammad while challenging readers to think critically about how Latins should regard Greek traditions of learning. It becomes clear that reflection on learning forms the true theme of the work not only from the Latin narrator's framing of the Greek speaker's account with critical remarks on Greek learning but also from the emphasis throughout the narrative on the teacher-pupil relationship between Nestorius and Muhammad.[131] In one remarkable passage, Muhammad even refers to his sessions with Nestorius, during which the pair cobbled together their dangerous new scriptures, as "your school" (*schola tua*).[132] Just as the polemical biography of Muhammad in the "Adelphus" narrative subverts

129 "Adelphus" 8; Virgil, *Aeneid* 2.371–72: *Androgeos offert nobis, socia agmina credens / inscius, atque ultro verbis compellat amicis.*

130 "Adelphus" 5: *Cuius haeresis sententia quia ratione caret, melius deputo eam te prorsus ignorare quam inde quicquam disputare. Saepe enim contingit id obesse si scitur, quod nil obest, verum prodest si nescitur.*

131 See, in addition to the Latin narrator's opening remarks already quoted, the critical comments by the Latin narrator upon the conclusion of the Greek speaker's account at "Adelphus" 6.

132 "Adelphus" 9.

the genre of Christian hagiography, so does the classroom learning depicted in this work represent a subversion of Latin intellectualism.

Walter the Chancellor's *Bella Antiochena* and the "Adelphus" narrative mark a new development in the Latin literature from Antioch. Although they were written in different genres and with diverging objectives, both works exhibit the beginnings of an engagement with other religious communities in and around Antioch. Walter was primarily concerned with the consequences for Latins of Eastern Christian moral transgressions, and he sought to offer with his history a guide for proper Christian conduct in the face of both internal and external threats. The "Adelphus" narrative, on the other hand, offers the first extensive treatment of Islam in a Latin work from Antioch. Yet this text too showed a preoccupation with the relationship between Latins and Eastern Christians in Antioch and warned Latins of the unreliability of Greek learning—a warning potentially directed at the likes of Stephen the Philosopher, who actively collaborated with an Orthodox Christian scholar. Despite the critical approaches of these works to other religious and cultural traditions, neither engages in an explicit discussion of religious doctrines. It did not take long, however, for Latin writers in the second half of the twelfth century to remedy this literary lacuna.

Episcopal Politics and Doctrinal Disputes: Gerard of Nazareth and Aimery of Limoges

The two central figures on the literary scene of Latin Antioch from the 1140s onward both held prominent positions in the ecclesiastical hierarchy. The careers of Gerard of Nazareth, bishop of Laodicea (1140–ca. 1161), and Aimery of Limoges, patriarch of Antioch (1140–ca. 1195), were closely connected.[133] Both churchmen became involved in the monastic culture on the Black Mountain, near Antioch; they shared an interest in developing ecumenical policies, but also participated in polemical activities centered on scriptural exegesis. Above all, Gerard and Aimery stressed the importance of providing a learned Latin response to Orthodox claims.

Before his ecclesiastical career, Gerard lived as a recluse in a small cell in Galilee, which may have been his native land.[134] There he became acquainted with several ascetics and monks, including the abbots of the monasteries on Mount Tabor and in Palmaria. He subsequently moved to the Principality of Antioch, where he joined a monastic community on the Black Mountain. By 1140 he had become

133 The limits of the career of Aimery of Limoges remain unclear; see Hamilton, "Aimery of Limoges, Patriarch," 285–86.

134 On the life of Gerard of Nazareth, see Kedar, "Gerard of Nazareth." Later sources that preserve fragments of his works (the so-called Magdeburg Centuriators, see below) introduce him as a native of Galilee who took up residence near Nazareth as a Benedictine monk.

bishop of the coastal city of Laodicea in the archdiocese of Antioch.[135] In his first recorded action as bishop, Gerard attended a synod in Antioch on 30 November 1140. The synod had been convened by a papal legate to rule on the complaints of two archdeacons against Ralph of Domfront, archbishop of Antioch. With Gerard's support, Ralph was found guilty of simony and deposed, paving the way for Aimery of Limoges to succeed him.[136]

Aimery had come to Antioch from the Limousin region in southwest central France. His uncle, Peter Armoin, castellan of Antioch, likely played an instrumental role in Aimery's meteoric rise in the ecclesiastical ranks of Antioch.[137] As a dean, Aimery witnessed the dispute between the abbey of Saint Paul and the canons of the Holy Sepulcher in 1140.[138] Although he was only a dean, Aimery subsequently benefited from the chaos caused by the conflict between Raymond of Poitiers (r. 1136–49) and Ralph of Domfront, as he ascended to the position of patriarch. However, Aimery soon found himself at the center of his own struggle with the new prince of Antioch, Reynald of Châtillon. After the disastrous rout of Raymond of Poitiers and his army by Nūr al-Dīn of Aleppo, Raymond's widow Constance married Reynald of Châtillon in 1153. He quickly used his newfound stature to confiscate church property, likely to meet the increased defensive expenditures required after the recent military setbacks. When Aimery protested, Reynald made a spectacular show of power: he seized the patriarch, positioned him on the citadel in full view of the populace, and had honey poured over his head to aggravate his torment by attracting insects.[139] Aimery subsequently left for Jerusalem in a self-imposed exile, where he remained for six years.

In the meantime, Gerard enjoyed considerable influence in Antiochene affairs as a confidant of Reynald. In 1159 Reynald met with the Byzantine emperor Manuel Komnenos in Mamistra to make amends for raiding Byzantine settlements in Cyprus. William of Tyre singles Gerard out as one of the individuals who counseled Reynald and accompanied him to the meeting.[140] However, the thirteenth-century French translation of William's text elaborates substantially on Gerard's actions.[141] In this version, Gerard takes the initiative in urging Reynald to beg for the emperor's mercy and subsequently persuades the emperor

135 Kedar, "Gerard of Nazareth," 71.

136 WT 15.16.11: *De provincia autem Antiochena, quoniam viciniores erant, affuerunt universi, quorum varia nimis et abinvicem dissona errant desideria . . . Geraldus Laodicensis* [*episcopus*]."

137 WT 15.16.60–67.

138 *Cart St-Sép*, 178–83, no. 77.

139 WT 18.1.

140 WT 18.23.42–43: *Usus ergo domesticorum consilio, assumptis ex eis pro arbitrio nonnullis, domino quoque Geraldo venerabili Laodicensium episcopo sibi facto itineris consorte, in Ciliciam . . . ad urbem Mamistram pervenit.*

141 *Guillaume de Tyr* 2:232. The discrepancy was first remarked by Kedar, "Gerard of Nazareth," 62.

to forgive Reynald his transgressions in return for a public display of humility. Although William of Tyre describes the occasion as a humiliating defeat for Latin Christendom (*Latinitas*), Gerard's involvement indicates that he was experienced in dealing with sensitive political and ecclesiastical affairs involving the Orthodox Greeks.[142]

Evidence for Gerard's career thins out not long after the settlement of Mamistra in 1159: that same year, or the year after, he witnessed two charters issued by Queen Melisende of Jerusalem, and the final record of his activities is his witness to a charter issued by King Baldwin III in 1161 in Nazareth.[143] While Gerard seems to have maintained a prominent position in church politics (his name appears in the witness lists in first, second, and third place, respectively), his association solely with the Kingdom of Jerusalem during these final years of his episcopacy has led to speculation that Gerard may have been driven from his see in Laodicea.[144] It is possible that the settlement at Mamistra called for the introduction of a Greek Orthodox bishop of Laodicea instead of or alongside the Latin bishop.[145] Like Aimery, Gerard may subsequently have entered a self-imposed exile and sought refuge in Jerusalem. Gerard probably died shortly thereafter.

Aimery, however, would go on to have an eventful career for another thirty years. Although Reynald of Châtillon had apparently promised Manuel Komnenos to restore an Orthodox patriarch to the see of Antioch, nothing came of this in the short term.[146] Instead, Aimery reassumed his position in Antioch after accompanying Baldwin III to a meeting with Manuel, and even took up governance of the city upon Reynald's imprisonment by Nūr al-Dīn in 1161. In 1164 Aimery's fortunes changed yet again, when Manuel demanded the reinstatement of an Orthodox patriarch in Antioch as a condition for paying the ransom of Bohemond III, the new prince of Antioch who had also been captured by Nūr al-Dīn. Some sixty-five years after the last Orthodox patriarch had been expelled from Antioch, the Byzantines finally succeeded in installing Athanasius VII as patriarch at the expense of the Latins. Aimery retreated to the patriarchal fortress of al-Quṣayr, only to reassume his office when Athanasius VII was killed in an earthquake in 1170. Aimery died possibly as late as 1196.[147]

Gerard of Nazareth and Aimery of Limoges faced intense conflict with the Greek Orthodox Church over the course of their ecclesiastical careers. In response, both developed Latin intellectual programs to counter Orthodox doctrine and

142 WT 18.23.56.

143 *UKJ* 1, nos. 194, 196, and 263.

144 Kedar, "Gerard of Nazareth," 62–63.

145 Jotischky, "Frankish Encounter," 112.

146 So claims the Byzantine historian John Kinnamos, *Epitome*, 4.20 (Brand, *Deeds of John*, 139); see the discussion in Hamilton, *Latin Church*, 174–75.

147 Hamilton, "Aimery of Limoges, Patriarch," 285–86.

praxis. No complete work of Gerard survives, but in 1983 B. Z. Kedar brought to light fragments and summaries of five of his works preserved among later writings.[148] Gerard's works may be subdivided into the genres of monastic hagiography, homily, exegesis, and polemic. Two of these works are a life of an abbot of the monastery of Palmaria and a survey of monastic and eremitical figures in the early decades of the twelfth century. Written in the style of the late antique *History of the Monks in Egypt*, these texts relate to Gerard's monastic beginnings in Galilee and on the Black Mountain near Antioch. It is the three remaining and closely related texts Gerard composed as bishop of Laodicea that will concern us here.[149]

A. Jotischky has argued that Gerard's three works, written during his episcopacy, constitute a coherent polemical program.[150] According to this reconstruction, one of Gerard's earliest works as bishop sparked an exegetical debate between Latins and Orthodox that ultimately revolved around contested episcopal authority. This work was a homily (now lost) for the convent of Saint Mary of Bethany titled *Ad ancillas Dei apud Bethaniam* (To the maidservants of God in Bethany). The convent was a recent royal foundation, from 1143, when, as William of Tyre reports, Queen Melisende established the convent to spare her sister Iveta the indignity of having to serve under an abbess.[151] Like the anonymous author of the *Tractatus de inventione*, Gerard may have been commissioned by the nuns to utilize his Latin learning to promote their convent.[152] Gerard's homily would have provided the new institution with a scriptural foundation to increase its stature and attract pilgrims. For this purpose, Gerard may have sought to associate the convent not only with the sisters Mary and Martha of Bethany but also with Mary Magdalene.

Another work by Gerard focuses precisely on this topic. In *De una Magdalena contra Graecos* (On the one [Mary] Magdalene against the Greeks), Gerard offers a polemical exegetical treatise propounding the common Latin view that identifies Mary of Bethany with Mary Magdalene, along with several unnamed women in the gospels, against the Orthodox contention that these are all separate persons. Drawing on a Latin patristic exegetical tradition that weaves through Ambrose, Augustine, Jerome, Gregory the Great, and Bede, Gerard connected several episodes from the gospels: the story of the unnamed woman anointing Jesus's head at the house of Simon the Leper in Bethany (Matthew 26:6–7; Mark 14:3); the unnamed female sinner who anointed Jesus's feet and wiped them clean with her hair in the house of Simon the Pharisee (Luke 7:37); the episode of Mary, sister of Martha and Lazarus, anointing Jesus's feet and wiping them with her hair (John

148 Kedar, "Gerard of Nazareth"; see also Kedar, "Latin Hermits."

149 See for the fullest treatment of these two works Jotischky, *Perfection of Solitude*, 17–46.

150 Jotischky, "Frankish Encounter."

151 WT 15.26.

152 See chap. 3.

12:1–3); and finally, Jesus's praise for Martha and Mary, who lived in an unidentified *castellum* (Luke 10:39). According to Gerard, these individuals referred to the same person named Mary, who was further identified with the woman from Magdala from whom Jesus cast out demons (Luke 8:2–3) and with the Mary who visited the empty tomb (Matthew 27:56; Mark 15:40; John 19:25). The Greek and Syrian Orthodox traditions, however, considered them separate individuals. In Laodicea and Antioch, the issue was not only an academic matter but had practical application, since Orthodox and Syrian Christians celebrated different feasts for Mary of Bethany and Mary Magdalene, whereas Latin Christians observed a single feast day.

In Jotischky's view, Gerard's treatise on Mary Magdalene represents a polemical response to Orthodox criticism on his earlier homily.[153] That these critics were likely Orthodox Christians from Gerard's own diocese is indicated by his final work. The title of this text is transmitted by John Hornby, a fourteenth-century Carmelite familiar with Gerard's works, as *Girardus episcopus Laodicensis contra Salam philosophum Grecum vel Cretum* (Gerard, bishop of Laodicea, against Sala, a Greek or Cretan philosopher).[154] According to the sixteenth-century Lutheran Church historians who summarized Gerard's works (known as the Magdeburg Centuriators), he wrote against a priest named Sala who had presumed to dedicate cemeteries—a privilege reserved for bishops. Worse still, Sala had introduced a Greek bishop to Laodicea in a direct challenge to Gerard's episcopal authority.[155] The Centuriators suggest that Gerard composed his treatise in response to Sala's reaction to his earlier work on Mary Magdalene:

> Gerard later defended this interpretation [concerning Mary Magdalene] in a specialized treatise against Sala the priest: when he [Sala] came to Laodicea and examined Gerard's treatise, he ostentatiously refuted it with great disdain. But he was unlearned and lacked wit, throwing about foot-and-a-half long words, which he delivered clumsily. Gerard, who was more learned and possessed a more concise style, gave him—that Sala who possessed no salient erudition—an excellent beating. First he provided Sala's words, then his refutation. We will quote just a few words of Gerard from his treatise against Sala. He said: "Since necessity obliges me to read the words of Sala, I feel like someone trying to chew pitch or some other sticky

153 Jotischky, "Frankish Encounter," 109.

154 Jotischky, "Gerard of Nazareth, Mary Magdalene," 223. Since the sixteenth-century Magdeburg Centuriators simply transmitted the title as *Contra Salam presbyterum* (Against the priest Sala), Kedar ("Gerard of Nazareth," 63) suggested that the priest Sala may have been associated with the Order of the Knights Templar, which clashed with both secular and ecclesiastical authorities as it arrogated an increasing number of privileges.

155 Kedar, "Gerard of Nazareth," 77.

substance, and with my teeth stuck I am barely able to swallow it. For as it is said in Job: "Surely it is not possible to eat something unsavory, that is not seasoned with salt?" [cf. Job 6:6][156]

While the Centuriators' account is obviously biased toward Gerard, some of the details are unlikely to be ideologically motivated: Sala's reaction to Gerard's earlier treatise on Mary Magdalene, the subsequent debate between the two churchmen, the location in Laodicea, and Gerard's method of reproducing his opponent's statements first before refuting them. The Centuriators' unflattering depiction of Sala likely channels Gerard's own disdain, given that they make the same pun on Sala's name that Gerard does in their quotation of him. Thus it is probable that their emphasis on Sala's boorishness—as opposed to Gerard's erudition—derives from Gerard's own treatise. From the little evidence the Centuriators provide, Gerard appears as a figure within a culture of lively debate, in which an embattled Latin bishop viewed an attack on his opponent's learning, literary style, and rhetorical abilities as the most viable opening gambit. The limited traces of Gerard's literary activity nevertheless paint a coherent picture: from a homily to a mildly defensive exegetical treatise and culminating in a polemical debate, Gerard utilized his Latin learning in a series of contentious disputes with Orthodox Greeks.

Unlike Gerard, Aimery of Limoges is not known to have composed any works.[157] Although William of Tyre characterized him as "an uneducated and not at all morally sound man" (*hominem absque litteris et conversationis non satis honeste*), Aimery's reputation has improved in recent decades.[158] Among the patriarch's other activities, scholars point to his intellectual interests as revealed in several epistolary exchanges with famed Pisan scholar Hugh Eterianus, who served as an advisor to Manuel Komnenos in Constantinople.[159] Two letters of Aimery to Hugh,

156 Kedar, "Gerard of Nazareth," 77: *Hanc sententiam postea defendit Gerardus peculiari libello contra Salam presbyterum: qui Laodiceam veniens, inspectoque tractatu Gerardi, insigni fastu refutationem ebuccinavit. Sed cum esset indoctus et insulsus, iactaretque sesquipedalia verba, quae inepte proferebat: ideo Gerardus literatior, et tersiori lingua praeditus, illum Salam, nihil salis eruditi habentem, egregie depectit, positis primum Salae verbis, deinde sua refutatione. Pauca tantum verba Gerardi de Salae scripto annotabimus. Sic inquit: Cum huius Salae scripta legere me cogit necessitas, videor mihi quasi picem vel aliquid glutinosum impeditis dentibus mandendo transglutire vix posse. Nam ut in Iob legitur: Nunquid insulsum edi potest, quod non est sale conditum?*

157 Lazar's (*La fazienda*) attribution to Aimery of the *Fazienda de Ultra Mar*, a Castilian paraphrase of the Hebrew Bible that also contains portions of Rorgo Fretellus's pilgrim guide, must be rejected now that the text has been redated to the thirteenth rather than the twelfth century. See Kedar, "Sobre la génesis."

158 Kedar, "Gerard of Nazareth," followed by Hiestand, "Un centre intellectuel," and Hamilton, "Aimery of Limoges, Patriarch."

159 See, e.g., Jotischky, "Frankish Encounter," 112. On Hugh Eterianus's activities in Constantinople, see Hamilton, Hamilton, and Hamilton, *Hugh Eteriano*, 109–53, and Cameron, *Arguing It Out*, 76–79.

which have only recently come to light, enable us to provide a more detailed chronology of the correspondence between the two than has previously been possible.[160]

Sometime between 1171 and 1176–77, Aimery received a copy of Hugh's correspondence with an unnamed member of the clergy of Pisa, almost certainly accompanied by Hugh's treatise *De anima corpore iam exuta* (On the soul, when it is freed from the body). In a letter to Hugh, Aimery praised his collection's "charming expression and substance" (*eloquii venusta facies, et sentenciarum tenor*) and proceeded to invite Hugh to come to Saint Peter's in Antioch. To sweeten the deal, Aimery offered the scholar "an income of a thousand bezants within eight days of your arrival" (*infra octo dies cum veneritis, redditibus mille bisantiorum vos assignabimus*), provided Hugh bring with him a gift of several other works: "Bring with you, therefore, by way of a magnificent gift, [John] Chrysostom, *On the Epistles of Paul*, and whatever can be found in the archives of the Greeks near you about the Nicene council, as well as histories of Greek emperors from the time in which Greece separated itself from the Latin community."[161] Apparently, Hugh was unmoved by the offer, for he remained by the emperor's side in Constantinople.

Sometime later, but presumably before 1176–77, Aimery sent another letter to Hugh. In this missive he again references the Pisan scholar's treatise on the soul, which the patriarch says he has reread and studied often and which deserves, in his view, "to be known to all the faithful." He once again expresses his hope that Hugh might join him in Antioch, but in the meantime he issues another request. He asks Hugh to translate a work—ostensibly a dialogue—written by the Greeks about the *filioque*. It is unclear which work exactly Aimery had in mind and whether or not Hugh complied. It is possible that one work, of which we have positive proof of having been dispatched by Hugh to the patriarch, was intended to fulfill the patriarch's requests. At some point in 1176–77, Hugh entrusted none other than Aimery's old nemesis, the "most glorious" (*gloriosissimi*) Reynald of Châtillon (in Hugh's words), with copies of *De sancto et immortali Deo* (On the holy and immortal God). Hugh had written this treatise in both Greek and Latin, outlining the Latin position on the *filioque* argument, at the request of his patron

160 Tarragona, Biblioteca Publica Provincial, 92, fol. 143r. As I argue elsewhere, internal evidence shows that the letters were in fact composed in the reverse order in which they occur in the manuscript. The second letter (in the manuscript) references Aimery's receipt of the *Libellus ad pisanae urbis clerum*—a collection of works almost certainly including Hugh's *De anima*—and issues an invitation to Hugh to come to Antioch, whereas the first letter (in the manuscript) refers to Aimery as "rereading" (*revolventes*) Hugh's *De anima* and presents Aimery as awaiting Hugh's company (*donec tui dominus copiam dederit*). The discussion below reflects this reconstructed chronology.

161 Tarragona, Biblioteca Publica Provincial, 92, fol. 143r: *Igitur crisostomum super epistolas pauli et quicquid de nicena sinodo in archivis grecorum penes vos inveniri potuerit, historias quoque grecorum imperatorum ab eo saltem tempore quo grecia a latina se divisit familiaritate loco magnifici muneris vobiscum afferte.*

Manuel Komnenos.[162] Upon receipt of this work, Aimery sent a grandiose thank-you note to Hugh:

> I believe that we, before all other Latins, have rightful cause to rejoice in the fact that the splendor of your learning has now shone its serene light over nearly all the world. For the closer we are to the Greeks, the safer we are by your keen knowledge that protects us. Moreover, I received with great enthusiasm the books on the procession of the Holy Spirit, which you sent written in both Greek and Latin. When soon after I had opportunity to devote myself to their study, I greatly admired your talent, eloquence, and knack for expression. I therefore place you ahead of the pagan philosophers of antiquity and put you on an even plane with the great teachers of the church, if the majesty of your affection [toward us] is not diminished by this. I have often wished for you to come to us, and I still persist in this aim—but just as I would rejoice in your arrival, so also is it a boon for us that you remained. For you live not only for yourself, but for us and the universal church, and you have made yourself the greatest defensive wall of all Latinity, giving us, as I said, cause for rejoicing; for we have such a great intermediary in you, whom learned Greece cannot refute, nor oppose with fallacious arguments.[163]

While Aimery could be expected to offer a hefty dose of flattery to the renowned scholar, his depiction of the relationship between Greeks and Latins in Antioch reveals his mindset in startling terms. Aimery presents the Greeks as dangerous to the Latins of Antioch (and possibly to the Latins of the Levant more generally),

162 Hugh Eterianus had entrusted his letter *per manum gloriosissimi Rainaldi*, which must refer to Reynald of Châtillon's only visit to Constantinople between September of 1176 and the summer of 1177. See Dondaine, "Hughes Éthérien," 71; Hamilton, "Aimery of Limoges, Patriarch," 289, n. 61; and Podolak and Bucossi, "Per una futura edizione," 288.

163 Aimery of Limoges, *Letter to Hugh Eterianus* 4–23: *Pro eo quod scientiae vestrae splendor iam prope toti mundo serenus irradiavit, non immerito nobis prae ceteris Latinis censemus esse gaudendum: quanto enim Graecis viciniores sumus, tanto sub vestrae protectionis elimata scientia reddimur securiores. Praeterea libros de processione Sancti Spiritus quos tam Graece quam Latine scriptos misistis cum magna suscepimus cordis alacritate, et mox, ut in perlegendis illis studii nostri curam potuimus adhibere, vestrum ingenium et facundiam et modum loquendi plurimum sumus admirati. Quare vos antiquis gentilium philosophis praeferimus et magnis Ecclesiae magistris, si vestrae dilectionis maiestas in hoc non laeditur, aequiparamus. Frequenter quidem optavimus ut veniretis ad nos et adhuc perseveramus in hoc ipso proposito, sed quemadmodum pro vestro gaudemus adventu, ita bonum est nobis quod remansistis: non solum enim vivitis vobis, sed nobis et universali Ecclesiae, proque tota Latinitate vos antemurale fortissimum opposuistis; unde non immerito, sicut diximus, nobis gaudendum est, utpote qui talem habemus mediatorem, cui nec docta Graecia resistere nec fabricatis sophismatum obiectionibus potest obviare.* I am grateful to P. Podolak for providing me with an advance copy of his critical edition of this letter.

who require protection in the form of Hugh's learned treatises. The relationship between Greeks and Latins is an intellectual battle in which Greek "fallacious arguments" (*fabricatis sophismatum obiectionibus*) must be opposed by Hugh's knowledge (*scientia*). For the patriarch of Antioch, evidently, Latin learning was the answer to countering "learned Greece" (*docta Graecia*).

Having established the importance of Hugh's activities to the Latins of Antioch, Aimery renews his earlier request for three additional works:

> Finally, there are three things for which I issue a request from your kindness. If you will take care that we obtain these, it will both be useful to all of Latinity and will earn you praise—a "monument, more durable than bronze" [Horace, *Odes* 3.30.1]. First of all, the treatise of John Chrysostom on the Epistles of Paul, from which some people have quietly stolen, claiming for themselves many things that belong to the author. Their presumptuousness, if you were to expend effort on this topic, would be worthy of ridicule, and their theft would be exposed, and their fraudulent claim would give way to a greater authority. Secondly, [I ask] for chronicles held among the Greeks since the time in which their emperors were split from the Roman Empire, all the way up to our time.[164] Third, [I ask] for the acts of the Nicene council, which I have heard are in the possession of the lord emperor.[165]

With these requests, Aimery appears to assemble materials for a polemical treatise directed against the Orthodox Greeks. B. Hamilton, however, has suggested that the letter may simply demonstrate the patriarch's desire to learn more about a sizeable segment of the Christian population of Antioch.[166] Viewing the letter in the broader context of Aimery's ecumenical policies toward the Maronites and Armenians, Hamilton argues that an irenic rather than a polemical purpose was not to be excluded. Indeed, Aimery proved instrumental in bringing the Maronites

164 Ciggaar ("Manuscripts as Intermediaries," 136) suggests that this work may refer to John Zonaras's early twelfth-century chronicle. However, given Aimery's circuitous description of the requested text, it is quite possible that Aimery did not have a specific work in mind and simply asked for "a chronicle" or "chronicles" by the Greeks that could shed light on the indicated period.

165 Aimery of Limoges, *Letter to Hugh Eterianus* 23–36: *Tria sunt denique pro quibus vestram postulatum accedimus dilectionem, quae si dederitis operam qualiter habeamus, et toti Latinitati proficuum et hoc ipsum vobis erit in praeconium vestrae laudis monimentum aere perennius: in primis pro tractatu sancti Iohannis Chrysostomi super Epistolas Pauli, de quo sibi, non auctori, plurima quidam ascribentes furtim subtraxerunt, quorum praesumptio, si labor vester in hoc desudaret, risu esset digna et furtum detegeretur et assertio fraudulenta maiori cederet auctoritati; secundo, pro chronicis quae habentur apud Graecos ex illo tempore quo imperatores eorum a Romano divisi sunt imperio usque ad nostra tempora; tertio, pro practica Nicaeni concilii quam audivimus esse penes dominum imperatorem.*

166 Hamilton, "Aimery of Limoges, Patriarch," 283; Hamilton, "Aimery of Limoges, Latin Patriarch."

into communion with the Roman Church in 1181 and probably mediated negotiations between Pope Lucius III and the Armenian catholicos Gregory IV in 1184. Moreover, while Aimery was ousted from his office by Athanasius VII, he developed a friendship with Michael Rabbo, patriarch of the West Syrian Church. Michael visited Antioch on a pilgrimage to Jerusalem in 1169 but decided to stop at Aimery's castle at al-Quṣayr rather than meet with Athanasius VII. He later explained his preference for meeting his Latin instead of his Greek counterpart by claiming that, unlike the Greeks, "the Franks never made any difficulty about matters of doctrine or tried to formulate it in one way only for Christians of differing race and language, but they accepted as a Christian anybody who venerated the cross without further examination."[167]

These comments are difficult to reconcile with the notion that Aimery planned an extensive polemical theological project to combat Orthodox doctrine. Nevertheless, Aimery demonstrated his interest in polemic when he inspired Michael to pen a treatise against Catharism for the occasion of the Third Lateran Council in 1179.[168] Michael's comments on the lack of Latin interest in polemical engagement may simply reflect a dynamic between the Latins and the West Syrians that did not extend to the Greeks. As opponents of the Greek Orthodox Church, whose connections with the Byzantine Empire presented serious ecclesiastical and political threats to both the Latin Church and the West Syrian Church, the two may have found useful allies in each other. The very fact of the parallel organization of the two churches may have favored the establishment of ties, whereas attempts to maintain unity between the Greek and Latin Churches served to heighten tensions.

Even when viewed on its own, Aimery's final letter to Hugh possesses an unmistakable polemical tone. Aimery employs siege imagery in referring to Hugh as the "strongest bulwark" (*antemurale fortissimum*) against Greek assault, resembling the rhetoric in Robert of Ketton's preface to his Latin translation of the Qur'an (1142). Addressing the Cluniac abbot Peter the Venerable, who had commissioned the work, Robert imparts a polemical purpose to the project in describing the need for Christianity to build up defenses (*munimen*), erect a defensive wall (*vallum*), and sharpen spears (*tela*).[169] Aimery's assemblage of Greek texts may have served a similar purpose as Peter the Venerable's so-called *Corpus Islamo-latinum* (including Robert of Ketton's Latin Qur'an), which formed the basis for Peter's own treatise refuting Islam.[170]

167 English translation from Hamilton, "Aimery of Limoges, Patriarch," 279.

168 Hamilton, "Aimery of Limoges, Patriarch," 279–80.

169 For the letter, see Cecini, *Alcoranus latinus*, 92–94. For Robert's use of bellicose imagery, see Martínez Gázquez, "Lenguaje de la violencia."

170 For an introduction to the *Corpus Islamo-latinum*, see Yolles and Weiss, *Medieval Latin Lives*, xix–xxiv.

Furthermore, the manner in which Aimery formulates his request to Hugh warrants closer inspection. To his first request for (presumably a Latin translation of) Chrysostom's homilies on the Epistles of Paul, Aimery adds a markedly hostile comment claiming that some people "have quietly stolen" (*furtim subtraxerunt*) from the venerable theologian. John Chrysostom (d. 407) was a native of Antioch, and there was an Orthodox Church of Saint John Chrysostom in the city.[171] In the eleventh century, the church father's writings inspired a specifically Antiochene school of study: renowned Orthodox figures such as Antony, the abbot of Saint Simeon the Younger, the *protospatharios* Ibrāhīm ibn Yūḥannā al-Anṭākī, and the notable translator and theologian ʿAbdallāh ibn al-Faḍl translated large amounts of Chrysostom's corpus into Arabic and wrote commentaries on his works.[172] In his accusation of plagiarism, Aimery appears to react against Orthodox theologians in Antioch who employed Chrysostom's writings to support their doctrine of the procession of the Holy Spirit. Ramping up the polemical tone, Aimery encourages Hugh to pen a treatise mocking his unnamed opponents for their—in his view—shameless use of Chrysostom.

Aimery may have possessed an expertise in Chrysostom's works, possibly even in the Greek originals. Early in his career as patriarch, he had sent a Greek manuscript of Chrysostom's homilies on Matthew to Pope Eugene III, who had them translated by the scholar Burgundio of Pisa in 1151. In the prologue to the translation, Burgundio expresses his confusion over Aimery's decision to dispatch the Greek original rather than a Latin translation and wonders whether the patriarch had failed to comply with the pope's request "due to laziness or because he did not know any translators" (*sive desidia sive inscitia interpretum*).[173] Aimery's motivation remains unknown; his failure to produce a Latin translation may have been the result of a misunderstanding or may perhaps indicate a lack of interest in cultivating relationships with learned Greek-speaking Christians. Yet it cannot be ruled out that Aimery, who later claimed to have studied both the Greek and Latin versions of Hugh Eterianus's treatise on the procession of the Holy Spirit, read Chrysostom's works in Greek.[174]

The timing of Aimery's final correspondence with Hugh may shed more light on his envisioned project. In 1174 King Amalric of Jerusalem had died, leaving

171 Bohemond II gave the Hospital of Saint John of Jerusalem a house with a garden near this church; see Hiestand, "Ein unbekanntes Privileg," 45.

172 For Antony of Saint Simeon the Younger and ʿAbdallāh ibn al-Faḍl, see Ibrahim, "Some Notes on Antonios"; for Ibrāhīm ibn Yūḥannā al-Anṭākī, see Mugler, "Ibrāhīm ibn Yūḥannā."

173 Burgundio of Pisa, *Prologus*, 817–18; Kedar, "Gerard of Nazareth," 69.

174 Hiestand ("Un centre intellectuel," 13) similarly takes a more positive view of Aimery's course of action, suggesting that Aimery may have anticipated that any translation he would send might raise questions over interpretation. Instead, he may have opted to send the pope the Greek original so that any problematic passages could be handled by a specialist at the papal court.

the thirteen-year-old leper Baldwin IV to manage the kingdom. The precarious alliance Amalric and his predecessor Baldwin III had maintained with the Byzantines was in danger of collapse, and it is probably in this context that Reynald of Châtillon, prince of Antioch, was sent to Constantinople in 1176 to renegotiate political ties with the Byzantines. While he was there, Hugh Eterianus entrusted Reynald with delivering his treatise on the procession of the Holy Spirit to Aimery. Shortly thereafter, in 1177–78, Manuel Komnenos dispatched Leontios, titular Greek Orthodox patriarch of Jerusalem, to the Kingdom of Jerusalem.[175] Aimery would have regarded the move with deep suspicion: having previously been displaced by a titular Greek Orthodox patriarch at Manuel's behest, Aimery had only regained his position due to the premature death of his rival Athanasius VII. With the threat of replacement hanging over him like a sword of Damocles, Aimery may well have regarded Leontios's visit to Jerusalem as Manuel's overture to reinstate a Greek Orthodox successor to Athanasius VII.[176] His Orthodox counterpart, Cyril II, was already waiting in the wings to assume Aimery's position, having been appointed titular patriarch of Antioch by Manuel. As we will discuss in the following chapter, the matter would not be settled until 1180; in the interim, Aimery may have decided to go on the offensive. Like Gerard, who adopted an academic approach to settling ecclesiastical disputes, Aimery may have decided to embark on an intellectual project in response to Orthodox encroachment. Accordingly, Aimery renewed his earlier request to Hugh for three works that could provide the basis for a doctrinal treatise. Aimery's tone in his last letter to Hugh strikes a note of urgency absent from his earlier correspondence. Whereas previously Aimery made the request almost as an afterthought and presented it as "a magnificent gift" (*loco magnifici muneris*), presumably to himself alone, he subsequently depicted Hugh's envisioned translations of the works as "useful to all of Latinity" (*toti Latinitati proficuum*) and added critical comments on Chrysostom's reception in (presumably) Orthodox circles. Whether or not Aimery ever completed the project remains unknown.

Despite limited evidence, Gerard of Nazareth and Aimery of Limoges emerge as prominent figures in the intellectual scene of twelfth-century Antioch. They both developed coherent intellectual programs and viewed Latin erudition as key in their conflicts with Orthodox Christians. Their elevated position in the church hierarchy exposed them to a far greater degree of political and ecclesiastical tension than that faced by writers like Ralph of Caen and Stephen the Philosopher. Compared to the incipient engagement with Eastern Christians by Walter the Chancellor and the "Adelphus" narrative, Gerard of Nazareth and Aimery of Limoges demonstrate the first substantive interest in doctrinal issues on the part

175 Rose, "Church Union Plans."
176 Hamilton, *Leper King*, 111–17.

of Latins. This development likely resulted from the increasing Byzantine pressure on Antiochene secular and ecclesiastical politics over the course of the twelfth century, as promoted by the emperors John II and Manuel Komnenos. Far from dampening enthusiasm, the ensuing controversies appeared to have spurred Latin intellectual activities in Antioch.

Antioch as a Conduit of Learning in the Latin East

The Latin literary tradition of Antioch that developed over the course of the twelfth century was not an isolated phenomenon cut off from western Europe or the rest of the Latin East. As C. Burnett has demonstrated, Antioch functioned as one of the links between Latin and Arabic cultures in the twelfth-century Mediterranean.[177] This was true from an early stage: in 1114, the renowned English scholar Adelard of Bath visited the Principality of Antioch, which may be where he found Thābit ibn Qurra's *Liber prestigiorum* (Book of spells), Abū Ma'šar's *Abbreviation of the Introduction to Astrology*, Pseudo-Ptolemy's *Centiloquium* (One hundred sayings), and even Euclid's *Elements*, all of which he translated from Arabic into Latin.[178] As Burnett has suggested, the two scholars may have met during this visit, and Stephen may even have been the one to furnish Adelard with the Arabic texts in question.[179] Stephen himself directed his works to a broad Latin intellectual community that extended across the Mediterranean to western Europe, where his translation of al-Maǧūsī's medical handbook enjoyed a respectable circulation.[180]

As R. Hiestand has shown, Aimery of Limoges appears as a conduit of Greek and Latin manuscripts between the Levantine East and Latin West in the second half of the twelfth century.[181] Years before his requests of texts from Hugh Eterianus, Aimery had sent a Greek manuscript of John Chrysostom's homilies on Matthew to Pope Eugene III, who had them translated by the scholar Burgundio of Pisa in 1151. Aimery was thus not merely a recipient of texts but also a distributor. In this light, it is distinctly plausible that Aimery was the source of Hugh Eterianus's Greek manuscript of a treatise by the ninth-century Melkite theologian Theodore Abū Qurra.[182] Moreover, Aimery may also have been involved

177 Burnett, "Antioch as a Link."

178 Adelard references a visit to Cilician Tarsus and Mamistra (which he described as situated *in partibus Antiochenis*, "in Antiochene territory"), both of which lay within the Principality of Antioch. His account of an earthquake during this visit dates his trip to 1114. See Adelard of Bath, *Questiones naturales* 50.1.

179 Burnett, "'Abd al-Masīḥ of Winchester," 113.

180 On the textual tradition of this work, see Haskins, *Studies in the History*, 131, nn. 8 and 9, and Burnett, "Antioch as a Link," 20–22 and 30.

181 Hiestand, "Un centre intellectuel," 9–16.

182 Burnett, "Antioch as a Link," 5–6.

in the circulation of a French text from Antioch. The late twelfth-century poet who reworked the French epic *Chanson des chétifs* (Song of the *chétifs*) claimed that the original poem had been composed at the Antiochene court of Raymond of Poitiers and was subsequently dispatched to western Europe by the patriarch, which presumably refers to Aimery.[183]

In addition to having links to the Latin West, Antioch also formed part of a closely knit network including the rest of the Latin East, especially the Kingdom of Jerusalem. With the exception of Walter the Chancellor and Stephen the Philosopher, all Latin authors who wrote in twelfth-century Antioch had a connection with the Kingdom of Jerusalem: Ralph of Caen directed his *Tancredus* to the patriarch of Jerusalem and may have moved there from Antioch; the Latin author of the "Adelphus" narrative situates the exchange in Antioch after his return from Jerusalem; Gerard of Nazareth moved to the Principality of Antioch after an earlier career (and possible upbringing) in Galilee; and finally Aimery of Limoges spent long stints in voluntary exile in Jerusalem before returning to Antioch. Even in the case of Walter the Chancellor, about whom precious little is known, the textual tradition of his work shows a close connection with the Kingdom of Jerusalem, while it is possible that Stephen the Philosopher moved there later in life. Two additional authors from twelfth-century Antioch, whose works have not been discussed here, also moved between these two areas: Rorgo Fretellus became an archdeacon of Antioch after holding the offices of chancellor and chaplain in Galilee, while Albert, archbishop of Tarsus, may have ended his career as archbishop of Nazareth (see appendix 1).

From this list, Galilee emerges as an area particularly well-connected to Antioch. The infrastructure for this network must at least in part have been provided by monastic institutions, which maintained frequent contacts with other institutions across the Levant. One example bears vivid testimony to this interconnected world as well as to the harsh realities of the Latin East. According to documents from 1183, the monks of Saint Paul of Antioch entered into a fraternal association with the monastic community of Mount Tabor in Galilee, stipulating that "if the Principality of Antioch should be overrun by the Turks and the prince exiled, the monks of Saint Paul will be received into Mount Tabor and will be provided for."[184] Fourteen years later, the monks of Saint Paul made similar arrangements with the abbey of Saint Mary of the Valley of Jehoshaphat in Jerusalem, which assured them that "if the land of Antioch falls into the hands of the Turks, Saint Mary will provide for the monks of Saint Paul."[185]

183 *Chanson des Chétifs*, 15–16.

184 *Cart Hosp*, 2:910–11, no. 22 (RRH no. 634; RRR no. 1137).

185 *Chartes Josaphat*, 92–94, no. 44 (RRH no. 738; RRR no. 1394).

But it was not only Latin Christian monasteries that connected Antioch with the rest of the Latin East. Antioch's diverse monastic communities made it a prime destination for those looking to find texts in a variety of languages. In 1179 Nerses of Lambron, the famed Armenian scholar and archbishop of Tarsus, encountered a Latin manuscript containing the *Rule of Saint Benedict* and Gregory the Great's *Dialogi* (Dialogues) at the abbey of Saint Paul in Antioch as well as a manuscript of Andrew of Caesarea's commentary on John's Revelation written in "the Lombard tongue." With the help of a Latin monk, Nerses subsequently translated the *Rule of Saint Benedict* into Armenian, leaving the translation of the life of Benedict (as found in the second book of the *Dialogi*) for another day.[186] This was the same monastery, we may recall, where Stephen the Philosopher had some fifty years earlier served as treasurer while he collaborated with an Eastern Christian scholar.

Another location that emerges as a center of textual exchange is the Black Mountain, some thirty kilometers northwest of Antioch. This part of the Amanus mountain range was densely populated with monasteries of various Eastern and Latin Christian communities, as attested by James of Vitry, bishop of Acre (1216–1227): "[The city] has to the north a certain mountain, commonly known as the 'Black Mountain,' on which there are many hermits of every people and ethnicity, and even more monasteries, of both Greek and Latin monks."[187] Gerard of Nazareth, as mentioned, spent the early part of his career there as a Benedictine monk before his episcopate, and may have interacted with other intellectuals there. Moreover, it was to a monastery on the Black Mountain that Nerses went to locate the Greek original of Andrew of Caesarea's commentary on John's Revelation.[188] Aimery may have procured some of his Greek manuscripts from an Orthodox monastery on the Black Mountain or alternatively from the Greek Orthodox monastery of Saint Simeon the Younger on the nearby Mons Admirabilis.[189] The patriarchs of Antioch appear to have had frequent access to this monastery: Aimery's predecessor, Ralph of Domfront, stayed there when Raymond of Poitiers prevented him from entering Antioch, and later he was imprisoned there by Raymond.[190] This monastery was renowned for its library; after a major fire in 1183, Michael Rabbo was relieved to discover that only books that "no one read" had perished.[191]

186 Nerses of Lambron, *Commentary on the Revelation*, 16–19.

187 James of Vitry, *Historia orientalis* 32.38–41: *Habet autem a septentrionali parte montem quendam qui vulgariter "montana Nigra" dicitur, in quo sunt multi eremite ex omni gente et natione et plura monasteria, tam grecorum quam latinorum monachorum.*

188 Nerses of Lambron, *Commentary on the Revelation*, 16–19.

189 Nasrallah, "Couvents de la Syrie."

190 Hiestand, "Un centre intellectuel," 14. For Ralph's captivity at Saint Simeon, see Hamilton, "Ralph of Domfront," 14–15 and 19.

191 Michael Rabbo, *Chronique de Michel le Syrien*, 3:392.

Antioch continued to function as a place of textual discovery and translation activity during the thirteenth century. Around 1220 the German scholar Oliver of Paderborn visited the monastery of Saint Simeon the Younger, where he consulted Georgian manuscripts with the help of a translator (*per interpretem*) and learned that Georgian Christians maintained the same order of the gospels and the Pauline epistles as Latins.[192] A decade later, the canon Philip of Tripoli translated an Arabic version of the pseudo-Aristotelian *Secretum secretorum* (Secret of secrets). In the prologue, he recounts that he discovered the manuscript in Antioch.[193] Philip's comment that the text was extremely rare among Arabs (and therefore among Latins) reveals the mindset of an early Poggio Bracciolini, experienced in finding the best places to hunt for manuscript treasures. Evidently Antioch was just such a potential treasure trove.

Conclusion

In the Latin works from twelfth-century Antioch, several tendencies emerge that differentiate them from the Latin literature of the Kingdom of Jerusalem. First, authors employed emphatic displays of learning rooted in a Latin school tradition. In particular, they cultivated a highly rhetorical brand of learning, as manifested in their interest in rhetorical theory, in the deployment of a style of writing characterized by rhetorical flourishes, and in the valorization of rhetorical mastery as a key component of both scientific and doctrinal discourse. Ralph of Caen and Walter the Chancellor's prosimetric works brim with rhetorical figures, while Stephen the Philosopher maintained an interest in rhetorical textbooks and presented scientific pursuit as a courtroom debate. In his dispute with a Greek priest, Gerard of Nazareth attacked his opponent's style, while Aimery of Limoges praised not the soundness of Hugh Eterianus's theological argument but his "talent, eloquence, and knack for expression"—sufficient cause, apparently, for Aimery to place Hugh on an even footing with the church fathers. In Antioch's diverse literary scene, Latin authors learned to place great value on eloquence and rhetorical skill.

Second, Latin writers engaged far more extensively with other intellectual and religious communities in Antioch than their counterparts in Jerusalem. To the extent that Latin authors in the Kingdom of Jerusalem drew on Eastern Christian, Muslim, or Jewish traditions, their engagement with them remained largely superficial and aimed at reinforcing Latin narratives. In Antioch, by contrast, Stephen the Philosopher not only touted his access to the "truth of the Arabs," but actively collaborated with a member of an Arabic-speaking Orthodox

192 Oliver of Paderborn, *Historia Damiatina* 63. For Georgian monasteries in and around Antioch, see Djobadze, *Materials for the Study*.

193 Williams, *Secret of Secrets*, 361.

Christian community. Even the highly critical "Adelphus" narrative admitted that the Greek tradition contained real truths and knowledge, though they required a vigilant Latin eye to discern them from falsehood. Finally, Aimery of Limoges's letters drew a picture of "learned Greece" as a formidable opponent to the Latin community in the Levant.

In Antioch we also observe a Latin interest in religious reform and doctrinal debate not paralleled in Jerusalem. In the first book of his history, Walter the Chancellor demonstrates an early attempt to reform the Eastern Christian populace and bring their cultural practices in line with those of their Latin rulers. Moreover, the increased involvement of the Byzantines in Antiochene secular and ecclesiastical affairs from the late 1130s onward prompted authors like Gerard of Nazareth and Aimery of Limoges to engage in discussion of doctrinal issues with the Greek Orthodox community. By contrast, as J. Rubin observed, there is no evidence for such interest in the Kingdom of Jerusalem before the thirteenth century.[194]

Two late thirteenth-century examples illustrate the degree to which these features of Latin literature in Antioch remained constant over time. In 1282 John of Antioch translated Cicero's *De inventione* and the *Rhetorica ad Herennium* into Old French for the first time in a sumptuously illuminated manuscript commissioned by William of Saint Stephen, a Hospitaller knight in Acre.[195] John of Antioch's translations demonstrate both continuity and change: they are translations of the same texts that Stephen the Philosopher had copied in 1121, yet the desire for a vernacular translation of these ancient school texts shows a fundamental shift in the literary culture of the Latin East. Importantly, the fact that these translations were not made directly on the basis of Stephen the Philosopher's Latin copies but from different textual witnesses shows that rhetorical study in Latin Antioch was more extensive than has been acknowledged.

Around 1265 Thomas Aquinas wrote a treatise directed to the cantor of Antioch called *Reasons for the Faith against Saracens, Greeks, and Armenians*, which addressed a range of Latin doctrinal concerns in the face of Islam as well as Greek and Armenian Orthodox Christianity.[196] The work underlines the sustained interest of senior Latin clergy in Antioch in doctrinal issues and also shows their continued success in persuading the greatest intellectuals of the Latin world to contribute their learning to their cause.

194 Rubin, *Learning in a Crusader City*, 139–40.

195 On William of Santo Stefano or Saint Étienne—his origins are a matter of dispute—see Burgtorf, *Central Convent*, 686; Folda, *Crusader Art*, 412; and Rubin, *Learning in a Crusader City*, 25.

196 For an introduction and translation, see Kenney, "Reasons for the Faith."

Chapter Five

EASTERN AND WESTERN LATIN LITERATURE IN WILLIAM OF TYRE

IN 1184 THE ARCHBISHOP OF TYRE surveyed the state of the Latin East. He concluded that the internal division among the Latins, coupled with a growing and unified external threat, created a situation so dire that he hesitated to put pen to parchment. A highly stylized passage expressing this view fits into a long tradition stretching back to Greek and Roman historiography, in which writers characteristically lamented the degeneration of their own time to promote the notion of decline. William of Tyre, the author of this passage, invokes this tradition by referencing the Roman historian Livy and the Jewish writer Josephus.[1]

To an extent, Livy and Josephus represent some of William's literary models for his grand chronicle, the *Historia*. More than that, they signify two distinct literary and cultural traditions, while highlighting the tension between William's continuing appeal to western European readership and patronage and his promotion of the exceptional status of the Christian populace of the Holy Land. Livy, whose Roman history began to resurface in the twelfth century, stood for the classical, Greco-Roman literary tradition. Josephus, on the other hand, was a Jewish native from Palestine who received patronage from the Roman emperors Vespasian and Titus. William may have conceived of himself as some combination of the two traditions: he enjoyed an extensive education in western Europe, including in classical literature, but, as a native of the Levant, he repeatedly appealed to patriotic sentiment and invoked an Arabic Christian writer as an authority.

As the capstone to this examination of Latin literature of the twelfth-century Levant, William's historical work represents the first truly extensive Levantine Latin literary project designed for both western European patrons and clerical and courtly audiences of the Latin East. William accomplished this delicate feat by, on the one hand, integrating the legend of Charlemagne into the history of the Crusades and appropriating the imperial biographical tradition associated with him. On the other hand, William used Christian Arabic texts and appealed to

1 WT 23.praef.

their intellectual authority. His access to these traditions parallels the intellectual relations between Latins and Eastern Christians in Antioch and may even indicate movement of manuscripts between Antioch and the Kingdom of Jerusalem. William's adoption of Eastern Christian historical framing and simultaneous claim to be writing a new, uniquely Latin history of the Latin East represents the most complex expression yet of Levantine Latinity.

Given the volume and scope of William's chronicle, it should be emphasized that this chapter is necessarily selective and relies firmly on an important and increasingly daunting body of scholarship. I have chosen these two strands of inquiry because I believe that they enable the identification of new developments in Levantine Latin literature. That is not to say, however, that they are the only features of William's Latinity worth discussing, as other readers of William may find equally valid aspects to which attention might be drawn.

Across the Sea and Back Again

The first Latin author in this study who is a confirmed native of the Levant, William of Tyre, was born in Jerusalem around 1130 to first- or second-generation Frankish settlers.[2] His family, which included at least one brother named Ralph, belonged to a social group in the Latin East known as burgesses,[3] who in the Kingdom of Jerusalem were free citizens, frequently merchants, who had their own legal court. Although they did not belong to the topmost echelon of Frankish society, as the backbone of the Frankish economy they must have possessed a certain degree of influence. Nevertheless, William's eventual rise to the office of archbishop—normally reserved for nobility—represented a considerable social advancement.

The 1130s and 1140s of William's early youth were a time of significant social and political change in the Kingdom of Jerusalem. On the one hand, the descendents of the barons who had acquired their lands and positions during the First Crusade vied with the continuous stream of new arrivals from western Europe. Fulk of Anjou's succession to the throne in 1131 signalled a tilt in the balance of power to European nobility and greater ties with Western courts. On the other hand, Armenian, Georgian, and Greek- and Arabic-speaking Christians became increasingly active at the Frankish courts in this period. Melisende—queen of Jerusalem, daughter of Baldwin II and the Armenian princess Morphia—was a

2 Gerard of Nazareth was reported by later sources to have been a native of Galilee; see chap. 4.

3 A charter from the Church of the Holy Sepulcher in 1175 lists William's brother Ralph (*Radulfus frater domni W[illelmi] Tyrensis archiepiscopi*) as a witness under "burgesses" (*burgenses*): *Cart St-Sép*, 311–12, no. 160 (RRH no. 531; RRR no. 946). For the social class of the burgesses, see Prawer, "Social Classes," and Nader, *Burgesses*. On the life of William of Tyre, see Edbury and Rowe, *William of Tyre*, 13–22, and the essays in Edgington and Nicholson, *Deeds Done*.

benefactor of the Armenian community of Jerusalem and commissioned from the scriptorium of the Church of the Holy Sepulcher sumptuous manuscripts betraying both Western and Eastern artistic influences. With her combined Frankish and Armenian heritage and her marriage to a newcomer to the Latin East, Melisende represented a combination of the disparate cultural elements that made up Frankish society in this period.

William received his early education in this dynamic and complex social and cultural context. He may have attended the school connected with the Church of the Holy Sepulcher in Jerusalem, where John of Pisa, who went on to become a cardinal in Rome, educated "young clergy" in 1136.[4] Other figures who may have played a role in William's early school days are Peter of Barcelona, prior of the Holy Sepulcher until 1148, and Geoffrey, prior and later abbot of the Templum Domini from 1136/37 onward.[5]

Around the age of fifteen or sixteen, William traveled to western Europe, where he spent the following nineteen years pursuing a remarkable course of study with some of the brightest minds of the twelfth century.[6] He began his studies in the liberal arts in Paris under Bernard of Moelan, Deacon Ivo of Chartres,[7] and Peter Helias, and also attended the disputations of Alberic de Monte, Robert of Melun, Mainer, Robert Amiclas, and Adam of Petit-Pont. Sometime afterward, William moved to Orléans to study classical literature with Hilary of Orléans and geometry with William of Soissons before moving back to Paris to study theology with Peter Lombard, author of the influential theological school text the *Sententiae* (*Sentences*), and later with Maurice of Sully, a former student of Abelard celebrated for his role in laying the foundations of the Notre-Dame de Paris. Finally, William spent four years studying law in Bologna with Martinus Hugo, Bulgar, and Jacobus—all former students of the renowned legal scholar Irnerius of Bologna.[8]

4 Mayer, "Guillaume de Tyr à l'école," based on the remarks in WT 16.17 and 18.8. A document from the cartulary of the chapter of the Holy Sepulcher bears the subscription *scriptum per manum Iohannis Pisani qui eo tempore ad Sepulchrum clericulos docebat*. See *Cart St-Sép*, no. 103, and Hotzelt, "Die Chorherren," 118. Buchthal (*Miniature Painting*, xxx) suggests that this may be the same person mentioned by William of Tyre (WT 16.17.26) as archdeacon of Tyre in 1146.

5 Krey, "William of Tyre," 10; see also Hiestand, "Zum Leben," 363–64. Krey also suggests Fulcher, patriarch of Jerusalem from 1146 to 1157, as playing a role, but Fulcher did not come into office until after William would have left to study in Europe.

6 Huygens, "Guillaume de Tyr étudiant." For William's study of the liberal arts and their impact on his thought and writings, see Schwinges, *Kreuzzugsideologie und Toleranz*, 286–90.

7 Not to be confused with Saint Ivo of Chartres, who died in 1116.

8 William claims to have studied both civil and canon law (WT 19.12.1): *iuris quoque tam ecclesiastici quam civilis prudentiam avidissime sum sequutus*. However, as Edbury and Rowe (*William of Tyre*, 15) point out, none of the teachers he mentions were canonists.

Returning to his homeland in 1165, William found the Kingdom of Jerusalem in drastically changed circumstances from when he left in the mid-1140s. The abject failure of the Second Crusade (1147–49), which had featured the participation of Conrad III of Germany and the French king Louis VII, soured relations between Jerusalem and the royal houses of western Europe. The young king Baldwin III instead began to favor an alliance with the Byzantines, resulting in a marriage with Theodora, niece to the Byzantine emperor Manuel Komnenos, in 1158 (presided over, incidentally, by Aimery of Limoges during his self-imposed exile in Jerusalem).

When he entered the Frankish political scene in the mid-1160s, William benefited from both his European education and his ties to the Latin East. He quickly proceeded through the clerical ranks, becoming canon of Acre in 1165 and archdeacon of Tyre in 1167. He also curried the favor of the royal court in Jerusalem in this period. King Amalric (r. 1163–1174), who had succeeded the childless Baldwin III, continued his brother's pro-Byzantine policies and sent William on a diplomatic mission to Manuel Komnenos in 1168. Two years later, William was appointed tutor to the future king Baldwin IV. Upon Amalric's death in 1174, the regent Raymond III of Tripoli appointed William chancellor of Jerusalem; a year later, he was elected archbishop of Tyre.

At this point, William might have expected his career to culminate in election to patriarch of Jerusalem. He possessed all the qualifications: a sound education, an illustrious ecclesiastical career, and support from the royal court in Jerusalem. Yet, when the patriarchal see fell vacant in 1180, Eraclius, archbishop of Caesarea, was elected instead.[9] William may simply have been unfortunate, for his rival was equally qualified. Nonetheless, the Old French continuation to William's history cast the patriarchal election and William's subsequent death in a sinister light, claiming that Eraclius had his former rival excommunicated from the church. When William traveled to Rome to appeal to Pope Alexander III, a physician allegedly poisoned William on Eraclius's orders.

While in the past some have accepted this account as largely true, the dramatic nature of the story as well as the factual inaccuracies it contains have made it subject to criticism by more recent scholars, who tend to view the account as a fabrication by partisans of William.[10] Regardless of the question of William's death, a likely explanation for his failure to obtain the Jerusalemite see lies in the shifting political balance during the last years of William's life, from the royal

9 On Eraclius, see Kedar, "Patriarch Eraclius."

10 For the former view, see Prutz, "Studien über Wilhelm von Tyrus," 106, and Röhricht, *Geschichte des ersten Kreuzzuges*, 391, who dates the excommunication to 2 April 1181. For the latter position, see Krey, "William of Tyre," 160; Mayer, "Zum Tode Wilhelms von Tyrus"; and Hiestand, "Zum Leben," 348.

pro-Byzantine party of Raymond III, count of Tripoli, to the powerful alliance of barons and European newcomers.

After succeeding his brother Baldwin III to the throne in 1163, Amalric had his first marriage, to Agnes of Courtenay, annulled to form an alliance with the Byzantines through a marriage to Maria Komnene in 1167. When William's career in the Jerusalemite court began in the late 1160s, he associated with the faction of Maria Komnene and her supporter Raymond III. Although this patronage benefited William in the short run, his connection to Maria may have harmed his long-term prospects, as the faction of Agnes eventually won out. Agnes enjoyed powerful support from her second husband, Reginald Grenier, lord of Sidon; Reynald of Châtillon, now lord of Oultrejourdain; Eraclius, then archbishop of Caesarea; and Gerard of Ridefort, master of the Knights Templar, as well as the more recent arrivals to the Latin East, Amalric of Lusignan and his younger brother Guy. Moreover, while Agnes had borne King Amalric a son and heir, Baldwin IV, Maria had only given him a daughter, Isabella. Since Baldwin IV (the "Leper King") was not expected to live long, the struggle for Isabella's hand in marriage grew fierce in the late 1170s. Baldwin IV's decision to marry Isabella to Guy of Lusignan in the summer of 1180 dashed the hopes of Maria's faction definitively, and in the fall of 1180 Eraclius, not William, was chosen to be patriarch of Jerusalem. William died sometime between 1184, the last date in his chronicle, and 1186, when Joscius was elected his successor as archbishop of Tyre.

The Scope and Structure of the History

William's *Historia* falls into two discrete units: books 1–8 give an account of the First Crusade, culminating in the capture of Jerusalem in 1099, while books 9–23 offer a history of the Kingdom of Jerusalem up to 1184.[11] William's account of the First Crusade innovatively begins the narrative not with the Council of Clermont in 1095, as was conventional, but with the Roman emperor Heraclius and the subsequent Muslim conquest of Jerusalem in 638. The organization of the second unit centers on the kings of Jerusalem. The first book, covering a king's rule, typically opens with the coronation ceremony, followed by a description of the physical traits and general character of the new king, while the second book concludes with a short eulogy describing the king's death.[12]

11 For an overview of the structure of William's work and the chronological range of each book, see the table in Propst, *Die geographischen Verhältnisse*, 1:9–10.

12 William deviates from this otherwise fixed structure in the last three books. Since Baldwin IV was not yet of age when his father Amalric left him the throne, Count Raymond III of Tripoli was regent from 1174 to 1176. Book 21 therefore contains two character portraits: that of Baldwin IV and of Raymond III. Moreover, since Baldwin IV's death in 1185 extended beyond the final redaction made by William in 1184, book 22 does not conclude with the death of the king, as one would

This clear-cut structure centered on the kings of Jerusalem found an important precedent in the organization set down by Fulcher of Chartres. By starting his history with the loss of Jerusalem to the Muslim conquests in the reign of Heraclius, however, William surpassed his predecessor and firmly established his work as a history of the Holy Land, while the increased scope of the work allowed him to address in greater depth the events that led to the First Crusade and the establishment of the Kingdom of Jerusalem. More importantly, William emphasized the Kingdom of Jerusalem's political and cultural continuity with the Roman Empire through Heraclius—a continuity also manifested in both implicit and explicit references to the Holy Roman emperor Charlemagne.

The History as a Product of Western Learning

In 1184, after he had written the bulk of a twenty-three-volume history of the Kingdom of Jerusalem, William composed a suitably elaborate prologue to the work. Addressing a broad but well-educated audience of "venerable brothers in Christ," the prologue showcases William's erudition and classical training. He quotes Cicero (twice) and the Roman comic Terence and paraphrases Boethius and Horace. In addition to impressing his readership, William positions himself and his work within a literary and intellectual tradition.

William's history of the Kingdom of Jerusalem is a product of both classical and medieval Latin intellectual culture. The second sentence of his prologue references a proverb involving the mythological figures Scylla and Charybdis. While evocative of classical antiquity, the proverb may have owed its popularity to the recent dissemination of Walter of Châtillon's *Alexandreis* (Poem on Alexander [the Great]), published just a few years earlier.[13] William's quotation of Cicero's *Tusculan Disputations* likewise does not necessarily indicate direct engagement with a classical author. The same quotation appears in the prologue to the ninth-century biography of Charlemagne authored by Einhard. Through his engagement with the work of Einhard, William also situated his history within a Frankish intellectual tradition.

In the prologue, William explains that a "most pressing love of his homeland" (*urgentissimus amor patrie*) drove him to take up the arduous task of writing history.[14] Almost as an afterthought, he adds that King Amalric insisted he compose the work. Amalric had also commissioned William to write another

---

expect, but with Baldwin IV handing over the throne to his nephew Baldwin V in 1183, as he was suffering from leprosy.

13 WT prol. 6; Walter of Châtillon, *Alexandreis* 5.301 (for the dating of the *Alexandreis*, see Townsend's comments at pp. 14–15; the likely date is 1178, or six years before William wrote his prologue).

14 WT prol. 66–67.

work, which does not survive, dealing with "Eastern rulers" from the time of Muhammad up to his own day:

> At his request, and while he himself supplied *Arabica exemplaria*, I also composed another history, from the time of the seducer Muhammad up to the current year, which is 1184 in the year of Our Lord, covering five-hundred and seventy years. I followed in particular the *auctor* Saʿīd ibn Baṭrīq, a venerable man and patriarch of Alexandria.[15]

William mentions this (now lost) history not only to promote his other work but also to emphasize the originality of his current project. Whereas his history of Eastern rulers relied on so-called *Arabica exemplaria* supplied by the king, he claims that no such sources existed for the history of the foundation of the Kingdom of Jerusalem:

> But for the present [history] I had no Greek or Arabic writing as my guide; and so, informed by reports alone—except for the few things of which I was an eyewitness—I have arranged a sequential narrative. I took as my starting point the exodus of heroic men and noble leaders, "amiable to the Lord," who at the Lord's summons left the Western kingdoms and laid claim to the Promised Land and almost all of Syria, "with a strong hand." I continued the history with great care, covering eighty-four years up to the reign of Lord Baldwin IV, the seventh in the sequence of kings (including Lord Duke Godfrey, who first obtained the kingdom).[16]

While William did rely on inherited Latin traditions on the First Crusade and the early decades of the Kingdom of Jerusalem (including, among others, the works of Fulcher of Chartres and Walter the Chancellor), he argues that there existed no Greek or Arabic historiographic tradition on which he could draw in writing the history of this uniquely Latin kingdom. His phrasing is marked: the medieval Latin term *auctor*, used here in reference to the Alexandrian patriarch Saʿīd ibn

15 WT prol. 84–89: *cuius etiam rogatu, ipso Arabica exemplaria ministrante, aliam Historiam a tempore seductoris Mahumet usque in hunc annum, qui est nobis ab incarnatione domini MCLXXXIIII, per annos quingentos septuaginta decurrentem conscripsimus, auctorem maxime sequuti virum venerabilem Seith, filium Patricii, Alexandrinum patriarcham.*

16 WT prol. 89–99: *In hac vero nullam Grecam aut Arabicam habentes preducem scripturam, solis traditionibus instructi, exceptis paucis que ipsi oculata fide conspeximus, narrationis seriem ordinavimus, exordium sumentes ab exitu virorum fortium et deo amabilium principum, qui a regnis Occidentalibus, vocante domino, egressi Terram Promissionis et pene universam Syriam in manu forti sibi vendicaverunt, et inde usque ad regnum domini Balduini quarti, qui in ordine regum, computato domino duce Godefrido, qui primus regnum obtinuit, locum habuit septimum, per annos LXXXIIII cum multa diligentia protraximus historiam.*

Baṭrīq, was an honorific title in learned medieval culture that is difficult to translate because of its complex web of associations of authorship and authority. As one scholar aptly puts it, the term indicated "a writer who is regarded as a master of his subject or as providing reliable evidence, an authority."[17]

The word *exemplar* (plural, *exemplaria*) likewise possessed notions of a literary model or authority. William's classically educated reader may have recognized the word from the poet Horace, who refers in his *Ars poetica* with condescension to those Roman poets who "night and day leaf through *exemplaria Graeca*," meaning Greek models of poetry.[18] In other contexts, the word *exemplaria* refers to original manuscripts serving as the basis for copies, while Jerome used *exemplaria Graeca* or *exemplaria Hebraea* to refer to Greek or Hebrew versions of scripture used for his Latin translation. For his work on the Latin Kingdom of Jerusalem, William claims to be his own *auctor* or literary authority, without recourse to *exemplaria* or literary models from other cultural and intellectual traditions.

However, William certainly looked to the ninth-century author Einhard as a model for imperial biography and utilized subsequent traditions to make a cogent connection between Charlemagne and the Kingdom of Jerusalem. Moreover, William also had access to a tenth-century Christian Arabic author from North Africa and his continuator in Antioch as well as a range of other Eastern Christian texts. His use of these two cultural and literary traditions reflects not only the course of his own life, divided between western Europe and the Levant, but also Levantine Latin culture more generally. William made a concerted effort to integrate the Frankish Levant within European frameworks of knowledge and history, possibly to appeal more successfully to European nobility for patronage. At the same time, he used his continental learning to promote the notion of a unified Christian identity of the Levant that encompassed both the Franks and the various local Greek- and Arabic-speaking Christian communities.

The Legend of Charlemagne, Proto-Crusader

Charlemagne was an ideal figure through whom William could engage his readership, both at home and abroad. By the second half of the twelfth century, legendary traditions on Charlemagne had become wildly popular across Europe in both Latin and vernacular literature.[19] These traditions frequently connected Charlemagne to the Holy Land and eventually presented him as a proto-Crusader.[20] This

17 Ziolkowski, "Cultures of Authority," 426.

18 Horace, *Ars poetica* 268.

19 On Charlemagne, see now Nelson, *King and Emperor*. On his reception in medieval literature, see Bastert, *Karl der Grosse*; Latowsky, *Emperor of the World*; and Purkis and Gabriele, *Charlemagne Legend*.

20 For Charlemagne in a Crusade context, see Latowsky, "Charlemagne."

connection was not a complete fabrication but was founded on Charlemagne's interest in maintaining favorable relations with Levantine Christians, as evidenced by an inventory of churches of the Holy Land Charlemagne commissioned to assess the extent of material aid the churches required.[21]

Moreover, Charlemagne entertained frequent diplomatic relations with Caliph Hārūn al-Rašīd on behalf of the Christians in the Holy Land. Royal annals record the arrival in Aachen of two different embassies sent by Hārūn al-Rašīd in 802 and 807 as the result of an initiative by Charlemagne in 799.[22] These diplomatic relations found wide circulation in Einhard's ninth-century *Life of Charlemagne*, which claimed that the caliph granted Charlemagne jurisdiction over the Church of the Holy Sepulcher.[23] A member of Charlemagne's inner circle, Einhard wrote a posthumous biography in the mold of Suetonius's treatments of Roman emperors along with elements drawn from saints' lives. The work was composed in the tumultuous reign of Charlemagne's son, Louis the Pious (814–840), and did much to consolidate the legend of Charlemagne as Holy Roman emperor and benefactor of Christians everywhere.[24]

Some seventy years after Charlemagne's death, Notker Balbulus, a monk from Saint Gall, dedicated his reworking of Einhard to Charles the Fat, Charlemagne's great-grandson (ca. 885). He embellished Einhard's account by claiming that Hārūn al-Rašīd was so impressed by the hunting dogs Charlemagne had sent him as a gift that he acknowledged Charlemagne to be a superior ruler. Wishing to offer him a fitting tribute, the caliph surrendered the entirety of the Holy Land to him, but for pragmatic reasons appointed himself its governor.[25]

From the tenth century onward, textual traditions on Charlemagne's relations with the Holy Land began to take on a life of their own. Around the year 968, Benedict, a monk at the monastery of Saint Andrew near Rome, embroidered the existing narratives by claiming that Charlemagne had himself traveled to the Holy Land out of concern for the Christians there, stopping over in Constantinople before returning to Rome.[26] Two late eleventh-century documents on the foundation of

21 For the relevant texts, see McCormick, *Charlemagne's Survey*, 199–217.

22 *Annales regni Francorum* 108, 117, 123.

23 For classic studies of Charlemagne's relations with the Holy Land, see Runciman, "Charlemagne and Palestine"; Borgolte, *Der Gesandtenaustausch*; Graboïs, "Charlemagne, Rome and Jerusalem"; Latowsky, "Foreign Embassies"; and Oellers, "Karl und die Christen."

24 Latowsky, *Emperor of the World*, 37–38.

25 Notker Balbulus, *Gesta Karoli Magni imperatoris* 64; see also Latowksy, *Emperor of the World*, 43–50. The terms used by Notker are *procurator* and *advocatus*, the latter of which was also the title Godfrey of Bouillon is reported by some sources to have assumed after the capture of Jerusalem.

26 Benedict of Monte Soratte, *Chronicon* (Zucchetti, *Il Chronicon di Benedetto*). See Sholod, "Charlemagne"; Stuckey, "Charlemagne as Crusader?," 137–38; and Gabriele, *Empire of Memory*, 41–44.

the monastery of Charroux (in the diocese of Poitiers) also refer to this journey but add that Charlemagne brought back with him a number of relics.[27]

By the time of the First Crusade, the legend of Charlemagne as patron of the Christians of the Holy Land was widely dispersed and could be utilized as precedent and justification for the Crusade. The anonymous author of the *Gesta Francorum* (ca. 1101) had claimed that the armies of Godfrey of Bouillon and his brother Baldwin of Boulogne had traveled to Constantinople on a road built by Charlemagne.[28] This detail brings the expedition into connection with Charlemagne and makes an implicit argument for a Frankish presence in the East by referencing legends of Charlemagne's supposed visit to the Holy Land by way of Constantinople. Charlemagne was felt to be present among the Crusaders through Godfrey and Baldwin, who traced their lineage back to him.[29] Much more explicit was the French chronicler Robert the Monk, author of the most popular Latin history of the First Crusade (ca. 1110). He reported that Pope Urban II urged his audience at the Council of Clermont to remember the deeds of their ancestors, of Charlemagne, Louis the Pious, and others, "who laid waste to the kingdoms of the pagans and extended the borders of the sacred church."[30] According to Robert, the Crusaders merely followed the example of their illustrious Carolingian forefathers.

William may have had at his disposal, in addition to this early tradition linking Charlemagne with the First Crusade, a growing body of literature from the Latin East. For example, Ralph of Caen explicitly refers to Charlemagne's connection to the Holy Land via the family of Godfrey and Baldwin and foreshadows that Baldwin of Boulogne would one day be king of Jerusalem:

27 The first is *Liber de constitutione* 1–7; the second occurs at 29–41. They are respectively referred to by scholars as the *Privilegium* (ca. 1045) and *Historia* (ca. 1095); see Gabriele, *Empire of Memory*, 27–28, 44–51.

28 *GF* 1.2; compare PT 33; *Balduini III Historia* 9 (via Robert the Monk, *Historia Iherosolimitana* 732); Ekkehard of Aura, *Hierosolymita* 19. On the routes taken to Constantinople during the First Crusade, see Koytcheva, "Logistics of the Early Crusades," and Murray, "Roads, Bridges and Shipping." It is unclear which road is meant here; possibly the Via Militaris, which was followed by Godfrey of Bouillon's party southward through the Balkans from Belgrade to Sardika (modern Sofia, Bulgaria) and eventually to Constantinople, but it was built by the Romans. Gabriele (*Empire of Memory*, 65, n. 97) suggests that this remark may indicate a connection with the *Descriptio qualiter*.

29 Compare the remark in the *Chanson d'Antioche*, 300, and see Aubé, *Godefroy de Bouillon*, 26–27; Winkler, *Le tropisme de Jérusalem*, 455–65; Crouzet-Pavan, *Le mystère des rois*, 128–37; and John, *Godfrey of Bouillon*, 15–18.

30 Robert the Monk, *Historia Iherosolimitana* 728: *Moveant vos et incitent animos vestros ad virilitatem gesta predecessorum vestrorum, probitas et magnitudo Karoli Magni regis et Ludovici filii eius aliorumque regum vestrorum, qui regna paganorum destruxerunt, et in eis fines sancte ecclesie dilataverunt.*

> Deriving his descent from Charlemagne, [Baldwin] was born divinely as one who was to take his seat on David's throne. Rightly and deservedly so did he, whose birth was illuminated by Charlemagne and his death by David, surpass Alexander.[31]

For Ralph, Baldwin's chief qualification for King David's throne consisted in his association with Charlemagne. His Carolingian lineage and connection to biblical kingship combined to surpass even classical ideals of rule and empire, as personified by Alexander the Great.

The pilgrim guide written by Rorgo Fretellus in Antioch (ca. 1137–38) provides more extensive evidence of the circulation of the legend of Charlemagne in the Latin East. In his lengthy description of Jerusalem, Rorgo relates the Templum Domini to the Herodian temple from the time of Jesus before referencing Charlemagne:

> [Jesus's] foreskin was presented to King Charlemagne in the Temple in Jerusalem by an angel from heaven, and it was brought by him to Gaul, to Aachen. Afterward it was transferred by Charles the Bald, son of Louis the Pious, to Aquitaine, to the region of Poitiers near Charroux, in a church which he built in honor of the holy Savior, enriching it with copious and generous grants under a monastic rule. The foreskin is solemnly venerated there even now.[32]

The relic of the Sacred Foreskin referenced by Rorgo is first mentioned in a document dating to the late eleventh century and belonging to the aforementioned abbey of Charroux.[33] To increase Charroux's prestige, the document gives an account of the abbey's treasures and relics, including a narrative explaining their origins. After Charlemagne founded the monastery (in reality, it had been established by Roger of Limoges), he embarked on a journey to Jerusalem in search of relics befitting the dignity of the new foundation.[34] There he fasted and prayed

31 RC 1142–45: *a magno illo rege Carolo genus trahens, super solium David sessurus divinitus trahebatur! Iure igitur ac merito Alexandrum vincebat, cuius illustrabant Carolus ortum, David occasum.*

32 RF 54: *Prepucium eius in Iherusalem in templo de celis ab angelo Karolo Magno regi presentatum fuit et ab eo delatum in Galiis: Aquisgrani. Postea quidem a Karolo Calvo, pii Lodovvici filio, translatum Aquitanie in pago Pictaviensi apud Carrosium, in ecclesia quam in honore sancti Salvatoris construxit, in eo largisque bonis et amplissimis sub monachali religione ditavit. Quod et tunc usque modo sollempniter ibi veneratur.*

33 Schwering-Illert, "Die ehemalige französische Abteikirche," 31–34; Cabanot, "Le trésor des reliques"; Palazzo, "Veneration"; Lützelschwab, "Zwischen Heilsvermittlung und Ärgernis"; Mattelaer, Schipper, and Das, "Circumcision of Jesus Christ"; Gabriele, *Empire of Memory*, 45–46.

34 *Liber de constitutione*, 29–41. For Charlemagne as the alleged founder of Charroux, see Gabriele, *Empire of Memory*, 24–25.

at the Church of the Holy Sepulcher for three days, along with the patriarch of Jerusalem.[35] On the third day, his piety was rewarded and the relic of the Sacred Foreskin appeared on the Holy Chalice. Charlemagne subsequently brought the relic to Charroux, where it performed numerous miracles.[36]

As opposed to the earlier version of the story, Rorgo Fretellus changes the site of the miracle from the Church of the Holy Sepulcher to the Templum Domini. The alteration is logical, given that Jesus was circumcised in the Temple, but this setting would not have held the same significance before the First Crusade, when the Church of the Holy Sepulcher formed the focal point for Christians in the West when they imagined Jerusalem. Rorgo, instead, adapted these preexisting narratives in a way that privileged the local topography and not the conceptions of a western Christian audience, thus fashioning stronger links between the biblical past, Frankish past, and Frankish present. As M. Gabriele observed of the legend of Charroux, the Charlemagne figure stands for a Carolingian Golden Age into which the eleventh-century abbey of Charroux is drawn.[37] Rorgo, in turn, used this legend to bring the Frankish Kingdom of Jerusalem into connection with Charlemagne and Carolingian kingship.

However, it was William of Tyre who made the most ambitious use of the legend of Charlemagne in the Latin East.

A Levantine Einhard

By the time William wrote his history of the Kingdom of Jerusalem in the second half of the twelfth century, he could draw on Charlemagne as a widely recognized figure with associations of Roman imperial dignity and Christian rule. More than that, Charlemagne was a symbol of a glorified Frankish past and was considered a proto-Crusader. William capitalized on these associations by repeatedly bringing his own work into connection with Charlemagne's biographer Einhard. In this way, William accomplished what no other writer in the Latin East had done: he constructed a coherent narrative in which the Latin East formed an organic and key component of Frankish literature and history.

35 The Charroux account refers to a Patriarch Basilius, possibly referring to a later patriarch named Basileus (820–838), who lived after Charlemagne's death (814).

36 Rorgo's text has been overlooked by scholars treating the legend of Charroux, who usually point to a late twelfth-century gloss on Peter Comestor's *Historia scholastica* as the earliest reception of the version related in the *Historia* of Charroux (Remensnyder, *Remembering Kings Past*, 155, n. 23). Some trace the source of the gloss to a pilgrim guide known as Innominatus VI or Pseudo-Bede, usually dated around 1187. However, this guide, including the passage on the Sacred Foreskin, derives almost verbatim from Rorgo's text or his source; see appendix 1. The fact that this story occurs in Rorgo indicates that the reception of this legend took place at least half a century earlier than previously assumed and had reached the Latin East.

37 Gabriele, *Empire of Memory*, 67.

William associated his literary project with Einhard in prominent ways. In the prologue to his history, William gives a rationale for his literary style, which, as ancient precepts teach, should be appropriate to the subject matter. For this, William adduces an authority from classical antiquity:

> For, as the excellent orator says in the first book of the *Tusculan* [*disputations*], "it is the mark of a man who immoderately abuses both literature and leisure to entrust his thoughts to writing, if he is unable either to arrange or polish them, or to entice the reader with any kind of delight."[38]

The "excellent orator" is, of course, Cicero. While the quotation is certainly apposite to William's point, there is more to it. The same quote was used by Einhard in the prologue to his biography of Charlemagne to argue that if Cicero's precept applied to Roman authors, then he too should follow it. According to Einhard, Charlemagne—his subject—stood in the tradition of Roman emperors, and therefore his biographer ought to follow the same literary conventions as Roman biographers.[39]

By quoting the same phrase from Cicero as Einhard, particularly in such a prominent position as the prologue (also like Einhard), William makes two implicit claims: first, that his own work stands in the same literary tradition as Einhard's *Life of Charlemagne*, which ultimately goes back to Roman imperial biography, and second, that his own subject matter is as dignified as Einhard's and bears a relation to it. William, like Einhard, subscribed to the notion that Roman political and cultural supremacy was passed on to other civilizations. William's claim is not directly tied to classical antiquity, but instead filtered through Carolingian models of empire and historiography. Because of Charlemagne's association with the Holy Land and the First Crusade, William could make a convincing case that the kings of Jerusalem—his subject matter—were successors to Charlemagne and every bit as dignified. By added implication, the literary culture of the Kingdom of Jerusalem—and therefore William's own literary pursuits—was heir (and possibly rival) to Carolingian courtly culture.

William most effectively associated the rulers of Jerusalem with Carolingian kingship by imitating Einhard's description of Charlemagne. Einhard, in turn, had drawn on the imperial biographies of the Roman author Suetonius to present Charlemagne as a composite of various Roman emperors. The most famous

38 WT prol. 42–46; Cicero, *Tusculanae disputationes* 1.3.6: *Nam, ut ait orator eximius in Tusculanarum primo, "mandare quemquam litteris cogitationes suas, qui eas nec disponere nec illustrare possit nec delectatione aliqua lectorem allicere, hominis est intemperanter abutentis et litteris et ocio."*

39 Einhard, *Vita Karoli Magni* 1.3. Note that William inverts the word order of the final phrase, which reads, in both Cicero and Einhard, *et otio et litteris*.

section of Einhard's biography deals with Charlemagne's physical appearance and personal traits:

> He was of a large and strong build, a tall stature, which nonetheless did not surpass proper proportion—for it is a fact that his height measured seven of his feet—, he had a round head, very large and lively eyes, a nose that somewhat exceeded the average size, charming grey hair, and a happy and cheerful face. His appearance, therefore, had great authority and dignity both when he was standing and sitting down; although his neck seemed stout and too short, and his belly to be overly protruding, still the proportionality of his other body parts hid these things. He had a firm gait and an entirely manly comportment; but a clear voice, such that it did not seem to match his physical appearance.[40]

We may compare this description with William's descriptive vignette of Godfrey of Bouillon:

> He had a tall body, such that he was considered shorter by the tallest but taller by those of average height, he was strong without parallel, possessing rather thick limbs, a manly torso, a charming face, somewhat blond hair and beard, and in facility with weapons and combat experience he was unique in everyone's opinion.[41]

William does not exactly copy word-for-word Einhard's physical description of Charlemagne, but he does adopt the descriptive framework, using the same grammatical structures.[42] William found in Einhard's description a model for royal biography that he used to compose descriptive vignettes of each of the Frankish rulers of Jerusalem at the start of their reign. The clearest example of William's imitation of Einhard is the description of Baldwin III, whose love of listening to histories and ancient *res gestae* (deeds done) echo Charlemagne's interests, while

40 Einhard, *Vita Karoli Magni* 22: *Corpore fuit amplo atque robusto, statura eminenti, quae tamen iustam non excederet—nam septem suorum pedum proceritatem eius constat habuisse mensuram—, apice capitis rotundo, oculis praegrandibus ac vegetis, naso paululum mediocritatem excedenti, canitie pulchra, facie laeta et hilari. Unde formae auctoritas ac dignitas tam stanti quam sedenti plurima adquirebatur; quamquam cervix obesa et brevior venterque proiectior videretur, tamen haec ceterorum membrorum celabat aequalitas. Incessu firmo totaque corporis habitudine virili; voce clara quidem, sed quae minus corporis formae conveniret.*

41 WT 9.5.44–48: *Fuit autem et corpore procerus, ita ut et maximis minor et mediocribus maior haberetur, robustus sine exemplo, membris solidioribus, torace virili, facie venusta, capillo et barba flavus mediocriter, in usu armorum et exercitio militari omnium iudicio quasi singularis.*

42 For the rhetorical structure of William's royal portraits (without reference, however, to the Einhardian tradition), see Giese, "Stadt- und Herrscherbeschreibungen," 398–400.

both Baldwin III's and Amalric's moderation in drink corresponds nearly verbatim to Einhard's depiction of Charlemagne.[43] By employing Einhard's descriptive framework, William elevated his source material and situated his own work within a renowned Frankish literary tradition.

In addition to drawing on Einhard for stylistic and structural elements, William integrated Levantine and Frankish history by selectively quoting from Einhard's biography and subtly changing the meaning of his words to fit his own agenda. In the opening chapter, for example, William offers a diachronic perspective on the relations between Christians and Muslims in the Levant and presents Eastern Christians as powerless under the tyranny of infidel rulers. Their plight improves dramatically as a result of the diplomatic relations between Charlemagne and Hārūn al-Rašīd. William quotes two extended passages from Einhard on the subject. The first passage forms part of Einhard's general treatment of Charlemagne's foreign policy, intended to demonstrate Charlemagne's sphere of influence and the high esteem he enjoyed among foreign rulers.[44] Einhard describes how even the mighty Hārūn al-Rašīd respected Charlemagne above all other rulers, so that, when Charlemagne's embassy, which he had sent with gifts to the Church of the Holy Sepulcher, pleaded with the caliph to surrender the church to Charlemagne's authority, the caliph did so willingly, and even sent back magnificent gifts to Charlemagne (including, famously, the elephant named Abul Abaz).

William changes the force of Einhard's words by introducing the quote with the claim that Charlemagne's frequent diplomatic efforts on behalf of Levantine Christians were so successful that "it appeared that they were governed more by Emperor Charles than by the aforementioned ruler [Hārūn al-Rašīd]."[45] William shortly afterward quotes another passage, in which Einhard portrays Charlemagne as a Christian ruler who looks out for the greater Christian community, distributing alms not only to the Christians in his own realm but even to those living in Syria, Egypt, Africa, Jerusalem, Alexandria, and Carthage.[46] Although Einhard's passage occurs in a longer list of Charlemagne's benefactions to Christians, including building and supporting churches in Aachen and Rome, William uses it here to demonstrate Charlemagne's active involvement in the political and religious life of the Levant.

William transforms the thrust of Einhard's passages, which were originally part of a larger narrative showcasing the various military, political, and religious

43 WT 16.2.16–18, 16.2.54–57 (=19.2.29–30, the description of King Amalric); Einhard, *Vita Karoli Magni* 24.1–2.

44 Einhard, *Vita Karoli Magni* 16.3, in WT 1.3.21–34.

45 WT 1.3.19–21: *ita ut magis sub imperatore Karolo quam sub dicto principe degere viderentur.*

46 Einhard, *Vita Karoli Magni* 27.1, in WT 1.3.38–47.

achievements of Charlemagne as a Christian emperor, to support his own argument that the Franks had always had a vested interest in the Christians of the Levant, and particularly that Charlemagne had such political influence that he became the de facto ruler of Jerusalem. For this motif, which did not originate with Einhard, William drew on later legends of Charlemagne. Resorting to both imperial biographical tradition and popular legend, William fashioned a trajectory whereby the Franks' participation in the First Crusade and the subsequent establishment of a Frankish Kingdom of Jerusalem seem a logical and inevitable consequence of the Christians' maltreatment at the hands of the Fatimids and the Seljuk Turks in the eleventh century.

Elsewhere William paraphrases Einhard to comment on the role of the Byzantines in the First Crusade. William paints a hostile picture of the Byzantine emperor Alexios Komnenos, claiming that he thwarted the Crusaders ("our men," he calls them) at every turn, intending deceit even when bestowing gifts. Predictably, William concludes that the Virgilian platitude *timeo Danaos et dona ferentis* (I fear the Greeks, even when they bear gifts) indeed rings true.[47] He explains Alexios's actions as motivated by a fearful suspicion: "Fearfully regarding the progress of all Latins, he did not permit their strength to grow or their might to expand, impeding them wherever he could."[48] William's words echo those of Einhard, who had offered the following explanation for the diplomatic animosities between Charlemagne and the Byzantine court: "For the might of the Franks had always been feared by the Romans and Greeks."[49] William notably alters Einhard's wording to refer not to Franks but to Latins, thereby changing an ethnonym to a linguistic marker with literary and religious connotations. The change may have been motivated in part by the fact that, in William's day, the term "Frank" had become more specialized. Where previously the word could be used to refer to Christians from western Europe more generally, over the course of the twelfth century it became associated specifically with the inhabitants of the Kingdom of France. Concurrently, the term "Latin" began to replace "Frank" as a marker of cultural and religious difference, in contradistinction to Christians who used non-Latin (usually Greek) rites. William's modification, therefore, signals a translation of Einhard's ninth-century cultural-political vocabulary to a late twelfth-century Levantine context.

By paraphrasing Einhard's interpretation of the diplomatic struggles between the Byzantines and the Franks, William presents the strained relationship

47 WT 11.6.15. The line is a quotation from Virgil, *Aeneid* 2.49. William again quotes this half-line at 20.2.7–8.

48 WT 11.6.15–18: *Suspectum enim habens omnium Latinorum generaliter processum, nec eorum vires multiplicari nec dilatari potestatem, ubicumque ministrare poterat impedimentum, patiebatur.*

49 Einhard, *Vita Karoli Magni* 16.4: *Erat enim semper Romanis et Graecis Francorum suspecta potentia.*

between Byzantines ("Greeks") and Latin Crusaders as a consequence of a much older, Carolingian dynamic. The Latin conquest and rule of the Levant had been anticipated by Charlemagne's Christian solidarity and supposed de facto rulership of the Holy Land, and thus twelfth-century Latin diplomatic conflicts with the Byzantines could be understood by turning to Einhard's ninth-century biography of Charlemagne. In this way, William constructed a Frankish framework for Levantine history out of Einhard's book.

William's prominent use of Einhard as a model for his Levantine history could have served several mutually compatible purposes. First, by stressing the links between Levantine and Frankish history and literature, William made the Latin East relevant to a western European audience. This was no small matter, since the declining military fortunes of the Latins made them dependent on material aid from the West for their continued survival. By showing western European readers how Levantine history fit into the big picture of Frankish history, William helped them understand both the cultural and political significance of the Latin East and the importance of the continued Latin presence in the Levant. Yet William also appealed to a Levantine patriotic sentiment among readers in the Latin East by associating their history and culture with the renown of Charlemagne. There was a ready audience for this kind of narrative in the Latin East, as evidenced by references to Charlemagne in Ralph of Caen and Rorgo Fretellus, and perhaps even by the later fragment of a French *chanson de geste* set in the time of Charlemagne.[50] As we will see, the same Levantine patriotism also comes to the fore in William's use and presentation of Eastern Christian writings.

The History as a Product of Eastern Learning

Although William went to considerable lengths to fit Levantine Latin history and literature into a broader Frankish framework, his chronicle was first and foremost an expression of Levantine patriotism.[51] In the prologue, William explicitly cites this sentiment as his central motivation in writing, referring to a "most pressing love of his homeland" (*urgentissimus amor patrie*).[52] The cultural boundaries of this patriotism, or indeed what precisely William considered his *patria* (homeland), remain unclear. Yet the pride William exhibits for his access to other Levantine traditions of learning indicate that his conception of *patria* extended beyond Latin culture.

50 A fragment of the late twelfth-century French poem *Fierabras* belonged to the Damascus Qubbat al-Ḫazna; see Giannini and Minervini, "Old French Texts," 337–38.

51 Edbury and Rowe, *William of Tyre*, 173; Schwinges, "Regionale Identität."

52 WT prol. 66–67.

William's expansive view of the Levant emerges from the opening words of the history proper: "Ancient histories teach, and so also do the traditions of the Easterners relate, that in the time in which Heraclius the Augustus governed the Roman Empire. . . ."[53] In the most prominent position possible, William chose to emphasize not only his use of what Latins in Europe would consider the "classics," but also Levantine traditions, and was thus in the process of constructing a new conception of what could constitute a "classic." This was not a development that was appreciated in Europe, where the French translation of William's history, made in early thirteenth-century Paris, pointedly dispensed with the reference to Eastern traditions, citing only *les anciennes estoires* (the ancient histories).[54] In the prologue, William mentions one of these "Eastern" sources by name: Saʿīd ibn Baṭrīq. As scholars have known for some time, his tenth-century Arabic chronicle and its eleventh-century continuation constituted William's most important Levantine sources outside of the Latin tradition.[55]

Saʿīd ibn Baṭrīq, also known by the Greek name Eutychios, was a Melkite, or Arabic-speaking Orthodox Christian, and patriarch of Alexandria in the tenth century. He composed a world chronicle in Arabic, spanning from creation until 938/939, under the title *Kitāb naẓm al-ǧawhar* (Book of the string of pearls).[56] He wrote from the perspective of North African and Levantine Christians under Muslim rule, and his Melkite community spoke Arabic and used Arabic rites. Unlike other Eastern Christian communities, such as West Syrian and East Syrian Christians, Melkites supported the doctrinal positions of the Council of Chalcedon (451), and thus maintained favorable relations with the Byzantine emperor and the patriarch of Constantinople. Even so, Saʿīd ibn Baṭrīq does not exempt Byzantine emperors from censure when explaining the causes for the rise of Islam, which in his view had relegated Orthodox Christianity in the Levant to a subservient position.

Rather than beginning his history of the Latin Kingdom of Jerusalem with the First Crusade, William takes as his starting point the Muslim conquest of the Levant in the seventh century. This decision reflects a view of history shaped by the lens of Eastern Christians such as Saʿīd ibn Baṭrīq. Throughout the first chapters of his work, William relies heavily on Saʿīd ibn Baṭrīq's chronicle. William similarly criticizes Byzantine court intrigue, resulting in Phokas's treacherous murder of Emperor Maurikios, and assigns a prominent role to Maria, Maurikios's daughter and wife of the Sassanian king Khosrow, who encourages her husband to

53 WT 1.1.1–3: *Docent veteres Historie, et idipsum etiam habent Orientalium traditiones, quod tempore quo Eraclius Augustus Romanum administrabat imperium. . . .*

54 *Guillaume de Tyr* 1:1.

55 See especially Möhring, "Zu der Geschichte."

56 The work is also known as *Kitāb al-taʾrīḫ al-maǧmūʿ ʿalā-l-taḥqīq wa-l-taṣdīq* (Book of history, compiled through investigation and verification).

invade Byzantine territories, including Syria, thus leaving the Levant vulnerable to Arab invasion.

A central episode in Saʿīd ibn Baṭrīq's chronicle concerns the Muslim conquest of Jerusalem in 638. The respectful exchange between Sophronios, patriarch of Jerusalem, and Caliph ʿUmar ibn al-Ḵaṭṭāb is meant to provide a blueprint for Christian-Muslim relations in safeguarding the integrity of churches and Christians' right to observe their own religion. According to Saʿīd ibn Baṭrīq, Sophronios permitted ʿUmar to build a mosque (*masǧid*) on the Temple Mount, thus leaving the area around the Church of the Holy Sepulcher to the Christians. Sometime afterward, Saʿīd ibn Baṭrīq asserts, Muslims violated this agreement by building a mosque next to the church, which they called the Mosque of ʿUmar.[57]

William, too, includes this episode, following Saʿīd ibn Baṭrīq in claiming that ʿUmar bestowed certain privileges upon the Christian community of Jerusalem. But where Saʿīd ibn Baṭrīq had the patriarch granting ʿUmar the Temple Mount area as the site for a planned mosque, William instead presents the caliph as requesting that the patriarch merely view the site of the Jewish Temple destroyed by the Roman emperor Titus. After being shown the remnants of the Temple, ʿUmar is described as "giving an order to build the Temple" (*Templum edificari precepit*) and grants the new institution extensive possessions for its maintenance. To this day, William claims, an inscription declares the edifice's founder and its dates of construction and completion.[58]

William's version of the encounter between patriarch and caliph exposes his Levantine Latin perspective and historiographical agenda. Like Saʿīd ibn Baṭrīq, William evinces a concern for the Christians of the holy city. But unlike Saʿīd ibn Baṭrīq, William does not describe the Dome of the Rock as a mosque, referring to it only as the Temple. His deviation from his source stems from the fact that the Franks of Jerusalem had appropriated the Dome of the Rock on the Temple Mount and referred to it as the Lord's Temple (Templum Domini). As discussed in chapter 3, the canons who administered this building closely associated their community with the Jewish Temple that stood there in the time of Christ, while arguing that the sizeable possessions and revenues allotted to the site as a Muslim sanctuary entitled them to both material and spiritual capital. Like the canons, William also emphasizes the possessions granted to the Dome of the Rock for its maintenance—an element that is absent from Saʿīd ibn Baṭrīq.

However, in identifying the founder of the Dome of the Rock, William hewed far more closely to his Christian Arabic source than to Latin tradition. Whereas Achard of Arrouaise's poem proposed a series of Christian Roman figures as potential originators, in book 1 William relies on Saʿīd ibn Baṭrīq's account in

57 Saʿīd ibn Baṭrīq, *Kitāb naẓm al-ǧawhar* 2:16–18 (Pirone, *Gli annali*, 335–37).

58 WT 1.2.30–52.

presenting ʿUmar ibn al-Ḳaṭṭāb as the founder. When returning to the subject in book 8 of his history, William confidently refers readers to this earlier passage, and once again backs up his argument with the observation that ʿUmar's role is attested by the Arabic inscription on the exterior of the Dome of the Rock—described by William as "ancient monuments of letters" (*antiqua litterarum monimenta*).[59] In fact, the inscription bears the name of Caliph al-Maʾmūn (who replaced the name of the actual founder, ʿAbd al-Malik, with that of his own).[60] William's error here does not necessarily impugn his ability to read Arabic, as has been suggested, but rather was the result of combining Saʿīd ibn Baṭrīq's account with the foundation narrative of the canons of the Templum Domini.[61]

William also had access to the continuation of Saʿīd ibn Baṭrīq's work by another Melkite Christian, Yaḥyā ibn Saʿīd al-Anṭākī.[62] Yaḥyā was also a native of Alexandria and may have been related to Saʿīd ibn Baṭrīq.[63] Probably under pressure from the anti-Christian policies of the Fatimid Caliph al-Ḥākim, Yaḥyā moved in the year 1015 to Antioch, where he continued to work on the chronicle until 1033/34, the likely date of his death.

Yaḥyā's portion of the chronicle centers on the rule of the Fatimids in the Levant during the tenth and eleventh centuries. The Fatimids initially maintained favorable relations with their Christian subjects and employed them in the uppermost echelons of courtly administration. Although he was the son of a Melkite mother, Caliph al-Ḥākim bi-Amr Allāh (985–1021) brutally disrupted these ties, culminating in the infamous sack of the Church of the Holy Sepulcher in 1009.[64]

In tracing the vicissitudes of Levantine Christians during the early Middle Ages, William also covered the reign of al-Ḥākim. He incorporated Yaḥyā's Melkite perspective into his narrative when describing al-Ḥākim's erratic and often ruthless character and relied closely on Yaḥyā's account of the destruction of the Church of the Holy Sepulcher. Earlier Crusade chronicles, including that of Fulcher of Chartres, spoke in more generalizing terms about the "defilement"

59 WT 8.3.51–52; at 1.2.49, William similarly describes the inscription as *litterarum vetustissima monimenta*.

60 Möhring, "Zu der Geschichte," 174. See, on the inscription, Milwright, *Dome of the Rock*. William's passage is the origin of the common conflation of the Dome of the Rock with the Mosque of ʿUmar, which is not on the Sacred Esplanade but next to the Church of the Holy Sepulcher.

61 Möhring, "Zu der Geschichte," 174.

62 For a list of correspondences between Yaḥyā ibn Saʿīd al-Anṭākī and William's chronicle, see Möhring, "Zu der Geschichte," 176–77.

63 According to the thirteenth-century writer Ibn ʾAbī Uṣaybiʿa, who also believed him to be the same person as the physician and apologist known as Abū l-Farağ Yaḥyā ibn Saʿīd ibn Yaḥyā, a claim generally discounted by modern scholars (see Swanson, "Yaḥyā ibn Saʿīd al-Anṭākī").

64 Samir, "Role of Christians"; Walker, "Al-Ḥākim."

of the Holy Sepulcher, but William's specificity reflects the lived experience of Levantine Christian communities.[65]

William's engagement with local Levantine tradition is manifest in his account of the subsequent efforts to restore the Church of the Holy Sepulcher. Again relying on Yaḥyā ibn Saʿīd al-Anṭākī, he relates the Byzantine emperor Romanos III's (r. 1028–1034) renewal of diplomatic relations with al-Ḥākim's son and successor, Caliph ʿAlī al-Ẓāhir (r. 1005–1036), to rebuild the churches of Palestine.[66] But unlike Yaḥyā, William assigns the initiative to the Christian populace of Jerusalem, who urgently appealed to the emperor's munificence. Apart from advancing a patriotic agenda, his emphasis on Jerusalemite Christians may have stemmed from local Melkite traditions, which may also have furnished him with details regarding the reconstruction of the Church of the Holy Sepulcher under the leadership of a Byzantine nobleman named Ioannes Karianites.[67]

For all his claims to write an original Latin work not reliant on Greek or Arabic histories of the Levant, for the first six chapters of his history William draws primarily on Christian Arabic, not Latin, texts. Yet there are other passages in his chronicle where William may have relied on Christian Arabic works.[68] In his character portrait of King Amalric (the same king who had supplied William with *Arabica exemplaria*), William describes Amalric as relishing conversations with "prudent and intelligent men who possessed familiarity with distant places and had experience with foreign customs."[69] One such conversation involved William himself, when the king stayed with him in Tyre. Between intermittent bouts of fever, the king asked William to provide him with a logical proof—without taking Christian scripture into account—for the future resurrection. In response, William proposes to walk the king through the logical steps necessary to answer his question:

> "Why don't you take on the role of such a person, so that we may try to find [an answer] regarding this matter?" "Agreed," he said. Then I said: "Do you confess that God is just?" He said: "I confess that nothing is more true." Then I said: "It is the mark of a just man to return good for good, and bad for bad." He said: "That is true." "In the present life, however, this

65 See FC 1.3.3 and Robert the Monk, *Historia Iherosolimitana* 728.

66 WT 1.6; Yaḥyā ibn Saʿīd al-Anṭākī, *Kitāb al-ḏayl* 532–34 (Pirone, *Cronache*, 371). William's reliance here on Yaḥyā has not, to my knowledge, been noted.

67 Ousterhout, "Rebuilding the Temple," 70.

68 Möhring ("Zu der Geschichte," 177–78) hypothesizes that William also used the Coptic *History of the Patriarchs of the Egyptian Church* for information about al-Ḥākim's Christian mother and uncle. Morton ("William of Tyre's Attitude," 15–16) suggests that at least some of this information may derive instead from a Western source.

69 WT 19.3.8–10.

does not happen, since some good persons suffer only misery and adversity in this world, while some wicked persons enjoy continuous happiness, as examples from daily life show us." He said: "That is beyond doubt." I continued: "Therefore, this will take place in some other life, since God is unable to not be one who gives just recompense. Therefore, there will be another life; and the Resurrection of this flesh, in which a person has deserved well or ill, in that must one receive reward and recompense."[70]

William's framing of the conversation within a description of Amalric as interested in conversing with "prudent and intelligent men" possessing knowledge of "distant places" and "foreign customs" indicates a non-Latin intellectual context. It is possible, as B. Z. Kedar has suggested, that Amalric's question reflects debates within Islamic discourse regarding the resurrection of the flesh.[71] But William surely includes himself among these "prudent and intelligent men" with whom the king enjoys conversing, and thus his own response to Amalric's query can be viewed as drawing on non-Latin traditions.

William may have availed himself of a body of Christian Arabic literature that addressed precisely these sorts of issues. In fact, William's argument, predicated on the divine attribute of justice, resembles that of an eleventh-century author from Antioch named ʿAbdallāh ibn al-Faḍl, a Melkite deacon and prolific author and translator of philosophical and religious texts, active in both Greek and Arabic. One short Arabic treatise by Ibn al-Faḍl could have been especially useful to William, the lengthy title of which translates to *An Essay Containing Ideas Useful for the Soul and Answers to Questions That People Frequently Ask and Dispute Which Are Extracted from the Sayings of the Holy Fathers and Select Philosophers*. In one passage, Ibn al-Faḍl similarly appeals to divine justice and retribution, claiming that earthly injustice exists to provide proof for the future resurrection:

As for the reason for disparity among people in terms of shortness and length of life, this is in order to establish proof of the Resurrection, the Creator's providence for the world, and that souls have a world other than

70 WT 19.3.34–49: *"Assumite ergo vobis huius hominis sic affecti personam et temptemus aliquid circa hoc invenire." "Placet," inquit. Tum ego: "Deum iustum confiteris esse?" Tum ille: "Nichil verius confiteor." Tum ego: "Iusti autem est pro bonis bona, pro malis mala retribuere." Tum ille: "Verum est." "In presenti autem vita non fit istud. Nam et boni quidam in presenti seculo nonnisi molestias patiuntur et adversa, mali vero quidam felicitate gaudent continua, sicut rerum cotidianarum exempla nos edocent." Tum ille: "Certum est." Ego vero processi: "Ergo in alia vita fiet, quia non potest deus non esse iustus retributor. Ergo alia vita erit et huius carnis Resurrectio, in qua meruit quis bonum vel malum, in ea debet recipere premium et remunerari."*

71 Kedar, "Intellectual Activities," 134.

> this one to which they go and receive recompense for their works, whether good or evil . . . if people were equal in this matter, then they would reject the existence of another world, and they would deny the providence and foreknowledge of the Creator and would imagine that creation was something natural and not something voluntary.[72]

While Ibn al-Faḍl's treatise may not necessarily have constituted William's exact source, the resemblances indicate the kind of work that may have informed his thinking. Alternatively, it is also plausible that William utilized a Latin source instead; Gregory the Great's sixth-century *Dialogues*, for instance, could have provided him with a literary model for constructing a dialogue on the subject of resurrection.[73]

In addition to Christian theology, William may also have drawn on Christian Arabic writings for his discussion of the origins of Shiʿa Islam. In a digression from his treatment of the Fatimid caliphate of Egypt, William explains that Shiʿites are adherents of ʿAlī, whereas Sunni Muslims follow Muhammad. According to William, ʿAlī opposed Muhammad, claiming that Gabriel had delivered revelation to Muhammad instead of ʿAlī by mistake. This account was not the product of William's imagination, but in fact formed the basis of an obscure Shiʿite sect known as the Ġurabiyya. Eleventh- and twelfth-century Sunni Muslim authors explain that the name derives from *ġurab*, the Arabic word for "raven," because ʿAlī and Muhammad were said to resemble each other like two ravens (hence Gabriel's error).[74] The story of Gabriel's alleged mistake also occurs among Christian Arabic authors, such as the eighth- and ninth-century Melkites Abraham of Tiberias and Qusṭā ibn Lūqā.[75] Among these Melkite sources, the identification of this doctrine as belonging to the sect of the Ġurabiyya is entirely absent, making it likely that, as elsewhere, William relied on a Christian Arabic rather than a Muslim source.

William's use of Christian Arabic works accompanies a radically new attitude, at least among Latin historiographers in the Levant, toward Arabic as a legitimate language capable of intellectual expression. William consistently refers to Arabic as a language in its own right (e.g., *Arabicum idioma*, *lingua Arabica*), acknowledges his own use of Greek and Arabic writings for his other history, and, for the first time in Levantine Latin writings, explicitly refers to an Arabic author with the important Latin title of *auctor*.[76] While Stephen the Philosopher had written at an

72 ʿAbdallāh ibn al-Faḍl, *An Essay* 140–41 (Noble, *An Essay*, 180).

73 See especially Gregory the Great, *Dialogi* 4.28. It is worth noting that the Nazareth catalogue lists "two books of Gregory's dialogue," though it is unclear which of the four books are meant here (see appendix 2).

74 Goldziher, "Ghurābiyya"; Anthony, "Ghurābiyya."

75 Abraham of Tiberias, *Dialogue* 127; Qusṭā ibn Lūqā, *Correspondence* 138.

76 WT 1.2.49, 11.30.12, 14.22.45, 15.25.14, 19.15.4, 21.6.14, 22.16.22.

early stage of the intellectual rewards of studying not only Latin but also works written in the Arabic language, and had implicitly termed the author of an Arabic medical treatise an *auctor*, no other Latin author in the Levant before William treated Arabic as a language of intellectual inquiry. Most barely even acknowledged the existence of Arabic as a language spoken and written in the Levant.[77]

A comparison between transliteration methods and discussions of toponyms in William of Tyre and Fulcher of Chartres proves especially instructive for showing related developments that took place over the course of the twelfth century. In chapter 2, we observed how, in one instance, William inversed Fulcher's literary/non-literary binary in giving preference to an Arabic rather than a Latinized toponym. In another remarkable passage, William even complains about the Latins' bastardization of Levantine place-names: "The masses call this place 'Scandalium,' using a bastardized pronunciation: for in Arabic, 'Alexander' is pronounced as *Scandar*, and Alexandrium *Scandarium*. The masses turned the 'r' into an 'l' and say 'Scandalium.'"[78] Elsewhere, William faults not just "the masses," but specifically "our Latins" (*nostri Latini*) for corrupting the name of the city Paneas (a Greek name, though not identified by William as such), complaining that his compatriots butcher the names of "almost all cities."[79]

William and Fulcher's differing attitudes toward Arabic also manifest in their diverging methods for representing Arabic words in Latin. A prime example forms both authors' treatment of the same historical episode in which two Muslim dignitaries are presented before the king of Jerusalem after the Latin conquest of Caesarea. Fulcher identifies the two figures as an *admiratus* and an *archadius*, likely referring to the offices of *amīr* (military commander) and *qāḍī* (judge).[80] He Latinizes the Arabic as much as possible, using words that somewhat resemble Latin words: *admiratus* bears a similarity to the Latin verb *admirari* and its derivatives, while *archadius* has the appearance of a Latinized Greek loanword. William, on the other hand, renders the two offices as *Emir* and *Cadius* and even provides

77 See chap. 4. In his preface to his translation of al-Maǧūsī's medical textbook, Stephen excoriates Constantine the African (though not by name) for removing the work's title and the name of its *auctor*: *Regalis dispositio*, pref. 14–16 (Burnett, "Antioch as a Link," 27–28). Rorgo Fretellus and the "Adelphus" narrative (RF 53; "Adelphus," 2), both from Antioch, referred to Arabic with the word "Saracen," thereby presenting the language as primarily part of speakers' religious identity as Muslims.

78 WT 11.30.10: *Hunc locum hodie appellatione corrupta populares appellant Scandalium: arabice enim Alexander Scandar dicitur et Alexandrium Scandarium, vulgares vero r in l conversa dicunt Scandalium.*

79 WT 19.10.27–30: *Dicitur autem et Paneas, sed nostri Latini, corrumpentes nomen sicut pene omnium aliarum urbium, Belinas vocant. Est autem ab oriente agro Damasceno contermina, iuxta quam fluentorum suorum Iordanis habet originem.* Ironically, this particular pronunciation likely resulted from the influence of Arabic, which does not have the letter "p."

80 FC 2.9.7: *admiratum ipsius urbis et episcopum, quem archadium praenominant, rex vivos habuit.*

short descriptions of the duties associated with each office.[81] Unlike Fulcher, William does not modify the Arabic *amīr* at all, choosing simply to transliterate the word into Latin, and only minimally modifies the Arabic *qāḍī* by adding a Latin case ending. William's is a fundamentally different attitude toward Arabic than Fulcher's and is, if anything, Arabicizing rather than Latinizing.

Levantine Christians as a Source for Arabic Texts

Having identified the kinds of Arabic texts William utilized, it is possible to hypothesize how William acquired and accessed them. William specified that it was King Amalric who supplied him with his *Arabica exemplaria*. Given the connection to the crown of Jerusalem, an ingenious explanation has been offered, based on a passage in the literary autobiography of Usāma ibn Munqiḏ. He was a twelfth-century Muslim diplomat from northern Syria active in various courts around the Levant. After entering Nūr al-Dīn's service in Damascus, Usāma summoned his family from Egypt. As they sailed northward along the coast, the ship was intercepted at Acre by King Baldwin III, the brother of the later king Amalric. Baldwin and his men wrecked the ship and robbed its passengers. While his family survived to report the incident to Usāma in Damascus, he bewailed the loss of his entire library, consisting of "4,000 bound volumes of the most precious tomes, whose loss was for me a heartache that lasted all my life."[82] R. B. C. Huygens suggested that Baldwin III seized Usāma's books and brought them to Jerusalem, where Amalric later placed them at William's disposal.[83]

This explanation fits in well with the prevailing view of the Latin East as an uncultured and uncouth society; whatever learning the Latins had been able to acquire, they took by force. But the distinctly Christian character of the Arabic texts utilized by William points to contacts with Levantine, Arabic-speaking Christians. More specifically, several of William's sources indicate a connection with Antioch: Saʿīd ibn Baṭrīq's history was likely brought to Antioch by Yaḥyā ibn Saʿīd al-Anṭākī, whose work was also used by William, and William may have looked to the Antiochene scholar Ibn al-Faḍl's treatment of the future resurrection.

Given the close ties between the Principality of Antioch and the Kingdom of Jerusalem (as discussed in chapter 4), there are several scenarios by which these Christian Arabic texts may have reached Amalric and later William. The first

81 WT 10.15.27–29: *procurator civitatis, qui lingua eorum dicitur Emir, et iuridicus, qui iuri dicendo preerat, qui etiam lingua eorum Cadius appellatur.*

82 Usāma ibn Munqiḏ, *Kitāb al-iʿtibār* 69 (Cobb, *Usama ibn Munqidh*, 35).

83 Huygens, *Latijn in Outremer*, 12. Williams ("Philip of Tripoli's Translation," 84–85, n. 20) suggests that these books may have been sold.

two kings of Jerusalem, Baldwin I and Baldwin II, had both at one point served as temporary rulers of Antioch, while the Latin patriarch of Antioch Aimery of Limoges paid frequent and lengthy visits to Jerusalem, including a six-year self-imposed exile in Jerusalem (1153–59) as the result of a dispute with Prince Reynald of Châtillon of Antioch. Aimery's presence in Jerusalem is potentially significant, for, as we have seen in the previous chapter, he displayed an active interest in both procuring and disseminating manuscripts from Antioch. Aimery sent Pope Eugene III a Greek manuscript of Chrysostom's homilies on Matthew, while the distinct possibility that Hugh Eterianus may have acquired from Aimery a Greek manuscript of a treatise by the ninth-century Melkite theologian Theodore Abū Qurra provides us with one potential example of the way in which Melkite texts could travel from Antioch to other parts of the Latin world.[84]

As we also noted in the previous chapter, Stephen the Philosopher worked closely in Antioch with an unnamed Arabic scholar, tentatively identified as one ʿAbd al-Masīḥ of Winchester, presumably a Melkite Christian.[85] Like Stephen, William may also have collaborated with an Arabic-speaking Christian. Twelfth- and thirteenth-century Latin translation activities in Iberia and Sicily frequently involved close collaboration with Arabic-speaking Jews, Christians, and Muslims.[86] These collaborators played a central role not just in the translation process but also in finding and selecting the texts to be translated. If mentioned at all, they are frequently left unnamed, as with Stephen the Philosopher's anonymous Arab. While William knew sufficient Arabic to translate simple place-names, his explanation of the term *mahdī* casts serious doubts on his ability to read and epitomize a lengthy chronicle fluently without assistance. He incorrectly explains that the Arabic word, a common term meaning "the guided one," indicates "one who flattens."[87] William's confusion stems from a misinterpretation of the participle as deriving from the triliteral root *mīm hā dāl* as opposed to *hā dāl ya̱*. The error is enlightening, for it shows that William did possess a degree of Arabic knowledge, while also demonstrating his linguistic limits. Like other Franks in the Levant, William may have been more familiar with the informal, spoken Arabic rather than the formal, written discourse.[88] Fortunately for William, in Jerusalem there would have been no shortage of individuals with the requisite linguistic skills to assist in reading some of the more extensive passages he drew on. Melkite Christians, for example, frequently held positions at the Frankish courts, most notably as physicians.

84 Burnett, "Antioch as a Link," 5–6.

85 Burnett, "ʿAbd al-Masīḥ of Winchester."

86 Gutas, "What Was There"; Hasse, "Social Conditions."

87 WT 19.21.31.

88 Lewis, "Medieval Diglossia"; Lewis, *Counts of Tripoli*, 217.

King Amalric was no exception and employed a Melkite physician named Abū Sulaymān Dāwūd to tend to his son, the future Baldwin IV, in the same period that William served as Baldwin's tutor.[89]

If Antioch was indeed the source of William's—and ultimately King Amalric's—Arabic texts, our picture of the intellectual and cultural dimensions of the Latin East requires some adjustment. First, Antioch may not have been the island of intellectual activity in the Levant it has often been perceived to be. Instead, Antioch's outward links with the Mediterranean, as illustrated by Aimery and Hugh's correspondence and by Stephen the Philosopher's connections with scholars across the Mediterranean, may also have extended across the Latin East to include Tyre and Jerusalem. Second, our understanding of Levantine intellectualism is further complicated if we accept the likelihood that William actively collaborated with someone at the Jerusalemite court or in his diocese in Tyre with proficiency in Arabic—probably a member of a local, Arabic-speaking Christian community.

Eastern and Latin Christians of Jerusalem as a "People of God"

Potential scholarly collaboration with Arabic-speaking Christians on William's part should be viewed alongside his increasing efforts to depict both Latin and Orthodox Christians in the Holy Land in an inclusive sense as a unified "People of God."

As we have already observed, the notion of a "People of God" was widely used by early Latin writers of the First Crusade to depict the Crusading army.[90] Fulcher of Chartres adapted the concept to apply not only to the Crusaders but also to subsequent settlers from the Latin East; as the canons of the Council of Nablus show, this broader conceptualization found currency among Fulcher's contemporaries across the Latin East. There are also some early indications that this divinely chosen people may have encompassed not only Latins but also Eastern Christians, although this sentiment is never explicitly articulated. Fulcher presented an eschatological vision of a Latin populace transformed by its proximity to Levantine culture, but his focus remained squarely on what this transformation meant for the Latins rather than Eastern Christians; in the conclusion to the first book of his history, Walter the Chancellor similarly depicted both Latin and Eastern Christian communities as unified in an "earthly paradise," yet strayed far from this characterization in his work's dour sequel.

89 On Abū Sulaymān Dāwūd, see Kohlberg and Kedar, "Melkite Physician," 114; Kedar, "La *Via sancti sepulchri*," 196–97; Cahen, "Indigènes et croisés"; Mitchell, *Medicine in the Crusades*, 35; and Edgington, "Oriental and Occidental Medicine," 200.
90 See chap. 2.

Given this earlier Latin discourse in the Levant, William's decision to apply the epithet of "People of God" to Eastern Christians represents a markedly new development.[91] In fact, William employs the phrase well before treating the First Crusade when writing about the Christians of the Holy Land during the Muslim conquests of the seventh century. He closely identifies with these Christians when explaining that, because "our sins required it, the holy city passed to various rulers."[92] In his discussion of Charlemagne's embassy to Hārūn al-Rašīd, William likewise refers to the Jerusalemite Christians, on whose behalf Charlemagne acted, as a "People of God" and frequently uses the phrase in dealing with the events leading up to the First Crusade.[93]

William continues his practice of referring to the Christians of the Holy Land as a "People of God" even when relying on established traditions on the First Crusade from which this designation is absent. Closely basing himself on the chronicle of Albert of Aachen (ca. 1119), William tells the story of Peter the Hermit, who allegedly undertook a pilgrimage to the holy city shortly before 1096. Symeon II, patriarch of Jerusalem, informs Peter of the persecutions afflicting "God's People living in the city [of Jerusalem]," and, explaining that their prayers have not yet been heard by the Lord because of their sins, he urges him to solicit aid from the West.[94] The patriarch's description of the Christians as "God's People" represents a significant departure from Albert of Aachen on William's part.[95]

The phrase next occurs when William describes the Council of Clermont in 1095 and introduces Adhémar of Le Puy, the papal legate who attended the council and accompanied the Crusaders. According to William, Adhémar "led the People of God on their expedition."[96] From this point onward, William continuously refers to the Crusaders as a "People of God." Immediately after the capture of Jerusalem, the Crusaders come face to face with the Christians of Jerusalem, resulting in a union of two peoples of God. This moment, too, is connected to Adhémar of Le Puy, who had passed away after the Crusader victory at Antioch. Following the conquest of Jerusalem, the deceased papal legate, along with many others who had fallen over the course of the Crusade, appears to the Crusaders

91 While Edbury and Rowe (*William of Tyre*, 151) have remarked on William's use of the term to describe the Crusaders, they did not note his application of the term to the pre-Crusade Christians of Jerusalem.

92 WT 1.3.1–4.

93 WT 1.3.18, 1.6.39, 1.6.58, 1.10.46.

94 WT 1.11.29.

95 As Edgington ("Albert of Aachen," 36) notes, Albert of Aachen generally avoids the term "People of God," even regarding the Crusaders.

96 WT 1.16.33–39.

as they first visit the holy sites. William interprets the apparition as a miraculous blessing, bestowed on "God's people in the holy city and its confines" that foretold the future resurrection.[97] Directly afterward, the local Christians come into view. They remember their plea to Peter the Hermit and give thanks to God for answering their prayers and inspiring Peter's appeals. From this point onward in William's narrative, the two peoples of God coalesce.

With William we encounter the novel notion that the "People of God" designated the Christian inhabitants of the Holy Land centuries before the First Crusade. William also drew on an early tradition that took shape over the course of the First Crusade, or immediately afterward at the latest, that conceived of the Crusaders as a People of God on their way to the Promised Land, led by Adhémar of Le Puy as a new Moses.[98] William thus combined two models of religious exceptionalism: that of the Crusaders, who had been chosen by God to liberate their brethren and inhabit the Promised Land, and that of Levantine Christians such as Saʿīd ibn Baṭrīq and Yaḥyā ibn Saʿīd al-Anṭākī, who presented their Christian community as suffering trials and tribulations mirroring those of the Israelites.

William's use of the term "People of God" may be connected to changes he implemented at a late stage. As several scholars have argued, William began revising his work in the early 1180s, when he had already written the bulk of his history.[99] These revisions included changing references to the Church of the Holy Sepulcher (*Ecclesia Sancti Sepulchri*) to the Church of the Resurrection (*Ecclesia Sancte/Dominice Resurrectionis*). With this change of nomenclature, William adopted the rebranding of this church by the Latin patriarch of Jerusalem Fulcher of Angoulême (1146–1157), who had overseen the completion of a rebuilding project to join the formerly separate choir church and the Church of the Resurrection into a single complex. Fulcher rededicated the church on the momentous date of 15 July 1149—the fiftieth anniversary of the Crusader capture of Jerusalem—and redesigned the liturgy for this commemorative feast to accompany the architectural changes.[100] From this point onward, Fulcher and his successors styled themselves "patriarch of the Church of the Resurrection" (*Ecclesiae Resurrectionis*

97 WT 8.22.21–26.

98 Several chronicles of the First Crusade compare Adhémar to Moses: RA 152; Robert the Monk, *Historia Iherosolimitana* 731; Baudri of Bourgueil, *Historia Hierosolymitana* 16; RC 2769–80.

99 Edbury and Rowe, *William of Tyre*, 85; Kedar, "Some New Light"; Spacey, "Refocusing the First Crusade."

100 Linder, "'Like Purest Gold,'" 31–32; Gaposchkin, "Echoes of Victory"; John, "Feast of the Liberation," 417–19; Aspesi, "Cantors of the Holy Sepulchre," 283–96; Salvadó, "Rewriting the Latin Liturgy."

patriarcha) in their seals and charters (see fig. 4 for an example). This appellation hews more closely to the Orthodox Christian appellation of the Church of the *Anastasis* in Greek or *Qiyāma* in Arabic, both meaning "resurrection"—a fact that is emphasized by the bilingual Latin and Greek inscriptions on the patriarchal seals from Fulcher onward.[101]

B. Z. Kedar has argued that William's putative revisions should be viewed against the background of the Third Lateran Council, which William attended in 1179. Given the emphasis at this council on Rome's supremacy in the ecclesiastical hierarchy, Kedar suggested that William endeavored to elevate the standing of the church of Jerusalem by adopting a nomenclature that emphasized the church's unique status as the site, not merely of an empty tomb, but of Christ's resurrection as well as of the future resurrection of mankind.[102]

Renaming the Church of the Holy Sepulcher in favor of the post-1149 appellation of the Church of the Resurrection was not the only change William made, but it seems to have gone hand-in-hand with his description of the local Christians of Jerusalem as a "People of God." Not only does the phrase appear alongside William's reference to the church as the Church of the Resurrection in several passages, but both the phrase and the new appellation do not occur beyond book 8 of the history, the point at which William's putative revisions appear to have ended.[103] The pairing of these two changes sheds new light on William's motivations in the later stages of his work, to include not only an effort to elevate the church of Jerusalem but also to depict its Christian population—Latin and Orthodox—as divinely elected. In this light, the new Latin appellation's resemblance to the Greek and Arabic nomenclature of the Church of the Resurrection served William's purpose in underscoring the notion that the elected status of Jerusalem's Christian inhabitants extended to include all of its various Christian communities (or, at the very least, of Latin and Orthodox communities). Following Kedar's interpretation, William may have wished to assert the church of Jerusalem's pride of place in the ecclesiastical hierarchy in response to the Third Lateran Council. In addition to serving patriotic sentiments, such a portrayal helped him make a case to western Europeans for their continued support of the Latin rulers of Jerusalem as protectors of the holy sites.[104] As Latin relations with Byzantines broke down toward the end of William's writing, securing aid from the West became increasingly urgent.

101 Mayer, *Siegelwesen*, 9; Hiestand, "Die Urkunden," 88; Schlumberger and Chalandon, *Sigillographie*, 75–76.

102 Kedar, "Some New Light," 9.

103 WT 1.15.40–52 (more precisely, the term here is *cultor dei populus*), 7.23.19–26, 8.22.11–21.

104 Kedar, "Some New Light," 9; cf. Edbury and Rowe, *William of Tyre*, 159–60.

Latins, Byzantines, and the Protection of the Holy Land

The second half of the twelfth century saw developing relations between the Latins and the Byzantines. This development was largely indebted to the policies of Emperor Manuel Komnenos (r. 1143–1180), who seized on the weakened position of the Latins following the failed Second Crusade (1147–49) to reestablish a strengthened Byzantine presence in the Levant.[105] In Antioch, as we saw in the previous chapter, Manuel reimposed Byzantine authority through a spectacular show of force in 1159 by publicly punishing Prince Reynald of Châtillon for his raids of Byzantine Cyprus. In the Kingdom of Jerusalem, by contrast, Manuel pursued a policy of strategic marriage alliance and soft power, while making sure to present himself as superior to the king of Jerusalem in public settings.[106] In 1161 he married Maria of Antioch, cousin to King Baldwin III and his brother Amalric. Upon Amalric's accession to the throne two years later, the king approached Manuel to negotiate a new marriage alliance, resulting in Amalric's marriage to Manuel's grandniece Maria Komnene in 1167.

Notably, Manuel also made the Byzantine presence felt in the cultural sphere of the Kingdom of Jerusalem. For instance, Manuel patronized Orthodox monasteries such as that of Mar Saba, situated halfway between Jerusalem and the Dead Sea, and it is likely that he used his influence to enable the readmittance of Greek Orthodox clergy to the Church of the Holy Sepulcher in 1173.[107] Above all, Manuel aimed to reclaim the coveted reputation of the Byzantine emperor as protector of the holy sites in and around Jerusalem. Accordingly, during the renovations to the Church of the Holy Sepulcher, Manuel funded the gilding of the slab on which Christ's body had reputedly been laid.[108] Another ostentatious act of patronage was Manuel's part in the project to redecorate the Church of the Nativity in Bethlehem, completed in 1169. Greek and Latin mosaics attest to the joint patronage of Manuel Komnenos and Amalric, but it is noteworthy that while the Latin depicts Manuel as a "generous benefactor" (*dator largus*), the Greek omits a similar reference to Amalric.[109]

However, Byzantine-Latin relations were not all one-way traffic: the joint patronage undertaken by Manuel and Amalric is indicative not only of Manuel's efforts to exert influence in the cultural and political sphere of the Kingdom of Jerusalem but also of Amalric's interest in close collaboration with the Byzantines.

105 Magdalino, *Empire of Manuel*, 72–76; Harris, *Byzantium and the Crusades*, 116–18.

106 For the relationship between art and politics in Byzantium, I draw on C. Hilsdale's work (*Byzantine Art and Diplomacy*) in a Palaiologan context.

107 Jotischky, "Greek Orthodox." See for other examples Runciman, *History of the Crusades*, 2:391. For the readmittance of Orthodox clergy, see Hamilton, *Latin Church*, 170–71.

108 Harris, *Byzantium and the Crusades*, 118.

109 De Sandoli, *Corpus inscriptionum crucesignetorum*, no. 260, 197–99; Hunt, "Art and Colonialism"; Jotischky, "Manuel Comnenus"; Folda, *Art of the Crusaders*, 347–64; MacEvitt, *Rough Tolerance*, 157–61.

After all, it was Amalric who had taken the initiative to negotiate his marriage to a Byzantine bride. Moreover, after a series of successful expeditions against the Fatimids in 1163/64 and 1168, Amalric was keen to use his alliance with the Byzantines to wrest Egypt from the weakened grasp of the Fatimids once and for all in a subsequent (and ultimately unsuccessful) campaign in 1169. Yet Amalric went much further than merely pursuing a Byzantine alliance and cultivated an image of himself as a Byzantine-style ruler. On the coins he issued, Amalric replaced the image of the Tower of David, which had featured on deniers issued by his predecessor, with a design of the Byzantine rotunda of the Church of the Holy Sepulcher—a move characterized by J. Folda as "made to enhance the identification of Jerusalem jointly with Crusader and Byzantine policy."[110] More tellingly, Amalric depicted himself on his seals wearing a Byzantine-style *loros*, a ceremonial dress reserved for the imperial family.[111] Amalric's self-representation is highly unusual from a western European perspective, yet viewed in a Byzantine context, Amalric acted similar to other Byzantine client rulers. One notable parallel is the early-twelfth-century Georgian king David IV ("the Builder"), who declared himself a *basileus* (the title employed by Byzantine emperors), seemingly in rivalry to the Byzantines, and is depicted in an icon from the monastery of Saint Catherine on Mount Sinai wearing the *loros* and identified with a Greek inscription as "Pious emperor of all the East."[112]

The rapprochement of Latins and Byzantines during Amalric's reign is reflected in both artistic and literary sources of the Kingdom of Jerusalem. In addition to the redecoration of the Church of the Nativity, two gospel books produced at the Church of the Holy Sepulcher in the late 1150s and 1160s feature visual designs that have been described as "intensely Byzantine."[113] Moreover, a Latin hymn interspersed with Greek, preserved among the famous collection of poems known as the *Carmina Burana*, attests to the Franks' optimism for an alliance with the Byzantines in the late 1160s.[114] The hymn, which has been overlooked by most scholars of this period, refers to Manuel as "emperor king of the Greeks" (*imperator rex grecorum*) and to Amalric as "king of our shared inheritance" (*rex communis nostre sortis*), thus stressing the Byzantines' and Latins' common interest as Christians in maintaining control of the Holy Land while emphasizing Amalric's position as king of Jerusalem.[115]

110 Folda, *Art of the Crusaders*, 335.

111 Mayer, "Das Pontifikale von Tyrus," 174–76.

112 On David's title, see Rapp, "Caucasia and Byzantine Culture," 21; on the Sinai icon, see Eastmond, *Royal Imagery*, 67–70.

113 Folda, *Art of the Crusaders*, 283; cf. 324 and 333.

114 Poem 51a in *Carmina Burana*, 1:186–88.

115 Kedar ("Intellectual Activities," 135) first suggested this poem's origins in the Latin East.

For William, whose career flourished in this climate of growing relations between Latins and Byzantines, an important function of writing history was not only promoting the preeminence of the church of Jerusalem and of its Christian population, as we have seen, but also establishing Latins as the proper stewards of the holy sites—a role for which the Byzantines were increasingly competing. Close diplomatic relations with the Byzantines held promise for the Latin rulers of Jerusalem, not necessarily out of an altruistic ecumenical sentiment, but because they hoped to leverage them to elevate their own image as Christian rulers of the Holy Land. In his history, William supports such a program by his tendentious framing of the diplomatic interactions between Byzantines and Latins. For instance, in his depiction of Amalric's state visit to the imperial court in Constantinople in March 1171, William emphasizes the lavish munificence with which Amalric was received (*cum summa honorificentia receptus est*), to a level that surpassed even Byzantine custom.[116] While the event was carefully staged to confirm Manuel's preeminence and Amalric's status as a client of the emperor following the collapse of their joint campaign in Egypt, William interpreted the proceedings as a confirmation of diplomatic relations among equals. The Byzantine opulence described by him in poeticizing terms—including a quotation from Ovid's description of the palace of the Sun, no less—served only to highlight the esteem with which the Byzantines supposedly regarded the Latin king.[117] William even interprets the veil that shielded the initial meeting of the two rulers from public view as necessary to keep Manuel's dignity intact before the imperial court, even though its purpose was likely to prevent Amalric's retinue from witnessing the king's necessary obeisance to the emperor.[118] Although William acknowledges that Amalric was subsequently positioned on a throne next to Manuel that was lower—but still honorable (*honesto*)—he portrays the renewal of the treaty in outspoken bilateral terms: "pacts were made by both parties to the satisfaction of both, put into writing, and sealed with the seals of each" (*pactis hinc inde ad placitam utrinque consonantiam redactis et scripto traditis utriusque bulla signato*).[119]

William similarly combined a depiction of Byzantine opulence and a favorable political outcome for the Latins when describing his own visit to the imperial court in 1179. Upon his return from the Third Lateran Council, William stopped in Constantinople for a lengthy stay of seven months. His account of his time at the court centers on the generosity shown to him by Manuel, the "magnificent emperor," and on the lavish wedding of Agnes, daughter of the French king

116 WT 20.23.5–14.

117 WT 20.23.16; Ovid, *Metamorphoses* 2.5.

118 Harris, *Byzantium and the Crusades*, 116.

119 WT 20.24.26–28; Magdalino, *Empire of Manuel*, 75, n. 185.

Louis VII, and Manuel's son Alexios I Komnenos. William includes an account of the wedding ceremony at the Great Palace, which he considers "not a minor part of the present history," and concludes the description with extensive praise of Constantinople's opulence and spectacle. That William assigns such prominence to this marriage likely stems from the promise this event held for future relations between Latins and Byzantines. In fact, a positive outcome for Latins followed soon after. Upon leaving Constantinople for Tyre, William stopped over in Antioch at Manuel's request. There he met with Manuel, Reynald of Châtillon, prince of Antioch, and Aimery of Limoges, Latin patriarch of Antioch. Subsequently, the Byzantine emperor made the unprecedented move of formally recognizing a Latin Christian as patriarch of Antioch. While several factors likely contributed to the emperor's decision, William implies that he himself had a part to play, given his sly comment that his time in the company of Manuel was "most useful to us and to our church."[120]

For William, relations between Latins and Byzantines thus helped to cement the position of Latins as rulers and protectors of the Holy Land. His use of Einhard as a biographical model served a similar purpose, as it elevated the standing of the kings of Jerusalem and situated them within a much longer Carolingian tradition of self-promotion as protectors of the Christians of the Holy Land and of rivals of the Byzantines. However, events toward the end of William's life drastically altered his outlook on Latin-Byzantine relations.

The Limits of William's "Ecumenism"

The rosy picture of Latin relations with Eastern Christians and Byzantines William paints at prominent moments in his history does not represent the totality of his sentiments. At times, disastrous turns of events frustrated William's idealized vision, revealing his prejudices and the tension between abstract ideals and practical realities.[121]

For example, William's attitude toward the Byzantines declined sharply in response to the anti-Latin policies of the imperial usurper Andronikos Komnenos, culminating in the massacre of the Latin inhabitants of Constantinople in 1182.[122] Although he maintained his praise of the recently deceased Manuel, William now presented him as the exception among Byzantines. William attempted to rewrite his earlier, more balanced and at times favorable assessments of the Byzantines

120 WT 22.4.2–3; for other possible factors in Manuel's decision, see Hamilton, "Aimery of Limoges, Latin Patriarch," 7.

121 So also Schwinges, *Kreuzzugsideologie und Toleranz*, 295–99.

122 WT 22.11–13; Edbury and Rowe, *William of Tyre*, 130–50.

by claiming that now at last their true designs were coming to light.[123] Here—and only here—in the last complete book of the history, William frames the differences between Latins and Byzantines in nakedly doctrinal and ecclesiastical, rather than political, terms.[124] He blames not only the Greek nobles who supported Andronikos but also the rest of the populace for harboring an insatiable hatred toward Latins, fueled by the "difference in [observing] the sacraments." In a return to the hostile language of the leaders of the First Crusade in their letter to the pope, in which they purportedly encouraged him to defeat the "Greek, Armenian, Syrian, and Jacobite heretics," William accuses the Byzantines of considering "anyone a heretic who does not follow their frivolous traditions, even though it is they who merit the title of heretics, when they produce and follow new and deadly ideas against the Roman Church and the faith of the apostles Peter and Paul."[125]

William's attitude toward Eastern Christians also requires some nuancing. On one occasion, for instance, William also applied the epithet of heretics to Maronite Christians. William describes their communion with the Roman Church in 1181 as a "conversion to the true faith," following their recanting of the supposedly monothelite heresies of their founder Maro.[126] His harsh language contrasts with the actions of his contemporary Aimery of Limoges, who had promoted the communion. Ironically, as R. W. Crawford has shown, William's attribution of monothelite beliefs (the notion that Christ possessed one will) to Maronites was not his own invention but derived from a passage from the work of another Eastern Christian author, the Melkite Saʿīd ibn Baṭrīq.[127]

On two occasions, William also expressed outright negative opinions of the Eastern Christian community he referred to as "Syrians." In 1182 a Frankish fortification in the Transjordan near the lands of Fulk of Tiberias was captured by Ṣalāḥ al-Dīn. According to William, a subsequent report attributed the loss to treason by the commanding officers, who were identified as "Syrians" (*Syri*). William goes on to blame Fulk for placing them in charge of this vital stronghold, given that they are "considered by us effeminate and weak" (*apud nos effeminati et molles habentur*).[128] As a similar description in the *Tractatus de locis* indicates, William's sentiments were not unique but seem to have been a more widely

123 WT 22.11.4–5.
124 Edbury and Rowe, *William of Tyre*, 149.
125 WT 22.11.30–35.
126 WT 22.9.
127 Crawford, "William of Tyre." However, given the evidence of monothelite support in the eleventh century (Roberts, *Reason and Revelation*, 52), it is possible that there was still grassroots support for monothelitism among Syrian Maronites in William's day.
128 WT 22.16.33–36.

shared prejudice among Franks.[129] The statement represents William's most explicit articulation of what the power dynamic between Latin and indigenous Christians should be: it was his opinion that Latins should be in charge, at least when it came to military affairs.

Earlier in his work, William had placed Latins above an even wider array of Levantine groups, which also included Syrians. In narrating King Baldwin III's death by poisoning in 1163, William recounts how, prior to falling ill, Baldwin had taken medicine given to him by one Barac, a physician of Count Raymond III of Tripoli. William anticipates that such trust in an individual who was obviously not a Latin Christian would likely baffle a Latin reader in Europe, going on to explain,

> For our Eastern rulers have (mostly at the behest of their wives) spurned the medicine and methods of healing of our Latins, trusting only Jews, Samaritans, Syrians, and Saracens, foolishly submitting to their care and entrusting themselves to them, even though they are utterly ignorant of the doctrine of medicine.[130]

This passage, even more so than the previous, establishes a dichotomy between "our Latins" (*nostri Latini*) and nearly all other groups living in the Latin East.[131] Moreover, William also disputes the intellectual authority of Eastern Christians, Jews, Samaritans, and Muslims—at least in the field of medicine. However, we should be wary of attaching too much weight to this single episode, for later on William depicts Greek and Syrian physicians as more competent—or at least more scrupulous—than their Latin counterparts. When suffering from a stomach ailment, King Amalric implores his Greek and Syrian physicians to administer a medicine they know will harm him; when he fails to sway them, he makes the same request to his Latin doctors and assures them that they will not suffer the consequences. They acquiesce, and shortly thereafter Amalric passes away.[132]

Written over a span of at least fifteen years, William's history shows him to have been a complicated thinker whose attitudes varied at different points in time and according to diverse situations. Although William may have perceived a

129 *Tractatus de locis* 124: *Alii sunt Suriani, armis inutiles.*

130 WT 18.34.6: *Nostri enim Orientales principes, maxime id efficientibus mulieribus, spreta nostrorum Latinorum phisica et medendi modo solis Iudeis, Samaritanis, Syris et Sarracenis fidem habentes, eorum cure se subiciunt inprudenter et eis se commendant, phisicarum rationum prorsus ignaris.* For another instance of non-Frankish physicians employed by Franks, see WT 20.31.27.

131 The prominent exception are the Armenians. The early absorption of Armenians into the royal family of the Latin kings of Jerusalem (with Baldwin II's marriage to Morphia) may have raised their esteem in the eyes of the Latin elite.

132 WT 21.31.27–37.

definitive rupture between Byzantines and Latins in 1182, the prologue to his work, which belongs to the final stage of composition (1184), exhibits a far more positive attitude toward the Eastern Christian population of the Levant.[133] He acknowledges, as we have seen, a Melkite author as a literary and intellectual authority and describes the pre-Crusade Levantine Christian populace as the "faithful."[134] Whatever insurmountable differences had arisen between Latins and Byzantines, the final stages of William's thought, as expressed in the prologue, indicate that he was hopeful when it came to those he considered his compatriots.

William and the Rise of Francophone Culture in the Latin East

William's monumental history was to be the last literary historical narrative of substance composed in Latin in the Levant during the Crusade era. That is not to say that Latin texts suddenly ceased to be written after the Battle of Hattin in 1187. In fact, original works belonging to the genres of religious polemic, ethnography, epistolography, law, the sermon, and monastic rules were composed in Latin throughout the following century.[135] Literary histories, however, were no longer produced in Latin; instead, the Latin East became fertile ground for the development of a new vernacular narrative tradition in French. Arguably the earliest original extended historical narrative in French, the *Chronique d'Ernoul* (Chronicle of Ernoul), may have been composed in the Latin East as early as the late twelfth century.[136] A French translation of William of Tyre's own history also found a ready audience in the Latin East. Although it was produced in the region of Paris in the early thirteenth century, it was soon copied (with lavish illustrations), adapted, and continued in Acre. The *Histoire ancienne jusq'à César* (Ancient history up to Caesar), a collection of classical and biblical narratives composed in early thirteenth-century Flanders, received similar interest in the Latin East.[137]

In the thirteenth-century Levant, French came to feature in nearly all the domains previously reserved to Latin: legal texts were composed in French, sometimes in an explanatory role subservient to Latin; classical rhetorical school texts were translated into French, accompanied by translated selections from Boethius

133 William gives the date of his writing as the year 1184 (WT prol. 85–86) and says that he divided the work into twenty-three books (WT prol. 118–19), indicating that he had already written book 22.

134 WT prol. 87 and 102.

135 For an overview of the Latin literature produced in thirteenth-century Acre, see Rubin, *Learning in a Crusader City*, 176–95. As Campopiano (*Writing the Holy Land*) has recently examined, a new literary tradition—which included Latin—was cultivated by the Franciscans in Jerusalem between ca. 1333 and 1530, when the area was no longer under Crusader rule.

136 Edbury, "Making Sense" and "Ernoul, *Eracles*."

137 Edbury, "French Translation"; Handyside, "*L'Estoire d'Eracles*"; Maraszak, *Manuscrits enluminés*.

on logic and an original treatise on logic in French; Vegetius's *De re militari* (On military matters), a classical Latin military treatise, was translated into French several times, as well as the more recently composed collection of edifying Latin lore and entertaining stories penned by Gervase of Tilbury (ca. 1215); medical learning, though not yet in any systematic form, features in a French pharmaceutical glossary; and, finally, French translations of selections of historical texts of the Bible were made.[138] Thus while the liturgical rites remained Latin, the thirteenth-century literary culture of the ruling class in the Latin East (or, for this period, Outremer) was less Latin than that of the previous century—or at least, not exclusively Latin.

The gravitational shift of literary production from Latin to the vernacular forms part of a larger trend across Europe, yet scholars have noted the relatively early development of such works and translations in the Levant as well as their groundbreaking nature.[139] Various factors contributed to these literary developments, including the rise of lay patronage, and remain the subject of an ongoing debate and fall outside the scope of the present study.[140] At the close of this inquiry, however, I would like to point to evidence from William of Tyre's Latin history that provides some context to these subsequent developments in the literature of the Latin East. As various remarks throughout his history indicate, William did not yet view French as a legitimate form of literary expression. In his description of Antioch, for instance, he complains that the promontory along the coast "is called *mons Parlier* by a vulgar name" (*vulgari appellatione dicitur mons Parlier*), seemingly referring to the French appellation.[141] Elsewhere, William provides the Greek and Arabic names of the city Baalbek in neutral terms (*grece* and *arabice*, respectively); he reports that "today" (*hodie*) it is called *Malbec*, and subsequently qualifies this toponym as "vulgar" (*hodie vulgo dicitur*).[142]

While William did not attribute to the French language the elevated status of literary expression he accorded to Latin, he did, as we have observed, acknowledge Arabic as a language in its own right, as an ancient idiom capable of intellectual expression. With the notable exception of Stephen the Philosopher, this is a significant leap from earlier authors in the Latin East, such as Fulcher of Chartres half a century earlier, who did acknowledge the use of Greek, Hebrew, and Syriac languages in the Levant but not Arabic. In 1230, some fifty years after William of Tyre stopped writing, the cleric Philip of Tripoli bolstered Arabic's status as a

138 For overviews of the French literature produced in thirteenth-century Acre, see Jacoby, "La littérature française"; Jacoby, "Knightly Values"; Rubin, *Learning in a Crusader City*, 176–95; and Morreale and Paul, "Introduction."

139 Morato and Schoenaers, "Medieval Francophone Literature"; Morreale and Paul, "Introduction."

140 Minervini, "What We Know."

141 WT 4.10.20.

142 WT 21.6.14–15; 21.8.18–19.

legitimate language among Latins. He did so by crediting it with its own distinctive modes of expression in the preface to his translation of the pseudo-Aristotelian philosophical work *Secretum secretorum* (Secret of secrets) from Arabic into Latin, thereby expanding upon Stephen the Philosopher's earlier discussion of the peculiarities of transliterating Arabic versus Greek into Latin.[143] As J. Rubin has observed, nearly the same formulation as that employed by Philip was used some fifty years later still (1282) by John of Antioch, but this time in the preface to a French translation of two ancient Latin rhetorical treatises.[144] John's groundbreaking approach in placing the Latin and French languages on an equal footing seems to have been preceded by a growing estimation of Arabic by the Franks, as can be traced in Latin works over the course of the twelfth and early thirteenth centuries. Seen in this light, the rapid rise of a French literary culture owed not only to the role of influential francophone patrons, such as Louis IX, king of France, but also to the multilingual environment of the Levant. As C. Aslanov has suggested, this environment may have proved conducive to the adoption of new attitudes by speakers toward their own spoken language and thus facilitated the early development of vernacular literature.[145]

Conclusion

William of Tyre's chronicle has long been recognized not only as a precious mine of historical data but also as one of the foremost achievements of narrative history from the Middle Ages. In their modern classic of Crusades historiography, P. W. Edbury and J. G. Rowe definitively established William's chronicle as a work of literature, composed according to the conventions and limitations of medieval Latin history writing, yet guided by William's own unique, and at times contradictory, preoccupations and perspectives. They praised the "organic unity" of William's narrative of the First Crusade, forming the first eight books of the chronicle, and the "unified conception on a scale unparalleled elsewhere [in the chronicle]." Nevertheless, they concluded that, when compared to the Latin tradition of Crusade narrative he relied on, "William was saying nothing new."[146]

While this assessment may hold largely true for the narrative portion extending from Urban II's speech to the conquest of Jerusalem, a broader study of Levantine Latinity enables new observations by putting William's chronicle into perspective, thus allowing a nuanced assessment of both continuities and revolutionary new

143 Williams, *Secret of Secrets*, 361; Stephen the Philosopher, *Medicaminum omnium Breviarium*, pref. (Burnett, "Antioch as a Link," 39).
144 Rubin, *Learning in a Crusader City*, 75–82.
145 Aslanov, "L'ancien français," followed by Rubin, *Learning in a Crusader City*, 81–82.
146 Edbury and Rowe, *William of Tyre*, 153, 158, 167.

developments. William's reframing of the Crusade in the opening chapters of his work, beginning not with Urban II's sermon at the Council of Clermont in 1095 but with the Muslim conquest of the Holy Land, drastically changed the conventional western European focus of the Crusade narrative and firmly situated its center in the Levant. To do so, William made innovative use of sources that had not been employed in Crusade narrative before.

In keeping with the Levantine perspective of his work, William drew on a history written from the point of view of Christians living in North Africa and the Levant composed in Arabic by the tenth-century Orthodox author Saʿīd ibn Baṭrīq as well as on a continuation of this work written in eleventh-century Antioch. A close examination of William's use of these two authors, as well as the incorporation of elements of Eastern Christian theological and polemical discourse elsewhere in William's chronicle, reveals his sophisticated engagement with Levantine Christian intellectual traditions. Rather than simply translating his sources wholesale, William adapted them and fused them with Latin traditions to suit his own agenda. At the same time, William's own limited competence in Arabic suggests that his access to Arabic sources may have been mediated through Arabic-speaking Christians, either in Tyre or at the royal court in Jerusalem, while the provenance of some of these works may suggest a connection with Antioch. Nevertheless, William's transliteration of Arabic, his many references to Arabic as a spoken and written language of the Levant, and, above all, his reference to a Christian Arabic writer as an *auctor* represent genuinely new developments in the Latin literature from the Levant, preceded only in the scientific writings of Stephen the Philosopher.

William innovated not only in his use of Christian Arabic sources but also by drawing on Einhard's ninth-century Latin biography of Charlemagne and subsequent legends to connect Levantine and Frankish history. He selectively quoted Einhard to present the ninth-century Holy Land as a virtual Frankish province, depicted Latin-Byzantine relations as part of a longer Frankish-Byzantine dynamic, and created a framework for his portraits of the kings of Jerusalem out of Einhard's description of Charlemagne. In this way, William made the case to his Latin readers in the West for the continued Latin presence in the Levant as the protectors of the holy sites, while appealing to a patriotic sentiment among readers in the Latin East by associating their history and culture with the renown of Charlemagne.

William's reframing of the Crusade thus not only sought to shape his contemporaries' understanding of the past but also to guide future attitudes toward the Latin settlement of the Levant. Yet even in his narrative of the First Crusade itself, William made at least one important change that supported this agenda: he modified his chief Latin authority on the Crusade to include a reference to the pre-Crusade Christian population of Jerusalem as a biblically inspired "People of God." In doing so, he adapted the existing notion of the Crusaders and their descendants as a chosen people and extended it to include also the Christians of the Levant prior to the Crusade.

Viewed within the Levantine Latin literary context of the twelfth century, William's innovations, even in the portions of his work typically considered derivative, vindicate his distinguished status in the literary landscape of the Latin East. However, the changed political situation almost immediately following William's writing greatly reduced the relevance of his distinctive project to promote Latin stewardship of the holy sites, the preeminence of the church of Jerusalem, and the divine election of its Christian populace. With the Kingdom of Jerusalem largely reduced to the city of Acre following the Battle of Hattin in 1187, and as Latins maintained only limited control of the holy sites in Jerusalem, William's work belonged to a world that no longer existed. Yet in the years that followed, his chronicle would enjoy new life in vernacular forms in cosmopolitan centers, not only in Acre, but across western Europe.

Conclusion

LEVANTINE LATINITY AS A LITERARY TRADITION

The Coherence of the Twelfth-Century Latin Tradition

UNTIL NOW, THE LATIN CULTURE OF the twelfth-century Levant has received largely negative appraisals of its literary and intellectual merits. Such assessments may result from a framing of the Latin East in unfavorable terms by treating the settlements as a protocolonial periphery with a limited capacity for reproducing the literary and intellectual trends of Europe. This study has sought to challenge this narrative by demonstrating that the writings from western European settlements in the twelfth-century Levant formed part of a distinctive and coherent Latin literary tradition. This tradition has been revealed and examined through an analysis of the development of textual traditions in the Latin East and of the methods authors used to tell stories about themselves, their institutions, and their place in the Levant and the rest of the Latin world.

Despite the probable loss of a considerable amount of Latin sources, an examination of the wide range of literary forms and genres found in the extant sources from the twelfth-century Latin East—including extended narratives in prose and poetry, abbreviated histories, sermons, liturgical texts, accounts of saints' relics, letters, polemical dialogue, and prefaces to philosophical and medical works—reveals various continuities that support the notion of a literary tradition here called Levantine Latinity. First, the extensive reception of Fulcher of Chartres's history in the Latin East in diverse contexts (the Church of the Holy Sepulcher and the royal court of Jerusalem) and genres (sermon, liturgy, and abbreviated history) points to the development over the course of the first half of the twelfth century of a remarkably consistent textual tradition centered on Fulcher's narrative. Compared to the critical assessment his work received in western Europe, this represents a development distinctive to the Latin East.

Second, the regular canons of two communities in the Kingdom of Jerusalem employed remarkably similar rhetorical strategies in the Latin literature composed to attempt to curb the intrusive influence of secular rulers and to elevate the relatively humble status of their respective sites. Despite differences in genre and in the formal characteristics of the texts they produced, both communities posited an unbroken historical continuity, as attested by local Jewish, Greek, and Syriac traditions, while drawing on biblical episodes to promote the notion that Latin Christians were divinely elected and superior to other Levantine communities. Moreover, both communities sought to enhance the prestige of their sites by associating them with a history of Christian martyrdom. They also argued that the Muslim institutions that predated their own provided a legitimate basis for continued material, political, and spiritual capital, while berating the Crusaders for looting the treasures bestowed upon their sites by Muslims. Finally, both communities of canons challenged the centrality claimed by the Church of the Holy Sepulcher within the sacred topography of the Holy Land and the Christian salvation narrative.

Meanwhile, the vibrant intellectual culture in the multiconfessional environment of twelfth-century Antioch stimulated the production of Latin literature characterized by emphatic displays of learning rooted in a Latin school tradition. Above all, authors cultivated a highly rhetorical brand of learning in works ranging from narrative history to religious polemic. Even Stephen the Philosopher, who viewed cosmology as his chief intellectual project, exhibited an interest in rhetorical study and presented philosophical reasoning as a rhetorical pursuit. As Byzantine involvement in Antiochene political and ecclesiastical affairs became more pronounced over the course of the twelfth century, Latin authors increasingly employed their rhetorical learning in religious polemic directed against the Greek Orthodox community of Antioch.

William of Tyre's twenty-three-book history of the Latin East exhibits both continuity and change within the Levantine Latin tradition. While previous discussions of the literature of the Latin East have tended to be dominated by William's imposing work, a broader study of Levantine Latinity enables new observations by putting William's chronicle into perspective, thus allowing a more nuanced assessment of both continuities and revolutionary new developments. For example, William followed Fulcher in organizing his history by the reigns of the rulers of the Latin East, yet innovated by beginning not with Urban II's sermon at the Council of Clermont in 1095 but rather with a summary of the history of Jerusalem under Muslim rule that drew on the Christian Arabic author Saʿīd ibn Baṭrīq. William similarly fused Levantine Arabic and Latin traditions in his retelling of the history of the Templum Domini: again he relied on Saʿīd ibn Baṭrīq, but deviated from this source to introduce details first encountered in Achard of Arrouaise's poem. Elsewhere, William drew on an early Levantine Latin tradition that presented Crusaders and Latin settlers as a biblically inspired "People of God," yet made a new contribution by also applying this epithet to the pre-Crusades Christian population of Jerusalem. While many of William's innovations involved Levantine Arabic or Latin traditions, others drew instead on narratives from the Latin West. For instance, William quotes Einhard, the ninth-century biographer of Charlemagne, and models his portraits of Latin rulers of Jerusalem on Einhard's description of Charlemagne. In this way, William was the first Levantine Latin author to construct a coherent narrative in which the Latin East forms an organic and key component of Frankish literature and history. This helped his Latin readers in the West understand the importance of the continued Latin presence in the Levant while also appealing to a Levantine patriotic sentiment among readers in the Latin East by associating their history and culture with the renown of Charlemagne. To do so, however, William recontextualized selective quotations and changed Einhard's wording to correspond more closely to the cultural-political reality of the Levant in the late twelfth century.

The notion of a Levantine Latin literary tradition is bolstered by the interconnectedness of both authors and texts to a degree not yet acknowledged by scholars.[1] Many authors were not confined to any one particular area but moved between the various Latin settlements in the Levant: Fulcher of Chartres left the County of Edessa for the Kingdom of Jerusalem, while at least five authors traveled between the Principality of Antioch and the Kingdom of Jerusalem. This movement of authors is reflected in the textual transmission of three early works: the joint transmission of the histories of Fulcher of Chartres, Walter the Chancellor, and Raymond of Aguilers connects the works of authors from the Kingdom of Jerusalem, the Principality of Antioch, and the County of Tripoli, respectively. This interconnectedness is also apparent in the rapid dissemination of narrative traditions across regions and genres. A passage from Fulcher's history was incorporated into a commemorative liturgy at the Church of the Holy Sepulcher at an early date, while the narrative of the canons of the church of Hebron may similarly have resulted in the rapid inclusion of the Feast of the Patriarchs in the liturgical calendars of two sacramentaries composed at the Church of the Holy Sepulcher. In Antioch, Rorgo Fretellus drew on a passage from a versification of Josephus's *Jewish War* composed one or two years earlier in Jerusalem by Geoffrey, abbot of the Templum Domini, thereby further demonstrating the capacity for Latin literature to connect communities across the Latin East.

Another previously unobserved salient feature of Levantine Latin literature is the tendency of literary works to cross genre boundaries, especially in regard to liturgy and literature. Fulcher of Chartres's history, as noted, was incorporated into a commemorative liturgy, while other works also evince a connection with liturgy. Two Latin histories from early twelfth-century Antioch include original poems in meters typically used in hymns, while elements in the poetry and prose

1 But compare MacEvitt's observation of the "easy flow of persons and practices across social and religious boundaries" between Levantine cultures in the twelfth-century Latin East (*Rough Tolerance*, 23).

compositions of the canons of the Templum Domini and of the church of Hebron, respectively, point to the introduction of commemorative traditions. These works' close connection with liturgy vindicates the recent surge of scholarly interest in liturgy and its role within the cultural and intellectual life of the Latin East, yet also points to fruitful new research directions.

Latin and Levantine Cultures

The notion of Levantine Latinity not only implies a coherence among Latin works composed in the Levant but also suggests that they were defined in part by their engagement with other Levantine cultures. In the diverse literary works examined in this study, Latin authors variously drew on and resisted Levantine Muslim, Christian, and Jewish traditions. As observed throughout, this Latin engagement with Levantine culture finds important contemporary parallels in the visual arts, where, for example, the increasingly Byzantine designs of illuminated manuscripts produced at the scriptorium of the Church of the Holy Sepulcher has long been established. However, given the inherent limits in interpreting visual evidence, an examination of the textual sources allows for a more nuanced appraisal of authors' attitudes and motivations. In fact, this study has revealed a range of Latin attitudes toward and levels of engagement with other Levantine literary and intellectual traditions. These observations, in turn, provide fresh insights into the changing ways authors valorized their own continued usage of the Latin idiom over the course of the twelfth century.

Some authors engaged in what I call the "Latinization" of Levantine history and geography by treating these topics predominantly in terms inherited from a Latin school tradition and by promoting Latin over Levantine intellectual traditions. For example, Fulcher of Chartres consistently imposed a Latinized biblical and Greco-Roman framework in referring to places and peoples, and while he did acknowledge the local languages of Greek, Hebrew, and Syriac, he eschewed Arabic as non-literary. While Fulcher did not promote Latin culture explicitly, one revealing comment shows that he considered Latin to be the default (and perhaps exclusive) literary discourse. His contemporary Achard of Arrouaise similarly failed to even raise the possibility that the building he and his fellow canons inhabited could have been constructed by anyone other than a Roman emperor (or, in the case of Helena, the mother of an emperor); to have cited Levantine traditions revealing the Muslim origins of the structure, as William of Tyre later did, would have played into the hands of those seeking to portray the site as a place of idolatry. Nonetheless, Fulcher and Achard acknowledged the role of Eastern Christians and Muslims in preserving relics and sites sacred to Christianity. Fulcher even utilized Jewish traditions on the sacred objects of the Temple (though he did not acknowledge his sources) and promoted close cooperation between Latins and

Eastern Christians, going so far as to present toward the end of his work an idealized vision of a hybrid Levantine culture that transcends Latinity as the fulfillment of a divine prophecy.

Some contemporaries of these authors, however, not only acknowledged Eastern Christian learning on Levantine history but even touted their privileged access to these traditions. Ansellus, cantor of the Church of the Holy Sepulcher, boasted to his former congregation in Paris of his conversations with the "elders of the Suriani" and claimed that "the Greeks possess many things, which the Latins do not." Writing for an audience in Paris, Ansellus seems to have wished to emphasize his access to knowledge that his readers did not possess. Moreover, in convincing his audience of the authenticity of the relics he had sent them, Ansellus may have felt that reliance on his own authority in this instance would have proved insufficient. The *inventio* account commissioned by the canons of the church of Hebron likewise accorded a central place to the narrative of a Greek monk and a Syrian priest to support the argument that the Latin canons were divinely elected and that their institution thus merited elevation to a bishopric. Unlike their fellow canons at the Templum Domini, the Eastern Christian narrative tradition (at least as reported by them) supported the claims of the canons of Hebron perfectly.

In Antioch, some Latin authors engaged far more substantively with Levantine traditions than their contemporaries in Jerusalem. Stephen the Philosopher translated into Latin an Arabic medical treatise originally composed by a tenth-century Muslim physician from Persia. He also collaborated with a Christian Arabic scholar to produce a translation-cum-commentary of an eleventh-century cosmological work of another Muslim scholar. In his prefaces, he promotes a far-reaching program to transform Latin intellectual culture by recourse to "the truth of the Arabs." This ambitious project, like that of all Levantine Latin writers, had both an intellectual and a religious component in that he viewed a Latin intellectual decline as part and parcel of a waning observance of the Latin Christian faith. Remarkably, for Stephen, ancient philosophical learning as preserved and developed by Muslims and Eastern Christians contained the cure to this perceived decline in Latin orthodoxy. Yet despite his revolutionary depiction of the Arabic, Greek, and Latin languages existing on the same plane, Stephen's learning was still rooted in and committed to the Latin tradition. He viewed himself as residing on the Latin periphery, diligently uncovering truths hidden in Arabic works for the betterment of Latinity—a concept that to him was coextensive with Europe.

Other Latin writers in Antioch were far less receptive to learning derived from Eastern Christian and Muslim sources. The author of the "Adelphus" narrative presented Greek erudition as deeply problematic and urged readers to employ their Latin learning to uncover the hidden truths of Greek writings rather than repeat them uncritically. Latin authors in Antioch who held prominent positions in the secular and ecclesiastical hierarchy harbored a similar mistrust of

Eastern Christian communities. As chancellor of the secular administration, Walter warned his fellow Latins against the moral decadence of the Eastern Christian populace of Antioch; several decades later, Gerard of Nazareth, bishop of Laodicea, and Aimery of Limoges, Latin patriarch of Antioch, debated doctrinal issues with the Greek Orthodox community of Antioch. Gerard publicized his account of a debate with a Greek priest, in which he impugned his opponent for his supposed lack of learning, while Aimery praised the Pisan scholar Hugh Eterianus as Latinity's champion in a doctrinal battle against "learned Greece" and gathered Greek materials, possibly in preparation for his own Latin polemical project.

With William of Tyre, a new feature of Levantine Latinity emerged: in his prominent reference to a Christian Arabic author from Alexandria as an *auctor*, or a literary and intellectual authority, William expressed the novel notion of a literary culture of the Levant that spanned Arabic and Latin. This development is reflected in William's consistent acknowledgment of Arabic as a literary language—unlike Fulcher of Chartres, for example—and in his tendency to transliterate Arabic into Latin rather than mold it into a Latinate form. On one occasion, William even gave preference to an Arabic toponym over a Latin one in stark contrast to Fulcher's practice. With the exception of Stephen the Philosopher some fifty years earlier, for the first time in the Latin East a member of the Frankish elite no longer perceived Latin to be the exclusive medium of literary expression. However, his claim that in writing a history of the Kingdom of Jerusalem he did not have any Greek or Arabic works available to guide him cuts two ways. While he acknowledged the literary and intellectual merits of these traditions for previous eras, William implied that, like the Latin Kingdom of Jerusalem, his chronicle was an original Latin accomplishment. With its originality and richness of thought and expression, William's chronicle forms the pinnacle of the Levantine Latin tradition yet also points to future developments in the literary culture of the Levant beyond Latinity.

Future Directions

In the decades that followed William's work, the Latin settlements of the Levant experienced profound changes, as Ayyubid and later Mamluk gains greatly reduced the lands controlled by the Latins in the Levant. Nevertheless, new Latin settlements were established in the eastern Mediterranean, beginning in formerly Byzantine Cyprus (1191) and followed, as a result of the Fourth Crusade (1204), by the founding of Latin settlements in large areas of the Peloponnese. These settlements maintained continuous contacts with the Latin West while forming part of a closely knit network that also extended to the Crusader settlements in the Levant. It has become increasingly apparent that, despite the political and humanitarian upheavals caused by conquest in the Levant and the eastern Mediterranean, these settlements developed vibrant intellectual cultures and a rich literary output in a variety of languages. However, many questions remain in the absence of a comprehensive and *longue durée* treatment of the literary and intellectual culture of the greater Latin East. For example, it is worth examining whether the literary developments identified in the present study were dead ends or continued in some form in other Crusader settlements. Did new agents of change lead to fundamentally different literary developments?

An equally valid form of inquiry might reexamine the dynamic between the Latin East and the Latin West. For instance, while it has often been taken for granted that the intellectual culture of Latin settlements in the Levant and the eastern Mediterranean was dependent on and derivative of developments in the Latin West, reappraisals of the cultural life in these settlements question the literary and intellectual influence of the Latin East on western Europe. For example, did William of Tyre's chronicle, in its Latin and vernacular forms, play a role in shaping historical narrative in western Europe? Does the fact that various translation projects originated in the Latin East—one thinks readily of Philip of Tripoli's widespread Latin translation of the pseudo-Aristotelian *Secretum secretorum* (Secret of secrets), but also of William of Moerbeke's Latin translations of ancient Greek philosophical works—change our understanding of the relationship between the Crusades, Latin expansion, and intellectual culture in western Europe?

These are just a few of the many remaining questions and possible avenues of inquiry. Far from presenting a conclusion, it is my hope that the present work will stimulate new conversations that will advance our understanding of the complicated and creative ways in which the settlers of the Latin East employed new forms of literary expression to entertain each other, to make sense of their place in the world, and to communicate on a continuous basis with an interconnected community across the Levant, the Mediterranean, and Europe.

APPENDIX I

An Overview of Latin Literature from the Twelfth-Century Levant

The following overview includes all known works written in Latin by settlers in the Levant from 1099 to 1187 except for letters, administrative and legal texts, and epigraphical sources.[1] Following J. Rubin's practice, this overview of twelfth-century Latin authors and texts is organized according to the likelihood that the texts in question were composed in the Latin East, in decreasing order.[2]

Works Certainly or Almost Certainly Composed in the Latin East

Achard of Arrouaise, *Super Templo Salomonis*[3]

The opening acrostic declares that the poem was composed by Achard, prior of the Templum Domini in Jerusalem, and addressed to King Baldwin: *Balduino regi prior Templi Acardus*. Although either King Baldwin I (r. 1100–1118) or Baldwin II (r. 1118–1131) could have been the intended addressee, a remark by Achard that he knows the identity of the robbers of the Templum Domini but chooses to suppress their names likely dates the poem to the reign of Baldwin I.[4]

1 The traditional resource for Latin literary epigraphy in the Kingdom of Jerusalem (de Sandoli, *Corpus inscriptionum crucesignatorum*) will in due course be replaced by a thorough reevaluation of Latin epigraphical culture in the Levant by E. Ingrand Varenne, as part of the European Research Council project GRAPH-EAST: Latin as an Alien Script in the Medieval "Latin East." In the meantime, see Ingrand Varenne, "Inscriptions" and "Transferts épigraphiques."

2 Rubin, *Learning in a Crusader City*, 176–95.

3 The poem survives in five manuscripts (including a short fragment), all dating between the mid-twelfth and the early thirteenth centuries. For an overview, see Lehmann's critical edition (AP 296–99).

4 AP ll. 811–15.

Balduini III Historia Nicaena
vel Antiochena necnon Ierosolymitana[5]

The poetic prologue to this abbreviated compilation of the histories of Fulcher of Chartres and Robert the Monk declares that the work was commissioned by King Baldwin III of Jerusalem in the third year of his reign, i.e., in 1146 or the years in direct proximity (depending on how the poet counted).[6] See appendix 3 for an edition of this prologue.

Fulcher of Chartres, *Historia Hierosolymitana*[7]

Internal evidence shows that Fulcher's history of the First Crusade and subsequent events in the Latin East (up to 1127) was written in Jerusalem. Fulcher describes his journey accompanying King Baldwin I in the Sinai Peninsula in 1100, and throughout his work he includes firsthand observations from Jerusalem.[8]

Geoffrey, Abbot of the Templum Domini,
Super libros Macchabeorum and *De septem libris Iosephi*[9]

The incipit of one manuscript witness attributes these poems to "Geoffrey, prior of the Temple," indicating the successor of Achard of Arrouaise.[10] The identification of his office as "prior" situates the poem's composition between 25 December 1135 and 24 December 1137, when the Templum Domini became an abbey. Geoffrey's presence in a witness list places him in Jerusalem at this time.[11]

Gerard of Nazareth, *De conversatione servorum Dei / De conversatione virorum Dei in Terra Sancta morantium*, *Vita abbatis Eliae*, *De una Magdalena contra Graecos*, *Ad ancillas Dei apud Bethaniam*, *Contra Salam presbyterum / Contra Salam philosophum Grecum vel Cretum*[12]

The sixteenth-century Lutheran scholars known as the Magdeburg Centuriators attributed these five works, belonging to the genres of monastic hagiography,

5 Martène's handwritten copy of the now lost manuscript is divided between Paris, BNF, fr. 9077, fols. 180r–205v, and fr. 9080, fols. 254r–257v. For a printed edition of the full text, see RHC HOcc 5.1:139–85. The metrical prologue was published earlier by Martène (*AmpColl* 5:536) and by Riant ("III. Poèmes").

6 *Balduini III Historia* 29–34.

7 The work survives in fifteen manuscripts, divided between the so-called first and second redactions. For the complex textual tradition, see Hagenmeyer (FC 91–104); Edgington, "'Bartolf of Nangis'"; Bull, "Historia Hierosolymitana."

8 FC 2.5; Epp, *Fulcher von Chartres*, 143–44.

9 Geoffrey's two poems survive in a total of eight manuscripts. For descriptions of the manuscript evidence and critical editions of the poems, see GA, *Mac*, and GA, *Ios*.

10 Oxford, Bodleian Library, Laud. misc. 406, fol. 1r.

11 *Cart Temp*, 99, no. 141 (RRH no. 173; RRR no. 364).

12 For an edition of the later summaries of these works and the few remaining fragments, see Kedar, "Gerard of Nazareth."

homily, exegesis, and polemic, of which they included extracts and summaries, to Gerard of Nazareth, bishop of Laodicea from ca. 1140 to 1161.[13] Quotations by Carmelites from the fourteenth through sixteenth centuries of the opening lines of Gerard's work on monks and hermits (*De conversatione servorum Dei / De conversatione virorum Dei in Terra Sancta morantium*) confirms one of these attributions.[14]

Manu plaudant omnes

This sequence (a type of liturgical verse originally sung immediately after the *alleluia*) is preserved in a liturgical fragment in a thirteenth-century manuscript.[15] The sequence was an original composition made for an office of the Feast of Jerusalem, commemorating the Crusader capture of the city on 15 July 1099. As A. Linder and M. C. Gaposchkin have argued, this liturgy represents an early version of the liturgy as used at the Church of the Holy Sepulcher in the beginning of the twelfth century.[16]

Ralph of Caen, *Tancredus*[17]

The preface to this history, addressed to Arnulf of Chocques, patriarch of Jerusalem (briefly in 1099 and later in 1112–1115 and 1116–1118), places the composition of at least the majority of this work in the Latin East sometime from 1112 to 1118. In another passage, Ralph declares *Tancredus* a product of Antioch, as opposed to competing works of Norman and Flemish origin.[18] A later addition to the work, referencing the death of Bohemond II of Antioch, dates after February 1130.[19] Some scholars have suggested that Ralph may have returned to Europe after his stay in the Latin East, since his autograph manuscript somehow ended up at the monastery of Gembloux, where it remained until it was salvaged from a fire in 1716. Traces of his work can also be found at Monte Cassino, where it could have been the source of the *Hystoria de via et recuperatione Antiochiae atque Ierusolymarum*. Moreover, Ralph mentions a visit to Rome.[20] Alternatively, Ralph may have visited Rome on his way to the Levant. Like the

13 Kedar, "Gerard of Nazareth" and "Latin Hermits."

14 Jotischky, "Gerard of Nazareth, John Bale."

15 London, British Library, Add. 8927, fols. 134r–135r. For the sequence, see *AH* 40:71–72, no. 60, and Linder, "Liturgy of the Liberation," 119–20. For an English translation and brief discussion, see Fassler, *Virgin of Chartres*, 154–55.

16 Linder, "Liturgy of the Liberation"; Gaposchkin, "Feast of the Liberation."

17 This work survives in a single manuscript, which is likely the author's autograph: Brussels, Bibliothèque royale, 5369–73. For a description and modern critical edition, see RC.

18 RC 1714–23.

19 RC 2149–89.

20 So d'Angelo (RC x). For the correspondences with Ralph in this text, see *Hystoria de via et recuperatione*, xxx–xxxiv. This text was previously known as *Belli Sacri Historia* or *Tudebodus imitatus et continuatus*. For the visit to Rome, see RC 201.

works of other authors who remained in the Latin East, Ralph's work may then have been brought to Europe by others.

Raymond of Aguilers, *Historia Francorum qui ceperunt Iherusalem*[21]

Several pieces of evidence place the composition of Raymond of Aguilers's work in the Latin East rather than the West. At the end of his work, Raymond still belongs to the retinue of Count Raymond IV of Toulouse, who never returned to his homeland, having died during the siege of Tripoli in 1105.[22] Raymond's account, moreover, was used by Fulcher of Chartres as early as 1106, so the text must have been accessible in Jerusalem at an early stage. Finally, Raymond's history was copied alongside two other works composed in the Latin East: the histories of Fulcher of Chartres and Walter the Chancellor. It has been suggested that this manuscript was copied in the Latin East.[23]

Rorgo Fretellus, *Descripcio cuiusdam de locis sanctis*[24]

Rorgo Fretellus is attested as a chancellor of the Principality of Galilee in 1119 and a chaplain of the church of Nazareth by 1121.[25] Sometime before 1137–38 he moved to Antioch, where he wrote the first recension of a pilgrim guide after having become a deacon there, which he dedicated to Jindřich Zdík, bishop of Olomouc. Shortly afterward, Rorgo was promoted to archdeacon and wrote a second recension of his work, which he addressed to Rodrigo González de Lara.[26] Rorgo subsequently disappears from the record.[27] The fact that Rorgo's two addressees for his different recensions can both be located in the Latin East in this period indicates that Rorgo composed the pilgrim guide there.[28] As P. Trovato has argued, Rorgo's

21 The work is transmitted in seven manuscripts; see the overview in the critical edition at RA 8–9.

22 See FC 1.32.1, 1.34.7.

23 Hagenmeyer (FC 91–92); Rubenstein, "Putting History to Use."

24 On the complicated and extensive textual tradition of this work (with over one hundred manuscript witnesses), see Boeren's critical edition (RF 1–52) and especially Trovato, "Sulla genealogia."

25 Rorgo Fretellus's life and work has been reconstructed by Hiestand, "Un centre intellectuel," 23–31; see also Yolles, *Latin Literature*, 131–38. For the document listing Rorgo as chancellor, see *Chartes Josaphat*, 32–33, no.7, and *UKJ* 1:219–20, no. 82 (RRH no. 87; RRR no. 188); but see discussions of authenticity in Mayer, *Bistümer*, 330–32, and Rheinheimer, *Das Kreuzfahrerfürstentum Galiläa*, 179. For the document listing a chaplain of Nazareth named "R.," who has been identified with Rorgo Fretellus (*R. capellanus Sancte Nazarene ecclesie*), see *Chartes Josaphat*, 35–36, no. 9 (RRH no. 97; RRR no. 205); Mayer, *Bistümer*, 333, 335–36.

26 A manuscript of the first recension identifies Rorgo as deacon of Antioch: Vienna, Österreichische Nationalbibliothek, 369. An epigrammatic colophon following the text of the second redaction in several manuscripts identifies Rorgo as archdeacon of Antioch; see the list at RF 66.

27 As Eck (*Die Kreuzfahrerbistümer Beirut und Sidon*, 131, n. 163) notes, he is probably not to be identified with one *Rorgo Acconensis episcopus*, who is recorded as attending a church council in Acre in 1148, since this Rorgo was a follower of Patriarch Fulcher of Jerusalem.

28 On Jindřich Zdík, see Kirstein, *Die lateinischen Patriarchen*, 271–72, and Petit, *Spirituality of the Premonstratensians*, 96–97. On Rodrigo González de Lara, see Kedar, "Iberia y el reino franco."

guide formed the basis for several subsequent anonymous works, including the so-called Innominatus VI and the *Descriptio locorum circa Hierusalem adiacentum* (Description of the sites in the vicinity of Jerusalem).[29]

Stephen the Philosopher, *Regalis dispositio*, *Medicaminum omnium breviarium*, *Liber Mamonis in astronomia*[30]

Stephen's copy of the *Rhetorica ad Herennium* contains a colophon indicating his presence in Antioch and the year 1121.[31] Another colophon situates Stephen's *Regalis dispositio* in Antioch in 1127. To this was appended the *Medicaminum omnium breviarium*, at the conclusion of which Stephen references its composition in Syria.[32] The colophons to the *Liber Mamonis* do not survive, but Stephen's references in the *Regalis dispositio* to a future project addressing "loftier matters" likely point to this work, which must therefore have been written in or after 1127.[33] Since Stephen the Philosopher should probably be identified with a treasurer named Stephen who lived in Antioch at least sometime during 1126–30, we may assign the composition of the *Liber Mamonis* to Antioch with a high degree of certainty.[34]

Tractatus de inventione[35]

The anonymous author of this text claims to have been commissioned by the canons of the church of Hebron to write an account of the discovery of the tombs of the patriarchs.[36] Since the author interviewed two of the canons and interacted with a Greek monk and Syrian priest from Sinai, this text was almost certainly composed in the Latin East.[37] As W. Zöller has suggested, we may tentatively assign the composition of the *Tractatus de inventione* to the period immediately following the death of Warmund, the years 1128–31, by combining archaeological and textual evidence.[38]

29 Trovato, "Sulla genealogia."

30 Stephen's *Regalis dispositio* and *Medicaminum omnium breviarium* are transmitted in eleven manuscripts and two early printed editions. For discussions and editions of the prefaces, see Burnett, "Antioch as a Link," 1–40. The *Liber Mamonis in astronomia* survives only in Cambrai, Médiathèque d'Agglomération, A 930. For a description, see SP, *Liber Mamonis* 16–17.

31 Milan, Biblioteca Ambrosiana, E. 7 sup., fol. 52r.

32 Burnett, "Antioch as a Link," 6–9.

33 *Regalis dispositio*, pref. 17 (Burnett, "Antioch as a Link," 28–29).

34 *Cart St-Sép*, 178–83, no. 77 (RRH no. 194; RRR no. 391); see also Hunt, "Stephen of Antioch," 172–73, and Burnett, "Antioch as a Link," 60.

35 This text, transmitted in five manuscripts, was first fully edited by Riant ("Invention de la sépulture") and later reedited by Huygens ("Inventio Patriarcharum") along with another version. For an English translation, see Whalen, "*Discovery of the Holy Patriarchs*."

36 *Tractatus de inventione* 1–2.

37 *Tractatus de inventione* 24–25, 28–30, 234–36.

38 Zöller, *Regularkanoniker*, 349–50.

Walter the Chancellor, *Bella Antiochena*[39]

Walter identifies himself in his history as "I, Walter the chancellor." The central focus of his narrative on Antioch and his intimate knowledge of the inner workings of Prince Roger's court show that he was the chancellor of Antioch.[40] He held office at least during the period of the events he describes, the outer limits of which are 1114–22; he must have left office by 1127, when one "Ralph the Chancellor" appears as a third witness to a charter issued by Bohemond II, prince of Antioch.[41]

William of Tyre, *Historia Hierosolymitana*[42]

William of Tyre spent his career from 1165 to 1184 in the Latin East, where he claims to have been commissioned by King Amalric of Jerusalem (r. 1163–1174) to write a history of the Kingdom of Jerusalem.[43] This monumental project occupied William for at least fifteen years: he reports that he had already begun writing in 1169, when he was archdeacon of Tyre; the last events occur in 1184, in the last days of his tenure as archbishop of Tyre.[44]

Works Probably Composed in the Latin East

The "Adelphus" Narrative[45]

This text describes an encounter between a Latin Christian and a Greek Christian in Antioch. The author claims to be on a return voyage from a visit to Jerusalem, though it is unclear from this wording whether the author was a resident of Antioch or if Antioch was merely a stop on the return trip of a pilgrimage to Jerusalem undertaken from somewhere in Europe, as has typically been assumed.[46] The author's identity is unknown; although the explicit in the lone manuscript witness attributes the work to one "Adelphus," the scribe's attribution likely derived from

39 Walter's history is transmitted in seven manuscripts, the oldest of which dates to 1137–46: Paris, BNF, lat. 14378. For the manuscript evidence, see Hagenmeyer's critical edition (WC 52–55) and Asbridge and Edgington's English translation (*Antiochene Wars*, 8–9).

40 WC 2 prol. 1.

41 *I libri iurium* 1.2:154, no. 337; Hiestand, "Ein unbekanntes Privileg," 44–46.

42 Nine manuscripts and one fragment of William's chronicle in Latin survive today, the oldest two of which are dated to the year 1200, while one manuscript dates to 1197–1207: Paris, BNF, lat. 17801 (1197–1207); Rome, BAV, lat. 2002 (1200); Chambéry, B 3240 (1200). For the manuscript tradition, see Huygens, "Le tradition manuscrite"; Huygens, "Editing William of Tyre"; WT 1:3–32.

43 WT prol. 84–89.

44 WT 20.17.38–39: *hec omnia scripto mandare iam conceperamus*. The first datable passages concern 1171; see WT 4.24.3–7 and 19.21.52–55; the events in the incomplete book 23, as well as the general prologue, all date to 1184.

45 The text is transmitted in a single manuscript, Trier, Stadtbibliothek 1897, described in Keuffer and Kentenich, *Beschreibendes Verzeichnis*, 8:277. See also Bischoff, "Ein Leben Mohammeds,"106.

46 "Adelphus" 2; Bischoff, "Ein Leben Mohammeds," 111; Tolan, *Saracens*, 138; González Muñoz, *Mahometrica*, 80.

a passage in which the Greek interlocutor addresses the author as *adelphe* (Greek for "brother"). This attribution in turn may have led subsequent scholars to identify the author with an otherwise unknown abbot named Adelphus.[47] In addition to the Antiochene setting, this narrative's inclusion of motifs unique to Levantine texts on Islam strongly points to an origin in the Latin East.[48]

Carmen Buranum 51a[49]

This short poem's hopeful references to joint military campaigns in Egypt by King Amalric and a Byzantine emperor place its composition within a specific historical context. Amalric had led successful expeditions against Fatimid Egypt in the years 1163/1164 and 1168, and after establishing an alliance with Manuel Komnenos, expected to find similar success in a subsequent campaign in 1169. Unfortunately for Amalric, that attempt failed at the siege of Damietta. Presumably the poem was composed in the wake of the success of 1168, and almost certainly before the campaign of 1169. The poem may have been commissioned by Amalric as a propaganda piece leading up to a new campaign into Egypt.[50] The refrain consists of macaronic, part-Greek, part-Latin verses in a variation on the *Trisagion*—a doxology in which praise is offered to God, reserved in the western liturgy for Good Friday. The combination of Greek and Latin verse, along with the characterization of Amalric as a "king of our shared inheritance," fits with the joint artistic program undertaken by Amalric and Manuel at the Church of the Nativity in Bethlehem in 1167–69. Two inscriptions there—one Latin, another Greek—attest to this project and acknowledge the roles of Amalric and Manuel as benefactors.[51]

(Ps.-)Fulcher, *Sermo de Ierosolimitana civitate quomodo capta est a Latinis*

The occasion for this sermon, the commemoration of the anniversary of the capture of Jerusalem by the Crusaders on 15 July 1099, situates its composition in Jerusalem, as do the preacher's references to the city's streets and neighborhoods.[52] The sole manuscript witness dates, on paleographical grounds, to the mid-twelfth century.[53] The scribe attributes the sermon to "Lord Fulcher." This could be an erroneous attribution to Fulcher of Chartres, quoted in the sermon, or it may

47 Bischoff, "Ein Leben Mohammeds," 106.

48 Yolles, "Latin Vigilance," 248.

49 This poem is found in the famous thirteenth-century collection from Benediktbeuern, known as the *Carmina Burana*. On this poem, see Wentzlaff-Eggebert, *Kreuzzugsdichtung*, 57–58; Spreckelmeyer, *Das Kreuzlied*, 76–80; Hartl, *Das Feindbild*, 85–86; and Trail in *Carmina Burana* 1:508.

50 Kedar, "Intellectual Activities," 135.

51 De Sandoli, *Corpus inscriptionum crucesignatorum*, 197–99, no. 260.

52 *Sermo domini Fulcheri* 161.

53 Paris, Bibliothèque Mazarine, 1711, fols. 336 and 319. The catalogue dates this section of the manuscript to the twelfth century more generally; see Molinier, *Catalogue des manuscrits*, 2:180–86, no. 59.

indicate Fulcher of Angoulême, archbishop of Tyre (1134–1146) and patriarch of Jerusalem (1146–1157).[54]

Tractatus de locis et statu sancte terre Ierosolimitane

As B. Z. Kedar has argued, this short geographical and ethnographical treatise was written sometime in the years 1168–87 by a visitor to the Kingdom of Jerusalem from western Europe.[55] The description corresponds to the Latin East before the Battle of Hattin in 1187 (but, given references to the bishopric of Hebron and the archbishopric of Petra, after 1168), while the author's remark about animals found in the Levant "that are common to ours" indicates his origins in western Europe. L. Minervini has further adduced the work's ethnographic division between Christians and non-Christians, rather than the typical Frankish division between Latins and non-Latin Christians, as reflective of a perspective from western Europe rather than the Latin East.[56] More recently, P. Trovato argued that a reference to the proclaimed union between the Armenian Church and the Roman Catholic Church is not a later interpolation, as Kedar suggested, but points rather to a compositional date shortly after 1198. However, J. Rubin's recent discovery of a manuscript omitting this statement may support Kedar's hypothesis that the text was subject to later revision.[57]

Works Possibly Composed in the Latin East

Albert of Tarsus, *Plange, Syon, et Iudea*[58]

As R. Hiestand has argued, this poetic lament may have been composed by Albert, archbishop of Tarsus and chancellor of Antioch, during a visit to the court

54 For the former view, see Kohler in *Sermo domini Fulcheri* 159; for the latter, see Pringle, *Churches*, 3:21, no. 283; Salvadó, "Liturgy of the Holy Sepulchre," 31; Aspesi, "Breviary of Lucca," 699–703; and Zöller, *Regularkanoniker*, 88.

55 Kedar in *Tractatus de locis*, 119–20.

56 Minervini, "La costruzione dell'identità," 95–96.

57 Trovato, *Everything*, 286–87; Trovato and Kedar, "New Perspectives"; Rubin, private communication.

58 A thirteenth-century scribe copied the poem at the end of an eleventh-century manuscript containing Jerome's letters with the addition of musical notation in the form of neumes: Salzburg, Bibliothek der Erzabtei St. Peter, a. IX 20, fol. 199r. For the poem, see Walther, *Initia*, no. 14145, and *AH* 33:315, no. 265. See also the editions in Schmuck, "Mittellateinische Kreuzlieder," 128–31; Spreckelmeyer, *Mittellateinische Kreuzzugslieder*, 20–22; and Szövérffy, *Secular Latin Lyrics*, 3:92–93. For commentary and discussion, see Wentzlaff-Eggebert, *Kreuzzugsdichtung*, 174–78; Spreckelmeyer, *Das Kreuzlied*, 219–27; and Hartl, *Das Feindbild*, 118–25. A shorter, abbreviated version of this hymn in four strophes and with a different opening (*Lugent Sion et Iudaea*), which leaves out the more topical material in the second half of the poem, is copied in another thirteenth-century manuscript: Zwettl, Bibliothek des Stiftes, 262, fol. 2r. For an edition, see *AH*, 21:165–66, no. 236, and Schmuck, "Mittellateinische Kreuzlieder," 131. I follow here the dating of Schmuck and Hiestand ("'*Plange, Syon et Iudea*,'" 127), rather than that of *AH*, which dates the hand to the twelfth century.

of William II of Sicily in November 1187 to solicit aid against Ṣalāḥ al-Dīn.[59] Hiestand combined references to events in the poem with a letter of Bohemond III of Antioch, which mentions that Albert was dispatched as an ambassador sometime after the beginning of Ṣalāḥ al-Dīn's siege of Jerusalem on 18 September 1187 but before the city's fall on 2 October. The poem's final words indicate that the poet composed the lament in Sicily rather than the Levant: "Sicily has taken in the tears of the [archbishop] of Tarsus" (*Suscepit Sicilia . . . lacrimas Tharsensis*). P. C. Jacobsen proposed an alternative theory of authorship, reading *Thyrensis* for *Tharsensis*, thereby identifying the author as the archbishop of Tyre rather than of Tarsus.[60] Jacobsen points out that there is no explicit evidence that Albert of Tarsus was sent to Sicily, while Joscius or Josias, archbishop of Tyre, stopped over in Sicily during his flight to France. Moreover, the fact that the lament quotes from Walter of Châtillon indicates for Jacobsen that it was not composed in Sicily, but rather in northern France.[61]

Gesta Francorum et aliorum Hierosolymitanorum[62]

This anonymous account of the First Crusade has variously been considered a derivative abbreviation of an earlier text (either that of Peter Tudebode or a shared source) and the first and most important history of the First Crusade.[63] Similar scholarly division surrounds the author's background, although the text has a clear bias in favor of Bohemond of Taranto. We do not know precisely when the *Gesta Francorum* was written, but it has been suggested to identify it as the "booklet" (*libellus*) that Ekkehard of Aura claims to have seen in Jerusalem in 1101.[64] More cogent evidence for its early circulation in Jerusalem is its use (or that of its source) in the histories of Raymond of Aguilers and Fulcher of Chartres. Raymond probably wrote his account before 1105, while Fulcher had written an early version of his history by 1106. Given the problematic nature of this work, it is impossible to locate its composition/compilation definitively in the Latin East.

59 Hiestand, "'*Plange, Syon et Iudea*.'"

60 Jacobsen, "Die Eroberung von Jerusalem," 361, n. 52.

61 Jacobsen, "Die Eroberung von Jerusalem," 363.

62 This work is transmitted in seven manuscripts; for a discussion, consult R. Hill's critical edition (*GF* xvi–xli).

63 For overviews, see Rubenstein, "What Is the *Gesta Francorum*"; Bull, "Western Narratives"; Kostick, "Further Discussion"; and Yolles, *Latin Literature*, 15–24.

64 Runciman, *History of the Crusades*, 1:329–30; *GF*, ix; Ekkehard of Aura, *Hierosolymita* 13.2.

The Letter of "Prester John"[65]

This letter, directed to the Byzantine emperor Manuel Komnenos, claims to have been sent by a "John, priest from India" (*Presbiter Iohannes de Indya*). The true authorship of this pseudepigraphic letter has been the subject of much debate. Most scholars agree that the letter was written by someone from western Europe, perhaps even by someone connected with the court of Frederick Barbarossa, such as Rainald of Dassel.[66] Others, however, have emphasized the role of Hugh, bishop of Jabala in the County of Tripoli, who in 1145 told the chronicler Otto of Freising about an East Syrian Christian king and priest named John, who lived in "the far East" (*in extremo Oriente*) and descended from the wise Magi of the gospels.[67]

Peter Tudebode, *Historia de Hierosolymitano itinere*[68]

The relationship between this account of the First Crusade and the *Gesta Francorum*, and the degree to which it represents an original text or constitutes an adaptation of the latter, continues to be the subject of scholarly debate.[69] Peter Tudebode—whether we regard him as an author or primarily an author-compiler—participated in the Crusade and presents his account of it up through the Battle of Ascalon in 1099. He offers no indication of his subsequent activities or the location of his literary activity. Although he seems to have been a Provençal like Raymond of Aguilers, he may have belonged to the contingent of Gaston of Béarn and returned home with him after the Battle of Ascalon.[70]

Ripoll Sermon and *Ripoll Hymn*

A late twelfth-century manuscript copied at the monastery of Ripoll in Catalonia contains several texts on the Crusades, including a fragment of Raymond of Aguilers's history and a compilation of several accounts of the First Crusade, followed by a sermon and a hymn.[71] Both sermon and hymn probably date to the first half of the twelfth century based on a series of corrections and revisions over a

65 This widespread work is transmitted in over one hundred manuscripts. For the manuscript tradition, consult Zarncke, "Der Priester Johannes," and Hamilton, "Note on the Manuscripts." See also B. Wagner's critical edition (*Epistola presbiteri Johannis* [Barber and Bate, *Letters from the East*, no. 33]).

66 For the letter's origins and cultural context, see Baum, *Die Verwandlungen*; see also the various contributions in Beckingham and Hamilton, *Prester John*, especially Hamilton, "Prester John."

67 Minervini, "Outremer," 641–42; d'Angelo (RC lxxxix).

68 Tudebode's history is transmitted in four manuscripts; for descriptions, see J. Hill and L. Hill's critical edition (PT 18–21).

69 For overviews, see Rubenstein, "What Is the *Gesta Francorum*"; Bull, "Western Narratives"; Kostick, "Further Discussion"; and Yolles, *Latin Literature*, 15–24.

70 Rubenstein, "What Is the *Gesta Francorum*," 189.

71 Paris, BNF, lat. 5132. For a description of the manuscript and its history, see Linder, "New Day, New Joy," 58–59.

considerable period of time. It has also been suggested that the reference to the Holy Lance would not have been topical at a later date.[72] Moreover, both sermon and hymn address participants of the First Crusade, making it likely that they were composed early in the twelfth century.[73] Although J. France initially suggested that the poem may have been composed at Ripoll, A. Linder argued that both sermon and hymn could only have been composed in Jerusalem.[74] More recent scholarly opinion, however, has tended to follow France's interpretation.[75]

Sortes regis Amalrici[76]

This astrological text occurs in various forms, considered to be different compilations of a core work consisting of twenty-eight questions. The compiler ascribes one portion of the text to "the physician of the most kind King Amalric" and references Amalric's campaign against the Kurdish lieutenant Shīrkūh in 1164.[77] B. Z. Kedar has suggested identifying the author with Abū Sulaymān Dāwūd, a Melkite physician in the service of Amalric,[78] but C. Burnett has concluded that he cannot have been the author and that no element in the text necessitates a Levantine origin. Burnett points to the distorted account of Amalric's campaigns against Shīrkūh, the lack of direct utilization of Arabic sources, and mistakes in the little Arabic it does contain; he suggests that the Levantine details may have been included "to lend a touch of exoticism."[79]

72 France, "Unknown Account," 782–83, and "Text of the Account," 643. For the reference to the Holy Lance, see *Ripoll Hymn*, strophe 16 (Linder, "New Day, New Joy," 63). See also Walther, *Initia*, no. 9812, where the hymn is dated as early as 1099, although presumably the commemorative Feast of the Liberation would not have taken place until a year after the conquest of Jerusalem at the earliest (i.e., 1100). Spreckelmeyer (*Das Kreuzlied*, 213) dates the hymn to 1100.

73 *Ripoll Sermon*, passim; *Ripoll Hymn*, strophes 6, 8, 18, 23 (Linder, "New Day, New Joy," 63).

74 France, "Unknown Account," 783; Linder, "New Day, New Joy," 58–59. Later, France ("Text of the Account," 642–43) suggested only that the collection of texts in the Ripoll manuscripts was assembled for commemorating the Feast of Jerusalem but did not specify whether he thought the texts themselves were composed at Ripoll rather than copied.

75 Dominguez, "Lírica y cruzadas," 153–86; Paul, *To Follow*, 269–70.

76 The complex nature of this work, which is transmitted in at least twenty-six manuscripts and has accrued various later additions and reworkings, is discussed at length by Burnett ("What Is the *Experimentarius*"), who also provides a critical edition. For earlier discussions, see Haskins, *Studies in the History*, 135–37, and Brini Savorelli, "Manuale di geomanzia"; see also the subsequent discussion in Donati, "È ancora verosimile."

77 Burnett, "*Sortes regis Amalrici*."

78 Kohlberg and Kedar, "Melkite Physician," 114; Kedar, "La *Via sancti sepulchri*," 196–97; cf. Minervini, "Outremer," 638. On the career of this physician, see Cahen, "Indigènes et croisés"; Micheau, "Les médecins orientaux," 96–100; Mitchell, *Medicine in the Crusades*, 35; Pahlitzsch, "Médecins sans frontières," 4–5; and Edgington, "Oriental and Occidental Medicine," 200.

79 Burnett "*Sortes regis Amalrici*," 237, and "Humanism and Orientalism." Earlier, Burnett ("What Is the *Experimentarius*," 94) had adduced evidence that medieval readers added exoticizing elements to the *Sortes*, even going so far as to describe Amaury as a "king of the Persians": *liber de 28 iudiciis, diversarum scilicet questionum Almericy regis Persarum*.

APPENDIX II

The Catalogue of Books of the Church of Nazareth

This list of books, labeled as pertaining to the "convent of the church of Nazareth," is copied on the verso of the last leaf of a codex that entered the holdings of the University of Erfurt as part of the Amplonius Collection.[1] The codex contains a collection of patristic homilies on various topics, as well as the *Liber scintillarum*—a compilation of patristic sayings made by Defensor of Ligugé, but here falsely attributed to Bede—and Gregory the Great's *Liber pastoralis*. Whereas the features of the main scribal hands throughout these portions of the manuscript are consistent with late twelfth-century hands, the hand that copied out the inventory of books has a slightly later appearance and may date to the early thirteenth century.[2]

In the transcription, I have resolved silently all abbreviations but marked scribal insertions and corrections with \ /; in the translation, I have italicized the titles of works and made clarifying insertions marked with < >, while editorial comments are identified with [ ].

1 Universität Erfurt, UB Erfurt, Dep. Erf., CA 4° 102, fol. 167v. The contents of this codex were first described by Amplonius Rating de Berka himself in his catalogue dating to 1412; see Schum, *Beschreibendes Verzeichniss*, 865. For modern catalogues describing the manuscript, see Schum, *Beschreibendes Verzeichniss*, 360–62; Gottlieb, *Über mittelalterliche Bibliotheken*, 154, n. 433; and Lehmann et al., *Mittelalterliche Bibliothekskataloge*, 2:93–94, no. 198. The Nazareth catalogue was transcribed in Beddie, "Some Notices of Books," and partially in Folda, *Crusader Art*, 402; see the corrections of Beddie's transcription in Lehmann, "Von Nazareth nach Erfurt." See also the discussions in Huygens, *Latijn in Outremer*, 12–14; Minervini, "Produzione e circolazione," 80–81; Tessera, "Dalla liturgia"; Kedar, "On Books and Hermits"; and Zöller, *Regularkanoniker*, 300–12.

2 Twelfth-century features of the main hands, such as the use of ampersands and "e caudata" are absent from the book catalogue. See also the remarks in Schum, *Beschreibendes Verzeichniss*, 361–62; and Zöller, *Regularkanoniker*, 301.

Transcription

hii sunt libri conventus nazarene ecclesie. Ieronimus super psalterum. Anbrosius super lucam. Matheus. iohannes. Apocalysis iohannis. Gregorius super ii. Libros ezechiel. Textus marci evand/gelisite. Gesta ponticifum. Isidorus ethimologiarum. Isidorus de summo bono. Dialogus Ieronimi presbiteri et vita patrum in eodem volumine. Liber quidam qui dicitur paradisus. Cur deus homo. Textus iiii. Evangeliorum. Epistole Ieronimi et Augustini in uno volumine. Duo libri canonum. XVcim libri beati Augustini etiam Gregorius super cantica canticorum in eodem volumine. Augustinus de trinitate. Augustinus super iohannem et Glosule super iohannem. Epistole magistri Ivonis. Elucidarium. Gregorius super moralia iob. Epistole pauli glosate. Augustinus de agone christiano. Episcopus Sidoniensis Augustinum de retractacione. Augustinum encheridion habet. Ieronimus de interpretacionibus nominum. Liber ieronimi questionum hebraicarum et de decem temptionibus. et de paralipomenon. et canticum de bofre. et lamentatio iheremie. et epistola ad dardanum de distanciis locorum. Epistola de veste sacerdotali. Registrum leonis pape. Alius isidorus de sumo bono.

Translation

These are the books of the convent of the Church of Nazareth: Jerome, *On the Psalms*; Ambrose, *On Luke*; <the gospel of> Matthew; <the gospel of> John; John's *Revelation*; Gregory <the Great,> *On the Two Books of Ezekiel*; the text of Mark the Evangelist; the *Deeds of the Popes*; Isidore, <the books of> the *Etymologies*; Isidore, *On the Highest Good*; the dialogue of the priest Jerome and the *Life of the Fathers* in the same volume; a certain book called *Paradise*; <Anselm of Canterbury,> *Why God Became Man*; the text of the four gospels; the letters of Jerome and Augustine in one volume; two books of canons; fifteen books of blessed Augustine <*On the Trinity*> as well as Gregory <the Great>, *On the Song of Songs*, in the same volume; Augustine *On the Trinity*; Augustine *On <the Gospel of> John* and glosses on <the gospel of> John; the letters of Master Ivo <of Chartres>; the *Elucidarium* <of Honorius Augustodinensis>; Gregory <the Great,> *Moral Commentary on Job*; the *Epistles of St. Paul* with glosses; Augustine, *On the Christian Struggle*; the bishop of Sidon has Augustine, *The Revisions*, <and> Augustine, *Handbook*; Jerome, *On the Interpretation of Names*; the book of Jerome, *Hebrew Questions* and *On the Ten Temptations <of the Israelites in the Desert>*; and *On Chronicles*; and the *Song of Bofre*; and the *Lamentation of Jeremiah*; and the *Letter of Dardanus on the Distances of Locations*; the *Letter on the Priestly Vestment*; the *Register* of Pope Leo; another <copy of> Isidore, *On the Highest Good*;

De egissipi .iiii. quaterniones et dimidius. V.ii. libri de sentenciis; ix \x/ libri de phisica. scintilarius. pastoralis Gregorii et duo libri dialogi Gregorii. duo libri de luna [l. marg.:] hi supradicti de divinitate. hi audem de grammatica. arimet\h/ica; magnus pricianus alius de constructione tres boetii \cum glosulis/. Duo oratii \cum glosulis/. Duo stacii \cum glosulis/. Persius. Duo salustii. eneis vird/gilii. Lucanus \cum glosulis/. iuvenalis duplex. Duo stacii achilleidos. Tullius de amicicia; tres prudencii; commenta boetii duo sedullii duo ovidii epistolarum ovidius de ponto. ovidius de amatoria arte duo ovidii stristium. Duo de remedio amoris. duo catones. v. sproperi. duo maximiani. duo donatuli[a]

four-and-a-half quires of Egissipus;[1] seven books of *Sentences*; ~~nine~~ ten books *On Physics*; the *Scintilarius* <and> *Pastoral Rule* of Gregory <the Great> and two books of the *Dialogues* of Gregory <the Great>; two books *On the Moon*. [l. marg.:] These aforementioned <books> are on theology, but these <books are> about literature: arithmetic; a large Priscian, another <book> *On Grammatical Construction*; three Boethiuses with glosses; two Horaces with glosses; two Statiuses with glosses; Persius; two Sallusts; Virgil's *Aeneid*; Lucan with glosses; two Juvenals; two <copies of> Statius' *Achilleid*; Cicero, *On Friendship*; three Prudentiuses; the commentaries of Boethius; two Seduliuses; two <copies of> Ovid's *Letters*;[2] Ovid, <*Letters*> *from Pontus*; Ovid, *The Art of Love*; two <copies of> Ovid's *Tristia*; two <copies of Ovid,> *Remedies of Love*; two Catos; five <copies of> Prosper of Aquitaine; two Maximians; two <copies of> the shorter <grammar of> Donatus.

a Marked as illegible by Beddie but transcribed as *donatuli* by Lehmann ("Von Nazareth nach Erfurt," 484).

1 The author and text here referred to are unclear. The text has been connected (see Boeren in RF, 86–93; and Zöller, *Regularkanoniker*, 309–11) with a short treatise on the geography of the Holy Land preserved in a seventeenth-century manuscript (Rome, BAV, Barberini lat. 2357) and titled *Tractatus de distantiis locorum terrae sanctae quem compilavit Eugesippus anno Domini MXXXX* (Treatise on the distances of places of the Holy Land, which Eugesippus compiled in the year 1040). This work seems to have a connection with the guide of Rorgo Fretellus, though the nature of the textual relationship remains unclear. Alternatively, the author listed here could refer to the "Hegesippus" (which could itself be a corruption of the name Josephus) to whom a Christianized reworking of Flavius Josephus's *Jewish War* was attributed during the Middle Ages.

2 Huygens (*Latijn in Outremer*, 14) interpreted this item as another copy of the *Epistulae ex Ponto*; alternatively, the item may refer to the *Heroides*. See, for instance, the reference to *in epistolis* for Ovid's *Heroides* in the late eleventh-century Blaubeuren catalogue, in distinction from the item *de Ponto*: Glauche, *Schullektüre im Mittelalter*, 102–3.

APPENDIX III

Prologue to *Balduini III Historia Nicaena vel Antiochena necnon Ierosolymitana*

Edmond Martène discovered this abbreviation of the histories of Robert the Monk and Fulcher of Chartres in 1718 in a thirteenth-century manuscript at the monastery of Himmerod and published the metrical prologue with emendations.[1] While the original manuscript was likely destroyed along with the monastery of Himmerod during the French Revolution, in 1881 Paul Riant rediscovered Martène's transcription and printed the prologue with additional emendations. An edition of the full text, based on Martène's complete transcription and on Riant's edition of the prologue, was published posthumously in the Recueil des Historiens des Croisades in 1895. The only major departure in this edition is the transposition of lines 27 and 28.

In the edition of the prologue provided here, I have restored Martène's earliest readings and noted variants from the various subsequent printed editions. With the exception of the problematic opening line, I have refrained from introducing additional emendations or conjectures. The meter is the quantitative dactylic hexameter with leonine or internal rhyme between the sixth (sometimes fifth) and fourteenth syllables. In the translation I have marked clarifying insertions with < >.

The following sigla are used and corrections in the manuscripts are noted with a superscript 1: e.g., M^1:

M = Martène's complete transcription, as preserved in Paris, BNF, fr. 9077, fols. 180r–205v and fr. 9080, fols. 254r–257v
A = Martène's neat copy of the prologue that was printed in the *Amplissima Collectio*, as found in Paris, BNF, fr. 9080, fol. 253r[2]
R = Riant's edition of the prologue[3]
C = Edition of the Recueil des Historiens des Croisades[4]

1 For Martène's account of the discovery, see *AmpColl*, 5:511–12.

2 *AmpColl*, 5:536.

3 Riant, "III. Poèmes."

4 RHC HOcc 5.1:139–85.

Edition

Historiam scriptus parvis[a] tenet iste[b] libellus[c];
Ut fuit urbs capta[d] Francorum gente Nicea[e]
Pro qua Francorum ceciderunt millia centum;
Quos Solyma stravit, princeps dum victus abivit,
Quodque labore fame[f] bello plures cecidere,
Urbem qui claram vicerunt Antiochenam,
Et qui Ierusalem pacis venerunt[g] ad urbem,
Ac Turcos sancto Domini pepulere sepulchro[h]
Auxilio Domini; sedesque[i] fit inclyta regni,
Hoc regno Reges reprimens populosque rebelles.
Hac pugna belli quicumque fuere peremti[j]
Quique labore viae[k] peregrinantes obiere
Christi militiae[l] coeli iungantur in arce.
Hoc Regnum solo Godefridus dux habet anno,
Annos octodecim[m] Balduinus eam regit urbem,
Hi duo Germani digni diademate regni,
Militia clari, fortes, bello metuendi,
Pauca gente sua gesserunt praelia[n] multa,
Illis infestas sternentes caede[o] catervas,
Perque Deum fortes fuerant[p] Babylonis in hostes,

Translation

This small book, written for the little ones, holds the historical narrative[1] of how the city Nicaea was captured <by> the people of the Franks, for which a hundred thousand Franks fell; these Prince Sulaymān[2] felled until he, having been conquered, departed; and <it holds the narrative relating> that more fell through hardship, hunger, and battle—those who conquered the illustrious city of Antioch and those who came to Jerusalem, City of Peace, and drove the Turks from the Holy Sepulcher of the Lord. And with the aid of the Lord it becomes the famed seat of a kingdom—<the Lord who> restrains the rebellious kings and peoples with this kingdom. May all those who were killed in this battle <and> who, on their pilgrimage, perished through the hardship of their voyage, be joined in the knighthood of Christ in the citadel of Heaven. Duke Godfrey held this kingdom for just one year, <but> Baldwin ruled that city for eighteen[3] years. These two brothers,[4] worthy of the royal crown, celebrated for their knightly valor, brave, fearsome in war, waged many battles with but few men of their own, laying low with bloodshed the troops hostile to them,

a parvis scriptis MA, parvis scriptus RC
b ille ARC
c libellis RC
d capta a ARC
e Nicaea M[1]AC
f famae M[1], famis A
g venerunt pacis RC
h Sepulcro RC
i Dominique sedes MA, Domini sedeque M[1]
j peremtis A perempti RC
k vie R
l militie R
m octodecem RC
n prelia R, proelia C
o cede R
p fuerunt RC

1 I have rejected all readings, as none make good sense or fit the rhyming scheme. The rhyme dictates that the second word must end on the same syllable as the final word in the line. Inverting the word order and case endings for *parvis* and *scriptus* produced a more meaningful sense; the alternative, with a redundant *parvus* describing the diminutive *libellus* and an unexplained case usage for *scriptis*, would mean "this small little book, contains a historical narrative <drawn from> writings (?)."

2 The writer mistakes Kiliç Arslan I, defeated by the Crusaders at the siege of Nicaea, for his father Suleyman I; cf. AA 1.17.1.

3 A slant rhyme with *urbem*; alternatively, it is possible that Martène (or the scribe of his lost manuscript) corrected an original reading of *octodecem*—this would have been a less common spelling but would have fit the rhyme.

4 There is potential wordplay here, as *germani* can mean both "brothers" and "Germans."

Dilataverunt regnum, quod tunc habuerunt
In Regno Christi nunc sint sine fine beati,
Imperium quorum cognatus sumsit[a] eorum,
Alter Balwinus[b], morum probitate decorus,
Quod per quindenos rexit feliciter annos,
Excepto solo quo captivus fuit anno,
Regnat pro socero Volco comes Andegavensis,[c]
Hic in tredecimo regni defungitur anno.
Post patrem ternis Baldwinus[d] tertius annis,
praefectus regno iam nomine clarus avito.
Qui compilavit simul et conscribere fecit
Hoc opus. Aeternae[e] sibi sit retributio vitae.
Incipit historia Nicena[f] vel Antiochena
Urbis praeclarae[g] nec non Ierosolymitanae [h].

and through God they were brave against the enemies from Babylon. They expanded the realm, which they then held; now may they be blessed without end in the kingdom of Christ. A relative of theirs has taken hold of their empire[5]—another Baldwin, renowned for his good morals. He governed this <empire> happily for fifteen years, except for the one year in which he was a captive. Fulk, count of Anjou, reigns in the place of his father-in-law[6]; he passed away in the thirteenth year of his reign. Following his father, Baldwin III has been at the head of the kingdom for three years, distinguished by the name of his grandfather. He compiled and had this work written down. May he receive the recompense of eternal life. The *History of Nicaea, Antioch, and of the Most Renowned City Jerusalem* begins.

a sumpsit RC
b Balduinus RC
c *Interpolation* R, *Transposed to l. 28* C
d Balduinus RC
e eterna R, aeterna C
f Nicaena AC
g preclare R
h Ierosolymitane R

5 The use of the word *imperium*, typically meaning "empire" in medieval Latin, is remarkable here.

6 Riant originally marked this line as an interpolation; in the RHC edition, it was transposed to line 28; although this would result in the correct number of years for Baldwin II's reign, it would directly contradict the statement in line 25 and leave King Fulk without an indication of the duration of his reign.

APPENDIX IV

Chronology

The following chronology of military and political events is selectively based on that of Barber, *Crusader States*, 359–66.

18–28 November 1095	Council of Clermont		
March 1098	Baldwin of Boulogne assumes rule of Edessa		
3 June 1098	Crusader conquest of Antioch		
15 July 1099	Crusader conquest of Jerusalem		
		Fall 1100	Fulcher of Chartres moves from Edessa to Jerusalem
25 December 1100	Baldwin of Boulogne crowned king of Jerusalem		
		1106	Fulcher of Chartres completes an early version of his history
September 1108	Treaty of Devol between Bohemond and Alexios I		
26 June 1109	Latin conquest of Tripoli		

Military/Political Chronology		*Literary/Cultural Chronology*	
		20 June 1112	Achard of Arrouaise first appears as prior of the Templum Domini
29 November 1114	Major earthquake in Syria		
		1114–18	Ralph of Caen composes bulk of *Tancredus*
14 September 1115	Roger of Antioch defeats Bursuq, lord of Hamadan		
		1115–19	Walter the Chancellor composes book 1 of the *Bella Antiochena*
28 June 1119	Roger of Antioch defeated at the Battle of the Field of Blood	June 1119	Canons of the church of Hebron claim to have discovered the tombs of the patriarchs
16 January 1120	Council of Nablus		
		1120–21	Ansellus, cantor of the Church of the Holy Sepulcher, sends two letters to the congregation of Paris on a relic of the True Cross
		1121	Stephen the Philosopher commissions a copy of the *Rhetorica ad Herennium* (and, almost certainly, Cicero's *De inventione*)
		1122–ca. 1127	Walter the Chancellor composes book 2 of the *Bella Antiochena*
July 1124	Capture of Tyre by the Franks and Venetians	1124	Fulcher of Chartres completes first redaction of his history

Military/Political Chronology		*Literary/Cultural Chronology*	
		1127	Fulcher of Chartres writes final portions of second redaction of his history; Stephen the Philosopher translates *Regalis dispositio*
		1128–31	Composition of the *Tractatus de inventione*
		1128–32	Two sacramentaries copied at the scriptorium of the Church of the Holy Sepulcher
		ca. 1135	Melisende Psalter commissioned
		25 December 1135–24 December 1137	Geoffrey, prior of the Templum Domini, revises Achard's poem and composes two poems of his own
		1137–38	Rorgo Fretellus, deacon of Antioch, authors a pilgrim guide for Jindřich Zdík
		1137–46	W. Grassegals presents a collection of the histories of Fulcher of Chartres, Walter the Chancellor, and Raymond of Aguilers to Louis VII
		1138	Rorgo Fretellus, now archdeacon of Antioch, revises his pilgrim guide for Rodrigo González de Lara
		1140	Aimery of Limoges elected patriarch of Antioch; Gerard of Nazareth first attested as bishop of Laodicea
		1141	Consecration of the Templum Domini
23–24 December 1144	Capture of Edessa by Zengi		
		1145–47	Baldwin III commissions *Historia Balduini III*

Military/Political Chronology		*Literary/Cultural Chronology*	
1147–49	Second Crusade		
		15 July 1149	Consecration of the Church of the Holy Sepulcher
		ca. 1151	Aimery of Limoges sends a Greek manuscript of Chrysostom's homilies on Matthew to Pope Eugene III
		1153–59	Aimery of Limoges stays in Jerusalem in self-imposed exile
1158	Marriage of Baldwin III and Theodora, niece of Manuel Komnenos; Reynald of Châtillon submits to Manuel Komnenos at Mamistra		
1163	First campaign of King Amalric in Egypt		
1164	Amalric's second campaign in Egypt		
1165	Athanasius Manasses installed as Orthodox patriarch of Antioch	1165	William of Tyre returns to the Latin East, becomes canon of Acre
1167	Amalric's third Egyptian campaign; Marriage of Amalric and Maria Komnena	1167	Frankish-Byzantine redecoration of the Church of the Nativity in Bethlehem
1168–69	Amalric's fourth and fifth Egyptian campaigns	ca. 1168–69	Composition of *Carmen Buranum* 51a
		ca. 1168–87	Composition of the core of the *Tractatus de locis*
		1169	William of Tyre has begun writing his chronicle
29 June 1170	Major earthquake in Syria, death of Athanasius	1170	William of Tyre appointed tutor to Baldwin IV
Spring 1171	Amalric's visit to Constantinople		

Military/Political Chronology		*Literary/Cultural Chronology*	
		1171–76/77	Aimery of Limoges receives a copy of Hugh Eterianus's treatise *De anima corpore iam exuta*
		1174	William of Tyre elected chancellor of Jerusalem
Summer 1176	Reynald of Châtillon released from Muslim captivity		
		1176–77	Hugh Eterianus sends a copy of *De sancto et immortali Deo* to Aimery of Limoges, via Reynald of Châtillon
1179	Third Lateran Council		
1180	Manuel Komnenos recognizes Aimery of Limoges as patriarch of Antioch		
1181	Maronites enter into communion with the Roman Church		
		1184	William of Tyre writes final portions of his chronicle
4 July 1187	Battle of Hattin		
		18 September–2 October 1187	Composition of the poem *Plange, Syon, et Iudea*
2 October 1187	Fall of the city of Jerusalem to Ṣalāḥ al-Dīn		

ABBREVIATIONS

AA	Albert of Aachen, *Historia Ierosolimitana*
AbhGött, Philol.-hist. Kl.	*Akademie der Wissenschaften, Göttingen, Philologisch-historische Klasse, Abhandlungen*
ADipl	*Archiv für Diplomatik, Schriftgeschichte, Siegel- und Wappenkunde*
AH	*Analecta hymnica medii aevi*, ed. G. M. Dreves, C. Blume, H. M. Bannister, 55 vols. (Leipzig, 1886–1922; repr. New York, 1961)
AHMA	*Archives d'histoire doctrinale et littéraire du moyen-âge*
AHR	*American Historical Review*
AmpColl	*Veterum scriptorum et monumentorum historicorum, dogmaticorum, moralium, amplissima collectio*, 9 vols., ed. E. Martène and U. Durand (Paris, 1724–33)
AOL	*Archives de l'Orient latin*
AP	Achard of Arrouaise, *Super Templo Salomonis*, ed. Lehmann
BAntFr	*Bulletin de la Société nationale des antiquaires de France*
BAV	Biblioteca Apostolica Vaticana
BEC	*Bibliothèque de l'École des Chartes*
BHL	*Bibliotheca hagiographica latina antiquae et mediae aetatis*, ed. Socii Bollandiani, 2 vols. (Brussels, 1898–1901 [1949]); Novum supplementum, ed. H. Fros, (Brussels, 1986)
BNF	Bibliothèque Nationale de France

Cart Hosp	*Cartulaire général de l'ordre des Hospitaliers de S. Jean de Jérusalem (1100–1310)*, ed. J. Delaville Le Roulx, 4 vols. (Paris, 1894–1906)
Cart St-Sép	*Le cartulaire du chapitre du Saint-Sépulcre de Jérusalem*, ed. G. Bresc-Bautier (Paris, 1984)
Cart Temp	*Cartulaire général de l'ordre du Temple, 1119?–1150*, ed. G. D'Albon (Paris, 1913)
CCCM	Corpus christianorum, Continuatio mediaevalis (Turnhout, 1971–)
CCSL	Corpus christianorum, Series latina (Turnhout, 1953–)
CE	*The Crusades: An Encyclopedia*, ed. A. V. Murray, 4 vols. (Santa Barbara, 2006)
Chartes Josaphat	*Chartes de Terre Sainte provenant de l'Abbaye de N.-D. de Josaphat*, ed. H. François Delaborde (Paris, 1880)
CHR	*Catholic Historical Review*
CMR	*Christian-Muslim Relations: A Bibliographical History*, ed. D. Thomas et al., 12 vols. (Leiden, 2009–18)
CSCO	Corpus scriptorum christianorum orientalium
CSEL	Corpus scriptorum ecclesiasticorum latinorum (Vienna, 1866–)
DA	*Deutsches Archiv für Geschichte des Mittelalters*
DHGE	*Dictionnaire d'histoire et de géographie ecclésiastiques*
DOMH	Dumbarton Oaks Medieval Humanities
DOML	Dumbarton Oaks Medieval Library (Washington, DC, 2010–)
DOP	*Dumbarton Oaks Papers*
EHR	*English Historical Review*
EI2 Online	*Encyclopaedia of Islam*, 2nd ed., ed. P. Bearman et al., Brill Online (Leiden, 2010), http://www.brillonline.nl/, accessed 30 October 2020
EI3 Online	*Encyclopaedia of Islam*, 3rd ed., ed. K. Fleet et al., Brill Online (Leiden, 2013), http://www.brillonline.nl/, accessed 30 October 2020
FC	Fulcher of Chartres, *Historia Hierosolymitana*, ed. Hagenmeyer

GA, *Ios*	Geoffrey, Prior of the *Templum Domini*, *De septem libris Iosephi*
GA, *Mac*	Geoffrey, Prior of the *Templum Domini*, *Super libros Machabeorum*, ed. Poleg
GF	*Gesta Francorum et aliorum Hierosolymitanorum*
GRBS	*Greek, Roman, and Byzantine Studies*
JEH	*Journal of Ecclesiastical History*
JMedHist	*Journal of Medieval History*
JQR	*Jewish Quarterly Review*
JRAS	*Journal of the Royal Asiatic Society*
JSAH	*Journal of the Society of Architectural Historians*
JW	John of Würzburg, *Peregrinatio*
JWarb	*Journal of the Warburg and Courtauld Institutes*
MedRenSt	*Mediaeval and Renaissance Studies*, Warburg Institute
MedSt	*Mediaeval Studies*, Pontifical Institute of Mediaeval Studies
MGH	Monumenta Germaniae Historica
ScriptRerGerm	Scriptores rerum Germanicarum in usum scholarum (Hanover, etc., 1839–)
ScriptRerGerm NS	Scriptores rerum Germanicarum, Nova series (Hanover, etc., 1839–)
SS	Scriptores (Hanover, etc., 1839–)
NA	*Neues Archiv der Gesellschaft für ältere deutsche Geschichtskunde*
OCP	*Orientalia christiana periodica*
OCT	Oxford Classical Texts
PL	Patrologiae cursus completus, Series latina, ed. J.-P.Migne, 221 vols. in 222 pts. (Paris, 1844–80)
PT	Peter Tudebode, *Historia de Hierosolymitano itinere*
RA	Raymond of Aguilers, *Historia Francorum qui ceperunt Iherusalem*
RBén	*Revue Bénédictine*
RBPH	*Revue belge de philologie et d'histoire*
RC	Ralph of Caen, *Tancredus*, ed. d'Angelo
REAug	*Revue des études augustiniennes*

RendPontAcc	*Atti della Pontificia accademia romana di archeologia, Rendiconti*
RF	Rorgo Fretellus, *Descripcio cuiusdam de locis sanctis*
RHC HOcc	Recueils des historiens des Croisades, Historiens occidentaux (Paris, 1844–95)
RHE	*Revue d'histoire ecclésiastique*
ROL	*Revue de l'Orient Latin*
RRH	*Regesta regni Hierosolymitani (MXCVII–MCCXCI)*, ed. R. Röhricht (Innsbruck, 1893)
RRR	*Revised Regesta Regni Hierosolymitani*, ed. H. E. Mayer et al., www.crusades-regesta.com, accessed 30 October 2020
RSCI	*Rivista di storia della Chiesa in Italia*
Sæwulf	*Peregrinatio*
Sermo domini Fulcheri	*Sermo domini Fulcheri de Ierosolimitana civitate quomodo capta est a Latinis*, ed. Kohler
SP, *Liber Mamonis*	Stephen the Philosopher, *Liber Mamonis in astronomia*
StItalFCl	*Studi italiani de filologia classica*
StMed	*Studi medievali*
UKJ	*Die Urkunden der lateinischen Könige von Jerusalem*, ed. H. E. Mayer, MGH Diplomata regum Latinorum Hierosolymitanorum, 4 vols. (Hanover, 2010)
WC	Walter the Chancellor, *Bella Antiochena*, ed. Hagenmeyer
WT	William of Tyre, *Historia Hierosolymitana*
ZDPV	*Zeitschrift des Deutschen Palästina-Vereins*

BIBLIOGRAPHY

Primary Sources

ʿAbdallāh ibn al-Faḍl. *An Essay Containing Ideas Useful for the Soul and Answers to Questions That People Frequently Ask and Dispute Which Are Extracted from the Sayings of the Holy Fathers and Select Philosophers*. Edited by P. Sbath. *Vingt traités philosophiques et apologétiques d'auteurs arabes chrétiens du IXᵉ au XIVᵉ siècle*, 131–48. Cairo, 1929.

———. *An Essay Containing Ideas Useful for the Soul and Answers to Questions That People Frequently Ask and Dispute Which Are Extracted from the Sayings of the Holy Fathers and Select Philosophers*. Translated by S. Noble. In *The Orthodox Church in the Arab World, 700–1700: An Anthology of Sources*, edited by S. Noble and A. Treiger, 171–87. DeKalb, IL, 2014.

Abraham of Tiberias. *Dialogue with ʿAbd al-Raḥmān al-Hāšimī*. Edited by G. B. Marcuzzo. *Le dialogue d'Abraham de Tibériade avec ʿAbd al-Raḥmān al-Hāšimī à Jérusalem vers 820: Étude, édition critique et traduction annotée d'un texte théologique chrétien de la littérature arabe*. Textes et Études sur l'Orient Chrétien 3. Rome, 1986.

Achard of Arrouaise. *Super Templo Salomonis*. Edited by P. Lehmann. "Die mittellateinischen Dichtungen der Prioren des Tempels von Jerusalem Acardus und Gaufridus." In *Corona quernea*, 296–330.

Adelard of Bath. *Quaestiones naturales*. Edited by C. Burnett. Translated by M. Lejbowicz, E. Ndiaye, and C. Dussourt. *L'un et le divers: Questions sur la nature (les causes des choses); avec le pseudépigraphe "Comme l'atteste Ergaphalau."* Paris, 2016.

"Adelphus." Edited and translated by J. Yolles and J. Weiss. In *Medieval Latin Lives of Muhammad*, 179–214. DOML 51. 2018.

Aimery of Limoges. *Letter to Hugh Eterianus on* De sancto et immortali Deo. Edited by P. Podolak. CCCM 298. 2020.

Albert of Aachen, *Historia Ierosolimitana*. Edited and translated by S. B. Edgington. Oxford, 2007.

Albertus of Tarsus. *Plange, Syon et Iudea*. Edited by C. Blume. *AH* 33:315, no. 265.

Annales regni Francorum. Edited by F. Kurze. MGH ScriptRerGerm. 1895.

Annales Rodenses. Edited by G. H. Pertz. MGH SS 16. 1859.

Anonymi Gesta Francorum et aliorum Hierosolymitanorum. Edited by H. Hagenmeyer. Heidelberg, 1890.

Anselm of Canterbury. *Opera*. Edited by F. S. Schmitt. 6 vols. Edinburgh, 1946–51.

Balduini III Historia Nicaena vel Antiochena necnon Ierosolymitana [Prologue]. Edited by E. Martène. In *AmpColl* 5:536. Reprinted in PL 155:1089–92.

———. Edited by P. Riant. RHC HOcc 5.1:139–85.

Baudri of Bourgueil. *Historia Ierosolimitana*. Edited by S. Biddlecombe. *The Historia Ierosolimitana of Baldric of Bourgueil*. Woodbridge, UK, 2014.

Benedict of Monte Soratte. *Chronicon*. Edited by G. H. Pertz. MGH SS 3. 1839.

———. *Chronicon*. Edited by G. Zucchetti. *Il Chronicon di Benedetto: Monaco di S. Andrea del Soratte e il Libellus de Imperatoria Potestate in urbe Roma*. Rome, 1920.

Burgundio of Pisa. *Prologus super opus beati Johannis Chrysostomi super Matthaeum*. Edited by E. Martène and U. Durand. In *AmpColl* 1:817–19.

Carmina Burana. Edited and translated by D. A. Trail. 2 vols. DOML 48–49. 2018.

Cassiodorus and Epiphanius. *Historia ecclesiastica tripartita*. Edited by W. Jacob and R. Hanslik. CSEL 71. 1952.

Chanson d'Antioche. Translated by S. B. Edgington and C. Sweetenham. Farnham, UK, 2011.

Chanson des Chétifs. Translated by C. Sweetenham. *The* Chanson des Chétifs *and* Chanson de Jérusalem*: Completing the Central Trilogy of the Old French Crusade Cycle*. Farnham, UK, 2016.

Cicero. *De officiis*. Edited by M. Winterbottom. OCT. Oxford, 1994.

Cicero. *Tusculanae disputationes*. Edited by M. Pohlenz. *M. Tulli Ciceronis scripta quae manserunt omnia*. Bibliotheca scriptorum Graecorum et Romanorum Teubneriana 44. Stuttgart, 1918. Reprint, Berlin, 2013.

Dante Alighieri. *De vulgari eloquentia*. Edited and translated by S. Botterill. *De vulgari eloquentia*. Cambridge, 1996.

Descriptio locorum circa Hierusalem adiacentum. Edited by M. de Vogüé. *Les Eglises de la Terre Sainte*, 414–33. Paris, 1860.

Einhard. *Vita Karoli Magni*. Edited by H. W. Garrod and R. B. Mowat. *Einhard's Life of Charlemagne: The Latin Text*. Oxford, 1915.

Ekkehard of Aura. *Hierosolymita*. Edited by H. Hagenmeyer. Tübingen, 1877.

Elzear Horn. *Ichnographiae monumentorum Terrae Sanctae*. Edited by E. Hoade and B. Bagatti. 2nd ed. Jerusalem, 1962.

Epistola presbiteri Johannis. Edited by B. Wagner. *Die "Epistola presbiteri Johannis": Lateinisch und deutsch; Überlieferung, Textgeschichte, Rezeption und Übertragungen im Mittelalter, mit bisher unedierten Texten*. Tübingen, 2000.

Flavius Josephus. *De bello Iudaico*. Edited by E. Cardwell. Oxford, 1837.

———. *Opera*. Edited by B. Niese. 7 vols. Berlin, 1885–95.

Fulcher of Chartres. *Historia Hierosolymitana*. Edited by H. Hagenmeyer. Heidelberg, 1913.

———. *Historia Hierosolymitana*. Translated by F. R. Ryan. *A History of the Expedition to Jerusalem 1095–1127*. Knoxville, 1969.

———. *Historia Iherosolymitana*. RHC HOcc 3:311–485.

Geoffrey, Prior of the Templum Domini. *De septem libris Iosephi*. Edited by J. Yolles. "Geoffrey, Prior of the *Templum Domini, On the Seven Books of Josephus*." *Crusades* 13 (2014): 77–118.

———. *Super libros Machabeorum*. Edited by E. Poleg. "On the Books of Maccabees: An Unpublished Poem by Geoffrey, Prior of the 'Templum Domini.'" *Crusades* 9 (2010): 13–56.

Gesta Francorum et aliorum Hierosolymitanorum. Edited by R. Hill. Oxford, 1967.

Gesta Francorum Iherusalem expugnantium. RHC HOcc 3:487–543.

Gilo of Paris. *Historia vie Hierosolimitane*. Edited and translated by C. W. Grocock, with J. E. Siberry. New York, 1997.

Guibert of Nogent. *Dei gesta per Francos*. Edited by R. B. C. Huygens. CCCM 127A. 1996.

———. *Dei gesta per Francos*. Translated by R. Levine. *The Deeds of God through the Franks: A Translation of Guibert de Nogent's* Gesta Dei per Francos. Woodbridge, UK, 1997.

Guillaume de Tyr et ses continuateurs: Texte français du XIIIe *siècle*. Edited by P. Paris. 2 vols. Paris, 1879–80.

Haimo of Auxerre. *Annotatio libri Isaiae prophetae*. Edited by R. Gryson. CCCM 135C. 2014.

Harawī, ʿAlī ibn Abī Bakr al-. *Kitāb al-Ishārāt ilā maʿrifat al-Ziyārāt*. Edited and translated by J. W. Meri. *A Lonely Wayfarer's Guide to Pilgrimage: ʿAlī ibn Abī Bakr al-Harawī's* Kitāb al-Ishārāt ilā maʿrifat al-Ziyārāt. Princeton, 2004.

Ps.-Hegesippus. *Historiae libri quinque*. Edited by V. Ussani. CSEL 66. 1932–60.

Historiae Hierosolymitanae secunda pars. RHC HOcc 5:549–85.

Hystoria de via et recuperatione Antiochiae atque Ierusolymarum (olim tudebodus imitatus et continuatus): I Normanni d'Italia alla prima crociata in una cronaca cassinese. Edited by Edoardo d'Angelo. Florence, 2009.

I libri iurium della Repubblica di Genova. 2 vols. Rome, 1996–2011.

Icelandic Pilgrim. Translated by J. Wilkinson, J. Hill, and W. F. Ryan. *Jerusalem Pilgrimage 1099–1185*, 220–222. London, 1988.

Innocent III. *Die Register Innocenz' III. 14. Jahrgang (1211/1212): Texte und Indices*. Edited by A. Sommerlechner. Graz, 2018.

Innominatus VI. Edited by W. A. Neumann. *Österreichisches Vierteljahrschrift für katholische Theologie* 7 (1868): 397–438.

James of Vitry. *Historia orientalis*. Edited and translated by J. Donnadieu. *Histoire orientale = Historia orientalis*. Turnhout, 2008.

James of Voragine. *Legenda aurea*. Edited by P. Maggioni. Florence, 1998–99.

Jerome. *Commentarii in Esaiam*. Edited by M. Adriaen. CCSL 73A. 1963.

———. *Commentarii in evangelium Matthaei*. Edited by D. Hurst and M. Adriaen. CCSL 77. 1969.

———. *Commentarii in Ezechielem*. Edited by F. Glorie. CCSL 75. 1964.

———. *Commentarii in prophetas minores*. Edited by M. Adriaen. CCSL 76–76A. 1969–70.

———. *Liber interpretationis hebraicorum nominum*. Edited by P. de Lagarde, G. Morin, and M. Adriaen. CCSL 72. 1959.

John Kinnamos. *Epitome*. Edited by A. Meineke. *Ioannis Cinnami Epitome rerum ab Ioanne et Alexio Comnenis gestarum*. Corpus scriptorum historiae byzantinae 25–26. Bonn, 1836.

———. *Epitome*. Translated by C. M. Brand. *Deeds of John and Manuel Comnenus*. New York, 1976.

John of Antioch. *La Rectorique de Cyceron*. Edited by E. Guadagnini. *La Rectorique de Cyceron tradotta da Jean d'Antioche: Edizione e glossario*. Pisa, 2009.

John of Würzburg. *Peregrinatio*. Edited by R. B. C. Huygens. *Peregrinationes tres: Saewulf, John of Würzburg, Theodericus*, 79–138. CCCM 139. Turnhout, 1994.

Liber de constitutione, institutione, consecratione, reliquiis ornamentis et privilegiis: Chartes et documents pour servir à l'histoire de l'Abbaye de Charroux. Edited by D. P. de Monsabert. *Archives historiques du Poitou* 39 (1910).

Manu plaudant. Edited by A. Linder. "The Liturgy of the Liberation of Jerusalem." *MedSt* 52 (1990): 110–31.

———. Edited by C. Blume. *AH* 40: 71–72, no. 60. Leipzig, 1902.

Matthew Paris. *Historia Anglorum*. Edited by F. Madden. Rerum Britannicarum Medii Aevi scriptores 44.1. London, 1866.

Metellus of Tegernsee. *Expeditio Jerosolimitana*. Edited by P. C. Jacobsen. Stuttgart, 1982.

Michael Rabbo. *Chronique de Michel le Syrien, Patriarche Jacobite d'Antioche (1166–1199)*. Translated by J.-B. Chabot. 4 vols. Paris, 1905. Reprint, Brussels, 1963.

Nerses of Lambron. *Commentary on the Revelation of Saint John*. Translated by R. W. Thomson. Louvain, 2007.

Notker Balbulus. *Gesta Karoli Magni imperatoris*. Edited by H. F. Haefele. MGH ScriptRerGerm NS 12. 1959.

Oliver of Paderborn. *Historia Damiatina*. Edited by H. Hoogeweg. *Die Schriften des Kölner Domscholasters, späteren Bischofs von Paderborn und Kardinal-Bischofs von S. Sabina, Oliverus*. Tübingen, 1894.

Otfrid of Weissenburg. *Evangelienbuch*. Edited by K. Pivernetz. *Otfrid von Weissenburg: Das 'Evangelienbuch' in der Überlieferung der Freisinger Handschrift (Bayerische Staatsbibliothek München, cgm. 14); Edition und Untersuchungen*. Göppingen, 2000.

Peter the Deacon. *Liber de locis sanctis*. Edited by R. Weber. CCSL 175. 1965.

Peter Tudebode. *Historia de Hierosolymitano itinere*. Edited by J. Hill and L. Hill. Paris, 1977.

Piacenza Pilgrim. Edited by P. Geyer. CCSL 175. 1965.
Qusṭā ibn Lūqā. *Correspondence with Ibn al-Munağğim Ḥunayn ibn Isḥāq*. Edited by S. K. Samir. Translated by I. Zilio-Grandi. *Una corrispondenza islamo-cristiana sull'origine divina dell'Islām*. Turin, 2003.
Ralph of Caen. *Tancredus*. Edited by E. d'Angelo. CCCM 231. 2011.
Raymond of Aguilers. *Historia Francorum qui ceperunt Iherusalem*. Edited by J. H. Hill and L. L. Hill. *Le "Liber" de Raymond d'Aguilers*. Paris, 1969.
Riccoldo of Montecroce. *Epistolae ad ecclesiam triumphantem*. Edited by R. Röhricht. "Lettres de Ricoldo de Monte-Croce." *AOL* 2 (1884): 258–96.
Ripoll Hymn. Edited by A. Linder. "A New Day, New Joy: The Liberation of Jerusalem on 15 July 1099." In *L'idea di Gerusalemme*, 46–64.
———. Edited by J. France. "The Text of the Account of the Capture of Jerusalem in the Ripoll Manuscript, Bibliothèque Nationale (Latin) 5132." *EHR* 103.408 (1988): 640–57.
Ripoll Sermon. Edited by A. Linder. "A New Day, New Joy: The Liberation of Jerusalem on 15 July 1099." In *L'idea di Gerusalemme*, 46–64.
———. Edited by J. France "The Text of the Account of the Capture of Jerusalem in the Ripoll Manuscript, Bibliothèque Nationale (Latin) 5132." *EHR* 103.408 (1988): 640–57.
Robert the Monk. *Historia Iherosolimitana*. Edited by D. Kempf and M. G. Bull. *The Historia Iherosolimitana of Robert the Monk*. Woodbridge, UK, 2013.
Rorgo Fretellus. *Descripcio cuiusdam de locis sanctis*. Edited by P. C. Boeren. *Rorgo Fretellus de Nazareth et sa Description de la Terre Sainte: Histoire et édition du texte*. Amsterdam, 1980.
Sæwulf. *Peregrinatio*. Edited by R. B. C. Huygens. *Peregrinationes tres: Saewulf, John of Würzburg, Theodericus*, 59–77. CCCM 139. Turnhout, 1994.
Sa'īd ibn Baṭrīq [Eutychius of Alexandria]. *Kitāb naẓm al-ğawhar*. Edited by L. Cheikho, B. Carra de Vaux, and H. Zayyat. *Eutychii patriarchae Alexandrini Annales*. CSCO, Scriptores Arabici, 6–7. Beirut, 1906–9.
———. *Kitāb naẓm al-ğawhar*. Translated by B. Pirone. *Gli annali / Eutichio, patriarca di Alessandria, 877–940*. Cairo, 1987.
Sermo domini Fulcheri de Ierosolimitana civitate quomodo capta est a Latinis. Edited by C. Kohler. "Un sermon commémoratif de la prise de Jérusalem par les croisés, attribué a Foucher de Chartres." *ROL* 8 (1900–1): 158–64. Reprinted in *Mélanges pour servir à l'histoire de l'Orient latin et des croisades*, 2:330–40. Paris, 1906.
Stephen the Philosopher. *Liber Mamonis in astronomia*. Edited and translated by D. Grupe. *Stephen of Pisa and Antioch: Liber Mamonis. An Introduction to Ptolemaic Cosmology and Astronomy from the Early Crusader States*. Munich, 2019.
Theoderich. *Peregrinatio*. Edited by R. B. C. Huygens. *Peregrinationes tres: Saewulf, John of Würzburg, Theodericus*, 142–97. CCCM 139. 1994.
Thomas of Froidmont. *Hodoeporicon*. Edited by P. G. Schmidt. "Peregrinatio periculosa: Thomas von Froidmont über die Jerusalem-Fahrten seiner Schwester Margareta." In *Kontinuität und Wandel: Lateinische Poesie von Naevius bis Baudelaire, Franco Munaro zum 65. Geburtstag*, edited by U. J. Stache, W. Maaz, and F. Wagner, 461–85. Hildesheim, 1986.
Tractatus de inventione. Edited by R. B. C. Huygens. "Inventio Patriarcharum." *Crusades* 4 (2005): 131–55.
Tractatus de locis. Edited by B. Z. Kedar. "The *Tractatus de locis et statu Sancte Terre Ierosolimitane*." In France and Zajac, *Crusades and Their Sources*, 111–33.
Tractatus eiusdem Breviarium. Edited by P. Riant. RHC HOcc 5.1:314–16.
Usāma ibn Munqiḏ. *Kitāb al-I'tibār*. Edited by P. K. Hitti. *Usāmah's Memoirs, Entitled* Kitāb al-i'tibār, *by Usāmah ibn-Munqidh*. Princeton, 1930.
———. *Kitāb al-I'tibār*. Translated by P. M. Cobb. *Usama ibn Munqidh: Warrior-Poet of the Age of Crusades*. Oxford, 2005.

Versus de viris illustribus dioecesis Tarvanensis. Edited by C. Moeller. "Les Flamands du Ternois au Royaume du Jérusalem." In *Mélanges Paul Fredericq: Hommage de la Société pour le Progrès des Études Philologiques et Historiques*, 189–202. Brussels, 1904.
Virgil. *Opera*. Edited by R. A. B. Mynors. OCT. Oxford, 1969.
Walter of Châtillon. *Alexandreis*. Translated by D. Townsend. *The Alexandreis of Walter of Châtillon: A Twelfth-Century Epic; A Verse Translation*. Philadelphia, 1996.
Walter the Chancellor. *Bella Antiochena*. Edited by H. Hagenmeyer. Innsbruck, 1896.
———. *Bella Antiochena*. Translated by T. S. Asbridge and S. B. Edgington. *Walter the Chancellor's* The Antiochene Wars. Brookfield, 1999.
Widukind of Corvey. *Res gestae Saxonicae*. Edited by D. G. Waitz. MGH SS 3. 1839.
William of Tyre. *Historia Hierosolymitana*. Edited by R. B. C. Huygens. *Willelmus Tyrensis, Archiepiscopus, Chronicon*. CCCM 63–63A. 1986.
Yaḥyā ibn Saʿīd al-Anṭākī. *Kitāb al-ḏayl*. Edited by I. Kratchkovsky. Translated by F. Micheau and G. Troupeau. *Histoire*. Patrologia Orientalis 47.4. 1997.
———. *Kitāb al-ḏayl*. Translated by B. Pirone. *Cronache dell'Egitto Fatimide e dell'Impero Bizantino (937–1033)*. Milan, 1997.

Secondary Sources

Abulafia, D., and N. Berend, eds. *Medieval Frontiers: Concepts and Practices*. Aldershot, 2002.
Agapitos, P. A., and L. Boje Mortensen, eds. *Medieval Narratives between History and Fiction: From the Centre to the Periphery of Europe, c. 1100–1400*. Copenhagen, 2012.
Aigrain, R. *L'hagiographie: Ses sources, ses méthodes, son histoire*. Paris, 1953.
Albu Hanawalt, E. *The Normans in Their Histories: Propaganda, Myth and Subversion*. Woodbridge, UK, 2001.
Ammirati, S. "The Latin Fragments from the Qubbat al-Khazna of Damascus: A Preliminary Palaeographical and Textual Survey." In *Palaeography between East and West: Proceedings of the Seminars on Arabic Palaeography at Sapienza University of Rome*, edited by A. D'Ottone Rambach, 95–117. *Rivista degli studi orientali*, n.s., 90, supplement 1. Pisa, 2018.
———. "Reconsidering the Latin Fragments from the Qubbat al-Khazna in the Great Mosque of Damascus." In D'Ottone Rambach et al., *The Damascus Fragments*, 321–30.
Amouroux-Mourad, M. *Le comté d'Edesse: 1098–1150*. Paris, 1988.
Andersen, H. "Markedness Theory: The First 150 Years." In *Markedness in Synchrony and Diachrony*, edited by O. M. Tomic, 11–46. Berlin, 1989.
Andersen Oftestad, E. *The Lateran Church in Rome and the Ark of the Covenant: Housing the Holy Relics of Jerusalem; With an Edition and Translation of the* Descriptio lateranensis ecclesiae *(BAV Reg. Lat. 712)*. Woodbridge, UK, 2019.
Andrews, T. L. *Mattʿēos Uṙhayecʿi and His Chronicle: History as Apocalypse in a Crossroads of Cultures*. Leiden, 2017.
Anthony, S. W. "Ghurābiyya." In *EI3 Online*. Leiden, 2013.
Antweiler, W. *Das Bistum Tripolis im 12. und 13. Jahrhundert: Personengeschichtliche und strukturelle Probleme*. Düsseldorf, 1991.
Archibald, E. *Apollonius of Tyre: Medieval and Renaissance Themes and Variations; Including a Text and Translation of the* Historia Apollonii Regis Tyri. Cambridge, 1991.
Asbridge, T. S. *The Creation of the Principality of Antioch, 1098–1130*. Woodbridge, UK, 2000.
Aslanov, C. *Evidence of Francophony in Mediaeval Levant*. Jerusalem, 2006.
———. "L'ancien français, sociolecte d'une caste au pouvoir: Royaume de Jérusalem, Morée, Chypre." In *Évolutions en français: Études de linguistique diachronique*, edited by B. Fagard, S. Prévost, B. Combettes, and O. Bertrand, 13–17. Berne, 2008.

Aspesi, C. "The Breviary of Lucca, Biblioteca Arcivescovile, MS 5: The Use of the Cathedral of Tyre." PhD diss., Notre Dame University, 2018.

———. "The Cantors of the Holy Sepulchre and Their Contribution to Crusade History and Frankish Identity." In *Medieval Cantors and Their Craft: Music, Liturgy and the Shaping of History, 800–1500*, edited by K. A.-M. Bugyis, A. B. Kraebel, and M. E. Fassler, 278–96. Woodbridge, UK, 2017.

Aubé, P. *Godefroy de Bouillon*. Paris, 1985.

Bale, A. *The Cambridge Companion to the Literature of the Crusades*. Cambridge, 2019.

———. "Reading and Writing in Outremer." In Bale, *Cambridge Companion to the Literature of the Crusades*, 85–101.

Bandt, C., and A. Rattmann. "Bruno Violet and the Exploration of the Qubbat al-Khazna around 1900." In D'Ottone Rambach et al., *The Damascus Fragments*, 105–26.

———. "Die Damaskusreise Bruno Violets 1900/1901 zur Erforschung der Qubbet el-Chazne." *Codices manuscripti* 76–77 (2011): 1–20.

Barber, M. *The Crusader States*. New Haven, 2012.

Barber, M., and K. Bate, eds. *Letters from the East: Crusaders, Pilgrims and Settlers in the 12th–13th Centuries*. Farnham, UK, 2010.

Bartlett, R., and A. MacKay, eds. *Medieval Frontier Societies*. Oxford, 1989.

Bastert, B. *Karl der Grosse in den europäischen Literaturen des Mittelalters: Konstruktion eines Mythos*. Tübingen, 2004.

Bates, M. L., and D. M. Metcalf. "Crusader Coinage with Arabic Inscriptions." In Setton et al., *A History of the Crusades*, 6:421–82.

Bauer, D., K. Herbers, and N. Jaspert, eds. *Jerusalem im Hoch- und Spätmittelalter: Konflikte und Konfliktbewältigung—Vorstellungen und Vergegenwärtigungen*. Frankfurt am Main, 2001.

Baum, W. *Die Verwandlungen des Mythos vom Reich des Priesterkönigs Johannes: Rom, Byzanz und die Christen des Orients im Mittelalter*. Klagenfurt, 1999.

Baumstark, A. *Geschichte der syrischen Literatur: Mit Ausschluss der christlich-palästinensischen Texte*. Bonn, 1922. Reprint, Bonn, 1968.

Beckingham, C. F., and B. Hamilton. *Prester John, the Mongols and the Ten Lost Tribes*. Ashgate, 1996.

Beddie, J. S. "Some Notices of Books in the East in the Period of the Crusades." *Speculum* 8 (1933): 240–42.

Berger, P. C. *The Crescent on the Temple: The Dome of the Rock as Image of the Ancient Jewish Sanctuary*. Leiden, 2012.

Bischoff, B. "Ein Leben Mohammeds (Adelphus?) (Zwölftes Jahrhundert)." In *Anecdota Novissima: Texte des vierten bis sechzehnten Jahrhundert*, 106–22. Stuttgart, 1984.

Boase, T. S. R. "The Arts in the Latin Kingdom of Jerusalem." *JWarb* 2 (1938): 1–21.

———. "Ecclesiastical Art in the Crusader States in Palestine and Syria: Architecture and Sculpture." In Setton et al., *A History of the Crusades*, 4:69–116.

———. "Ecclesiastical Art in the Crusader States in Palestine and Syria: Mosaic, Painting, and Minor Arts." In Setton et al., *A History of the Crusades*, 4: 117–39.

Boehm, L. "Die *Gesta Tancredi* des Radulf von Caen: Ein Beitrag zur Geschichtsschreibung der Normannen um 1100." *Historisches Jahrbuch* 75 (1956): 47–72.

Bohak, G., and S. Ammirati. "The Latin *Iliad* in the Cairo Genizah (T-S Misc. 27.2 c–e)." Cambridge University Library, February 2019. http://www.lib.cam.ac.uk/collections/departments/taylor-schechter-genizah-research-unit/fragment-month/fotm-2019/fragment-0.

Boje Mortensen, L. "Roman Past and Roman Language in Twelfth-Century English Historiography." In *Conceptualizing Multilingualism in England, c. 800–c. 1250*, edited by E. M. Tyler, 309–20. Turnhout, 2010.

———. "Sanctified Beginnings and Mythopoetic Moments: The First Wave of Writing on the Past in Norway, Denmark, and Hungary, c. 1000–1230." In *The Making of Christian Myths in the*

Periphery of Latin Christendom (c. 1000–1300), edited by L. Boje Mortensen, 247–73. Copenhagen, 2006.
Borgolte, M. *Der Gesandtenaustausch der Karolinger mit den Abbasiden und mit den Patriarchen von Jerusalem*. Munich, 1976.
Borgolte, M., and B. Schneidmüller, eds. *Hybride Kulturen im mittelalterlichen Europa: Vorträge und Workshops einer internationalen Frühlingsschule*. Berlin, 2010.
Bouras-Vallianatos, P. "Galen's Reception in Byzantium: Symeon Seth and His Refutation of Galenic Theories on Human Physiology." *GRBS* 55 (2015): 431–69.
Boyadjian, T. M. *The City Lament: Jerusalem across the Medieval Mediterranean*. Ithaca, NY, 2018.
Bradbury, J. "Geoffrey V of Anjou, Count and Knight." In *The Ideals and Practice of Medieval Knighthood III: Papers from the Fourth Strawberry Hill Conference, 1988*, edited by C. Harper-Bill and R. Harvey, 21–38. Woodbridge, UK, 1990.
Braund, D. *Georgia in Antiquity: A History of Colchis and Transcaucasian Iberia, 550 BC–AD 562*. Oxford, 1994.
Bresc-Bautier, G. "L'envoi de la relique de Vraie Croix à Notre-Dame de Paris en 1120." *BEC* 129 (1970): 387–97.
Brett, M. "Badr al-Ğamali and the Fatimid Renascence." In *Egypt and Syria in the Fatimid, Ayyubid and Mamluk Eras*, edited by U. Vermeulen and J. Van Steenbergen, 4:61–78. Leuven, 2005.
Brini Savorelli, M. "Un manuale di geomanzia presentato da Bernardo Silvestre da Tours (XII secolo): *l'Experimentarius*." *Rivista critica di storia della filosofia* 14 (1959): 283–342.
Brockelmann, C., et al., eds. *Die Transliteration der arabischen Schrift in ihrer Anwendung auf die Hauptliteratursprachen der islamischen Welt*. Leipzig, 1935.
Bruce, S. G. *Cluny and the Muslims of La Garde-Freinet: Hagiography and the Problem of Islam in Medieval Europe*. Ithaca, 2015.
Buchthal, H. *Miniature Painting in the Latin Kingdom of Jerusalem*. Oxford, 1957.
Buck, A. D. *The Principality of Antioch and Its Frontiers in the Twelfth Century*. Woodbridge, UK, 2017.
———. "Settlement, Identity, and Memory in the Latin East: An Examination of the Term 'Crusader States.'" *EHR* 135.573 (2020): 1–32.
Bull, M. G. "Historia Hierosolymitana." *CMR* 3:406.
———. "Overlapping and Competing Identities in the Frankish First Crusade." In *Le concile de Clermont de 1095 et l'appel à la croisade: Actes du Colloque universitaire international de Clermont-Ferrand (23–25 juin 1995)*, 195–211. Rome, 1997.
———. "The Western Narratives of the First Crusade." *CMR* 3:16–25.
Burgtorf, J. *The Central Convent of Hospitallers and Templars: History, Organization, and Personnel (1099/1120–1310)*. Leiden, 2008.
Burnett, C. "'Abd al-Masīḥ of Winchester." In *Between Demonstration and Imagination: Essays on the History of Science and Philosophy Presented to John D. North*, edited by L. Nauta and A. Vanderjagt, 159–69. Leiden, 1999.
———. "Antioch as a Link between Arabic and Latin Culture in the Twelfth and Thirteenth Centuries." In Draelants et al., *Occident et Proche-Orient*, 1–78. Reprinted in Burnett, *Arabic into Latin*, no. iv.
———. *Arabic into Latin in the Middle Ages: The Translators and Their Intellectual and Social Context*. Farnham, UK, 2009.
———. "Humanism and Orientalism in the Translations from Arabic into Latin in the Middle Ages." In Speer and Wegener, *Wissen über Grenzen*, 22–31.
———. "A Note on the Origins of the *Physica Vaticana* and the *Metaphysica media*." In *Tradition et traduction: Les textes philosophiques et scientifiques grecs au Moyen Age latin*, edited by R. Beyers, J. Brams, D. Sacré, K. Verrycken, 59–69. Louvain, 1999.
———. "The *Sortes regis Amalrici*: An Arabic Divinatory Work in the Latin Kingdom of Jerusalem?" *Scripta Mediterranea* 19–20 (1998–1999): 229–37.

———. "Stephen, the Disciple of Philosophy, and the Exchange of Medical Learning in Antioch." *Crusades* 5 (2006): 113–29.

———. "The Transmission of Arabic Astronomy via Antioch and Pisa in the Second Quarter of the Twelfth Century." In *The Enterprise of Science in Islam: New Perspectives*, edited by J. P. Hogendijk and A. I. Sabra, 23–51. Cambridge, MA, 2003.

———. "What Is the *Experimentarius* of Bernardus Silvestris? A Preliminary Survey of the Material." *AHMA* 44 (1977): 79–125.

Cabanot, J. "Le trésor des reliques de Saint-Sauveur de Charroux, centre et reflet de la vie spirituelle de l'abbaybe." *Bulletin de la société des antiquaires de l'Ouest et des musées de Poitiers*, 4th ser., 16 (1981): 103–23.

Cadderi, A. *Conone di Preneste: Cardinale legato di Pasquale II, Gelasio II, Callisto II (?–1122).* Centro studi francescani del Lazio. Rome, 1974.

Cahen, C. "Indigènes et croisés: Quelques mots à propos d'un médecin d'Amaury et de Saladin." *Syria* 15 (1934): 351–60.

———. *La Syrie du nord à l'époque des croisades et la principauté franque d'Antioche.* Paris, 1940.

Cameron, A. *Arguing It Out: Discussion in Twelfth-Century Byzantium.* Budapest, 2016.

Campopiano, M. *Writing the Holy Land: The Franciscans of Mount Zion and the Construction of a Cultural Memory, 1300–1550.* Cham, 2020.

Cantarella, G. M. "La frontiera della crociata: I Normanni del Sud." In *Il Concilio di Piacenza e le Crociate*, 225–46. Piacenza, 1996.

Catlos, B. *Muslims of Medieval Latin Christendom, c. 1050–1614.* Cambridge, 2014.

Cecini, U. *Alcoranus latinus: Eine sprachliche und kulturwissenschaftliche Analyse der Koranübersetzungen von Robert von Ketton und Marcus von Toledo.* Berlin, 2012.

Chartrou, J. *L'Anjou de 1109 à 1151: Foulque de Jérusalem et Geoffroi Plantegenêt.* Paris, 1928.

Ciggaar, K. N. "Cultural Identities in Antioch (969–1268): Integration and Disintegration—New Texts and Images." In Borgolte and Schneidmüller, *Hybride Kulturen*, 105–22.

———, ed. *East and West in the Medieval Eastern Mediterranean 1: Antioch from the Byzantine Reconquest until the End of the Crusader Principality; Acta of the Congress Held at Hernen Castle in May 2003.* Leuven, 2006.

———. "Manuscripts as Intermediaries: The Crusader States and Literary Cross-Fertilization." In Ciggaar, Davids, and Teule, *EWCS 1*, 131–51.

Ciggaar, K. N., A. Davids, H. G. Teule, eds. *EWCS 1 = East and West in the Crusader States: Context—Contacts—Confrontations; Acta of the Congress Held at Hernen Castle in May 1993.* Louvain, 1996.

Ciggaar, K. N., and H. Teule, eds. *EWCS 2 = East and West in the Crusader States: Context—Contacts—Confrontations 2.* Louvain, 1999.

Ciholas, P. *Omphalos and the Cross: Pagans and Christians in Search of a Divine Center.* Macon, 2003.

Copeland, R., and I. Sluiter. *Medieval Grammar and Rhetoric: Language Arts and Literary Theory, AD 300–1475.* Oxford, 2009.

Corona quernea, Festgabe Karl Strecker zum 80. Geburtstage dargebracht. Leipzig, 1941.

Crawford, P. "Poulains." *CE* 3:984.

Crawford, R. W. "William of Tyre and the Maronites." *Speculum* 30.2 (1955): 222–28.

Crouzet-Pavan, É. *Le mystère des rois de Jérusalem: 1099–1187.* Paris, 2013.

Curtius, E. R. *Europäische Literatur und lateinisches Mittelalter.* Bern, 1948.

Dalché, P. G. "Géographie arabe et géographie latine au XIIe siècle." *Medieval Encounters* 19 (2013): 408–33.

———. *La Géographie de Ptolémée en Occident.* Turnhout, 2009.

Daniel, N. *Islam and the West: The Making of an Image.* Oxford, 1993.

De Ghellinck, J. *L'essor de la littérature latine au XIIe siècle.* Brussels, 1946.

de Sandoli, S., ed. *Corpus inscriptionum crucesignatorum Terrae Sanctae (1099–1291): Testo, traduzione e annotazioni*. Jerusalem, 1974.

———. *Itinera Hierosolymitana crucesignatorum (saec. XII–XIII): Textus Latini cum versione Italica*. 3 vols. Jerusalem, 1978.

Demyttenaere, B., and L. C. Meijer. "Walter van Terwaan over de Passie van Karel en de Wraak Gods: Genre, Compositie, Stijl en Tekst van de *Vita Karoli*." *RBPH* 88 (2010): 935–81.

Dereine, C. "Chanoines." *DHGE* 12 (1953): 353–405.

———. "Conon de Préneste." *DHGE* 13 (1956): 461–71.

Derolez, A. "The Abbey of Saint-Bertin, the *Liber Floridus*, and the Origin of the *Gesta Francorum Hierusalem expugnantium*." *Manuscripta* 57.1 (2013): 1–28.

Di Cesare, M. "The Qubbat al-Ṣaḫrah in the 12th Century." *Oriente moderno* 95 (2015): 233–54.

Djobadze, W. *Materials for the Study of Georgian Monasteries in the Western Environs of Antioch on the Orontes*. Louvain, 1976.

Dominguez, C. "Lírica y cruzadas en el ámbito hispanomedieval: Una lectura de las cantigas gallego-portuguesas desde la Literatura Comparada." In *Iberia Cantat: Estudios sobre poesía hispánica medieval*, edited by J. Casas Rigall and E. M. Díaz Martínez, 153–86. Santiago de Compostela, 2002.

Donati, M. T. "È ancora verosimile l'attribuzione dell'*Experimentarius* a Bernardo Silvestre?" *Medioevo* 12 (1986): 281–344.

Dondaine, A. "Hughes Éthérien et Léon Toscan." *AHMA* 19 (1952): 67–134.

Dondi, C. *The Liturgy of the Canons Regular of the Holy Sepulchre of Jerusalem: A Study and a Catalogue of the Manuscript Sources*. Turnhout, 2004.

D'Ottone Rambach, A. "Manuscripts as Mirrors of a Multilingual and Multicultural Society: The Case of the Damascus Find." In *Negotiating Co-Existence: Communities, Cultures and Convivencia in Byzantine Society*, edited by B. Crostini and S. La Porta, 63–88. Trier, 2013.

D'Ottone Rambach, A., K. Hirschler, and R. Vollandt, eds. *The Damascus Fragments: Towards a History of the Qubbat al-khazna Corpus of Manuscripts and Documents*. Beirut, 2020.

Draelants, I., A. Tihon, and B. van den Abeele, eds. *Occident et Proche-Orient: Contacts scientifiques au temps des Croisades. Actes du colloque de Louvain-la-Neuve, 24 et 25 mars 1997*. Turnhout, 2000.

Eastmond, A. *Royal Imagery in Medieval Georgia*. University Park, PA, 1998.

Eck, T. *Die Kreuzfahrerbistümer Beirut und Sidon im 12. und 13. Jahrhundert auf prosopographischer Grundlage*. Frankfurt am Main, 2000.

Edbury, P. W. "Crusader Sources from the Near East (1099–1204)." In *Byzantines and Crusaders in Non-Greek Sources, 1025–1204*, edited by M. Whitby, 23–38. Oxford, 2007.

———. "Ernoul, *Eracles*, and the Collapse of the Kingdom of Jerusalem." In Morreale and Paul, *French of Outremer*, 44–67.

———. "The French Translation of William of Tyre's *Historia*: The Manuscript Tradition." *Crusades* 6 (2007): 69–105.

———. "Making Sense of the *Annales de Terre Sainte*: Thirteenth-Century Vernacular Narratives from the Latin East." In *Crusader Landscapes in the Medieval Levant: The Archaeology and History of the Latin East*, edited by M. Sinibaldi, K. J. Lewis, B. Major, and J. A. Thompson, 403–13. Cardiff, 2016.

Edbury, P. W., and J. Folda. "Two Thirteenth-Century Manuscripts of Crusader Legal Texts from Saint-Jean d'Acre." *JWarb* 57 (1994): 243–54.

Edbury, P. W., and J. G. Rowe. *William of Tyre, Historian of the Latin East*. Cambridge, 1988.

Edgington, S. B. "Albert of Aachen and the *chansons de geste*." In France and Zajac, *Crusades and Their Sources*, 23–37.

———. "Antioch: Medieval City of Culture." In Ciggaar, *East and West in the Medieval Eastern Mediterranean 1*, 247–60.

———. "The *Gesta Francorum Iherusalem expugnantium* of 'Bartolf of Nangis.'" *Crusades* 13 (2014): 21–35.

———. "Oriental and Occidental Medicine in the Crusader States." In *The Crusades and the Near East: Cultural Histories*, edited by C. Kostick, 189–215. London, 2011.

Edgington, S. B., and H. J. Nicholson, eds. *Deeds Done beyond the Sea: Essays on William of Tyre, Cyprus and the Military Orders Presented to Peter Edbury*. Farnham, UK, 2014.

Ellenblum, R. *Frankish Rural Settlement in the Latin Kingdom of Jerusalem*. Cambridge, 1998.

Elm, K. "Das Kapitel der Regulierten Chorherren vom Hlg. Grab in Jerusalem." In *Umbilicus mundi: Beiträge zur Geschichte Jerusalems, der Kreuzzüge, des Kapitels vom Hlg. Grab in Jerusalem und der Ritterorden*, edited by K. Elm, 107–37. Sint-Kruis, 1998.

———. "Die Eroberung Jerusalems im Jahre 1099: Ihre Darstellung, Beurteilung und Deutung in den Quellen zur Geschichte des Ersten Kreuzzugs." In Bauer et al., *Jerusalem im Hoch- und Spätmittelalter*, 31–54.

———. "*Nec minori celebritate a catholicis cultoribus observatur et colitur:* Zwei Berichte über die 1119/20 erfolgte Auffindung und Erhebung der Gebeine der Patriarchen Abraham, Isaak und Jakob." *Zeitschrift für Religions- und Geistesgeschichte* 94.4 (1997): 318–44.

———. "'*O beatas idus ac prae ceteris gloriosas!*' Darstelling und Deutung der Eroberung Jerusalems 1099 in den *Gesta Tancredi* des Raoul von Caen." In *Es hat sich viel ereignet, Gutes wie Böses: Lateinische Geschichtsschreibung der Spät- und Nachantike*, edited by G. Thome and J. Holzhausen, 152–78. Munich, 2001.

Epp, V. "Die Entstehung eines 'Nationalbewußtseins' in den Kreuzfahrerstaaten," *DA* 45 (1989): 596–604.

———. *Fulcher von Chartres: Studien zur Geschichtsschreibung des ersten Kreuzzuges*. Düsseldorf, 1990.

Erdmann, C. "Leonitas." In *Corona quernea*, 15–28.

Esposito Frank, M. "Dante's Muhammad: Parallels between Islam and Arianism." *Dante Studies* 125 (2007): 185–206.

Fassler, M. E. *The Virgin of Chartres: Making History through Liturgy and the Arts*. New Haven, 2010.

Faulhaber, C. B. "Libraries." In *Medieval Iberia: An Encyclopedia*, edited by E. M. Gerli, 484–86. New York, 2003.

Fohlen, J. "Un nouveau manuscrit de l'Eglise de Sidon à la Bibliothèque Vaticane (Vat. lat. 2220)." *Scriptorium* 38 (1984): 302–4.

Folda, J. *The Art of the Crusaders in the Holy Land, 1098–1187*. New York, 1995.

———. *Crusader Art in the Holy Land: From the Third Crusade to the Fall of Acre, 1187–1291*. New York, 2005.

———. "Crusader Art in the Twelfth Century: Reflections on Christian Multiculturalism in the Levant." *Mediterranean Historical Review* 10 (1995): 80–91.

———. "A Crusader Manuscript from Antioch." *RendPontAcc* 42 (1969–70): 283–98.

———. "Crusader Painting in the 13th Century: The State of the Question." *Atti del XXIV congresso internazionale di Storia dell'Arte*, 2:103–15. Bologna, 1982.

———. "Melisende of Jerusalem: Queen and Patron of Art and Architecture in the Crusader Kingdom." In *Reassessing the Roles of Women as 'Makers' of Medieval Art and Architecture*, edited by T. Martin, 1:429–77. Leiden, 2012.

Foreville, R. "L'école de Caen au XIe siècle et les origines normandes de l'Université d'Oxford." In *Études médiévales offertes à M. le doyen Augustin Fliche*, 81–100. Paris, 1952.

———. "Un chef de la première croisade: Arnoul Malecouronne." *Bulletin Philologique et Historique du Comité des Travaux Historiques et Scientifiques* (1953–54): 377–90.

France, J. "The Text of the Account of the Capture of Jerusalem in the Ripoll Manuscript, Bibliothèque Nationale (Latin) 5132." *EHR* 103.408 (1988): 640–57.

———. "An Unknown Account of the Capture of Jerusalem." *EHR* 87.345 (1972): 771–83.

France, J., and J. G. Zajac, eds. *The Crusades and Their Sources: Essays Presented to Bernard Hamilton*. Aldershot, 1998.
Frolow, A. *La relique de la Vraie Croix: Recherches sur le développement d'un culte*. Paris, 1961.
Gabriele, M. *An Empire of Memory: The Legend of Charlemagne, the Franks, and Jerusalem before the First Crusade*. Oxford, 2011.
Gabrieli, F., ed. *Arab Historians of the Crusades*. London, 2010.
Galadza, D. "Greek Liturgy in Crusader Jerusalem: Witnesses of Liturgical Life at the Holy Sepulchre and St Sabas Lavra." *JMedHist* 43.4 (2017): 421–37.
Gaposchkin, M. C. "The Echoes of Victory: Liturgical and Para-Liturgical Commemorations of the Capture of Jerusalem in the West." *JMedHist* 40 (2014): 237–59.
———. "The Feast of the Liberation of Jerusalem in London, British Library Additional 8927 Reconsidered." *MedSt* 77 (2015): 127–81.
———. *Invisible Weapons: Liturgy and the Making of Crusade Ideology*. Ithaca, 2017.
———. "Louis IX, Crusade and the Promise of Joshua in the Holy Land." *JMedHist* 34 (2008): 245–74.
García-Guijarro, L. "Some Considerations on the Crusaders' Letter to Urban II (September 1098)." In *Jerusalem the Golden: The Origins and Impact of the First Crusade*, edited by S. B. Edgington and L. García-Guijarro, 151–71. Turnhout, 2014.
Garipzanov, I. H., ed. *Historical Narratives and Christian Identity on a European Periphery: Early History Writing in Northern, East-Central, and Eastern Europe (c. 1070–1200)*. Turnhout, 2011.
Garrison, E. B. "A Twelfth-Century Bible: A Jerusalem (?) Masterpiece." *Studies in the History of Mediaeval Italian Painting* 8 (1958): 300–309.
Gasnault, P. "L'homéliaire de l'*ecclesia Sydonensis*." *BAntFr* (1967): 276–82.
Gaunt, S. "French Literature Abroad: Towards an Alternative History of French Literature." *Interfaces* 1 (2015): 25–61.
George-Tvrtković, R. *A Christian Pilgrim in Medieval Iraq: Riccoldo da Montecroce's Encounter with Islam*. Turnhout, 2012.
Georgopoulou, M. "Orientalism and Crusader Art: Constructing a New Canon." *Medieval Encounters* 5 (1999): 289–321.
Gerish, D. E. "Remembering Kings in Jerusalem: The Second Crusade, the *Historia Nicaena vel Antiochena*, and Royal Identity." In *The Second Crusade: Holy War on the Periphery of Latin Christendom*, edited by J. T. Roche and J. Møller Jensen, 51–90. Turnhout, 2015.
Giannini, G., and L. Minervini. "The Old French Texts of the Damascus Qubba." In D'Ottone Rambach et al., *The Damascus Fragments*, 331–62.
Giese, W. "Stadt- und Herrscherbeschreibungen bei Wilhelm von Tyrus." *DA* 34 (1978): 381–409.
———. "Untersuchungen zur *Historia Hierosolymitana* des Fulcher von Chartres." *Archiv für Kulturgeschichte* 69 (1987): 62–115.
Giordanengo, C. *Le registre de Lambert, évêque d'Arras (1093–1115)*. Paris, 2007.
Glaesener, H. "Raoul de Caen, historien et écrivain." *RHE* 46 (1951): 1–21.
Glauche, G. *Schullektüre im Mittelalter: Entstehung und Wandlungen des Lektürekanons bis 1200 nach den Quellen dargestellt*. Munich, 1970.
Goitein, S. D., ed. *A Mediterranean Society: The Jewish Communities of the Arab World as Portrayed in the Documents of the Cairo Geniza*. 6 vols. Berkeley, 1967–1993.
Goldziher, I. "Ghurābiyya." In *EI2 Online*. Leiden, 2010.
González Muñoz, F. *Mahometrica: Ficciones poéticas latinas del siglo XII sobre Mahoma*. Madrid, 2015.
Gottlieb, T. *Über mittelalterliche Bibliotheken*. Leipzig, 1890.
Grabar, O. *The Dome of the Rock*. Cambridge, MA, 2006.
Graboïs, A. "Charlemagne, Rome and Jerusalem." *RBPH* 59.4 (1981): 792–809.
Graf, G. *Geschichte der christlichen arabischen Literatur*. 5 vols. Rome, 1944–53.

Gutas, D. "What Was There in Arabic for Latins to Receive? Remarks on the Modalities of the Twelfth-Century Translation Movement in Spain." In Speer and Wegener, *Wissen über Grenzen*, 3–21.

Hagenmeyer, H., ed. *Epistulae et chartae ad historiam primi belli sacri spectantes: Die Kreuzzugsbriefe aus den Jahren 1088–1100*. Innsbruck, 1901.

Hamilton, B. "Aimery of Limoges, Latin Patriarch of Antioch (c. 1142–c. 1196) and the Unity of the Churches." In Ciggaar and Teule, *EWCS 2*, 1–12.

———. "Aimery of Limoges, Patriarch of Antioch: Ecumenist, Scholar and Patron of Hermits." In *The Joy of Learning and the Love of God: Studies in Honor of Jean Leclercq*, edited by E. R. Elder, 269–90. Kalamazoo, 1995.

———. "Knowing the Enemy: Western Understanding of Islam at the Time of the Crusades." *JRAS*, 3rd ser., 7.3 (1997): 373–87.

———. *The Latin Church in the Crusader States: The Secular Church*. London, 1980.

———. *The Leper King and His Heirs: Baldwin IV and the Crusader Kingdom of Jerusalem*. Cambridge, 2000.

———. "A Note on the Manuscripts of the Latin Text of the Prester John Letter." In Beckingham and Hamilton, *Prester John*, 39.

———. "Prester John and the Three Kings of Cologne." In *Studies in Medieval History Presented to R. H. C. Davis*, edited by H. Mayr-Harting and R. I. Moore, 177–91. London, 1985. Reprinted in Beckingham and Hamilton, *Prester John*, no. VII.

———. "Ralph of Domfront, Patriarch of Antioch (1135–40)." *Nottingham Medieval Studies* 28 (1984): 1–21.

———. "Women in the Crusader States: The Queens of Jerusalem (1100–1190)." In *Medieval Women: Dedicated and Presented to Professor Rosalind M. T. Hill on the Occasion of Her Seventieth Birthday*, edited by D. Baker, 143–73. Oxford, 1978.

Hamilton, J., S. Hamilton, and B. Hamilton, eds. *Hugh Eteriano: Contra Patarenos*. Leiden, 2004.

Handyside, P. "A Crusader Manuscript from Antioch? Reappraising the Provenance of Biblioteca Apostolica Vaticana, ms. Pal. lat. 1963." *Crusades* 16 (2017): 65–78.

———. "*L'Estoire d'Eracles* in Outremer." In Morreale and Paul, *French of Outremer*, 68–85.

Harris, J. *Byzantium and the Crusades*. London, 2014.

Hartl, I. *Das Feindbild der Kreuzzugslyrik: Das Aufeinandertreffen von Christen und Muslimen*. Bern, 2009.

Haskins, C. H. *Studies in the History of Mediaeval Science*. Cambridge, MA, 1924.

Hasse, D. "The Social Conditions of the Arabic-(Hebrew-)Latin Translation Movements in Medieval Spain and in the Renaissance." In Speer and Wegener, *Wissen über Grenzen*, 68–86.

Haye, T. *Lateinische Oralität: Gelehrte Sprache in der mündlichen Kommunikation des hohen und späten Mittelalters*. Berlin, 2005.

Heffernan, T. J. *Sacred Biography: Saints and Their Biographers in the Middle Ages*. New York, 1988.

Heinzelmann, M. *Translationsberichte und andere Quellen des Reliquienkultes*. Turnhout, 1979.

Hexter, R. J. "Ovid and the Medieval Exilic Imaginary." In *Writing Exile: The Discourse of Displacement in Greco-Roman Antiquity and Beyond*, edited by J. F. Gaertner, 209–36. Leiden, 2007.

Hexter, R. J., and Townsend, D., eds. *The Oxford Handbook of Medieval Latin*. Oxford, 2012.

Hiestand, R. "Boemondo I e la prima Crociata." In *Il Mezzogiorno normanno-svevo e le Crociate (Atti delle quattordicesime giornate normannosveve, Bari, 17–20 ottobre 2000)*, edited by G. Musca, 65–94. Bari, 2002.

———. "Der lateinische Klerus der Kreuzfahrerstaaten: geographische Herkunft und politische Rolle." In *Die Kreuzfahrerstaaten als multikulturelle Gesellschaft: Einwanderer und Minderheiten im 12. und 13. Jahrhundert*, edited by H. E. Mayer and E. Müller-Luckner, 43–68. Munich, 1997.

———. *Die päpstlichen Legaten auf den Kreuzzügen und in den Kreuzfahrerstaaten: Vom Konzil von Clermont (1095) bis zum 4. Kreuzzug.* 3 vols. Kiel, 1972.
———. "Die Urkunden der lateinischen Patriarchen von Jerusalem und Antiochia im 12. Jahrhundert." In *Die Diplomatik der Bischofsurkunde vor 1250*, edited by C. Haidacher and W. Köfler, 85–95. Innsbruck, 1995.
———. "Ein unbekanntes Privileg Fürst Bohemunds II. von Antiochia für das Hospital vom März 1127 und die Frühgeschichte der antiochenischen Fürstenkanzlei." *ADipl* 43 (1997): 27–46.
———. "*Gaufridus abbas Templi Domini*: An Underestimated Figure in the Early History of the Kingdom of Jerusalem." In *The Experience of Crusading*, edited by P. Edbury and J. Phillips, 1:48–59. Cambridge, 2003.
———. "Legat, Kaiser und Basileus: Cuno von Praeneste und die Krise des Papsttums von 1111–1112." In *Aus Reichsgeschichte und Nordischer Geschichte: Festschrift Karl Jordan*, edited by H. Fuhrmann, K. Wriedt, and H. E. Mayer, 141–52. Stuttgart, 1972.
———. *Papsturkunden für Kirchen im Heiligen Lande.* Göttingen, 1985.
———. "'*Plange, Syon et Iudea*'—Historische Aussage und Verfassersfrage." *Mittellateinisches Jahrbuch* 23 (1988): 126–42.
———. "Un centre intellectuel en Syrie du Nord? Notes sur la personnalité d'Aimeri d'Antioche, Albert de Tarse et *Rorgo Fretellus*." *Le Moyen Âge* 101 (1994): 7–36.
———. "Zum Leben und zur Laufbahn Wilhelms von Tyrus." *DA* 34 (1978): 345–80.
Hillenbrand, R. "Medieval Muslim Veneration of the Dome of the Rock." In *Tomb and Temple: Re-imagining the Sacred Buildings of Jerusalem*, edited by R. Griffith-Jones and E. Fernie, 125–45. Woodbridge, UK, 2018.
Hilsdale, C. J. *Byzantine Art and Diplomacy in an Age of Decline.* Cambridge, 2014.
Hirschler, K. "Books within Books: The Link between Damascene Reuse Fragments and the Qubbat al-Khazna." In D'Ottone Rambach et al., *The Damascus Fragments*, 439–74.
———. "Saleroom Fiction versus Provenance: Historicising Manuscripts via Their Marginal and Material Logic (Schøyen Fragments 1776)." *Journal of Islamic Manuscripts* 13.1 (2022): 1–54.
Hodgson, N. R. "Reinventing Normans as Crusaders? Ralph of Caen's *Gesta Tancredi*." *Anglo-Norman Studies* 30 (2007): 117–32.
———. *Women, Crusading and the Holy Land in Historical Narrative.* Woodbridge, UK, 2007.
Holzner-Tobisch, K., ed. *Die Vielschichtigkeit der Straße: Kontinuität und Wandel im Mittelalter und der frühen Neuzeit.* Vienna, 2012.
Hotzelt, W. "Die Chorherren vom Heiligen Grabe in Jerusalem." In *Das Heilige Land in Vergangenheit und Gegenwart: Gesammelte Beiträge und Berichte zur Palästinaforschung*, edited by V. Cramer and G. Meinertz, 2:107–36. Cologne, 1940.
Hunt, L.-A. "Art and Colonialism: The Mosaics of the Church of the Nativity in Bethlehem (1169) and the Problem of 'Crusader Art.'" *DOP* 45 (1991): 69–85.
———. "The Syriac Buchanan Bible in Cambridge: Book Illumination in Syria, Cilicia and Jerusalem in the Later Twelfth Century." *OCP* 57 (1991): 331–69.
Hunt, R. W. "Stephen of Antioch." *MedRenSt* 2 (1950): 172–73.
Huygens, R. B. C. "Editing William of Tyre." *Sacris Erudiri* 27 (1984): 461–73.
———. "Guillaume de Tyr étudiant: Un chapitre (XIX, 12) de son 'Histoire' retrouvé." *Latomus* 21 (1962): 811–29.
———. "Inventio Patriarcharum." *Crusades* 4 (2005): 131–55.
———. *Latijn in Outremer: Een blik op de Latijnse letterkunde der kruisvaarderstaten in het Nabije Oosten.* Leiden, 1964.
———. "La tradition manuscrite de Guillaume de Tyr." *StMed*, 3rd ser., 5 (1964): 281–371.
Ibrahim, H. "Jean Chrysostome arabe: Histoire de la traduction et réception." *Chronos: Revue d'Histoire de l'Université de Balamand* 40 (2019): 153–208.
———. "Some Notes on Antonios and His Arabic Translations of John of Damascus." In Roggema and Treiger, *Patristic Literature*, 158–79.

Ingrand Varenne, E. "The Inscriptions of the Latin Kingdom of Jerusalem: New Corpus and Perspectives." In *Crusading and Archaeology: Some Archaeological Approaches to the Crusades*, edited by V. R. Shotten-Hallel and R. Weetch, 328–344. Crusades Subsidia 14. London, 2020.

———. "Transferts épigraphiques: Les inscriptions de l'abbaye du Val de Josaphat à Jérusalem." *Transferts culturels France-Orient latin (XII*[e]*–XIII*[e] *s.)*, edited by M. Aurell, M. Galvez, E. Ingrand-Varenne, 75–100. Paris, 2021.

Jacobsen, P. C. "Die Eroberung von Jerusalem in der mittellateinischen Dichtung." In Bauer et al., *Jerusalem im Hoch- und Spätmittelalter*, 335–65.

Jacoby, D. "Knightly Values and Class Consciousness in the Crusader States of the Eastern Mediterranean." *Mediterranean Historical Review* 1 (1986): 158–86.

———. "La littérature française dans les états latins de la Méditerranée orientale à l'époque des croisades: Diffusion et création." In *Essor et fortune de la chanson de geste dans l'Europe et l'Orient latin: Actes du IX*[e] *Congrès international de la Société Rencesvals pour l'étude des épopées romanes, Padoue-Venise, 29 août–4 septembre 1982*, 617–46. Modena, 1984.

Jaeger, C. S. *The Envy of Angels: Cathedral Schools and Social Ideals in Medieval Europe, 950–1200*. Philadelphia, 1994.

———. *The Origins of Courtliness: Civilizing Trends and the Formation of Courtly Ideals, 939–1210*. Philadelphia, 1985.

Jefferson, R. J. W. "Deconstructing 'the Cairo Genizah': A Fresh Look at Genizah Manuscript Discoveries in Cairo before 1897." *JQR* 108.4 (2018): 422–48.

John, S. "The Feast of the Liberation of Jerusalem: Remembering and Reconstructing the First Crusade in the Holy City, 1099–1187." *JMedHist* 41 (2015): 409–31.

———. *Godfrey of Bouillon: Duke of Lower Lotharingia, Ruler of Latin Jerusalem, c. 1060–1100*. London, 2018.

———. "Royal Inauguration and Liturgical Culture in the Latin Kingdom of Jerusalem, 1099–1187." *JMedHist* 43.4 (2017): 485–504.

Jotischky, A. *Crusading and the Crusader States*. 2nd ed. New York, 2017.

———. "Ethnographic Attitudes in the Crusader States: The Franks and the Indigenous Orthodox People." In *East and West in the Crusader States: Context—Contacts—Confrontations 3; Acta of the Congress Held at Hernen Castle in September 2000*, edited by K. Ciggaar, A. Davids, and H. Teule, 1–19. Leuven, 2003.

———. "The Fortunes of War: An Eleventh-Century Greek Liturgical Manuscript (Sinai gr 512) and Its History." *Crusades* 9 (2010): 173–84.

———. "The Frankish Encounter with the Greek Orthodox in the Crusader States: The Case of Gerard of Nazareth and Mary Magdalene." In *Tolerance and Intolerance: Social Conflict in the Age of the Crusades*, edited by M. Gervers and J. M. Powell, 100–14, 168–72. Syracuse, NY, 2001.

———. "Gerard of Nazareth, John Bale and the Origins of the Carmelite Order." *JEH* 46.2 (1995): 214–36.

———. "Gerard of Nazareth, Mary Magdalene and Latin Relations with the Greek Orthodox in the Crusader East in the Twelfth Century." *Levant* 29 (1997): 217–26.

———. "Greek Orthodox and Latin Monasticism around Mar Saba under Crusader Rule." In *The Sabaite Heritage in the Orthodox Church from the Fifth Century to the Present*, edited by J. Patrich, 85–96. Leuven, 2001.

———. "Manuel Comnenus and the Reunion of the Churches: The Evidence of the Conciliar Mosaics in the Church of the Nativity in Bethlehem." *Levant* 26 (1994): 207–24.

———. *The Perfection of Solitude: Hermits and Monks in the Crusader States*. University Park, PA, 1995.

Kazhdan, A. P., et al., eds. *Oxford Dictionary of Byzantium*. Oxford, 1991.

Kedar, B. Z. *Crusaders and Franks: Studies in the History of the Crusades and the Frankish Levant*. London, 2016.

———. "The Crusading Kingdom of Jerusalem—the First European Colonial Society? A Symposium." In *The Horns of Ḥaṭṭīn*, edited by B. Z. Kedar, 341–66. Jerusalem, 1992.
———. *The Franks in the Levant, 11th to 14th Centuries*. Aldershot, 1993.
———. *Franks, Muslims and Oriental Christians in the Latin Levant: Studies in Frontier Acculturation*. Aldershot, 2006.
———. "Gerard of Nazareth: A Neglected Twelfth-Century Writer in the Latin East; A Contribution to the Intellectual and Monastic History of the Crusader States." *DOP* 37 (1983): 55–77.
———. "Iberia y el reino franco de Jerusalén." *Ad limina* 8.8 (2017): 39–61.
———. "Intellectual Activities in a Holy City: Jerusalem in the Twelfth Century." In *Sacred Space: Shrine, City, Land; Proceedings from the International Conference in Memory of Joshua Prawer*, edited by B. Z. Kedar and R. J. Zwi Werblowsky, 127–39. London, 1998. Reprinted in Kedar, *Franks, Muslims*, no. IX.
———. "The Jerusalem Massacre of July 1099 in the Western Historiography of the Crusades." *Crusades* 3 (2004): 15–75.
———. "The Latin Hermits of the Frankish Levant Revisited." In *Come l'orco della fiaba: Studi per Franco Cardini*, edited by M. Montesano, 185–202. Florence, 2010.
———. "La *Via sancti sepulchri* come tramite di cultura araba in Occidente." In *Itinerari medievali e identità europea: Atti del Congresso Internazionale di Parma, 27–28 febbraio 1998*, edited by R. Greci, 181–201. Bologna, 1999.
———. "On Books and Hermits in Nazareth's Short Twelfth Century." In *Nazareth: Archaeology, History and Cultural Heritage*, edited by M. Yazbak and S. Sharif, 43–53. Nazareth, 2012.
———. "The Origins of the Earliest Laws of Frankish Jerusalem: The Canons of the Council of Nablus, 1120." *Speculum* 74 (1999): 310–35. Reprinted in Kedar, *Franks, Muslims*, no. I.
———. "The Patriarch Eraclius." In Kedar et al., *Outremer*, 177–204. Reprinted in Kedar, *The Franks in the Levant*, no. VIII.
———. "Sobre la génesis de la Fazienda de Ultra Mar." *Annales de historia antigua y medieval* 28 (1995): 131–36.
———. "Some New Light on the Composition Process of William of Tyre's *Historia*." In Edgington and Nicholson, *Deeds Done beyond the Sea*, 3–11.
———. "The Subjected Muslims of the Frankish Levant." In *Muslims under Latin Rule, 1100–1300*, edited by J. M. Powell, 135–74. Princeton, 1990.
Kedar, B. Z., and C. Aslanov. "Problems in the Study of Trans-Cultural Borrowing in the Frankish Levant." In Borgolte and Schneidmüller, *Hybride Kulturen*, 277–85.
Kedar, B. Z., H. E. Mayer, and R. C. Smail, eds. *Outremer: Studies in the History of the Crusading Kingdom of Jerusalem Presented to Joshua Prawer*. Jerusalem, 1982.
Kenney, J. "Reasons for the Faith against Muslim Objections (and One Objection to the Greeks and Armenians) to the Cantor of Antioch." *Islamochristiana* 22 (1996): 31–52.
Keuffer, M., and G. Kentenich. *Beschreibendes Verzeichnis der Handschriften der Stadtbibliothek zu Trier*. 9 vols. Trier, 1888–.
Kirschberger, T. *Erster Kreuzzug und Ethnogenese: In novam formam commutatus—ethnogenetische Prozesse im Fürstentum Antiochia und im Königreich Jerusalem*. Göttingen, 2015.
Kirstein, K.-P. *Die lateinischen Patriarchen von Jerusalem: Von der Eroberung der Heiligen Stadt durch die Kreuzfahrer 1099 bis zum Ende der Kreuzfahrerstaaten 1291*. Berlin, 2002.
Kletter, K. "The Christian Reception of Josephus in Late Antiquity and the Middle Ages." In *A Companion to Josephus*, edited by H. Howell Chapman and Z. Rodgers, 360–80. Chichester, 2016.
Kohlberg, E., and B. Z. Kedar. "A Melkite Physician in Frankish Jerusalem and Ayyubid Damascus: Muwaffaq al-Din Ya'qub b. Siqlab." *Asian and African Studies* 22 (1988): 113–26. Reprinted in Kedar, *Franks in the Levant*, no. XII.
Kohler, C. "Chartes de l'abbaye de Notre-Dame de la Vallée de Josaphat en Terre-Sainte (1108–1291)." *ROL* 7 (1899): 108–222.

———. "Un nouveau récit de l'invention des Patriarches Abraham, Isaac et Jacob à Hebron." *ROL* 4 (1896): 477–502.
Köhler, M. A. *Alliances and Treaties between Frankish and Muslim Rulers in the Middle East: Cross-Cultural Diplomacy in the Period of the Crusades*. Leiden, 2013.
König, D. G. *Arabic-Islamic Views of the Latin West: Tracing the Emergence of Medieval Europe*. Oxford, 2015.
———. "Latin-Arabic Entanglement: A Short History." In *Latin and Arabic: Entangled Histories*, edited by D. G. König, 31–121. Heidelberg, 2019.
Kool, R. "A Deposit of Twelfth-Century Medieval Seals at Caesarea: Evidence of the Cathedral Archive of St Peter." In *In laudem hierosolymitani: Studies in Crusades and Medieval Culture in Honour of Benjamin Z. Kedar*, edited by I. Shagrir, R. Ellenblum, and J. Riley-Smith, 181–89. Aldershot, 2007.
Korobeinikov, D. "Orthodox Communities in Eastern Anatolia in the Thirteenth and Fourteenth Centuries: Part 1, The Two Patriarchates: Constantinople and Antioch." *Al-Masāq* 15 (2003): 197–214.
Kostick, C. "A Further Discussion on the Authorship of the 'Gesta Francorum.'" *Reading Medieval Studies* 35 (2009): 1–14.
Koytcheva, E. "Logistics of the Early Crusades in the Balkans on *Via Militaris*." In Holzner-Tobisch, *Die Vielschichtigkeit der Straße*, 209–32.
Krey, A. C. "William of Tyre: The Making of an Historian in the Middle Ages." *Speculum* 16.2 (1941): 149–66.
Lafontaine-Dosogne, J. "Le monastère du Sinaï: Creuset de culture chrétienne (X^e–XIIIe siècles)." In Ciggaar, Davids, and Teule, *EWCS 1*, 103–29.
Lamoreaux, J. C. "Ibrāhīm ibn Yūḥannā al-Anṭākī." *CMR* 2:611–6.
Lapina, E. "The Maccabees and the Battle of Antioch." In *Dying for the Faith, Killing for the Faith: Old-Testament Faith-Warriors (1 and 2 Maccabees) in Historical Perspective*, edited by G. Signori, 147–59. Leiden, 2012.
Latiff, O. *The Cutting Edge of the Poet's Sword: Muslim Poetic Responses to the Crusades*. Leiden, 2017.
Latowsky, A. "Charlemagne, Godfrey of Bouillon, and Louis IX of France." In Bale, *Cambridge Companion to the Literature of the Crusades*, 200–14.
———. *Emperor of the World: Charlemagne and the Construction of Imperial Authority, 800–1229*. Ithaca, 2013.
———. "Foreign Embassies and Roman Universality in Einhard's *Life of Charlemagne*." *Florilegium* 22 (2005): 25–57.
Lazar, M., ed. *La fazienda de Ultra Mar: Biblia romanceada et itinéraire biblique en prose castillane du XIIe siècle*. Salamanca, 1965.
Lees, J. "The *Historia Hierosolymitana* of Fulcher of Chartres: Reform, Papacy and the Kingdom of Jerusalem." PhD diss., University of Liverpool, 2019.
Lehmann, P. "Die mittellateinischen Dichtungen der Prioren des Tempels von Jerusalem Acardus und Gaufridus." In *Corona quernea*, 296–330.
———. "Vom Leben des Lateinischen im Mittelalter." *Bayerische Blätter für das Gymnasialschulwesen* 65 (1929): 65–82.
———. "Von Nazareth nach Erfurt." *Zentralblatt für Bibliothekswesen* 50 (1933): 483–84.
Lehmann, P., et al. *Mittelalterliche Bibliothekskataloge Deutschlands und der Schweiz*. 4 vols. Munich, 1918–39.
Lewis, K. J. *The Counts of Tripoli and Lebanon in the Twelfth Century: Sons of Saint-Gilles*. New York, 2016.
———. "Medieval Diglossia: The Diversity of the Latin Christian Encounter with Written and Spoken Arabic in the 'Crusader' County of Tripoli, with a Hitherto Unpublished Arabic Note

from the Principality of Antioch (MS, AOM 3, Valletta: National Library of Malta, no. 51v." *Al-Masāq* 27.2 (2015): 119–52.

L'idea di Gerusalemme nella spiritualità cristiana del Medioevo: Atti del Convegno internazionale in collaborazione con l'Istituto della Görres-Gesellschaft di Gerusalemme. Vatican City, 2003.

Linder, A. "'Like Purest Gold Resplendent': The Fiftieth Anniversary of the Liberation of Jerusalem." *Crusades* 8 (2009): 31–51.

———. "The Liturgy of the Liberation of Jerusalem." *MedSt* 52 (1990): 110–31.

———. "A New Day, New Joy: The Liberation of Jerusalem on 15 July 1099." In *L'idea di Gerusalemme*, 46–64.

———. "An Unpublished Charter of Geoffrey, Abbot of the Temple in Jerusalem." In Kedar et al., *Outremer*, 119–29.

Lock, P. *The Routledge Companion to the Crusades.* New York, 2006.

Lohrmann, D. "Échanges techniques entre Orient et Occident au temps de croisades." In Draelants et al., *Occident et Proche-Orient*, 117–43.

Lützelschwab, R. "Zwischen Heilsvermittlung und Ärgernis—das *preputium Domini* im Mittelalter." In *Reliques et sainteté dans l'espace médiéval*, edited by J.-L. Deuffic, 601–28. Saint-Denis, 2005.

MacEvitt, C. *The Crusades and the Christian World of the East: Rough Tolerance.* Philadelphia, 2008.

———. "Processing Together, Celebrating Apart: Shared Processions in the Latin East." *JMedHist* 43.4 (2017): 455–69.

———. "What Was Crusader about the Crusader States?" *Al-Masāq* 30.3 (2018): 317–30.

MacGregor, J. B. "The First Crusade in Late Medieval *exempla*." *Historian* 68 (2006): 29–48.

Magdalino, P. *The Empire of Manuel I Komnenos, 1143–1180.* Cambridge, 1993.

———. "The Porphyrogenita and the Astrologers: A Commentary on *Alexiad* VI.7.1–7." In *Porphyrogenita: Essays on the History and Literature of Byzantium and the Latin East in Honour of Julian Chrysostomides*, edited by J. Herrin, 15–31. Aldershot, 2003.

Maier, A. "Die Handschriften der Ecclesia Sidonensis." *Manuscripta* 11 (1967): 39–45.

———. "Die Homiliare der 'Ecclesia Sidonensis.'" *Manuscripta* 12 (1968): 22–25.

———. "Noch einmal zu den Codices der 'Ecclesia Sidonensis.'" *Manuscripta* 12 (1968): 106–7.

Mallett, A. "The 'Other' in the Crusading Period: Walter the Chancellor's Presentation of Najm al-Dīn Il-Ghāzī." *Al-Masāq* 22.2 (2010): 113–28.

Manitius, M. *Geschichte der lateinischen Literatur des Mittelalters.* 3 vols. Munich, 1911–31.

Manselli, R. *Italia e Italiani alla I Crociata.* Rome, 1993.

Maraszak, É. *Les manuscrits enluminés de l'Histoire ancienne jusqu'à César en Terre sainte: Saint Jean d'Acre, 1260–1291.* Dijon, 2015.

Marino, A. *The Biography of "the Idea of Literature": From Antiquity to the Baroque.* Albany, 1996.

Martínez Gázquez, J. "El lenguaje de la violencia en el prólogo de la traducción latina del Corán impulsada por Pedro el Venerable." *Cahiers d'études hispaniques médiévales* 28 (2005): 243–52.

Mattelaer, J. J., R. A. Schipper, and S. Das. "The Circumcision of Jesus Christ." *Journal of Urology* 178.1 (2007): 31–34.

Matzke, M. "Pisa." *CE* 3:964–66.

Mayer, H. E. *Bistümer, Klöster und Stifte im Königreich Jerusalem.* Schriften der MGH 26. Stuttgart, 1977.

———. "Das Pontifikale von Tyrus und die Krönung der lateinischen Könige von Jerusalem." *DOP* 21 (1967): 141–232.

———. *Das Siegelwesen in den Kreuzfahrerstaaten.* Munich, 1978.

———. "Die Herrschaftsbildung in Hebron." *ZDPV* 101.1 (1985): 64–81.

———. "Die Hofkapelle der Könige von Jerusalem." *DA* 44 (1988): 489–509.

———. *Die Kanzlei der lateinischen Könige von Jerusalem.* Hanover, 1996.

———. "Guillaume de Tyr à l'école." *Mémoires de l'Académie des sciences, arts et belles-lettres de Dijon* 117 (1985–86): 257–65.

———. *Marseilles Levantehandel und ein akkonensisches Fälscheratelier des 13. Jahrhunderts.* Tübingen, 1972.

———. "Studies in the History of Queen Melisende of Jerusalem." *DOP* 26 (1972): 95–182.

———. "Une lettre de sauf-conduit d'un roi croisé de Jérusalem pour un marchand musulman." In *La présence latine en Orient au Moyen Âge*, edited by G. Brunel and M.-A. Nielen, 27–35. Paris, 2000.

———. *Von der Cour des Bourgeois zum öffentlichen Notariat: Die freiwillige Gerichtsbarkeit in den Kreuzfahrerstaaten.* Schriften der MGH 70. Wiesbaden, 2016.

———. "Zum Tode Wilhelms von Tyrus." *ADipl* 5–6 (1959–60): 182–201.

Mayer, H. E., and C. Sode. *Die Siegel der lateinischen Könige von Jerusalem.* Wiesbaden, 2014.

McCormick, M. *Charlemagne's Survey of the Holy Land: Wealth, Personnel, and Buildings of a Mediterranean Church between Antiquity and the Middle Ages.* DOMH. Washington, DC, 2011.

Meijns, B. "De *pauperes Christi* van Watten: De moeizame beginjaren van de eerste gemeenschap van reguliere kanunniken in Vlaanderen (vóór 1072–ca. 1100)." *Jaarboek voor Middeleeuwse Geschiedenis* 3 (2000): 44–91.

Merisalo, O., ed. *Frontiers in the Middle Ages: Proceedings of the Third European Congress of the Medieval Studies (Jyväskylä, 10–14 June 2003).* Turnhout, 2003.

Metcalf, D. M. *Coinage of the Crusades and the Latin East in the Ashmolean Museum Oxford.* 2nd ed. London, 1995.

———. "Six Unresolved Problems in the Monetary History of Antioch, 969–1268." In Ciggaar, *East and West in the Medieval Eastern Mediterranean 1*, 283–318.

Meyer, W. *Gesammelte Abhandlungen zur mittellateinischen Rythmik.* 3 vols. Berlin, 1905.

Micheau, F. "Les médecins orientaux au service des princes latins." In Draelants et al., *Occident et Proche-Orient*, 95–115.

Milis, L. *L'ordre des chanoines reguliers d'Arrouaise: Son histoire et son organisation, de la fondation de l'abbaye-mère (vers 1090) à la fin des chapitres annuels (1471).* 2 vols. Bruges, 1969.

Milwright, M. *The Dome of the Rock and Its Umayyad Mosaic Inscriptions.* Edinburgh, 2016.

Minervini, L. "La costruzione dell'identità franca nell'Oriente latino nel *Tractatus de locis et statu terre Sancte* (ca. 1170–1186)." In *Lo sguardo sull'altro, lo sguardo dell'altro: L'alterità in testi medievali*, edited by M. Cassarino, 89–103. Soveria Mannelli, 2011.

———. "La français dans l'orient Latin (XIIIe–XIVe siècles): Éléments pour la caractérisation d'une scripta du Levant." *Revue de linguistique romane* 74 (2010): 119–98.

———. "Modelli culturali e attività letteraria nell'Oriente latino." *Studi medievali* 43.1 (2002): 337–48.

———. "Outremer." In *Lo spazio letterario del Medioevo: 2, Il Medioevo volgare*, edited by P. Boitani, M. Mancini, A. Varvaro, 1:611–48. Rome, 2001.

———. "Produzione e circolazione di manoscritti negli stati crociati: Biblioteche e 'scriptoria' latini." In *Il viaggio dei testi: Medioevo romanzo e orientale III*, edited by A. Pioletti and F. Rizzo Nervo, 79–96. Venice, 1999.

———. "What We Know and Don't Yet Know about Outremer French." In Morreale and Paul, *French of Outremer*, 15–29.

Mitchell, P. D. *Medicine in the Crusades: Warfare, Wounds, and the Medieval Surgeon.* Cambridge, 2004.

Moeller, C. "Les Flamands du Ternois au Royaume du Jérusalem." In *Mélanges Paul Fredericq: Hommage de la Société pour le Progrès des Études Philologiques et Historiques*, 189–202. Brussels, 1904.

Möhring, H. "Zu der Geschichte der orientalischen Herrscher des Wilhelm von Tyrus: Die Frage der Quellenabhangigkeiten." *Mittellateinisches Jahrbuch* 19 (1984): 170–83.

Molinier, A. *Catalogue des manuscrits de la Bibliothèque Mazarine*. 4 vols. Paris, 1885.
Mollat, G. *Lettres communes des papes d'Avignon*. Bibliothèque des écoles françaises d'Athènes et de Rome. 3rd ser. 16 vols. Paris, 1904–47.
Morato, N., and D. Schoenaers. "Medieval Francophone Literature and Its Path to Universality." In *Medieval Francophone Literary Culture Outside France: Studies in the Moving Word*, edited by N. Morato and D. Schoenaers, 1–30. Turnhout, 2018.
Morin, G. "Hégésippe en rimes latines." *RBén* 31 (1914): 174–78.
Morreale, L. K., and N. L. Paul, eds. *The French of Outremer: Communities and Communications in the Crusading Mediterranean*. New York, 2018.
———. "Introduction." In Morreale and Paul, *French of Outremer*, 1–14.
Morton, N. "The Defence of the Holy Land and the Memory of the Maccabees." *JMedHist* 36 (2010): 275–93.
———. *The Field of Blood: The Battle for Aleppo and the Remaking of the Medieval Middle East*. New York, 2018.
———. "Walter the Chancellor on Ilghazi and Tughtakin: A Prisoner's Perspective." *JMedHist* 44.2 (2018): 170–86.
———. "William of Tyre's Attitude towards Islam: Some Historiographical Reflections." In Edgington and Nicholson, *Deeds Done Beyond the Sea*, 13–23.
Muehlberger, E. "The Legend of Arius' Death: Imagination, Space and Filth in Late Ancient Historiography." *Past and Present* 227 (2015): 3–29.
Mugler, J. "Ibrāhīm ibn Yūḥannā and the Translation Projects of Byzantine Antioch." In Roggema and Treiger, *Patristic Literature*, 180–97.
———. "A Martyr with Too Many Causes: Christopher of Antioch (d. 967) and Local Collective Memory." PhD diss., Georgetown University, 2019.
Muldoon, J., and F. Fernández-Armesto, eds. *The Expansion of Latin Europe*. 12 vols. Farnham, UK, 2007–19.
Müller, S. "Gute Geschichte/n: Literarische Selbsterfindungen und die Geschichte der Literatur des Mittelalters." *Interfaces* 1 (2015): 92–109.
Munk Olsen, B. *I classici nel canone scolastico altomedievale*. Spoleto, 1991.
———. *L'étude des auteurs classiques latins aux XIe et XIIe siècles*. 5 vols. Paris, 1982–2020.
Munro, D. C. "The Speech of Pope Urban II. At Clermont, 1095." *AHR* 11.1 (1905): 231–42.
Muratova, X. "Western Chronicles of the First Crusade as Sources for the History of Art in the Holy Land." In *Crusader Art in the Twelfth Century*, edited by J. Folda, 47–70. Jerusalem, 1982.
Murray, A. V. "Biblical Quotations and Formulaic Language in the Chronicle of William of Tyre." In Edgington and Nicholson, *Deeds Done beyond the Sea*, 25–34.
———. *The Crusader Kingdom of Jerusalem: A Dynastic History 1099–1125*. Oxford, 2000.
———. *The Crusades: An Encyclopedia*. 4 vols. Santa Barbara, 2006.
———. "Ethnic Identity in the Crusader States: The Frankish Race and the Settlement of Outremer." In *Concepts of National Identity in the Middle Ages*, edited by S. Forde, L. Johnson and A. V. Murray, 59–73. Leeds, 1995.
———. "Franks and Eastern Christians in the Principality of Antioch, 1099–1187: Ethnicity and Identity." In *East and West in the Medieval Eastern Mediterranean 3: Antioch from the Byzantine Reconquest until the End of the Crusader Principality*, edited by K. Ciggaar and V. van Aalst, 113–26. Louvain, 2018.
———. "Franks and Indigenous Communities in Palestine and Syria (1099–1187): A Hierarchical Model of Social Interaction in the Principalities of Outremer." In *East Meets West in the Middle Ages and Early Modern Times: Transcultural Experiences in the Premodern World*, edited by A. Classen, 291–310. Berlin, 2013.
———, ed. *The North-Eastern Frontiers of Medieval Europe: The Expansion of Latin Christendom in the Baltic Lands*. Farnham, UK, 2014.

———. "Roads, Bridges and Shipping in the Passage of Crusade Armies by Overland Routes to the Bosporus 1096–1190." In Holzner-Tobisch, *Die Vielschichtigkeit der Straße*, 183–208.

Nader, M. *Burgesses and Burgess Law in the Latin Kingdoms of Jerusalem and Cyprus (1099–1325)*. Aldershot, 2006.

Nasrallah, J. "Couvents de la Syrie du Nord portant le nom de Siméon." *Syria* 49 (1972): 127–59.

Nelson, J. *King and Emperor: A New Life of Charlemagne*. London, 2019.

Nicholson, H. J. "Women's Writing and Cultural Patronage." In Bale, *Cambridge Companion to the Literature of the Crusades*, 72–84.

Nicholson, R. L. *Joscelyn I, Prince of Edessa*. Urbana, 1954.

Noble, S., and A. Treiger, eds. "Christian Arabic Theology in Byzantine Antioch: ʿAbdallāh ibn al-Faḍl al-Anṭākī and His Discourse on the Holy Trinity." *Le Muséon* 24 (2011): 371–417.

———. *The Orthodox Church in the Arab World, 700–1700: An Anthology of Sources*. DeKalb, IL, 2014.

Norberg, D. L. *An Introduction to the Study of Medieval Latin Versification*. Washington, DC, 2004.

Oellers, A. C. "Karl und die Christen im Heiligen Land." In *Ex Oriente: Isaak und der weisse Elefant; Bagdad-Jerusalem-Aachen; Eine Reise durch drei Kulturen um 800 und heute*, edited by G. Minkenberg, W. Dreßen, and A. C. Oellers, 3:108–21. Mainz am Rhein, 2003.

Orme, N. *Medieval Schools*. New Haven, 2006.

Otter, M. "Functions of Fiction in Historical Writing." In *Writing Medieval History*, edited by N. Partner, 109–30. London, 2005.

Ousterhout, R. "Rebuilding the Temple: Constantine Monomachus and the Holy Sepulchre." *JSAH* 48.1 (1989): 66–78.

Pahlitzsch, J. *Graeci und Suriani im Palästina der Kreuzfahrerzeit: Beiträge und Quellen zur Geschichte des griechisch-orthodoxen Patriarchats von Jerusalem*. Berlin, 2001.

———. "Médecins sans frontières: Médecins melkites, juifs et samaritains en Égypte et en Syrie à l'époque des croisades." *Trivium* 8 (2011): 1–16.

Pahlitzsch, J., and D. Baraz. "Christian Communities in the Latin Kingdom of Jerusalem (1099–1187 CE)." In *Christians and Christianity in the Holy Land: From the Origins to the Latin Kingdoms*, edited by O. Limor and G. G. Stroumsa, 205–35. Turnhout, 2006.

Palazzo, R. P. "The Veneration of the Sacred Foreskin(s) of Baby Jesus—A Documented Analysis." In *Multicultural Europe and Cultural Exchange*, edited by J. P. Helfers, 155–76. Turnhout, 2005.

Parsons, S. T., and L. M. Paterson, eds. *Literature of the Crusades*. Woodbridge, UK, 2018.

Paul, N. L. *To Follow in Their Footsteps: The Crusades and Family Memory in the High Middle Ages*. Ithaca, NY, 2012.

Peters, G. *The Story of Monasticism: Retrieving an Ancient Tradition for Contemporary Spirituality*. Grand Rapids, 2015.

Petit, F. *Spirituality of the Premonstratensians: The Twelfth and Thirteenth Centuries*. Translated by V. Szczurek. Trappist, KY, 2011.

Podolak, P., and S. Bucossi. "Per una futura edizione di Ugo Eteriano: Censimento della tradizione manoscritta e problemi di cronologia." *Sacris erudiri* 56 (2017): 274–346.

Poleg, E. "On the Books of Maccabees: An Unpublished Poem by Geoffrey, Prior of the 'Templum Domini.'" *Crusades* 9 (2010): 13–56.

Porteous, J. "Crusader Coinage with Greek or Latin Inscriptions." In Setton et al., *A History of the Crusades*, 6:354–420.

Prawer, J. *Crusader Institutions*. Oxford, 1980.

———. *The History of the Jews in the Latin Kingdom of Jerusalem*. Oxford, 1988.

———. *The Latin Kingdom of Jerusalem: European Colonialism in the Middle Ages*. London, 1972.

———. "Social Classes in the Crusader States." In Setton et al., *History of the Crusades*, 5:119–47.

Pringle, D. *The Churches of the Crusader Kingdom of Jerusalem: A Corpus*. 4 vols. Cambridge, 1993–2009.
Propst, H. *Die geographischen Verhältnisse Syriens und Palästinas nach Wilhelm von Tyrus, Geschichte der Kreuzzüge*. 2 vols. Leipzig, 1927.
Prutz, H. "Studien über Wilhelm von Tyrus." *NA* 8 (1883): 91–132.
———. *Kulturgeschichte der Kreuzzüge*. Berlin, 1883.
Purkis, W. J. "'Zealous Imitation': The Materiality of the Crusader's Marked Body." *Material Religion* 14.4 (2018): 438–53.
Purkis, W. J., and M. Gabriele, eds. *The Charlemagne Legend in Medieval Latin Texts*. Cambridge, 2016.
Rapp, S. H., Jr. "Caucasia and Byzantine Culture." In *Byzantine Culture: Papers from the Conference "Byzantine Days of Istanbul," Held on the Occasion of Istanbul Being European Cultural Capital 2010, Istanbul, May 21–23 2010*, edited by D. Sakel, 217–34. Ankara, 2014.
Remensnyder, A. G. *Remembering Kings Past: Monastic Foundation Legends in Medieval Southern France*. Ithaca, NY, 1995.
Rey, E. *Les colonies franques en Syrie aux XIIe et XIIIe siècles*. Geneva, 1883.
Reynolds, S. *Medieval Reading: Grammar, Rhetoric and the Classical Text*. Cambridge, 1996.
Rheinheimer, M. *Das Kreuzfahrerfürstentum Galiläa*. Frankfurt, 1990.
———. "Tankred und das Siegel Boemunds." *Schweizerische numismatische Rundschau* 70 (1991): 75–93.
Riant, P. "Invention de la sépulture des Patriarches Abraham, Isaac et Jacob à Hébron le 25 juin 1119." *AOL* 2 (1884): 411–21. Reprinted in RHC HOcc 5.1:302–14.
———. "III. Poèmes." *AOL* 1 (1881): 549–50.
Riley-Smith, J. "Some Lesser Officials in Latin Syria." *EHR* 87 (1972): 1–26.
Roberts, A. M. *Reason and Revelation in Byzantine Antioch: The Christian Translation Program of Abdallah ibn al-Fadl*. Berkeley, 2020.
Rödig, T. *Zur politischen Ideenwelt Wilhelms von Tyrus*. Frankfurt am Main, 1990.
Rodriguez, J., ed. *Muslim and Christian Contact in the Middle Ages: A Reader*. Toronto, 2015.
Roggema, B., and A. Treiger, eds. *Patristic Literature in Arabic Translations*. Leiden, 2020.
Röhricht, R. *Geschichte des ersten Kreuzzuges*. Innsbruck, 1901.
———. "Lettres de Ricoldo de Monte-Croce." *AOL* 2 (1884): 258–96.
Rose, R. B. "Church Union Plans in the Crusader Kingdoms: An Account of a Visit by the Greek Patriarch Leontios to the Holy Land in A.D. 1177–1178." *CHR* 73.3 (1987): 371–90.
Rubenstein, J. "Guibert of Nogent, Albert of Aachen and Fulcher of Chartres: Three Crusade Chronicles Intersect." In *Writing the Early Crusades: Text, Transmission and Memory*, edited by M. Bull and D. Kempf, 24–37. Woodbridge, UK, 2014.
———. "Holy Fire and Sacral Kingship in Post-Conquest Jerusalem." *JMedHist* 43.4 (2017): 470–84.
———. "Lambert of Saint-Omer and the Apocalyptic First Crusade." In *Remembering the Crusades: Myth, Image and Identity*, edited by N. Paul and S. Yeager, 69–95. Baltimore, 2012.
———. *Nebuchadnezzar's Dream: The Crusades, Apocalyptic Prophecy, and the End of History*. Oxford, 2019.
———. "Putting History to Use: Three Crusade Chronicles in Context." *Viator* 35 (2004): 131–68.
———. "What Is the *Gesta Francorum*, and Who Was Peter Tudebode?" *Revue Mabillon*, 2nd ser., 16 (2005): 179–204.
Rubin, J. *Learning in a Crusader City: Intellectual Activity and Intercultural Exchanges in Acre, 1191–1291*. Cambridge, 2018.
Runciman, S. "Charlemagne and Palestine." *EHR* 50.200 (1935): 606–19.
———. *A History of the Crusades*. 3 vols. Cambridge, 1951–54.
Russo, L. "Tancredi e i Bizantini: Sui Gesta Tancredi in expeditione Hierosolymitana di Rodolfo di Caen." *Medioevo Greco* 3 (2002): 193–230.

Sabbadini, R. "Spogli Ambrosiani Latini." *StItalFCl* 11 (1903): 165–388.
Salvadó, S. "The Augustinian Reform, the Panormia Glosses, and Reading the Bible in the Medieval Latin Liturgy of Jerusalem." *REAug* 62.1 (2016): 27–55.
———. "The Liturgy of the Holy Sepulchre and the Templar Rite: Edition and Analysis of the Jerusalem Ordinal (Rome, Bib. Vat., Barb. Lat. 659) with a Comparative Study of the Acre Breviary (Paris, Bib. Nat., Ms. Lat. 10478)." PhD diss., Stanford University, 2011.
———. "Rewriting the Latin Liturgy of the Holy Sepulchre: Text, Ritual and Devotion for 1149." *JMedHist* 43.4 (2017): 403–20.
Samir, S. K. "The Role of Christians in the Fatimid Government Services of Egypt to the Reign of al-Hafiz." *Medieval Encounters* 2.3 (1996): 177–92.
Saxer, V. "Le calendrier de l'église latine d'Antioche à l'usage du patriarche Opizo Ier Fieschi." *RSCI* 26 (1972): 105–23.
Schein, S. "Between Mount Moriah and the Holy Sepulchre: The Changing Traditions of the Temple Mount in the Central Middle Ages." *Traditio* 40 (1984): 175–95.
———. *Gateway to the Heavenly City: Crusader Jerusalem and the Catholic West (1099–1187)*. Burlington, VT, 2005.
Schlumberger, G., and F. Chalandon. *Sigillographie de l'Orient latin*. Paris, 1943.
Schmuck, A. "Mittellateinische Kreuzlieder: Poetische Werbung zum Kreuzzug." PhD diss., Universität Würzburg, 1954.
Schreckenberg, H. *Die Flavius-Josephus-Tradition in Antike und Mittelalter*. Leiden, 1972.
Schreckenberg, H., and K. Schubert. *Jewish Historiography and Iconography in Early and Medieval Christianity*. Assen, 1992.
Schum, W. *Beschreibendes Verzeichniss der Amplonianischen Handschriften-Sammlung zu Erfurt*. Berlin, 1887.
Schwering-Illert, G. "Die ehemalige französische Abteikirche Saint-Sauveur in Charroux (Vienne) in 11. und 12. Jh.: Ein Vorschlag zur Rekonstruktion und Deutung der romanischen Bauteile." PhD diss., Universität Bonn, 1963.
Schwinges, R. C. *Kreuzzugsideologie und Toleranz: Studien zu Wilhelm von Tyrus*. Stuttgart, 1977.
———. "Regionale Identität und Begegnung der Kulturen der Stadt und 'Kreuzfahrerkönigreich' Jerusalem." In *Päpste, Pilger, Pönitentiarie: Festschrift für Ludwig Schmugge zum 65. Geburtstag*, edited by A. Meyer, C. Rendtel, and M. Wittmer-Butsch, 237–51. Tübingen, 2004.
Setton, K. M., et al., eds. *A History of the Crusades*. 6 vols. Madison, 1969–89.
Shagrir, I. "*Adventus* in Jerusalem: The Palm Sunday Celebration in Latin Jerusalem." *JMedHist* 41 (2015): 1–20.
Shagrir, I., and M. C. Gaposchkin, eds. *Liturgy and Devotion in the Crusader States*. *JMedHist* 43.4 (2017).
Sholod, B. "Charlemagne: Symbolic Link between the Eighth and Eleventh Century Crusades." *Studies in Honor of M. J. Bernardete: Essays in Hispanic and Sephardic Culture*, edited by I. A. Langnas and B. Sholod, 33–46. New York, 1965.
Skottki, K. "Of 'Pious Traitors' and Dangerous Encounters: Historiographical Notions of Interculturality in the Principality of Antioch." *Journal of Transcultural Medieval Studies* 1 (2014): 75–115.
Smail, R. C. *Crusading Warfare (1097–1193): A Contribution to Medieval Military History*. Cambridge, 1956.
Smith, T. W., and A. D. Buck, eds. *Remembering the Crusades in Medieval Texts and Songs*. Cardiff, 2019.
Spacey, B. C. "Refocusing the First Crusade: Authorial Self-Fashioning and the Miraculous in William of Tyre's *Historia Ierosolymitana*." In Parsons and Paterson, *Literature of the Crusades*, 57–61.
Spear, D. S. "The School of Caen Revisited." *Haskins Society Journal* 4 (1992): 55–66.

Speer, A., and L. Wegener, eds. *Wissen über Grenzen: Arabisches Wissen und lateinisches Mittelalter.* Berlin, 2006.
Spreckelmeyer, G. *Das Kreuzlied des lateinischen Mittelalters.* Munich, 1974.
———. *Mittellateinische Kreuzzugslieder: Texte und Melodien.* Göppingen, 1987.
Steffens, F. *Lateinische Paläographie: 125 Tafeln in Lichtdruck mit gegenüberstehender Transkription nebst Erläuterungen und einer systematischen Darstellung der Entwicklung der lateinischen Schrift.* Berlin, 1929.
Stuckey, J. "Charlemagne as Crusader? Memory, Propaganda, and the Many Uses of Charlemagne's Legendary Expedition to Spain." In *The Legend of Charlemagne in the Middle Ages: Power, Faith, and Crusade,* edited by M. Gabriele and J. Stuckey, 137–52. New York, 2008.
Swanson, M. N. "Abū l-Faraj Yaḥyā ibn Saʿīd ibn Yaḥyā." *CMR* 3:257–60.
———. "Arabic Hagiography." In *The Ashgate Research Companion to Byzantine Hagiography,* edited by S. Efthymiadis, 1:345–68. Farnham, UK, 2011.
———. "Yaḥyā ibn Saʿīd al-Anṭākī." *CMR* 2:657–61.
———. "Yūḥannā al-Anṭākī." *CMR* 3:274–6.
Szövérffy, J. *Secular Latin Lyrics and Minor Poetic Forms of the Middle Ages: A Historical Survey and Literary Repertory from the Tenth to the Late Fifteenth Century.* 4 vols. Concord, NH, 1994.
Talbot, C. H. "Stephen of Antioch." In *Dictionary of Scientific Biography,* edited by C. C. Gillispie, 13:38–39. New York, 1976.
Tessera, M. R. "Dalla liturgia del Santo Sepolcro alla Biblioteca di Sidone: Note sulla produzione libraria latina di Oltremare nel XII–XIII secolo." *Aevum: Rassegna di scienze storiche, linguistiche e filologiche* 79 (2005): 407–15.
———. "La croce del legato: Conone di Preneste, il papato e i riflessi della Missione in Oriente." In *Legati, delegati e l'impresa d'Oltremare (secoli XII–XIII),* edited by M. P. Alberzoni and P. Montaubin, 139–60. Turnhout, 2014.
Thiolier-Méjean, S. *La prise de Jérusalem par Vespasien: Une légende médiévale entre Languedoc et Catalogne.* Paris, 2012.
Tokay, E. "Continuity and Transformation: Theosis in the Arabic Version of Gregory Nazianzen's Oration on Baptism (Oration 40)." PhD diss., Cardiff University, 2013.
Tolan, J. V. "Anti-Hagiography: Embrico of Mainz's *Vita Mahumeti.*" *JMedHist* 22 (1996): 25–41.
———. *Saracens: Islam in the Medieval European Imagination.* New York, 2002.
Traube, L. *Vorlesungen und Abhandlungen.* 3 vols. Munich, 1909–20.
Treiger, A. "ʿAbdallāh ibn al-Faḍl al-Anṭākī." *CMR* 3:100–1.
———. "The Beginnings of the Graeco-Syro-Arabic Melkite Translation Movement in Antioch." *Scrinium* 16 (2020): 1–27.
———. "Greek into Arabic in Byzantine Antioch: ʿAbdallāh ibn al-Faḍl's 'Book of the Garden' (Kitāb ar-rawḍa)." In *Ambassadors, Artists, Theologians: Byzantine Relations with the Near East from the Ninth to the Thirteenth Centuries,* edited by Z. Chitwoog and J. Pahlitzsch, 227–38. Mainz, 2019.
Trovato, P. *Everything You Always Wanted to Know about Lachmann's Method.* Padua, 2014.
———. "Sulla genealogia e la cronologia di alcuni testi di età crociata: Rorgo Fretellus e dintorni (l'alte Compendium, Eugesippus, l'Innominatus VI o pseudo-Beda, la *Descriptio locorum circa Hierusalem adiacentium*)." *Annali dell'Universita di Ferrara Sezione Lettere* 7.1 (2012): 247–68.
Trovato, P., and B. Z. Kedar. "New Perspectives on *Tractatus de locis et statu sancte terre Jerosolimitane.*" *Storie e linguaggi* 4.2 (2018): 1–32.
Tyerman, C. *The Invention of the Crusades.* London, 1998.
Van Drival, E. *Cartulaire de l'abbaye de Saint-Vaast d'Arras rédigé au XIIe siècle.* Arras, 1875.
Vessey, D. W. T. C. "William of Tyre and the Art of Historiography." *MedSt* 35 (1973): 433–55.
Vincent, L. H., E. J. H. Mackay, and F. M. Abel. *Hébron: Le Haram el-Khalîl; Sépulture des patriarches.* 2 vols. Paris, 1923.

Walker Bynum, C. *Docere verbo et exemplo: An Aspect of Twelfth-Century Spirituality*. Ann Arbor, 1979.

Walker, P. E. "Al-Ḥākim and the Dhimmīs." *Medieval Encounters* 21 (2015): 345–63.

Walther, H., ed. *Initia carminum ac versuum Medii Aevi posterioris Latinorum: Alphabetisches Verzeichnis der Versanfänge mittellateinischer Dichtungen*. 2nd ed. Göttingen, 1969.

Watson, N. "The Idea of Latinity." In Hexter and Townsend, *Oxford Handbook*, 124–48.

Weitzmann, K. *Studies in the Arts at Sinai: Essays*. Princeton, 1982.

Weltecke, D. "On the Syriac Orthodox in the Principality of Antioch during the Crusader Period." In Ciggaar, *East and West in the Medieval Eastern Mediterranean 1*, 95–124.

Wentzlaff-Eggebert, F. W. *Kreuzzugsdichtung des Mittelalters: Studien zu ihrer geschichtlichen und dichterischen Wirklichkeit*. Berlin, 1960.

Wetherbee, W. "Philosophy, Cosmology, and the Twelfth-Century Renaissance." In *A History of Twelfth-Century Western Philosophy*, edited by P. Dronke, 21–53. Cambridge, 1988.

Whalen, B. E. "*The Discovery of the Holy Patriarchs*: Relics, Ecclesiastical Politics and Sacred History in Twelfth-Century Crusader Palestine." *Historical Reflections* 27.1 (2001): 139–76. Reprinted in Whalen, *Pilgrimage in the Middle Ages*, 210–21.

———, ed. *Pilgrimage in the Middle Ages: A Reader*. Toronto, 2011.

Williams, M. *Fiery Shapes: Celestial Portents and Astrology in Ireland and Wales 700–1700*. Oxford, 2010.

Williams, S. J. "Philip of Tripoli's Translation of the Pseudo-Aristotelian *Secretum Secretorum* Viewed within the Context of Intellectual Activity in the Crusader Levant." In Draelants et al., *Occident et Proche-Orient*, 79–94.

———. *The Secret of Secrets: The Scholarly Career of a Pseudo-Aristotelian Text in the Latin Middle Ages*. Ann Arbor, 2003.

Winkler, A. *Le tropisme de Jérusalem dans la prose et la poésie (XIIe–XIVe siècle): Essai sur la littérature des croisades*. Paris, 2006.

Winterbottom, M. "*De inventione*, and *ad Herennium*." In *Texts and Transmission: A Survey of the Latin Classics*, edited by L. D. Reynolds, 98–100. Oxford, 1983.

Yeager, S. M. *Jerusalem in Medieval Narrative*. Cambridge, 2008.

Yolles, J. "Geoffrey, Prior of the *Templum Domini*, *On the Seven Books of Josephus*." *Crusades* 13 (2014): 77–118.

———. "Josephus in the Twelfth-Century Latin East." In *The Reception of Flavius Josephus in the Middle Ages*, edited by P. Hilliard and K. Kletter. Leiden (forthcoming).

———. "Latin Literature and Frankish Culture in the Crusader States (1098–1187)." PhD diss., Harvard University, 2015.

———. "Latin Vigilance and Greek Invention in Twelfth-Century Antioch: A New Interpretation of 'Adelphus.'" *Mittellateinisches Jahrbuch* 55.2 (2020): 240–66.

———. "The Maccabees in the Lord's Temple: Biblical Imagery and Latin Poetry in Frankish Jerusalem." In *The Uses of the Bible in Crusader Sources*, edited by E. Lapina and N. Morton, 421–39. Leiden, 2017.

Yolles, J., and J. Weiss, eds. *Medieval Latin Lives of Muhammad*. DOML 51. 2018.

Zajac, W. G. "Captured Property on the First Crusade." In *The First Crusade: Origins and Impact*, edited by J. Phillips, 153–86. Manchester, 1997.

Zarncke, F. "Der Priester Johannes." *AbhGött, Philol.-hist. Kl.* 7 (1879): 827–1039; 8 (1883): 1–186.

Ziolkowski, J. M. "Cultures of Authority in the Long Twelfth Century." *Journal of English and Germanic Philology* 108.4 (2009): 421–48.

———. "Towards a History of Medieval Latin Literature." In *Medieval Latin: An Introduction and Bibliographical Guide*, edited by F. A. C. Mantello and A. G. Rigg, 505–36. Washington, DC, 1996.

Zöller, W. "The Regular Canons and the Liturgy of the Latin East." *JMedHist* 43.4 (2017): 367–83.

———. *Regularkanoniker im Heiligen Land: Studien zur Kirchen-, Ordens- und Frömmigkeitsgeschichte der Kreuzfahrerstaaten*. Berlin, 2018.

GENERAL INDEX

Page numbers in *italics* indicate illustrations.